LINCOLN

As I would not be a slave, so I
would not be a master. This ex:
presses my idea of democracy. —
Whatever differs from this, to the
extent of the difference, is no
democracy. —

A. Lincoln—

LINCOLN

A Picture Story of His Life

BY STEFAN LORANT

REVISED AND ENLARGED EDITION

W · W · NORTON & COMPANY · INC · NEW YORK

sbn 393 07446 3

Library of Congress Catalog Card No. 69-11484

PRINTING HISTORY
Lincoln, His Life in Photographs 1941 60,000 copies
Lincoln, a Picture Story of His Life 1952 25,000 copies
The Life of Abraham Lincoln 1954 275,000 copies
Lincoln, a Picture Story of His Life (revised) 1957 26,000 copies
New, enlarged, and thoroughly revised edition, September 1969, 11,000 copies
Second printing, October 1969, 14,000 copies

For

LILI DARVAS

NOTES AND ACKNOWLEDGMENTS

With this volume, my research on Lincoln photographs, a task which I began twenty-eight years ago, comes to an end. Not that there are no more new items to be discovered (though I doubt that any more genuine Lincoln photographs or any significant manuscripts could come to light), but even if there were I do not think that they would basically alter our picture of Lincoln.

I published my *Lincoln, His Life in Photographs*, a slim volume of 160 pages, in 1941. When Bob Davis, the celebrated columnist of the New York *Sun,* wrote, "You have unwittingly prepared the scene for a thousand biographies" I accepted it as a friendly compliment, not to be taken too seriously. At that time I was not aware that my experimentation with new techniques made the book "the first modern pictorial biography," a model for countless other volumes in both America and Europe.

Though the work was amazingly well received, I was dissatisfied with it. I felt I could do better. Thus, after the first 60,000 copies were sold I made up my mind to start afresh. It took more than a decade before my new presentation was ready. In 1952 my *Lincoln, A Picture Story of His Life,* a book of 256 pages, came out. The reviews were enthusiastic, and yet I was still not content. After the first 25,000 copies had been sold I persuaded my publisher to allow me to revise the book. The result was the 1957 edition, a volume of 304 pages. Still I felt I could improve upon it, so after another dozen years and 26,000 copies later, here I am trying again. This time the volume has 336 pages, or more than twice as many as my first effort. And this time I do not feel that I will have to do another revision.

What is new in it? First, fresh reproductions have been made of all the key Lincoln photographs, and the pictures have been enlarged and presented over the full area of the page (see pages 55, 66, 72, 82, 85, 89, 93, 97, 98–99, 111, 115, 122, 151, 194, 198, 208, 212, and 258–59).

The known material has been enhanced by "a hitherto unknown photograph and a bit of doggerel in his own hand" (see pages 190–91). This is the first time that the Alexander Gardner photograph taken on August 9, 1863, and the doggerel written by Lincoln on July 19, in the same year, have been printed.

The thirty-two new pages include sections dealing with Lincoln's life portraits painted in the summer of 1860 (pp. 100–5), with the Volk busts modeled from life (pp. 96–97), and with the early cartoon assaults on Lincoln (pp. 130–31).

Other additions are: "After the Nomination" (pp. 98–99), "The Attacks of a Baltimore Dentist" (pp. 168–69), "The Butt of Ridicule" (pp. 182–83), "Southern Thrusts" (pp. 206–7), "Another Brady Sitting" (pp. 208–11), "A French Merchant Sketches Lincoln" (pp. 222–23), "The Bixby Letter" (p. 236), "The Photographer of Lincoln" (pp. 296–97), "The Family" (pp. 302–3), "Lincoln's Head on Other Bodies" (pp. 304–7), and "Is This Lincoln?" (pp. 308–11).

A score of newly discovered pictures and unknown letters in Lincoln's hand were added to the former illustrations. Much of the text has been rewritten to incorporate the findings of the latest research; the chronology of Lincoln photographs has been revised with many new and improved reproductions; the contents and bibliography have been brought up to date; and an index has been added.

In 1941 when I began my initial research my first step was to see Frederick Hill Meserve, the pioneer Lincoln-photograph expert. Mr. Meserve had been collecting Lincoln plates and prints since the turn of the century, and in 1911 he issued 102 copies of a privately printed volume, *The Photographs of Abraham Lincoln,* which contained a hundred small photographic prints of Lincoln pasted in, four to a page. In 1917 and again in 1937 he sent out supplements, adding sixteen more photographs to the previous hundred. (And in 1950 and in 1955 he had two further supplements with sixteen more pictures.) I remember my first meeting with him in his downtown office in New York. He took *carte-de-visite* Lincoln photographs out of his wallet and waved them before my eyes by the dozen. His desk drawer was also full of them. I bought many of his pictures and I still cherish the canceled check with his endorsement.

The Meserve photographs were too small—I wanted much larger prints. Arthur Brown, the genial owner of Brown Brothers, who had numerous Lincoln plates in his files, provided me with lifesize enlargements of them. With this the search for negatives and prints began. At the New York Public Library Dorothy Miller, Ivor Avallino, and Sylvester Vigilanti dug into the library's prints for me; at the Museum of the City of New York, Grace Mayer helped.

From New York my path led to Washington. At that time the Lincoln photographs in the Library of Congress were stored in a little space indeed—a couple of boxes. Carl Stange, Milton Kaplan, and Virginia Daiker saw to it that I got reproductions of the original prints. At the National Archives Josephine Cobb secured for me enlargements from the Archives' original Brady plates. In the old Handy studio (Levin Handy was Brady's nephew) the late photographer's daughters, Mrs. Mary Handy Evans and Mrs. Alice Handy Cox, carried on the business. They sold me prints made directly from the original Brady negatives.

My next stop was Chicago, where I got additional prints from the Historical Society and from the famous Lincoln collector Oliver Barrett.

And then to Springfield. The Abraham Lincoln Association was in its prime, with less than a thousand members; its secretary was Harry Pratt, with whom I soon became friends. He took me to the home of Logan Hay, the prime organizer of the Lincoln community, and over the luncheon table we talked about our man till nightfall. I secured many photographs and copies of Lincoln letters from the Association's files.

At the Lincoln tomb I met Herbert Fay Wells, its custodian, who had amassed an incredible conglomeration of newspaper clippings, pictures, and other paraphernalia about Lincoln between the narrow wall-spaces of the tomb. He gave me some exquisite prints, as did the photographer Herbert Georg.

At the Illinois State Historical Society I made the acquaintance of Paul Angle and Jay Monaghan, who was then working on his Lincoln bibliography, and I also met Margaret Flint and Ernest East, all Lincoln students; they helped in my search.

The last stop on that first trip was Fort Wayne and the Lincoln National Life Foundation, where Dr. Louis A. Warren, its director, came to my assistance. On my return home I found that I possessed reproductions of all the Lincoln photographs known until then.

In letters and meetings with Lincoln scholars I sought further guidance. Carl Sandburg, Lauriston Bullard, William Townsend, Benjamin Thomas, James Randall, William Baringer, Ralph Newman, and many others shared their time and their knowledge with me.

For the present work I retraced my steps of twenty-eight years before. Alas, many of the old Lincoln scholars were gone. Mr. Meserve was no more, nor were Arthur Brown, Lauriston Bullard, William Townsend, Benjamin Thomas. But in Washington Josephine Cobb was still at her post, as were Virginia Daiker and Milton Kaplan. In Chicago Paul Angle was still at the Historical Society, and in Springfield I renewed old friendships with Margaret Flint and King Hostick. At Oak Ridge Cemetery, a stone's throw from Lincoln's tomb, I paid my respects at the grave of Harry Pratt and his wife Dolores, and at the graves of Ernest East and Oliver Barrett. In Fort Wayne I visited Louis Warren, who in the twenty-eight-year interval had changed little; he was busy planting 1,500 gladiolus bulbs in his back garden, and I talked to his knowledgeable successor, Gerald McMurtry, the present editor of *Lincoln Lore*, who showed me the treasures of his institution. I also went to see the McLellan collection at Brown University in Providence, as I had twenty-eight years before.

It was not only a sentimental journey, but another check to see whether I really had the best photographic prints on Lincoln and also whether I had missed anything. I was confident I had not.

The question I am most often asked is, "But how do you find these unknown pictures?" In the span of my research I came upon and printed six different Lincoln photographs which had not been known before. My first find was a standing Lincoln taken by Brady on February 9, 1864 (I published it in my first book in 1941; see page 212 in this volume). I discovered it among the copyrighted photographs in the Library of Congress which other sleuths had failed to look into. (When I presented a print of it to Mr. Meserve, he dispatched his daughter posthaste to check at the Library to see whether I had missed others.)

My second find was more exciting. I was corresponding with Emerson Carpenter Ives, the grandson of Francis B. Carpenter, the painter who had stayed in the White House for six months in 1864 and who wrote a delightful book about his experiences. I had a hunch that Carpenter might have had more material than he had put into his book. Mr. Ives told me that indeed there was a diary of his grandfather's and also other mementos, and he invited me to visit him at his summer home near Pawling, New York, where he kept the material.

When I arrived at his place, he led me into his rustic kitchen where under a table in a corner there was a good-sized metal container. He pulled it out and spilled its contents onto the kitchen table—letters, pictures, and drawings galore, the treasures of his grandfather.

I was curious about a battered brown Kodak box. Mr. Ives told me it contained some old broken glass negative; "I really don't know what it is," he said.

As I opened it and unwrapped the small glass negative, broken at the edges and packed in paper, I recognized with a thrill that it was a Brady plate—Lincoln was sitting in the well-known "Brady chair." I was allowed to make enlargements of the plate, and I recall the excitement when I looked at the first pictures in the darkroom and saw that it was one of Lincoln's most telling likenesses, a magnificent pose and expression. I published the photograph with a story on Carpenter in the *Saturday Evening Post* on July 19, 1947 (see picture on page 221).

My next Lincoln find came unexpectedly. One day in 1947 Katherine Dougan, the secretary of the Lincoln Joint Stock Land Bank in Lincoln, Nebraska, wrote to me that the widow of the photographer A. M. Byers had willed to the University of Nebraska an ambrotype which her father took of Lincoln in 1858. Mr. Lundy, the director of the library, sent me a copy of it via Mrs. Clara L. Craig, the reference librarian. It showed Lincoln in a white linen duster on the very day he defended Duff Armstrong with the help of an almanac. *Life* magazine printed the picture and my story about it on February 9, 1948 (see picture on page 71).

A year later, on February 13, 1949, I had in the *New York Times Magazine* the cut-out Lincoln head of Mr. Ives, which Carpenter had kept among his treasures (see page 324), and on September 15, 1952, in *Life* I published the long-lost photograph of Lincoln in his coffin, the discovery of a fifteen-year-old boy in the Illinois State Historical Library (see page 275).

The sixth of my "firsts" is printed in this volume on page 190 — the magnificent photograph taken by Alexander Gardner. It appeared with my article in *Look* Magazine the first week of October prior to publication herein.

In my search I was encouraged and assisted by many experts who with great kindness made the task easier.

Kurt E. Brandenburg and Eleanor S. Brockenbrough of the Confederate Museum in Richmond sent new reproductions of Southern caricatures against Lincoln.

Josephine Cobb, specialist in iconography at the National Archives, with whom I have enjoyed an almost thirty-year-long professional friendship, was most generous in allowing me to read her research notes on the early photographs and on the dating of Lincoln photographs. She answered my numerous questions with unfailing patience.

Virginia Daiker and Milton Kaplan of the Library of Congress, whose advice I have sought repeatedly in the past three decades, were as helpful and cooperative as ever.

Robert H. Dumas, librarian of the Decatur Public Library, allowed me to make a new reproduction of his library's Barnwell photograph.

Margaret A. Flint, assistant State Historian of the Illinois State Historical Library, was as always most solicitous with her time and advice. And James T. Hickey, the curator of the Lincoln Collection of the Illinois State Historical Library, sent me much-appreciated copies of a number of Lincoln's unpublished letters.

King V. Hostick, also an old friend, let me have a copy of his second-inaugural photograph, for which I am most grateful.

A special and most heartfelt thanks goes to David A. Jonah, Librarian and Director of the Brown University Libraries, for sending me the new Lincoln photograph and the doggerel in Lincoln's hand. And I am profoundly grateful to John Hay, grandson of Lincoln's secretary, for allowing me to reproduce the photograph which he inherited from his father earlier this year.

Susan M. Levy at the University of Chicago Library kindly put a copy of the Lincoln portrait in the university's collection at my disposal.

R. Gerald McMurtry, Director of the Lincoln National Life Foundation, and Mrs. Ruth P. Higgins of the same institution were most cordial and gracious in sending me prints and photographs from the Foundation's collection.

I am indebted to Beaumont Newhall, Director of the George Eastman House in Rochester, on whose sound judgment about photographic matters I have learned to rely, for presenting me the magnificent new reproduction of Brady's "Cooper Union" photograph.

Mrs. Paul M. Rhymer of the Chicago Historical Society gave me superb enlargements of photographs in the Society's collection.

Mrs. Frances H. Stadler of the Missouri Historical Society in St. Louis sent information on the Pierre Morand sketches now in the Society's collection.

My thanks go to the photographic experts who with superb craftsmanship and imagination made new reproductions from the original Lincoln plates and prints: Kenneth Carroll of the Herbert Georg Studio in Springfield, Illinois; Hy Lewis of Royaltone, Inc., in Jersey City; A. Hoffmann of Eddowes Company, New York; R. P. Petersen in New York; and Richard Gilson, Joel Librizzi, and John Rice in Pittsfield, Massachusetts.

Evan W. Thomas, my editor at W. W. Norton & Company, stood at my side and steered the work into safe harbor. And the unfailing good humor and human understanding of Rose Franco was a tremendous asset during the time the book was put to bed. I also thank John Woodlock, the director of production at Norton, who expertly saw to it that the complicated process of preparing the book for the printer went so smoothly.

Fritz Walker, the head of the Murray Printing Company, the printer of the book, and Kenneth Adams, who supervised the details of production, made my task easy and pleasant. It was as always a delight to work with them. The high quality of printing is due to their efforts.

John Furbish assisted me in the research and in the preparation of the layouts, doing it most efficiently and intelligently.

My wife, Laurie, took over the chores of typing and the checking of the manuscript. Her suggestions and criticism were always pertinent, and I have followed them to the letter. And I would be remiss not to mention my two little sons, Christopher and Mark, who with wild enthusiasm volunteered to color the pictures with their crayons.

STEFAN LORANT

September 17, 1969
"Farview"
Lenox, Massachusetts

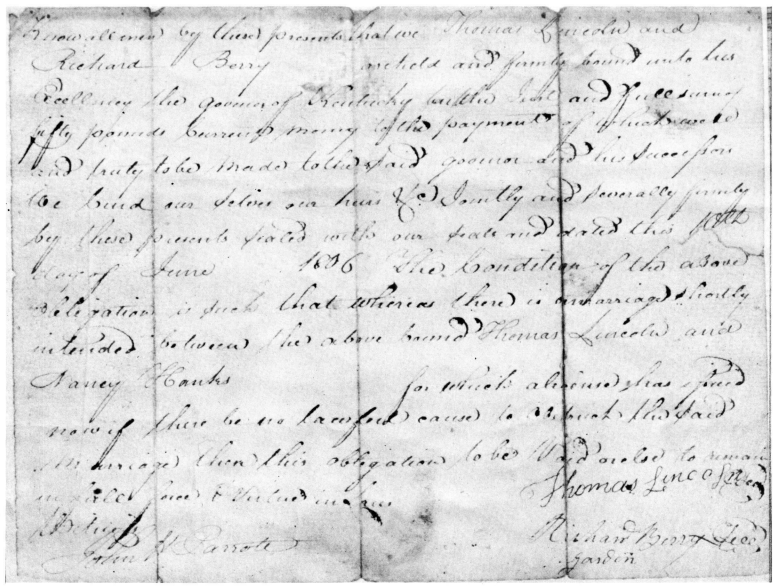

THE MARRIAGE BOND OF THOMAS LINCOLN, issued on June 10, 1806, two days before he married Nancy Hanks. According to Kentucky law, no marriage license could be issued without a bond. signed by two responsible citizens. Usually the first signature was that of the bridegroom and the second that of the bride's father or some close friend—here Richard Berry, in whose cabin the wedding took place. This friend, signing himself "guardian," assumed the bride's interest only for the purpose of the license.

THOMAS LINCOLN TAKES A WIFE

THOMAS LINCOLN was twenty-eight years old, and still he had no wife. Both his sisters, both his brothers were married; only Tom remained single. Three years before—in 1803—he had bought a 238-acre tract near Elizabethtown, the county seat of Hardin County in Kentucky, for one hundred and eighteen pounds "in hand paid."

It was the very year that another Thomas, President Thomas Jefferson, purchased some land, too, one million square miles of land—the Louisiana Wilderness—paying for it more than eleven million dollars in good U. S. currency. The country grumbled: Why

THE PLACE OF THE WEDDING, Richard Berry's cabin near Beechland, Ky., where Thomas Lincoln and Nancy Hanks married.

should the government buy more land? Wasn't there enough of it already? If each of the seven million two hundred thousand inhabitants of the country (which included the one million nine hundred thousand slaves), should desire to live on the land to till, sow, and harvest, there would still be plenty of it left for the future population.

Yes, it was a rich country all right; one could make a good living. Seventeen states formed the Union, the income of its inhabitants amounted to nearly eight million dollars in a year, and the national debt was some 57 million. Democracy was triumphant, even though the Federalist newspapers denounced it. If the New York *Herald* thundered that since Jefferson's accession to the Presidency the country had seen "a political intolerance as despotic, as wicked and capable of bitter persecution" and "an adherence to an insidious policy, which has at length brought the nation into the most unexampled state of distress and debasement," the people took such rantings in their stride.

Neither Thomas Lincoln nor the men and women with whom he talked in Elizabethtown believed that they lived under a despotic tyrant. For them democracy was the wave of the future; let the Federalists shout themselves hoarse.

Thomas was a carpenter by trade, doing the rough carpenter work of the pioneers. One of his biographers described him as "compactly built, inclined to stoutness. His face was round, complexion swarthy, hair black and coarse, eyes brown. He was improvi-

THOMAS LINCOLN'S STORE ACCOUNT. He traded with Bleakley and Montgomery at Elizabethtown, and together with Isaac Bush he took produce down to New Orleans for that firm in the spring of 1806. Returning from the trip in May, he settled his account with the store on the sixteenth, receiving enough money so he could think about taking a wife. The Bleakley and Montgomery ledgers and day book, now in the collection of the Lincoln National Life Foundation in Fort Wayne, Indiana, reveal Thomas Lincoln's purchases before and after his marriage. Thomas had a good credit rating, buying on the cuff, and on occasion he was also charged with sums for his friends and relatives. The entries disprove stories of those Lincoln biographers who described him as a shiftless moneywaster.

Thomas bought carpentering tools quite often and once a fiddle string for his violin. On New Year's Day, 1805, at the time he was wooing Nancy Hanks, he purchased a hat for one pound and sixteen shillings, which at 16⅔ cents a shilling came to $2.50.

THREE WEEKS BEFORE HIS WEDDING —on May 20, 1806—Thomas made all kinds of purchases in preparation for the big day.

dent, yet in a slow and plodding way industrious . . . good natured, inoffensive, law-abiding, notably honest, without a vestige of book learning, he was able only to write his name in a painful scrawl; but he preferred to make his mark and usually did so." Later, when books were written about his famous son, the biographers got into the habit of sketching Thomas as a nomadic, shiftless, good-for-nothing creature. The sparse record of his life shows nothing of the kind. He was a sober, industrious, hard-working man, not a great success in life, but neither was he a failure.

His forebears came from England, and they got their name from the place from which they came. Lindum—established 86 A.D.—was the name of a colony in the time when the Romans occupied the British Isles. During the centuries the name underwent changes from Lincum-Colonia and Lindum Colony to Lindcolm, Lindcoln, and finally Lincoln.

Samuel Lincoln, a weaver's apprentice, left the Old Country in 1637 and settled in Hingham, Massachusetts. From there the Lincolns spread into New Jersey, Pennsylvania, and Virginia and westward along the wilderness road into Kentucky. It was in that state that the twenty-eight-year-old Thomas Lincoln lived in 1806, the year he made up his mind to get married.

Thomas—so the story goes—presented himself to Sarah Bush and asked her to be his wife but was refused. The rejection did not discourage him; soon thereafter he proposed again—and to another girl. This time it was twenty-two-year-old Nancy Hanks, a woman with a "remarkable keen perception" as her cousin Dennis Hanks remembered her: "shrewd, smart . . . highly intellectual by nature," with a strong memory and accurate judgment, kind and affectionate, "spiritually and ideally inclined." All this was probably true, but it was also true that she could neither read nor write. Whenever she signed a legal document she made a cross mark on the page.

Her mother, Lucy, married Henry Sparrow in 1791, some years after her daughter's birth. Who Nancy's real

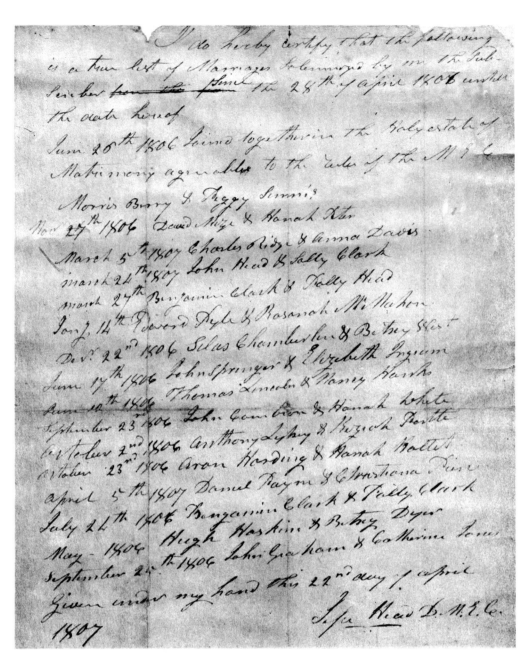

MARRIAGE RETURN of the Reverend Jesse Head, Deacon in the Methodist Episcopal Church, certifying to the marriage of Thomas Lincoln and Nancy Hanks on June 12, 1806.

father was is not known. (Lincoln is supposed to have told his law partner Billy Herndon that he believed him "a well-bred Virginia planter.")

Nancy was willing and Thomas married her on June 12, 1806, at Richard Berry's place—a little cabin close to Beechland in Washington County. A neighbor, the Reverend Jesse Head, performed the ceremony, pronouncing that Thomas Lincoln and Nancy Hanks had "joined together in the Holy Estate of Matrimony agreeable to the rules of the Methodist Episcopal Church." It was of small consequence that Jesse

Head was a Methodist while both the bride and bridegroom were Baptist. Marriage vows were marriage vows.

The ceremony over, came the "infare." One of the guests recalled later that bear meat was served, and venison, wild turkey, and duck; "maple sugar lumps tied on a string to bite off for coffee or whiskey"; a sheep was roasted over an open fire; and there was gaiety, singing, and dancing. When the sun rose in the sky and the celebration was over, the husband lifted his bride on his horse and took her to Elizabethtown to his house.

11

THE CABIN
WHERE LINCOLN WAS BORN

FOR A year and a half after their marriage Thomas Lincoln and his wife lived in and around Elizabethtown. Their first child, a daughter whom they named Sarah, was born on February 10, 1807. Before long, Thomas had enough money to buy a 300-acre tract, for which he paid $200, all in cash. The place was eighteen miles from Elizabethtown, out in the open country, on Nolin Creek, where neighbors were sparse and life was lonely. There Thomas moved with his wife and little daughter in the winter of 1808.

On the land there was already a little cabin, built on a knoll near a spring, a sinking spring it was called, and that is how the farm got its name of Sinking Spring Farm.

The months in the winter dragged; they moved as slow as honey poured on bread. And Nancy was expecting her second child. January went by and February came. On the twelfth of that month, a Sunday, Thomas walked to the next cabin, two miles away, where his sister-in-law lived, and as he came into the room he said kind of slow:

"Nancy got a boy baby."

Ten-year-old Dennis Hanks heard the words, ran quickly to the Lincoln cabin, and the events of that Sunday morning burned themselves sharply into his

memory. Decades later he could still remember it vividly—and this is how he told it:

"Mother got flustered," recalled Dennis, "an' hurried up 'er work to go over to look after the little feller, but I didn't have nothin' to wait fur, so I cut an' run the hull two mile to see my new cousin.

"Nancy was layin' thar in a pole bed lookin' purty happy. Tom'd built up a good fire and throwed a b'ar skin over the kivers to keep 'em warm. . . .

"Mother come over and washed him an' put a yaller flannen petticoat an' a linsey shirt on him, an' cooked some dried berries with wild honey for Nancy, an' slicked things up an' went home. An' that's all the nuss'n either of 'em got."

It was this way that the infant in the Kentucky cabin entered the world. And what a world it was!

Europe trembled under Napoleon's heel; England was fighting France; thrones were shaking; a new order was in the making.

In the United States, President Jefferson cut off trade with the belligerents hoping to keep the country from war, but his Embargo Act was not a success. American business and American exports were hurt. A rebellious Congress forced Jefferson to revoke the "ruinous" embargo and substitute it with "Non-

A replica of the cabin

THE CABIN was eighteen feet wide and sixteen feet long, built in pioneer fashion. Its floor was packed-down dirt. The cooking was done at the fireplace, a clay chimney carried away the smoke.

Reconstruction in the Chicago Historical Society

INSIDE THE CABIN. The view from the bed of cornhusks and bearskins, where Lincoln was born. The single door swung on leather hinges, and light came in through a solitary window.

THE BIRTHPLACE. "I was born February 12, 1809, in the then Hardin County, Kentucky, at a point within the new County of Larue, a mile or a mile and a half from where Hodgen's mill now is," wrote Abraham Lincoln in his autobiographical sketch. His father bought the farm for two hundred dollars and the purchase price included the little cabin situated near to a sinking spring.

Intercourse." The President signed the act on March 1, 1809, two and a half weeks after the birth of Nancy's baby boy. Three days later his successor, James Madison, was inaugurated.

The winds of discontent blew from one part of the country to the other. The New England merchants, their goods in their warehouses, grumbled; the ship- owners, with ships tied up at the wharves, fumed; artisans looking in vain for jobs, farmers suffering under the decreasing market and low prices grew rebellious. There was talk that the country would soon be at war. "What a bad time to live," moaned some people. But people are seldom satisfied, they always must grumble.

13

THE LINCOLN HOME AT NOLIN CREEK. A faithful reproduction of Abraham Lincoln's birthplace, with small carved figures of the family. Thomas Lincoln is carrying water from the sinking spring while Nancy with her two children—Sarah and Abraham—sits on the bench next to the door of the cabin. It was a lovely spot in the Kentucky Wilderness, lovely and lonely, quiet and serene.

THE SEVEN YEARS IN KENTUCKY

THE LINCOLNS stayed at their Nolin Creek place for two corn years. The soil was barren, it did not yield a living, so Thomas went looking for greener pastures. He bought another tract of land ten miles away, at Knob Creek on the old Cumberland Trail, and there he moved with his family in 1811. Abraham was then two years old. Dennis Hanks, who was there, remembered those days:

"It didn't seem no time till Abe was runnin' 'round in buckskin moccasins and breeches, a tow-linen shirt an' coon-skin cap. That's the way we all dressed then. We couldn't keep sheep fur the wolves, an' pore folks didn't have sca'cely any flax except what they could get tradin' skins. We wasn't much better off'n the Indians, except 't we tuk an interest in religion an' polytiks. We et game an' fish an' wild berries an' lye hominy, an' kep' a cow. Sometimes we had corn enough to pay fur grindin' meal an' sometimes we didn't, or thar wasn't no mill nigh enough. When it got so we could keep chickens, an' have salt pork an' corn dodgers an' gyarden sass an' molasses, an' have jeans pants an' cowhide boots to w'ar, we felt as if we was gittin' along in the world. But that was some years later."

And Dennis recalled:

"Abe never give Nancy no trouble after he could walk except to keep him in clothes. Most o' the time we went bar foot. Ever wear a wet buckskin glove? Them moccasins wasn't no putection ag'inst the wet. Birch bark with hickory soles, strapped on over yarn socks, beat buckskin all holler, fur snow. Abe 'n me got purty handy contrivin' things that way. An' Abe was right out in the woods, about as soon's he was weaned, fishin' in the crick, settin' traps fur rabbits an' muskrats, goin' on coon-hunts with Tom an' me an' the dogs, follerin' up bees to find bee trees, an' drappin' corn fur his pappy. Mighty interestin'

14

A photograph of the dilapidated cabin long after the Lincolns lived in it

THE LINCOLN HOME AT KNOB CREEK. In the year of 1811 Thomas Lincoln moved with his wife and two children to another farm, ten miles northeast from his former place. The new home was on the Main Street of the Kentucky Wilderness—the much traveled road from Louisville to Nashville. Here the Lincolns lived for the next five years; here another boy, who died in infancy, was born.

life fur a boy, but thar was a good many chances he wouldn't live to grow up."

Yes, it seemed a "mighty interestin' life." When he was six, Abraham was sent to school—a cabin with a dirt floor, no windows, one door. It was two miles up the road, and each day he and his sister Sarah went trudging along to get their education. The children had no books; all they had to do was to repeat what the teacher said— it was a "blab" school.

But more than in school he learned from his surroundings, from the deep hollows and ravines, from the majestic cedar trees and clear waters of the creek, from the lush meadows and rolling fields, from the land around him, peaceful and tranquil, virgin and pristine, as on the day of its creation.

A photograph of the building taken about a hundred years after Lincoln attended classes

THE SCHOOLHOUSE where in the fall of 1816 Abraham Lincoln's education began. In this windowless cabin with a dirt floor young Abe started to learn how to read and write.

15

MOVING TO INDIANA

LAND TITLES in Kentucky were a plague on the settlers, and Thomas Lincoln had more than his share of trouble.

Three times he had to fight for the land he bought. Once he was deceived about the prior claim of the original owner, another time he discovered errors in the original survey, and the third time, an ejectment suit was brought against him and nine of his neighbors.

Troubled by these difficulties, he was ready to move to Indiana, a state with a Federal land survey, where land titles were safe and where a man, once he bought a home, could hold on to it.

Thus, on a winter morning in 1816, a year so cold that people remembered it as "eighteen-hundred-and-froze-to-death," Thomas helped his wife onto a horse, himself mounted another, and with a child before each of them, they set out for Indiana.

With them went their relatives, the Sparrows, and Dennis Hanks, Nancy's cousin. Dennis had a good memory and a vivid imagination. To his old age he remembered those early days and was happy to talk about them. This is Dennis's recollection of their departure from Kentucky:

"Nancy emptied the shucks out o' the tow-linen ticks, an' piled everything they had wuth takin' on the backs o' two pack hosses. Tom could make new pole beds an' puncheon tables an' stools easier 'n he could carry 'em. Abe toted a gun, an' kep' it so dry on the raft crossin' the Ohio, that he shot a turkey hen with it the fust day we got to Indiany. He couldn't stop talkin' about it till Tom hollered him to quit."

The little group headed for the rich and fertile forest country near Little Pigeon Creek, a mile and a half east of Gentryville.

"Tom brought his tools, an' four hundred gallons o' whiskey to trade fur land with Mr. Gentry. It was in Spencer County, back a piece from the Ohio River. We had to chop down trees to make a road to the place, but it was good land, in the timber, whar the women could pick up their fire-wood, an' on a crick with a deer lick handy, an' a spring o' good water."

HE WAS FOND OF READING. His cousin Dennis Hanks, who lived with the Lincolns in Indiana, recalled:

The men worked, building the cabin and clearing the forest, becoming familiar with their new surroundings. A year passed and another. In the fall of the second year the Sparrows died, then Nancy Lincoln, wife of Thomas

A drawing from a photograph taken in the eighteen seventies

A LINCOLN CABIN IN INDIANA. In the winter of 1816 Thomas Lincoln, with his wife and two children, Sarah and Abraham, left Kentucky for Indiana. They settled at Pigeon Creek in Perry County. At first they lived in a cabin which Thomas had rebuilt to fit their need. Twelve years later, in 1829, he erected the above cabin with the help of his son Abraham. But the family never moved into it. The cabin stood until 1874, when it was dismantled and taken first to Rockfort and then to Cincinnati, where it was sold piecemeal as souvenirs.

16

Diorama in the Chicago Historical Society

"I never seen Abe after he was twelve 'at he didn't have a book in his hand or in his pocket. He'd put a book inside his shirt an' fill his pants pockets with corn dodgers an' go off to plow or hoe.

When noon came he'd set under a tree, an' read an' eat. An' when he come to the house at night, he'd tilt a cheer back by the chimbley, put his feet on the rung, an' set on his back-bone an' read."

and mother of Sarah and Abraham, was carried away by the "milk-sickness."

Dennis said: "Oh Lord, oh Lord, I'll never furgit it, the mizry in that cabin in the woods when Nancy died.

"Abe an' me helped Tom make the coffin. He tuk a log left over from makin' the cabin, and I helped him whipsaw it into planks an' plane 'em. Me 'n Abe held the planks while Tom bored holes an' put 'em together with

pegs Abe'd whittled. There wasn't sca'cely any nails in the kentry an' little iron, except in knives an' guns an' cookin' pots. Tom's tools was a wonder to the hull deestrict. 'Pears to me like Tom was always makin' a coffin

17

fur someone. We laid Nancy close to the deer run in the woods. Deer was the only wild critters the women wasn't afeerd of. Abe was som'ers 'round nine year old, but he never got over the mizable way his mother died."

For the next year Abraham's twelve-year-old sister Sarah cooked the meals and took care of the household. It was hard for Tom to live in the wilderness without a wife to look after the children. So he went back to Elizabethtown to find one.

Once more he looked up Sarah Bush, whom he had courted before he married Nancy. Since then Sarah, who had married Daniel Johnston, the jailer, had become a widow, her husband having died, leaving her with three children.

According to a contemporary witness, this is what happened when Thomas Lincoln visited Sarah Bush Johnston.

"Well, *Miss* Johnston," said Thomas, "I have no wife, and you have no husband. I came a purpose to marry you. I knowed you from a gal, and you knowed me from a boy. I have no time to lose; and, if you are willin' let it be done straight off."

And Sarah replied:

"Tommy, I know you well, and have no objection to marrying you; but I cannot do it straight off, as I owe some debts that must first be paid."

Thomas paid the debts, and the next morning—December 2, 1819—they were married. And soon his new wife and her three children, John, Elizabeth, and Matilda, "an' a four-hoss wagon load o' goods; feather pillers and chists o' drawers, an' a flax wheel, an' a soap kettle, an' cookin' pots an' pewter dishes," set out for Pigeon Creek.

What the new Mrs. Lincoln found there was not too encouraging. A little cabin without windows and floor, with a few pieces of crude furniture around, two unkempt children—Sarah, aged twelve, and Abraham, aged ten. And

there was Dennis, who, since the death of the Sparrows, lived there as well.

In Dennis's opinion "Aunt Sairy sartinly did have faculty. I reckon we was all purty ragged an' dirty when she got there. The fust thing she did was to tell me to tote one o' Tom's carpenter benches to a place outside the door, near the hoss trough. Then she had me an' Abe an' John Johnston, her boy, fill the trough with spring water. She put out a big gourd full o' soft soap, an' another one to dip water with, an' told us boys to wash up fur dinner. You jist naturally had to be somebody when Aunt Sairy was around. She had Tom build 'er a loom, an' when she heerd o' some lime burners bein' 'round Gentryville, Tom had to mosey over an' git some lime an' whitewash the cabin. An' he made 'er an ash-hopper fur lye, an' a chicken house nothin' could git into. Then— te-he-he-he! she set some kind of a dead-fall trap fur him an' got Tom to jine the Baptist Church. Cracky, but Aunt Sairy was some punkins!

"Before winter he'd put in a new floor, he'd whipsawed an' planed off so she could scour it; made some good beds an' cheers, an' tinkered at the roof so it couldn't snow in on us boys that slep' in the loft. Purty soon we had the best house in the kentry. Thar was eight of us then to do fur, but Aunt Sairy had faculty an' didn't 'pear to be hurried or worried none.

"An' it wasn't only in things to make us comfable an' well thought of. She didn't have no eddication herself, but she knowed what l'arnin' could do fur folks. She wasn't thar very long before she found out how Abe hankered after books. She heered him talkin' to me, I reckon. 'Denny,' he'd say, 'the things I want to know is in books. My best friend's the man who'll git me one.' Well, books wasn't as plenty as wild cats, but I got one by cuttin' cordwood. It had a lot o' yarns in it. One I ricollect was about a feller that got near some darned fool rock that drawed all the nails out o' his boat an' he got a duckin'. Wasn't a blamed bit o' sense in that yarn."

And Dennis remembered that "Abe'd lay on his stummick by the fire, an'

IN THE FALL OF 1818 LINCOLN'S MOTHER DIED. Thirty-four-year-old Nancy Hanks was buried in Indiana soil, leaving behind her husband and her two young children. "Oh Lord, oh Lord," remembered Dennis Hanks, "I'll never furgit it, the mizry in that cabin in the woods when Nancy died." There was no church in the neighborhood, and the winter passed before Rev. David Elkins, pastor of the Little Mount Church back in Kentucky— where Nancy Hanks had once worshiped—came to Indiana and preached her funeral sermon.

read out loud to me an' Aunt Sairy, an' we'd laugh when he did, though I reckon it went in at one ear an' out at the other with 'er, as it did with me. Tom'd come in an' say: 'See here, Abe, your mother can't work with you abotherin' her like that,' but Aunt Sairy always said it didn't bother her none, an' she'd tell Abe to go on. I reckon that encouraged Abe a heap.

" 'Abe,' sez I, many a time, 'them yarns is all lies.'

" 'Mighty darned good lies,' he'd say, an' go on readin' an' chucklin' to hisself, till Tom'd kiver up the fire fur the night an' shoo him off to bed.

"I reckon Abe read that book a dozen times an' knowed all the yarns by heart. He didn't have nothin' much else to read, excep' Aunt Sairy's Bible. He cut four cords o' wood onct to git one stingy little slice of a book. It was a life of Washington; an' he'd lay over the Statoots of Indiany half the night. We'd git hold o' a newspaper onct in a while, an' Abe larned Henry Clay's speeches by heart. He liked the stories in the Bible, too, an' he got a little book o' fables som'ers. I reckon it was them stories he read that give him so many yarns to tell. I asked him onct after he'd gone to lawin' an' could make a jury laugh or cry by firing a yarn at 'em.

" 'Abe,' sez I, 'whar did you got so blamed many lies?' An' he'd always say, 'Denny, when a story l'arns you a good lesson, it ain't no lie. God tells truth in parables. They're easier fur common folks to understand an' ricollect.' His stories was like that.

"Seems to me now I never seen Abe after he was twelve 'at he didn't have a book in his hand or in his pocket. He'd put a book inside his shirt an' fill his pants pockets with corn dodgers an' go off to plow or hoe. When noon came he'd set under a tree, an' read an' eat. An' when he come to the house at night, he'd tilt a cheer back by the chimbley, put his feet on the rung, an' set on his back-bone an' read. Aunt Sairy always put a candle on the mantel-tree piece fur him, if she had one. An' as like as not Abe'd eat his supper thar, takin' anything she'd give him that he could gnaw at an' read at

A PAGE FROM LINCOLN'S EXERCISE BOOK. His stepmother said: "Abe read all the books he could lay his hands on, and when he came across a passage that struck him, he would write it down on boards if he had no paper and keep it there till he did get paper, then he would rewrite it, look at it, repeat it. He had a copybook, a kind of scrapbook, in which he put down all things and then preserved them." In the corner of this page he wrote the lines: "Abraham Lincoln his hand and pen he will be good but god knows When."

the same time. I've seen many a feller come in an' look at him, Abe not knowin' anybody was 'round, an' sneak out agin like a cat, an' say: 'Well, I'll be darned.' It didn't seem natural, no-how, to see a feller read like that. Aunt Sairy'd never let the childern pester him. She always declared Abe was goin' to be a great man some day, an' she wasn't goin' to have him hendered."

THE FOURTEEN YEARS IN INDIANA

His LIFE in Indiana Lincoln summed up in the laconic sentence: "There I grew up." Yes, he grew up there in that "wild region, with many bears and other wild animals, still in the woods," not only in body—which shot up to over six feet in height—but in mind as well. There he went to school "by littles," as he recalled, there he learned "*readin'*, *writin'*, and *cipherin'* to the Rule of Three."

The names of his schoolmasters were Andrew Crawford, James Swaney and Azel W. Dorsey. At Crawford's school he was about ten years old, at Swaney's he was fourteen, and at Dorsey's he was in his seventeenth year. Sometimes, when money became scarce in the Lincoln household, Abe would stop studying and work either with his father on the farm or for neighbors.

His aggregate schooling, as he himself confessed, "did not amount to one year."

One of his schoolmates—Nathaniel Grigsby—whose brother Aaron afterward married Sarah, Lincoln's sister—tells of those early schooldays:

"He was always at school early and attended his studies. He was always at the head of his class, and passed us rapidly in his studies. He lost no time at home, and when he was not at work was at his books. He kept up his studies on Sunday, and carried his books with him so that he might read when he rested from labor."

His great love was books. He read not many of them, but what he read, he remembered. "Abe could easily learn and long remember, and when he did learn anything he learned it

well and thoroughly," said his stepmother. His favorite books were the *Bible* and *Aesop's Fables*, and he always kept these two books within reach, reading and rereading them again and again. "These two volumes furnished him with the many figures of speech and parables which he used with such happy effect in his later and public utterances." The other books he read were: *Robinson Crusoe*, Bunyan's *Pilgrim's Progress*, a *History of the United States*, and Weems' *Life of Washington*, and later Franklin's *Autobiography* and Weems' *Life of Marion*.

To his schoolmates he often repeated long passages from books which he was reading. He was—so his stepsister recalled—an indefatigable preacher. "When father and mother would go to church," said Matilda, "Abe would take down the Bible, read a verse, give out a hymn, and we would sing. Abe was about fifteen years of age. He preached, and we would do the crying. Sometimes he would join in the chorus of tears. One day my brother, John Johnston, caught a land terrapin, brought it to the place where Abe was preaching, threw it against the tree, and crushed the shell. It suffered much—quivered all over. Abe then preached against cruelty to animals, contending that an ant's life was as sweet to it as ours to us." And he sat down and wrote an essay in which he protested against cruelty to animals. He also wrote poetry.

What did he look like? He was tall and was growing rapidly. Before he was seventeen he measured 6 feet 2 inches, and weighed about 160 pounds. His body was slim, but wiry, his skin shriveled and yellow, his arms were large and muscular, his legs long.

"He wore buckskin breeches," says Kate Gentry, one of the girls who was with him at Crawford's school, "linsey-woolsey shirt, and a cap made of

An imaginary sketch by an unknown artist

HOW HE EARNED HIS FIRST DOLLAR. "I was about eighteen years of age," recalled Lincoln, "and had constructed a flatboat large enough to take the few barrels of things we had gathered to New Orleans. A steamer was going down the river . . . when two men with trunks came down to the shore in carriages, and asked: 'Will you take us and our trunks out to the steamer?' I was very glad to have the chance of earning something, and supposed that both of them would give me a couple of 'bits.' The trunks were put in my boat, the passengers seated themselves on them, and I sculled them out to the steamer. They got on board, and I lifted the trunks and put them on the deck. The steamer was about to put on steam again, when I called out, 'You have forgotten to pay me!' Each of them took from his pocket a silver half-dollar and threw it on the bottom of my boat. I could scarcely believe my eyes as I picked up the money. You may think it was a very little thing, and in these days it seems to me like a trifle, but it was a most important incident in my life. I could scarcely credit that I, the poor boy, had earned a dollar in less than a day: that by honest work I had earned a dollar. I was a more hopeful and thoughtful boy from that time."

Painted around 1860; now in the Chicago Historical Society

"ABE COULD SINK AN AXE DEEPER IN WOOD than any man I
ever saw," recalled William Wood, a Lincoln neighbor. "He was a
strong man, physically powerful; he could strike with a mall a
heavier blow than any other man." This painting, "The Railsplitter,"
was carried about in Republican rallies during the 1860 contest.

the skin of a squirrel or coon. His
breeches were baggy and lacked by
several inches meeting the tops of his
shoes, thereby exposing his shin-bone,
sharp, blue, and narrow!"

He had to work. As soon as he was
able to earn wages, he was hired out
among the neighbors. Mrs. Josiah
Crawford said that Lincoln worked for
her husband, daubing the cabin, clearing land, and making rails. "When he
worked for us, he read all our books,
would sit up late in the night, kindle
up the fire, read by it, cipher by it."
Another of Lincoln's employers, John
Romine, recalled that he "used to get
mad at him" because he "was always
reading and thinking . . . I say Abe
was awful lazy; he would laugh and

talk and crack jokes and tell stories all
the time, didn't ever work but did
dearly love his pay."

Once Lincoln was asked whether he
could kill a hog and he replied that he
felt like the Irishman with the violin:
"that he had never done it, but he
would try."

"If you will risk the hog," he said,
"I will risk myself."

As the years went by and he grew
up, he would go in the evening to the
store of William Jones in Gentryville.
"He was so odd, original and humorous and witty that all the people in
town would gather around him," recalled Dennis Hanks. He would keep
them there till midnight or longer telling stories and cracking jokes."

He liked the company of men more
than that of the girls. "He was not very
fond of girls, as he seemed to me,"
said his stepmother, and John Hanks
asserted: "I never could get him in
company with women; he was not a
timid man in this particular, but did
not seek such company."

His life at home was simple. His
relations to his father were not too
warm, but he got on well with his stepmother and the children she brought
in the house. He loved her and she was
deeply fond of him.

"He was the best boy I ever saw,"
said she. "I never gave him a cross
word in all my life. . . . His mind and
mine, what little I had, seemed to run
together, move in the same channel."

THE MIGRATION TO ILLINOIS WAS LONG AND TEDIOUS. The roads were bad; they would thaw out during the daytime and freeze over at night. One day the little dog which trotted behind the wagon fell behind and was not missed until the oxen crossed a stream. To turn back would have taken too much time, so the whining little animal was left to its fate. "But I could not endure the idea of abandoning even a dog," said Lincoln later. "Pulling off shoes and socks I waded across the stream and triumphantly

MOVING TO ILLINOIS

"WELL! LEMME see. Yes, I reckon it was John Hanks 'at got res'less an' lit out fur Illinois, an' wrote fur us all to come, an' he'd git land fur us," said Dennis Hanks, explaining why Thomas Lincoln decided to leave Indiana. "Tom was always ready to move. He never had his land in Indiany all paid fur, anyhow. So he sold off his corn an' hogs an' piled everything into ox wagons an' we all went, Linkhorns an'

Hankses an' Johnstons, all hangin' together. I reckon we was like one o' them tribes o' Israel that you can't break up nohow. An' Tom was always lookin' fur the land of Canaan. Thar was five famblies of us, an' Abe. It tuk us two weeks to git thar, raftin' over the Wabash, cuttin' our way through the woods, fordin' rivers, pryin' wagons an' steers out o' sloughs with fence rails, an' makin' camp. Abe cracked a

joke every time he cracked a whip, an' he found a way out o' every tight place, while the rest o' us was standin' 'round scratchin' our fool heads. I reckon Abe an' Aunt Sairy run that movin' an' good thing they did, or it'd 'a' been run into a swamp an' sucked under."

In his recollection Dennis put the blame on "shiftless" Tom Lincoln as the one who was eager to leave Indiana; by then he had forgotten that he himself was just as anxious to move as Tom. He cursed the land. "I'm goin' to git out o' here and hunt a country where the 'milk-sick' is not; it's like to ruined me," he was heard to say.

returned with the shivering animal under my arm. His frantic leaps of joy and other evidences of a dog's gratitude amply repaid me for all the exposure I had undergone."

Yes, there was the frightful plague of milk sickness that winter in Indiana. Dennis lost four milk cows and eleven calves in one week; how many of Thomas Lincoln's perished, we do not know. But we do know that his farm was not paying, and as John Hanks sent messages of the wonderful land in Illinois, he was willing to give it a try. By the middle of February, 1830, he had sold his farm for $125—and once more he and his family were on the move.

Thirteen people went with the wagons, drawn by ox teams and filled with bedding, furniture, ovens, skillets, and all the household goods the migrants possessed. Thomas Lincoln, his wife Sarah, his son Abraham, and her son John D. Johnston made four. (Sarah, the elder sister of Abraham was no longer living. Married to Aaron Grigsby, she had died in childbirth two years before.) Dennis Hanks, who nine years before had married Sarah Bush Lincoln's fifteen-year-old daughter Elizabeth, was with his wife and four children in another wagon; Squire Hall, the husband of Matilda Johnston, Sarah Bush Lincoln's second daughter, his wife and child were in still another.

It was a tedious journey, "painfully slow and tiresome," recalled Lincoln later.

Abraham, who around this time had completed his twenty-first year and was lawfully free of his father's command, drove one of the teams. Before they left, he bought $30 worth of merchandise, investing all his savings in it. There were knives, forks, needles, pins, threads, buttons, and other things which he peddled all the way, making a handsome profit on his investment.

The wagons reached the county of Macon in Illinois sometime in March, and Thomas Lincoln settled with his family "on the north side of the Sangamon River, at the junction of the timberland and prairie, about ten miles westerly from Decatur. Here they built a log cabin, into which they removed, and made sufficient of rails to fence ten acres of ground, fenced and broke the ground, and raised a crop of sown corn upon it the same year." This is how Lincoln remembered his entry to Illinois.

"In the autumn all hands were greatly afflicted with ague and fever, to which they had not been used, and by which they were greatly discouraged, so much so that they determined to leave the county. They remained, however, through the succeeding winter, which was the winter of the very celebrated 'deep snow' of Illinois."

When spring came the Lincolns were on the move again—Thomas at last finding his harbor in Coles County where he remained the rest of his days.

The reassembled cabin at the Chicago Sanitary Fair, photographed on June 8, 1865

THE LINCOLNS' FIRST HOME IN ILLINOIS. Thomas Lincoln stopped at first in Macon County, where, with his son's help, he erected this cabin. Dennis Hanks (with beard) and John Hanks posed before it in 1865, when the cabin was shown in Chicago. Of those early days Dennis remembered: "It was a purty kentry up on the Sangamon, an' we was all tuk with the idy that they could run steamboats up to our cornfields and load; but we had fever an' ager turrible. . . . Abe helped put up a cabin fur Tom on the Sangamon, clear fifteen acres fur corn an' split walnut rails to fence it in."

23

FLOATING DOWN THE MISSISSIPPI

ONCE BEFORE, Lincoln had taken produce down the Mississippi. This was in the spring of 1828—three months after his sister Sarah died. At that time James Gentry had asked him to go with his son Allen on a flatboat to New Orleans. Said Lincoln: "I was a hired hand merely, and I and the son of the owner, without other assistance, made the trip. The nature of part of the cargo-load, as it was called, made it necessary for us to linger and trade along the sugar coast; and one night we were attacked by seven negroes with intent to kill and rob us. We were hurt some in the melée, but succeeded in driving the negroes from the boat, and then 'cut cable,' 'weighed anchor,' and left."

Three years later Lincoln was again hired, together with John Hanks and his stepbrother John D. Johnston, to go down the river. They were to get 50 cents a day in addition to the $60 for the trip. Their boss was Denton Offutt, "a brisk and venturesome business man, whose operations extended up and down the Sangamon River for many miles." Offutt asked the three men to meet him at Springfield as soon as the snow should go off. Lincoln remembered: "When it did go off, which was about the first of March, 1831, the country was so flooded as to make traveling by land impracticable; to obviate which difficulty we purchased a large canoe, and came down the Sangamon River in it."

The young men found Offutt, but no boat. Offutt said he would pay them

TAKING PRODUCE TO NEW ORLEANS. In 1828, while living in Indiana, nineteen-year-old Abraham Lincoln was hired by

each $12 per month if they would build one. They got the timber out of the trees and began making it at Sangamo Town, seven miles northwest of Springfield. They finished it in about four weeks, and loaded it with barrels of pork and corn and live hogs.

Lincoln later told the story: "Offutt bought thirty odd large fat live hogs, but found difficulty in driving them from where purchased them to the

An imaginary sketch from 1912 by Alice Myers Casey

THE TALE HOW LINCOLN CAME INTO CONTACT WITH SLAVERY. On his second trip to New Orleans, according to John Hanks, Lincoln visited the slave market and saw, for the first time, Negroes in chains—whipped and scourged. "Slavery ran the iron into him then and there," says Hanks, who "remembered" being in New Orleans with Lincoln—though in an autobiographical sketch Lincoln clearly said: "Hanks had not gone to New Orleans . . . but turned back from St. Louis." However it may be, Hanks recalled that he watched with Lincoln the auction of a comely mulatto girl. As she was undergoing a thorough examination by the bidders, Lincoln cried out: "By God, boys, let's get away from this. If ever I get a chance to hit that thing [meaning slavery], I'll hit it hard."

A 19th-century representation by W. J. Wilson

James Gentry to take a boatload of cargo to New Orleans. He and the son of Gentry made the trip alone and were attacked on

the way by seven Negroes. Three years later, in 1831, together with his stepbrother, John D. Johnston, and John Hanks, Lincoln

was again taking produce to New Orleans. this time for Denton Offutt, who hired him as a clerk for his New Salem store.

boat, and thereupon conceived the whim that he could sew up their eyes and drive them where he pleased. No sooner thought of than decided, he put his hands, including A., at the job, which was completed." But the "blind" hogs were just as difficult to handle; in the end they had to be tied and hauled on carts to the boat.

At last the three men went off with their cargo. At New Salem they met

with their first reverse. Their vessel stranded on the Rutledge's mill dam; they had to borrow another boat and change their goods into it. John Hanks recalled that they "rolled the barrels forward, bored a hole in the end of the boat over the dam—water ran out and thus we got over."

The voyage thereafter was uneventful; they reached New Orleans and disposed of their cargo.

In his third-person autobiography Lincoln wrote: "During this boat enterprize acquaintance with Offutt, who was previously an entire stranger, he conceived a liking for A. and believing he could turn him to account, he contracted with him to act as clerk for him, on his return from New-Orleans, in charge of a store and mill at New-Salem, then in Sangamon, now in Menard County."

25

AT NEW SALEM

THE PLACE where Abraham Lincoln came in July, 1831, to stop "indefinitely and for the first time, as it were, by himself" was New Salem—a tiny frontier village on the Sangamon River. Founded two years earlier, it was laid out by men who, with the unbounded optimism of the pioneers, hoped and believed that their river could be navigated. The two early settlers—James Rutledge and the nephew of his wife, John M. Camron —built a dam over the Sangamon, erected a saw and grist mill and waited for good tidings. Soon other settlers came; Samuel Hill and John McNeil opened a store not far from the mill,

then William Clary established a "grocery"—the frontier term for a saloon. A mill, a store, and a saloon were the usual foundation of a pioneer village; so New Salem began its life.

When twenty-two-year-old Lincoln arrived, there were already a few houses standing, with a handful of families living in them. It was a small community, and it did not grow to be big. In its heyday New Salem did not harbor more than a hundred people, but the population of another village in the northern part of the state, called Chicago, had no more either.

Lincoln sauntered around, made himself acquainted, and awaited the

PEOPLE LIKED TO LISTEN TO HIS STORIES. A short while after Lincoln came to New Salem, an election was held. "As things were dragging a little," remembered one of the villagers, "the new man began to spin out a stock of Indiana yarns." One of them went like this: "There was an old preacher in Indiana who used to appear before his congregation in a coarse linen shirt and baggy pantaloons with flap in front. His shirt was held in position by a single button, and that was at the collar, and as to suspenders —he had none. One day when rising in his pulpit to announce his text: 'I am the Christ, whom I shall represent today,' a little blue lizard ran up underneath his pantaloons. At first the old Baptist took little notice of the intruder; he slapped at it once or twice, that was all. But then, while he was continuing his text, the little fellow passed the equatorial line and was romping in the higher regions. The harassed preacher loosened the button on his waist-band and off came the baggy pantaloons. But by then the lizard was already underneath the shirt. This was too much. The poor man tore open the collar button and, with a sweep of his arm, threw off his shirt. There he stood before the dazed congregation. The silence was interrupted by an old lady in the back who got up and said in a loud voice: 'If you represent Christ then I'm done with the Bible.'"

Woodcarving by Carl Hallsthammer in the Illinois State Historical Library

HERE HE WORKED. The Offutt store in New Salem where Lincoln worked as a

arrival of his boss—Denton Offutt; and when Offutt came, the store was opened. It was similar to other frontier stores—stocked with goods and foodstuffs which were needed most. Situated on the bluff above the river—not far from the mill—the men of the neighborhood came there to meet, gossip, and debate. A few steps from it was the saloon owned by Bill Clary, whose brother founded the Clary's Grove settlement. The young men of that place made quite a reputation for themselves as a wild and reckless, hard-drinking and hard-fighting crowd.

26

clerk in the year 1831. It was situated on the bluff above the river, not far from Bill

Clary's grocery ("grocery" was the frontier term for a saloon), where the neighbor-

hood youth — and a carefree, boisterous youth it was—met to talk, drink and play.

Their leader, Jack Armstrong, was one of the strongest men in the neighborhood.

But for Denton Offutt no one could be more powerful than his clerk, Lincoln. He opened his mouth wide and let everybody know that his man could lick anyone, whoever it might be. The boys at Clary's Grove took the bait, and it was not long before Jack Armstrong challenged Offutt's clerk to a wrestling match.

The hours in the store passed pleasantly. If a customer came in, he lingered for a talk, and when nobody

was in the store, Lincoln settled down to read and study. Mentor Graham, the teacher, introduced him to mathematics and suggested he study grammar.

When spring came, Lincoln—"encouraged by his great popularity among his immediate neighbors"— decided to run for the State Legislature. Helped by Mentor Graham and John McNeil, he carefully composed a circular announcing his candidacy and setting forth his policies. In it he advocated internal improvements ("I believe the improvement of the Sangamo River to be vastly important and highly

desirable to the people of this country"), usury laws (". . . the practice of loaning money at exorbitant rates of interest" should be given attention), and aid to education ("That every man may receive at least a moderate education, and thereby be enabled to read the histories of his own and other countries, by which he may duly appreciate the value of our free institutions. . . .").

What interested the men of New Salem most was the improvement of navigation. If the Sangamon could be made navigable, the future of their village was safe; it meant not only

HIS FRIENDS IN NEW SALEM
PHOTOGRAPHS MADE IN THEIR LATER YEARS

SAMUEL HILL, grocer and leading businessman of New Salem was a thrifty person. The Methodist preacher, Peter Cartwright, said he believed Hill had no soul until a quarter was put to his lips and his soul "came up to get it."

JOHN M. CAMRON, one of the founders of New Salem, was a millwright by trade, and an ordained Presbyterian minister. When young Abraham Lincoln first arrived in New Salem in the summer of 1831, he boarded at Camron's house.

JAMES SHORT. When Lincoln could not pay his debts and the sheriff ordered the sale of his personal possessions, it was "Uncle Jimmy" who supposedly bid for the surveying instruments and returned them to his unlucky friend.

HANNAH ARMSTRONG, the wife of Jack Armstrong, was a special favorite of Lincoln. He often visited the Armstrong cabin, bringing candy to the children and rocking a cradle while she mended his clothes or got him something to eat.

MARY ANN RUTLEDGE, mother of Ann, Lincoln's traditional sweetheart, lived to a ripe old age and loved to talk of New Salem days. As Ann and her mother had a family resemblance, this is how Ann might have looked had she lived longer.

NANCY GREEN, the wife of Judge Bowling Green, was always at hand when Lincoln was in trouble. Villagers recalled that after Ann Rutledge died, Lincoln stayed with the Greens, and it was Nancy who nursed him back to sanity.

WILLIAM G. GREENE was hired by Denton Offutt to assist Lincoln in the store and at the mill. "Slicky Bill" and Lincoln slept in the store, and so strong was their intimacy that "when one turned over the other had to do likewise."

MENTOR GRAHAM, the teacher, helped Lincoln with his studies. In later years he said that of all his 5,000 pupils, Lincoln was the "most studious, diligent, straightforward young man in the pursuit of knowledge and literature."

JACK KELSO, with whom Lincoln boarded at one time, was an easygoing man who liked to fish, hunt, and most of all to read poetry. The latest research casts doubt on the authenticity of this portrait. It may be that of John A. Kelso.

cheaper goods, but more accessible markets.

It was around this time that the news reached them about the steamer *Talisman,* which, chartered by Captain Vincent Bogue, was ready to "deliver freight from St. Louis at the landing on the Sangamon River, opposite the town of Springfield, for thirty-seven and a half cents for 100 pounds"—or for less than half the overland charge. The villagers looked with great optimism toward this event.

Captain Bogue asked that a few men with long-handled axes meet him at the river mouth, to go before the *Talisman* and cut off overhanging limbs and clear the obstructions from the Sangamon. One of the men who responded was Lincoln. He and the others walked on the shore, and the *Talisman* followed them up the river till it reached Portland Landing, about seven miles from Springfield. The people were jubilant—at last it was proved that the river could be navigated.

For a week the *Talisman* lay anchored, then—as the water receded—it started on the return trip. Rowan Herndon was to pilot her to Beardstown, and he had chosen Lincoln as an assistant. They moved out with great hopes, but the going turned out to be slow. The Sangamon had so little water that the pilots could barely keep the boat under way. And when they reached New Salem, part of the dam had to be torn down. The villagers' hearts sank.

The excitement about the *Talisman* had barely spent itself when New Salem heard that Black Hawk, an Indian chief, had recrossed the border of Illinois with five hundred of his armed braves and was spreading terror along the frontier. The Governor asked for a thousand mounted volunteers to fight them, and Lincoln was among those who answered the call. The enlisted men met at the farm of Dallas Scott, on Richland Creek, formed a company and elected him as their captain.

Captain Lincoln was in the war for three months; he re-enlisted twice. "I was out of work," he said, "and there being no danger of more fighting, I

Painted for Esquire *in 1949 by Harold von Schmidt*

THE CELEBRATED WRESTLING BOUT OF NEW SALEM. Jack Armstrong was the leader of the Clary's Grove boys, a reckless roisterous, fearless crowd. When Denton Offutt bragged that his clerk was the strongest man in the neighborhood, Armstrong challenged Lincoln to a wrestling match. Rowan Herndon, who was there, remembered that after the two wrestlers had been striving a long time without either man prevailing, Lincoln said: "Jack, let's quit. I can't throw you—you can't throw me." So the match ended. From then on, the Clary's Grove boys accepted the newcomer. He was no longer an outsider in the village but one who "belonged."

could do nothing better than enlist again." Of military matters he knew little. Once when his company reached a narrow gate and he could not remember the proper command, he ordered: "Halt! This company will break ranks for two minutes and form again on the other side of the gate."

The nearest he and his group came to the war was at Kellogg's Grove where they buried five white men killed by the Indians. Lincoln later recalled: "I remember just how those men looked as we rode up the little hill where their camp was. The red light of the morning sun was streaming upon them as they lay heads toward us on the ground. And every man had a round, red spot on top of his head, about as big as a dollar where the redskins had taken his scalp. It was frightful, but it was grotesque, and the red sunlight seemed to paint everything all over. I remember that one man had on buckskin breeches."

In the middle of July Lincoln was mustered out of service at White River, Wisconsin, and returned home.

He arrived in New Salem sometime in July—in time to wind up his campaign for the election. In Pappsville he made a speech to a large crowd attending a sale, looking somewhat odd as he stood before the crowd, wearing flax and tow-linen pantaloons which were five inches too short in the legs, a calico shirt, short brogans, blue yarn socks, and an old-fashioned straw hat without a band.

While he stood on the platform, a fight broke out among the listeners. Lincoln descended, and seizing the bully who had started the mêlée by the neck and seat of his trousers, threw him—according to an eyewitness—twelve feet away. Then he returned to the platform, ending his speech with the memorable sentences:

"Fellow citizens, I presume you all know who I am—I am humble Abraham Lincoln. I have been solicited by my friends to become a candidate for the Legislature. My politics are short and sweet, like the old woman's dance. *(turn to page 32)*

THE VILLAGE OF NEW SALEM

THE PIONEER VILLAGE OF NEW SALEM—Lincoln's home from 1331 to 1837—was founded in 1829 by James Rutledge and John M. Camron, who built a dam on the river for a saw and grist mill.

THE DOUBLE HOUSE OF JOSHUA MILLER AND JOHN KELSO. Miller was a blacksmith and wagon maker; Kelso, his brother-in-law, was the easygoing, poetry-reading philosopher of the village.

THE MILLER BLACKSMITH SHOP was spacious, and one of the busiest places in the village. Here Miller's anvil forged horse shoes, different kinds of farm implements and household fittings.

THE INTERIOR OF THE ONSTOT HOUSE had a quiet dignity. There were stone fireplaces, chimneys and mantels, brick hearths, floors of sawn boards, and iron locks, door latches and hinges.

THE RUTLEDGE TAVERN. James Rutledge and a nephew of his wife, John Camron, founded New Salem in 1829. A year later the Legislature granted permission to build a dam, and thus the pros-

perity of the village began. To accommodate the newcomers, Rutledge converted his place into a tavern. Here Lincoln boarded at one time and fell in love with Ann, daughter of the house.

The pictures of the homes were taken at the New Salem village
which was restored on the initiative of William Randolph Hearst,
who in 1906 purchased the site and conveyed it first to the Old

THE HOME OF HENRY ONSTOT, the cooper, was built in 1835 when good workmanship and materials were not hard to get. As barrels were in great demand, Onstot could afford a good home.

SAM HILL'S RESIDENCE was the finest in the village, the only one with two stories and a porch. It was built of good materials, had doors front and rear; Sam was a wealthy man.

THE HOME OF ROBERT JOHNSON, the wheelwright. He was not a man of means; his home was a simple one. The floors were of puncheon, and latches, hinges and other fittings were of wood.

THE RESIDENCE OF DR. FRANCIS REGNIER, eccentric son of a French physician, was first used as a saloon. The doctor lived there only about two years, later kept the place as an office.

THE HILL-McNEIL STORE, in the center of the village, opened in the fall of 1829. Three years later the partnership was dissolved, as legend had it, because both men were in love with Ann Rutledge.

Hill continued the business by himself, and John McNeil became engaged to Ann. But then he left New Salem to visit his family in the East; by the time he returned to the village, Ann had died.

Salem Chautauqua Association at Petersburg, then by them to the State of Illinois to be used as a state park. The Illinois General Assembly voted funds to restore the village, opening it in 1933.

I am in favor of a national bank. I am in favor of the internal improvement system and a high protective tariff. These are my sentiments and political principles. If elected I shall be thankful; if not, it will be all the same."

He was not elected, and he found himself "without means and out of business." The Offutt store faded out, and Lincoln was wondering what to do. He "thought of learning the blacksmith trade—thought of trying to study law—rather thought he could not succeed at that without a better education."

"Before long, strangely enough," so he later recalled, "a man offered to sell, and did sell, to Abraham and another as poor as himself, an old stock of goods, upon credit. They opened as merchants; and he says that was *the* store. Of course they did nothing but get deeper and deeper in debt." It was not long before "the store winked out," and once more he had nothing to do. Luckily, he could land the job of the postmaster, succeeding Samuel Hill, "the office being too insignificant to make his politics an objection."

To be postmaster in New Salem was not so hard. One had plenty of time on hand, one could read the newspapers which came to the village, one could think and ponder. That Lincoln was not too businesslike we gather from a letter of Mathew S. Marsh, who wrote to his brother at that time: "The Post Master is very careless about leaving his office open and unlocked during the day—half the time I go in and get my papers, etc. Without anyone being there. . . ."

His pay was little, depending upon the receipts of the office; it was never more than $50 to $75 a year. To supplement it he split rails, helped at the mill, gave a hand at harvesting, tended store for Sam Hill, and took whatever came his way.

John Calhoun, the county surveyor, promised to make him his assistant. For days and nights Lincoln threw himself into studying Flint's *Treatise on Geometry, Trigonometry and Rectangular Surveying* and Gibson's *Treatise on Practical Surveying.* He bought a compass and chain, and with the help of Mentor Graham, he mastered surveying. "This procured bread, and kept soul and body together."

A surveyor usually got $2.50 for establishing each quarter-section of land, and less if his work was less. For traveling expenses he charged $2 a day. Often the pay was in goods. Thus, for one of his first surveys Lincoln re-

Reconstructed house in New Salem

THE BERRY-LINCOLN STORE. When Lincoln returned from the Black Hawk War and was defeated for the Legislature, he started a store. His partner was resourceful William F. Berry, a lad who had served in his company. But the two young men could not make the grade. They got deeper and deeper in debt, and gradually "the store winked out."

NINETEEN-YEAR-OLD ANN SHOPS IN THE

On the shelves all kinds of dry goods, furs, mittens, hides, pots, plates, and glassware. The store carried sugar, salt, and coffee, all imported through St. Louis, and very expensive; eggs, hops, vegetables, honey, butter, cheese, and bacon. If one needed firearms, one could buy them, and saddles, ox yokes, and tools.

That Ann Rutledge, whose name American folklore everlastingly links with that of Abraham Lincoln, visited the store and did some of her shopping there is probable. In 1832, when the store came into being, Ann

Diorama in the Chicago Historical Society

ERRY-LINCOLN STORE, WHERE TWENTY-THREE-YEAR-OLD ABRAHAM WAITS ON HER.

was nineteen years old and engaged to John McNeil—who later confessed to her that his real name was McNamar—a prosperous young man and a partner in Sam Hill's store. But one day John left New Salem to visit his family in New York, and as the weeks grew into months and he did not return, Ann felt she was free to do as she pleased.

Lincoln—according to the story which William H. Herndon perpetrated in his celebrated lecture of 1866—was in love with Ann, courted her, and asked her to marry him. Ann consented. To one of her brothers she said: "As soon as his studies are completed, we are to be married."

But it was not to be. In the summer of 1835 she became ill with typhoid fever. For weeks she lingered between life and death, and on August 25 she died, twenty-two years old. Legend had it that Lincoln almost lost his mind over her death and that it took weeks before he recovered. Speaking of her grave, Lincoln supposedly said to a friend: "My heart lies buried there."

THE LEAN-TO WHERE LINCOLN slept in the store was a typical frontier addition.

in my view, might tend most to the advancement of justice.

But, Fellow-Citizens, I shall conclude.—Considering the great degree of modesty which should always attend youth, it is probable I have already been more presuming than becomes me. However, upon the subjects of which I have treated, I have spoken as I thought. I may be wrong in regard to any or all of them ; but holding it a sound maxim, that it is better to be only sometimes right, than at all times wrong, so soon as I discover my opinions to be erroneous, I shall be ready to renounce them.

Every man is said to have his peculiar ambition. Whether it be true or not, I can say for one that I have no other so great as that of being truly esteemed of my fellow men, by rendering myself worthy of their esteem. How far I shall succeed in gratifying this ambition, is yet to be developed. I am young and unknown to many of you. I was born and have ever remained in the most humble walks of life. I have no wealthy or popular relations to recommend me. My case is thrown exclusively upon the independent voters of this county, and if elected they will have conferred a favor upon me, for which I shall be unremitting in my labors to compensate. But if the good people in their wisdom shall see fit to keep me in the background, I have been too familiar with disappointments to be very much chagrined.

Your friend and fellow-citizen,
            A. LINCOLN.
New Salem, March 9, 1832.

POLITICIAN. In the spring of 1832, less than a year after his arrival in New Salem, Lincoln, encouraged "by his great popularity among his immediate neighbors," ran for the State Legislature. The twenty-three-year-old politician announced his candidacy in the *Sangamo Journal* and for the first time put his political beliefs in print. He lost the election, the only time he was "ever beaten on a direct vote of the people."

SOLDIER. On April 21, 1832, Lincoln enrolled as militiaman in the expedition against the Indian Chief Black Hawk, who with five hundred braves crossed the Mississippi River into Illinois, creating fear and apprehension along the border. Lincoln's company, constituted of New Salem men, elected him as their captain. For three months he served in the "war," chasing after Indians without seeing one. On July 10 he was mustered out.

ceived two buckskins, which Hannah Armstrong "foxed" on his pants to protect them from briars.

A year went by, and another one. In the spring of 1834 Lincoln decided to try once more for the Legislature. This time he was chosen, so Lincoln erroneously remembered, "by the highest vote cast for any candidate." In reality he ran second.

During the campaign, Major John T. Stuart, a practicing lawyer in Springfield whom he had met in the Black Hawk War, encouraged him to take up the study of law. So, after he won the election, Lincoln "borrowed books of Stuart, took them home with him, and went at it in good earnest. He studied with nobody. He still mixed in the surveying to pay board and clothing bills."

Fall came, the time when the Legislature was to convene. Lincoln borrowed some money, bought himself a new suit, and set out for Vandalia to present himself. He was twenty-five years old, and—according to legend—in love with Ann Rutledge, the daughter of the man who founded New Salem. He had known her ever since he first came to the village, ever since he first boarded with the Rutledges. At that time Ann was not free; she was engaged to John McNeil, the partner in Sam Hill's grocery store. But in 1832 McNeil—who revealed to Ann that his real name was McNamar—had gone back East to see his parents and had failed to return. So Ann and Lincoln became engaged.

Their romance—if it was one—lasted only for a short while. In the summer of 1835 Ann became ill. For weeks she lingered between life and death, then she died. Lincoln, so the story goes, "slept not . . . ate not, joyed not." Ann's brother remembered that "His mind wandered from its throne . . . walked out of itself along the uncolumned air, and kissed and embraced the shadows and illusions of the heated brain." To a friend the young lover confessed that his heart was buried in the girl's grave.

Thus runs the legend of Lincoln's romance as told by William H. Herndon in his celebrated lecture a year after Lincoln's death. Whether it is the truth, who would say? While Lincoln was alive, there was only one story about the romance—in the *Menard Axis* (February 15, 1862), the newspaper in Petersburg, the neighboring town to New Salem.

One of the New Salem men, Isaac Cogdal, recalled a talk with Lincoln shortly before he left Springfield in 1860. This is how he remembered it:

Cogdal: "Is it true that you fell in love and courted Ann Rutledge?"

Lincoln: "It is true—true indeed I did. I have loved the name of Rutledge to this day."

"Is it true," asked Cogdal again, "that you ran a little wild about the matter?"

"I did really. I ran off the track; it was my first. I loved the woman dearly and sacredly. She was a handsome girl—would have made a good loving wife—was natural and quite intellectual, though not highly educated. I did honestly and truly love the girl. . . ."

Those who are familiar with Lincoln's character do not believe that such a dialogue was ever spoken. Still, the Ann Rutledge romance fired the imagination of later Americans, has become part of the folklore, and will remain so as long as the name of Abraham Lincoln is remembered.

At the frontier village of New Salem, Lincoln stayed for almost six years. They were fruitful, important years. There he became acquainted with the works of Shakespeare and the poetry of Burns, studied grammar and mastered mathematics, made his fledgling efforts in speechmaking and politics. There he learned to know the people, made friendships, fell in love. There he tried his hand at many trades —storekeeper, store owner, postmaster, surveyor.

He came there without a penny, "a piece of floating driftwood," as he told of himself, and left after six years with more than a thousand dollars of debt—but what he learned there could not be measured in material goods. The people, their thoughts and feelings, became etched deep in his soul—to remain there forever. His later greatness was built on this foundation.

POSTMASTER. On May 7, 1833, after the failure with his store, Lincoln became Postmaster of New Salem, an office which he retained for the next three years. He was well liked, friendly and obliging. If he knew someone was waiting for a letter, he would put it in the crown of his hat and deliver it, even though he had to walk many miles to do so. But—as the above Lincoln letter shows—the Postmaster also had his troubles.

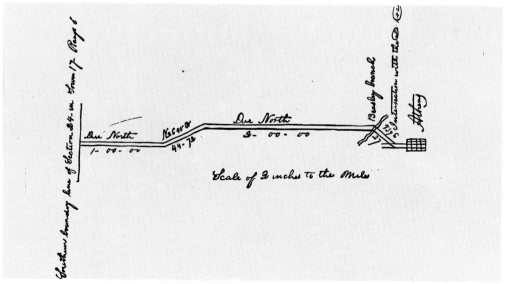

SURVEYOR. In the latter part of 1833 Lincoln secured employment as deputy to John Calhoun, the county surveyor. He had to earn money; the pay of the Postmaster was not enough to keep "soul and body together." Studying night and day, he mastered surveying, bought a horse on credit, "procured a compass and chain . . . and went at it." Several of the surveys like that above, which Lincoln made while in New Salem, have survived.

LEGISLATOR IN VANDALIA

THE Ninth General Assembly of the Sovereign State of Illinois, to which Lincoln was elected, convened at Vandalia the first day of December, 1834, and continued in daily session till the second week of February the following year. The young legislator from Sangamon County submitted his first proposal "to limit the jurisdiction of Justices of the Peace" a few days after the opening of the Legislature, and gave notice to the Speaker "that on Thursday next, or some day thereafter, I shall ask leave to introduce a bill entitled 'An act to authorize Samuel Musick, to build a toll bridge across Salt Creek in Sangamon County.'"

During his first term the new legislator was rather shy and silent with very little to say. But he had his eyes and ears open, he observed, watched and learned; and he acquired friends. It was in Vandalia that Lincoln first met the newly elected Democratic member from Morgan County, twenty-three-year-old Stephen A. Douglas.

At the next election Sangamon County re-elected Lincoln, and he returned to Vandalia as the leader of the "long nine," the seven tall Representatives and two Senators from his home county.

In the ensuing session, which enacted a record number of bills, legislating aids to an enormous internal improvement system, Lincoln took a prominent part. He proved himself a resourceful parliamentarian, a clever practitioner of logrolling, using all the tricks and wiles of the trade. His ambition was—so he said—to become the "DeWitt Clinton of Illinois."

His efforts to remove the seat of government from Vandalia were shrewd. A contemporary historian

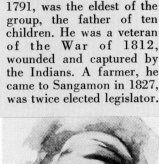

NINIAN W. EDWARDS, born in 1809, was the youngest of the long nine and one of the least popular. "Constitutionally an aristocrat," wrote one of his colleagues about him, "he hated democracy . . . as the devil is said to hate holy water."

WILLIAM F. ELKIN, born in 1792, moved from Kentucky to Ohio and then to Indiana, settling in the Sangamon region in 1825. A farmer, with fifteen children, he was elected to the Legislature three years after he came to the county.

JOHN DAWSON, born in 1791, was the eldest of the group, the father of ten children. He was a veteran of the War of 1812, wounded and captured by the Indians. A farmer, he came to Sangamon in 1827, was twice elected legislator.

ROBERT LANG WILSON was born in Pennsylvania in 1805. From there he came by way of Ohio and Kentucky to Sangamon County in 1833. A self-made lawyer, he practiced in the village of Athens, ten miles from Springfield.

ARCHER G. HERNDON, born in 1795, was elected to the Senate along with Job Fletcher. Tavernkeeper and strong proslavery man, he called his son William (who later became Lincoln's law partner) "a damned abolitionist pup."

JOB FLETCHER, born in 1793, came to the Sangamon country as early as 1819. Besides being a farmer, he taught school and was the first justice of the peace in the county. He was elected to the House in 1826 and the Senate in 1836.

THE "LONG NINE" FROM SANGAMON

In 1836 Sangamon County sent seven Whig Representatives and two Senators to the Illinois Legislature. As most of them were tall men—their total height was fifty-four feet—they became known as "the long nine." Six-foot-four Lincoln, the tallest, was their leader. Pictures of Andrew McCormick, a three-hundred-pound stonecutter, and Dan Stone, a college-educated Vermonter who had started on his political career in Ohio, could not be found.

THE THIRD STATE HOUSE of Vandalia, where Lincoln served as a legislator. Built in 1836 in the hope that the capital would remain there, it was barely ready for the regular session of the Legislature.

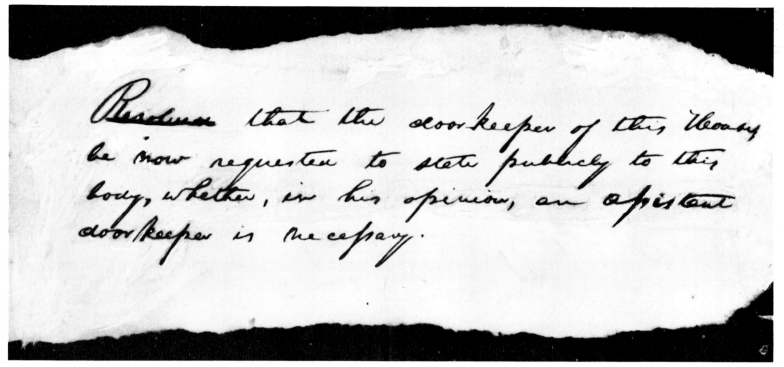

IS AN ASSISTANT DOORKEEPER NECESSARY? A suggested resolution in the Vandalia Legislature, in Lincoln's handwriting, asking the doorkeeper of the House "to state publicly to this body, whether, in his opinion, an assistant doorkeeper is necessary."

noted that the Sangamon County delegation under Lincoln's leadership "from the beginning of the session, threw itself as a unit in support of, or opposition to, every local measure of interest, but never without a bargain for votes in return on the seat of government question." Thus the capital of Illinois became Springfield.

It was during this session that Lincoln made a protest against the state's position on the slavery issue. He and his colleague Dan Stone declared that slavery was "founded on both injustice and bad policy." Yet they did not think that the abolitionists' agitation would help matters. They held that the abolitionists were increasing rather than abating the evils of slavery.

Professor William E. Baringer gives this fine analysis of the young legislator's years in the small Illinois capital.

"In the muddy village of Vandalia he learned and practiced the subtleties of his trade under the example and tutelage of experienced politicians. Here for the first time he mingled in polite society with men and women of wealth, culture, education; here he debated and heard discussed every phase of national and state politics and economic theory, probing problems of slavery and abolition, banking states' rights, executive powers and patronage, temperance, internal improvements, public lands, tariff, education, capital punishment, judicial procedure, financial panic. As a formative influence the Vandalia period was of first importance in the astonishing career of Abraham Lincoln."

CHARTER'S TAVERN, the inn at Vandalia, where Lincoln boarded when a legislator. Many of the fifty-five Representatives and twenty-six Senators who made up the Illinois Legislature stayed in this hostelry.

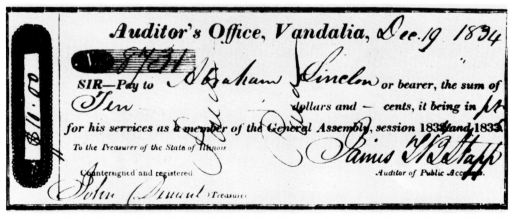

ONE OF LINCOLN'S SALARY WARRANTS for his services as legislator in the Illinois General Assembly. During his four terms in the Legislature—eight years—Lincoln received $1,762 as salary and $188 for traveling expenses, altogether a total of $1,950.

IN LOVE

WITH

A FAT GIRL

THE MAN who observed Lincoln for more than two decades—William H. Herndon—said about his law partner's feeling toward the weaker sex: "Mr. Lincoln had a strong, if not terrible passion for women. He could hardly keep his hands off a woman; and yet, much to his credit, he lived a pure and virtuous life." Judge David Davis, another man who knew him well, confirmed this opinion. "Mr. Lincoln's honor saved many a woman," said he.

Herndon and Davis may have been right. But how much could friends really know about the love life of such a reticent man as Lincoln was?

A year had passed since Ann Rutledge's death, and Lincoln was courting again. The object of his attention was Mary Owens, a girl from Kentucky, 29 years old, weighing about 170 pounds. "She was tall, portly, had large blue eyes and the finest trimmings I ever saw," remembered a man of New Salem. "She was jovial, social, loved wit and humor, had a liberal English education, and was considered wealthy." And there was still more to say about her: "None of the poets or romance writers have ever given us a picture of a heroine so beautiful as a good description of Miss Owens in 1836 would be."

Lincoln met Mary for the first time in 1833, when she came to visit her married sister in New Salem. Mary's sister, Mrs. Bennett Abell, was a good friend of his, and she thought that it was time for Lincoln to marry. When

LINCOLN WRITES TO MARY OWENS. This is the second of the three letters which remain of his quaint romance. Written in Springfield on May 7, 1837, whence Lincoln had removed the previous month, it is a warning to Mary in case she would be willing to marry him. "You would have to be poor without the means of hiding your poverty," Lin-you have said to me may have been in jest, or I may have misunderstood it. If so, then let it be forgotten; if otherwise, I much wish you would think seriously before you decide. For my part I have already decided. What I have said I will most positively abide by, provided you wish it. My opinion is that you had better not do it. You have not been accustomed to hardship, and it may be more severe than you now imagine.

I know you are capable of thinking correctly on any subject, and if you deliberate maturely upon this, before you decide, then I am willing to abide your decision.

You must write me a good long letter after you get this. You have nothing else to do, and though it might not seem interesting to you, after you had written it, it would be a good deal of company to me in this "busy wilderness". Tell your sister I don't want to hear any now about selling out and moving. That gives me the hypo whenever I think of it.

Yours &c

Lincoln

MARY OWENS, the girl Lincoln proposed to marry in 1837. She was a year older than he, and according to her own description she had "fair skin, deep blue eyes, and dark curling hair; height five feet, five inches; weight about a hundred and fifty pounds."

Of their meeting he noted: "I knew she was called an 'old maid,' and I felt no doubt of the truth of at least half of the appelation; but now, when I beheld her, I could not for my life avoid thinking of my mother; and this, not from withered features, for her skin was too full of fat, to permit its contracting into wrinkles; but from her want of teeth, weatherbeaten appearance in general, and from a kind of notion that ran in my head that *nothing* could have commenced at the size of infancy, and reached her present bulk in less than thirty-five or forty years; and, in short, I was not at all pleased with her. But what could I do? I had told her sister that I would take her for better or for worse; and I made a point of honor and conscience in all things, to stick to my word, especially if others had been induced to act on it, which in this case, I doubted not they had, for I was now fairly convinced, that no other man on earth would have her, and hence the conclusion that they were bent on holding me to my bargain. Well, thought I, I have said it, and, be consequences what they may, it shall not be my fault if I fail to do it. At once I determined to consider her my wife; and this done, all my powers of discovery were put to the rack, in search of perfections in her, which might be fairly set-off, against her defects. I tried to imagine she was handsome, which, but for her unfortunate corpulency, was actually true. Exclusive of this, no woman that I have seen, has a finer face. I also tried to convince myself, that the mind was much more to be valued than the person; and in this, she was not inferior, as I could discover, to any with whom I had been acquainted."

All this sounds like "sour grapes." In reality, Lincoln wooed her, wanted to marry her, and it was Mary who declined.

coln tells her, and adds: "Whatever woman may cast her lot with mine, should any ever do so, it is my intention to do all in my power to make her happy and contented." But once more he sounds a warning. "My opinion is that you had better not do it. You have not been accustomed to hardship, and it may be more severe than you now imagine."

her sister left New Salem to return home, there was some teasing about her. Mrs. Abell told Lincoln that she would bring Mary back if he would promise to marry her. Lincoln promised—whether in fun or in earnest, we don't know—and was looking forward to Mary's return.

On the 7th of November, 1836—election day—she came back to New Salem. The prospective bridegroom was on hand to greet her, and from then on—so the people of the village said—"wherever she went, he was at her side." They walked and they talked, they visited people and took part in quilting bees and outings.

One day they were riding together with other young people to visit the Bowling Greens. Coming to a treacherous branch of the stream, all the men gallantly helped their ladies to cross safely—all of them save Lincoln, who rode on, never even looking back at Mary. "You are a nice fellow," chided Mary when she caught up with him on the other side. "I suppose you did not care whether my neck was broken or not." He said laughingly that he knew she was "plenty smart to take care of herself." But Mary wondered. Was this the man she was to marry?

In December, a month after her return, when Lincoln left for Vandalia to take up his legislative duties, there was no definite understanding between them.

They wrote to each other and, as lovers do, they quarreled. "The longer I can avoid the mortification of looking in the Post Office for your letter and not finding it, the better. You see I am mad about that *old letter* yet. I don't like very well to risk you again," wrote Lincoln. Yet he ended his note with the plea: "Write back as soon as you get this, and if possible [say] something that will please me, for really I have not been pleased since I left you."

The following March, after the recess of the Legislature, Lincoln returned to New Salem where he saw Mary again and noted: "She was the same, and so was I." And though he said of himself that he was as "firm as the surge-repelling rock" in his reso-

lution to be wedded to her, he was "continually repenting the rashness" which had led him to make it. He hesitated, procrastinated, delayed saying the final word. "I really dreaded as much, perhaps more, than an Irishman does the halter," said he later.

Soon afterward, in April, Lincoln left New Salem for Springfield, where his doubts got the better of him. He feared that he would make a bad husband. In a letter written on May 7 he warned her that if they would marry, she would be poor without the means of hiding her poverty. And while he would promise to do all in his power to make her happy and contented, as to their marriage his advice was: "My opinion is you had better not do it. You have not been accustomed to hardship, and it may be more severe than you imagine."

What Mary answered, we do not know, but we know that in the middle of August Lincoln went to see her in New Salem, probably made a definite

AFTER HIS RETURN FROM NEW SALEM, where he visited Mary, Lincoln wrote her this letter in which he said: "I want . . . more than anything else, to do right with you, and if I *knew* it would be doing right, as I rather suspect it would, to let you alone, I would do it." He left it for Mary to decide. "If you feel in any degree bound to me,

40

proposal, and then in the evening of that very day he returned to Springfield, from where he wrote her a strange and confusing letter.

"You must know that I cannot see you, or think of you, with entire indifference," wrote Lincoln. "I want, at this particular time, more than anything else, to do right with you, and if I *knew* it would be doing right, as I rather suspect it would, to let you alone, I would do it." But what would be the right thing? To marry her or to give her up? He did not know. So he suggested: "If you feel yourself in any degree bound to me, I am now willing to release you, provided you wish it; while, on the other hand, I am willing, and even anxious to bind you faster, if I can be convinced that it will, in any considerable degree, add to your happiness."

Mary knew her own mind. She told her strange suitor that she had no desire to marry him. Lincoln was perplexed, asked her a second time, supposing at first she was turning him down "through an affectation of modesty," but Mary once more said no with even "greater firmness than before." He "tried it again and again, but with the same success, or rather with the same want of success."

Now that Mary had rejected him, Lincoln's attitude toward her changed. He was no longer ready to give her up; he wanted to have her as his wife, and he was mortified "almost beyond endurance." Yet Mary was firm; her "no" could not be changed.

After the affair was over, Lincoln wrote a curious letter, trying to analyze his emotions and explain his part in the matter. As it was dated April 1, it could be taken as an April Fool's Day letter, and that is how the recipient, Mrs. Browning, regarded it. But it is not difficult to perceive beyond the jocular narrative how seriously Lincoln was involved and how hurt he had been by Mary's refusal.

"I was mortified," he wrote to his friend Mrs. Browning, "in a hundred different ways. My vanity was deeply wounded by the reflections, that I had so long been too stupid to discover her intentions, and at the same time never doubting that I understood them perfectly; and also, that she whom I had taught myself to believe nobody else would have, had actually rejected me with all my fancied greatness; and to cap the whole, I then, for the first time, began to suspect that I was really a little in love with her. But let it all go. I'll try and outlive it. Others have been made fools of by the girls; but this can never with truth be said of me. I most emphatically, in this instance, made a fool of myself. I have now come to the conclusion never again to think of marrying, and for this reason; I can never be satisfied with any one who would be block-head enough to have me."

Mary Owens returned to Kentucky, married and raised a family. When—three decades later—she was asked why she refused to become the wife of Lincoln, she answered: "Mr. Lincoln was deficient in those little links which make up the chain of woman's happiness—at least it was so in my case."

I am now willing to release you, provided you wish it; while, on the other hand, I am willing, and even anxious to bind you faster, if I can be convinced that it will, in any considerable degree, add to your happiness." When Mary told Lincoln that she would not marry him, the rejected lover was mortified. He then knew that he really loved her.

A photograph taken around 1858 by Preston Butler

THE SPRINGFIELD WHICH ABRAHAM LINCOLN SAW when he lived there. This is the west side of the Square. The next to last building housed the office of the Lincoln-Herndon law firm, where Lincoln practiced law for sixteen years. Notice the sign of J. H. Adams, the hatter, in front of the third house—a top hat on a pole —and the boards in the plank street, which are clearly visible.

MOVING TO SPRINGFIELD

ON APRIL 15, 1837, Lincoln left New Salem, riding to Springfield, where he was to settle. He had little money—all his earthly belongings he carried in his saddlebags. He was twenty-eight years old—and strangely enough he had twenty-eight more years to live— to the day. Six weeks before—as legislator in Vandalia—he had been the chief mover behind the acceptance of an Act which was to remove the capital from Vandalia to Springfield.

When he arrived at Springfield, to take up his new duties as a partner in the law office of John T. Stuart, whom he first met in the Black Hawk War, the city boasted about 1,500 inhabitants. A census taken the previous year counted nineteen dry-goods stores, six retail groceries, one wholesale grocery, four hotels, four coffee houses, four drug, two clothing, and two shoe stores. There were two newspapers— the *Sangamo Journal*, edited by Simeon Francis, the organ of the Whigs, and the *Illinois Republican*, under George R. Weber, the mouthpiece of the Democrats.

THE ADVERTISEMENT in the *Sangamo Journal* on April 15, 1837, announcing that Abraham Lincoln had become a partner in the law office of John T. Stuart.

If one needed medical help, eighteen doctors ("including steam doctors") were on call, and to look after one's legal entanglements, eleven lawyers were at hand.

A photograph taken around 1858 by Preston Butler

THE EAST SIDE OF THE SPRINGFIELD SQUARE. The last house on the left is the Stephen T. Logan building, where on the top floor the Federal Court met after 1855 and where Lincoln tried over ninety cases. The first house on the right belonged to A. M. Converse. The building next to it was gutted by fire in the early part of 1858; the unrepaired damage can still be seen in the photograph.

Life—so the housewives complained —was expensive. A pound of butter came as high as 8 cents, for a dozen eggs one had to pay 6 cents, beef was 3 cents a pound and pork 2 cents. But the most expensive items were coffee and sugar, as these had to be imported by long and difficult routes. For a pound of coffee 20 cents was charged, for a pound of sugar, 10 cents.

Laborers and domestic servants were hard to get. A good farmhand could command $120 a year besides his keep, and female help earned as much as $2 weekly.

The only cheap commodity was land —there was plenty of it—an acre cost not more than $1.25.

Joshua Fry Speed, who soon became Lincoln's most intimate friend, left a

Frank Leslie's Illustrated Newspaper, *December 22, 1860*

THE STUART-LINCOLN LAW OFFICE—on the second floor in Hoffman's Row. It was sparsely furnished, with a bed on the right. As the first floor of the building harbored the Circuit Court of Sangamon County, the office was occasionally used as a jury room.

James P. Hawthorn
vs
David Wooldridge

The defendant, David Wooldridge, being sworn says that he verily believes that the said plaintiff is unable to pay the costs of this suit, and that the officers of this court will be in danger of of losing their costs in said suit unless the said plaintiff be ruled to give security therefor. He states that said plaintiff is a young man and without family and that he has not, to the said defendants knowledge, any real, or personal property out of which the costs could be made.

David Wooldridge

James P. Hawthorn to David Wooldridge Dr
To Boarding from the first day of April until the first of November 1835 at $1-50 cents per week being 30 weeks & 4 days — $45.75
To use of waggon & team from first of Ap. to till first of November 1836 — $90.00
1834 To 11 bushels of wheat @ 75. — 8.25
1836. Jan.y 8 Cash lent — 100.00
May & June. Breaking 10 acres of Prairy — 20.00
To money lent to enter lands ... $264,00
... in the name of ...
... — 50.00

LINCOLN'S FIRST LAW SUIT. On October 5, 1836, Lincoln filed a plea in his first lawsuit, representing David Wooldridge. He wrote an affidavit, which his client signed, asking the court to have the plaintiff deposit a bond to secure the costs of the case.

[18 June 1838]

The county of Sangamon.
To Stuart & Lincoln Dr

To furnishing room for Grand an Petit juries at July & October terms of 1837 and March term of 1838 — $36-00

BILL OF STUART AND LINCOLN FOR USE OF THE OFFICE AS A JURY ROOM.

vivid account of how Lincoln, who "had ridden into town on a borrowed horse," came into his store, set his saddlebags on the counter, and inquired "what the furniture for a single bedstead would cost." Speed figured that it would come to $17, to which Lincoln answered: "It is probably cheap enough; but I want to say that, cheap as it is, I have not the money to pay. But if you will credit me until Christmas, and my experiment here as a lawyer is a success, I will pay you then. If I fail in that I will probably never pay you at all."

The tone of the stranger's voice was such that Speed felt pity for him. Struck by his gloomy and melancholy face, Speed told him:

"As so small a debt seems to affect you so deeply, I think I can suggest a plan by which you will be able to attain your end without incurring any debt. I have a very large room and a very large double bed in it, which you are perfectly welcome to share with me if you choose."

"Where is your room?" asked Lin-

TWO FRIENDS

JOHN T. STUART, who encouraged him to study law and then offered him a partnership in his office, met and grew fond of Lincoln during the Black Hawk campaign. Their friendship deepened at Vandalia, where both men served in the Legislature.

coln. "Upstairs," said Speed, pointing to the stairs leading from the store to his room. Without saying anything more the stranger took his saddlebags on his arm, went upstairs, set them down on the floor, came down again, and with a beaming face, all pleasure and smiles, exclaimed, "Well, Speed, I am moved."

So Lincoln's life in Springfield began. During the day he attended court or worked at his office in the upper story of a building just north of the present Court House Square, writing declarations and pleas, entering fees in the firm's account books, doing all the chores of a junior partner. (An entry of $2.25 for a wood saw in the firm's ledger indicates that the junior partner did the sawing, for no payment for having wood sawed is recorded.)

He had plenty to do—the practice was large, even though the litigations were limited in importance. At the July, 1837, term of the Sangamon Circuit Court, Stuart and Lincoln had 66 cases as compared to 45 for Logan and

IN SPRINGFIELD

JOSHUA F. SPEED, a prosperous Springfield merchant, to whose store Lincoln came to buy bedding, offered to share his quarters and large double bed. Lincoln put his belongings in the room and exclaimed happily: "Well, Speed, I am moved."

THE STUART-LINCOLN ACCOUNT BOOK. As Lincoln was the junior partner, and perhaps because of his legible handwriting, it was he who entered the fees. The average was $5—only two or three cases brought $50. At times goods were taken instead of money. One entry in the fee book shows a fifteen-dollar deduction for "credit by coat to Stuart."

Baker, their nearest competitor. The cases were small—there were no great corporations yet—and the charges amounted to five dollars on the average. During the whole of 1837 only two or three of the fees, divided equally between the two partners, reached fifty dollars.

In the evenings Lincoln stayed "at home" at the Speed store, where young men came and discussed politics. "The thing of living in Springfield is rather a dull business after all; at least it is so to me," he wrote to Mary Owens

three weeks after his arrival. "I am quite as lonesome here as I ever was anywhere in my life. I have been spoken to by but one woman since I've been here, and should not have been by her, if she could have avoided it. I've never been to church yet, nor probably shall not be soon. I stay away because I am conscious I should not know how to behave myself."

But his blue mood was of short duration. Soon he accustomed himself to his new surroundings, and felt comfortable in his new life.

LINCOLN PENNED THIS LETTER on January 3, 1842, and handed it to his friend Joshua Speed to read on the journey to Louisville. Speed was trying to make up his mind whether he should marry black-eyed Fanny Henning or not, and Lincoln told him: "I know what the painful point with you is, at all times when you are unhappy. It is an apprehension that you do not love her as you should. What nonsense!" *(The Speed letters are published through the courtesy of the Illinois State Historical Library.)*

TO MARRY

In his letters to his friend Joshua Fry Speed, state legislator Lincoln reveals a great indecision about making Mary Todd his wife. But

THE Illinois General Assembly was to meet in Springfield, its new capital, on December 9, 1839, for the first time. In honor of it, a grand cotillion ball was held, and it was at this ball that Abraham Lincoln, the leading Whig member of the lower House, first set his eyes on the girl he was to marry.

Twenty-one-year-old Mary Todd of Kentucky had come from Lexington to Springfield only a short while before to visit her eldest sister, the wife of Ninian W. Edwards, Lincoln's colleague in the Legislature. Elizabeth Todd Edwards, mistress of an elegant mansion and an arbiter of Springfield's

social life, had married off her sister Frances to well-to-do William S. Wallace—and was now ready to find a husband for Mary, next in line of the Todd sisters. This did not seem to be too difficult. Mary had a good education; she spoke French, played the piano, was well versed in literature, and was an attractive girl with a great charm and a caustic wit.

At the ball Lincoln approached her. "Miss Todd," he said, "I want to dance with you the worst way." And as Mary remembered it, "He certainly did."

From that evening on, they became steady com-

LINCOLN WAS OVERJOYED when Speed wrote after his marriage that he was "far happier than [he] ever expected to be." In his reply Lincoln said: "That much I know is enough . . . I am not going beyond the truth, when I tell you, that the short space it took me to read your last letter, gave me more pleasure, than the total sum of all I have enjoyed since that fatal first Jany. '41."

A FEW WEEKS BEFORE LINCOLN MARRIED, he wrote Speed: "You have now been the husband of a lovely woman nearly eight months. That you are happier now than you were the day you married her I well know; for without you would not be living . . . I have your word for it too. . . . But I want to ask a closer question. 'Are you now in *feeling* as well as *judgement*, glad you are married as you are?' . . . I feel impatient to know."

OR NOT

when Speed's marriage to Fanny Henning in 1842 proved a success, Lincoln decided that he would dare to take the plunge as well.

panions; they read books and poetry together and they enjoyed discussing political problems. Mary's sister observed that every time Lincoln came to visit, it was usually Mary who led the conversation. "Mr. Lincoln would sit at her side and listen. He scarcely said a word, but gazed on her as if irresistibly drawn toward her by some superior and unseen power."

Their courtship matured during the winter months, and when summer came, it seemed as if they had made up their minds.

But after Mary said the word, Lincoln must have become uneasy. As with Mary Owens three years before, so he now probably behaved with Mary Todd.

There was no doubt that he was under the spell of her, that he loved her as much as he was able to love—but as soon as she consented to become his wife, he began to see a hundred reasons why a marriage between them might not work out. In such a mood he composed a letter, showing it first to the friend with whom he boarded. Joshua Speed knew more of women than did Lincoln, and he advised him: "Don't write—that will give her an advantage

47

THE HOUSE WHERE LINCOLN MARRIED. On November 4, 1842, thirty-three-year-old Abraham Lincoln became the husband of twenty-three-year-old Mary Todd in the Ninian Edwards' mansion.

THE PEOPLE OF THE STATE OF ILLINOIS.

To any Minister of the Gospel, or other authorised Person---GREETING.

THESE are to License and permit you to join in the holy bands of Matrimony *Abraham Lincoln* and *Mary Todd* of the County of Sangamon and State of Illinois, and for so doing, this shall be your sufficient warrant.

Given under my hand and seal of office, at Springfield, in said County this 4th day of Novmr 1842

N W Matheny Clerk

Solemnized on the same 4th day of Nov. 1842. *Charles Dresser*

THE MARRIAGE CERTIFICATE. The Reverend Charles Dresser performed the wedding ceremony according to the requirements of the Episcopal Church, the bridegroom looking "as pale and trembling as being driven to slaughter." When Lincoln repeated the vow: "With this ring I thee endow with all my goods and chattels, lands, and tenements," the old Judge Thomas C. Browne burst out for all to hear: "God Almighty, Lincoln! the statute fixes all that."

THE GLOBE TAVERN IN SPRINGFIELD, where the Lincolns started their married life, charged them for board and room four dollars a week. Here, nine months later, their first child was born.

over you." And throwing the letter in the fireplace, he told his troubled roommate: "If you have the courage of manhood, go see Mary yourself, tell her, if you do not love her, the facts, and that you will not marry her; but be quick about it, say little and leave soon."

Lincoln went, and it was not till midnight that he returned and related to Speed what had taken place. After he had told Mary that he desired to end their relationship, she seemed so unhappy that Lincoln took her in his arms and kissed her. "Well, if I am in again, so be it. It's done, and I shall abide by it," said he to Speed.

Lincoln and Mary Todd seem to have gone through the emotional upheavals, the well-established routine for lovers ever since the Lord created Adam and Eve. They quarreled; they made up, and quarreled again.

Was it jealousy? Was it because Mary flirted with other men, because she was seen arm in arm with Stephen A. Douglas? Or was it the incompatibility of their temperaments that caused the clashes?

On New Year's Day, 1841—Lincoln later referred to it as that fatal first of January—they parted again, and this time it was "forever." The break between the two lovers seemed to be final.

Herndon asserted in his biography that the wedding was set for that day; cakes baked, dinner ready, guests assembled, the minister waiting, but Lincoln failed to appear. It is a vivid, romantic story—one fixed in the minds of generations of Americans—and entirely untrue.

There was no wedding date set; there was only a quarrel, leaving Lincoln in a desperate mood. Mary's sister asserted that after the engagement was broken, "Lincoln went crazy as a loon," to which Herndon added that Lincoln's state of mind was such that "knives and razors, and every instrument that could be used for self-destruction were removed from his reach." This is most certainly an exaggeration.

Lincoln confided to his law partner, Stuart: "I am now the most miserable man living. If what I feel were equally distributed to the whole human family, there would not be one cheerful face on the earth. Whether I shall ever be better I can not tell; I awfully forbode I shall not. To remain as I am is impossible; I must die or be better, it appears to me."

In his despondent mood he communicated with a well-known doctor in Cincinnati, describing his symptoms. The doctor replied that he could not suggest any remedies without seeing him, so Lincoln consulted his friend Dr. Anson G. Henry in Springfield, who suggested that ancient remedy for lovers —a change of scenery.

Lincoln, broken-hearted, was ready to go any-

THE WOMAN HE MARRIED. The earliest daguerreotype of Mary Todd, taken around 1848 when she was twenty-eight years old and the mother of two boys.

Reproduced from the cleaned daguerreotype in the Library of Congress

This memorandum witnesseth that Charles Dresser and Abraham Lincoln of Springfield Illinois, have contracted with each other as follows. The said Dresser is to convey to or procure to be conveyed to, said Lincoln, by a clear title in fee simple, the entire premises (ground and improvements) in Springfield, on which said Dresser now resides, and give him possession of said premises, on or before the first day of April next — for which said Lincoln, at or before the same day, is to pay to said Dresser twelve hundred dollars, or what said Dresser shall then at his own option accept as equivalent thereto. and also to procure to be conveyed to said Dresser, by a clear title in fee simple, the entire premises (ground and building) in Springfield, on the block immediately West of the Public square, the building on which is now occupied by H. A. Hough as a shop, being the same premises some time since conveyed by N. W. Edwards & wife to said Lincoln & Stephen T. Logan — Said Dresser takes upon himself to arrange with said Hough for the possession of said shop and premises —

Jany 16.th 1844

(signed duplicates)

Charles Dresser
A Lincoln

HE BUYS A HOUSE. Memorandum of the contract in Lincoln's handwriting for the purchase of his Springfield house. The seller was the Reverend Charles Dresser, the same who had married him, and the final purchase price was $1,500, not the $1,200 mentioned.

interest of his fellowmen, was what he desired to live for."

But the air of the country, the quiet walks through the meadows, the peaceful talks with Speed, the books he read, soon put him in a better frame of mind. His melancholy lifted and when, a few weeks later, he returned to Springfield, he was in a much happier spirit.

On New Year's Day, 1842—one year after he broke his engagement to Mary—his friend Speed was leaving for Kentucky, and Speed felt very like Lincoln the year before. He, too, was worried, indecisive and hesitant whether he should marry Fanny Henning, the girl he was then courting.

Lincoln urged Speed not to break off the engagement, but to marry her. And Speed followed the advice.

On the eve of his wedding, Lincoln wrote his friend, which was more revealing of his condition than that of Speed.

"I incline to think it probable," he said, "that your nerves will fail you occasionally for a while; but once you get them fairly graded now, that trouble is over forever. . . . If you went through the ceremony *calmly*, or even with sufficient composure not to excite alarm in any present, you are safe, beyond question, and in two or three months, to say the most, will be the happiest of men."

Two weeks later he once more reassured Speed that "our *forebodings*,

where. He asked his law partner, Stuart, who was at that time serving as Congressman in Washington, to secure him a consular job in South America. Stuart tried, but could not get the desired appointment. So instead of going to Bogota, Lincoln visited his friend Speed on his farm near Louisville.

He arrived in Kentucky in a much depressed state. He felt useless, declaring that "he had done nothing to make any human being remember that he had lived; and that to connect his name with the events transpiring in his day and generation, and so impress himself upon them as to link his name with something that would redound to the

THIS IS WHAT THE HOUSE LOOKED LIKE when Lincoln bought it in 1844. It was a one-and-a-half-story cottage, built in 1839 on a 50x152-foot lot which also contained a woodshed, privy, and a place for the carriage. In 1856 it was enlarged to two stories.

for which you and I are rather peculiar, are all the worst sort of nonsense."

So they seemed to be. Speed replied that he enjoyed married life and was happy, which news gave Lincoln "more pleasure, than the total sum of all I have enjoyed since that fatal first of Jany. '41."

Many months went by after Speed's marriage, and still the memory of Mary Todd was haunting Lincoln; he was missing her. One day he unburdened himself to Speed that he could not be happy "for the never-absent idea, that there is *one* still unhappy whom I have contributed to make so. That still kills my soul."

Speed insisted that he should either make up with her and marry her or turn away from her entirely. For Lincoln it was not such a clear-cut matter. Turning the alternatives over in his mind he answered his friend:

"But before I resolve to do the one thing or the other, I must regain my confidence in my own ability to keep my resolves when they are made. In that ability, you know, I once prided myself as the only, or at least the chief, gem of my character; that gem I lost —how, and when, you too well know. I have not yet regained it; and until I do, I can not trust myself in any matter of such importance."

Not long after this letter, Lincoln was asked to a party given by Mrs. Simeon Francis, the wife of the editor of the *Sangamo Journal*. When he

THE FRONT PARLOR of the house was separated by a large door which could be opened up, making the two rooms into one. Here Mrs. Lincoln liked to receive her friends, and it was this room that Lincoln used most frequently to confer with his political associates.

THE SITTING ROOM of the Lincoln house located on the northeast corner of Eighth and Jackson Streets. Lincoln, with his wife and infant son, moved into their home on May 2, 1844, living there for seventeen years—until they left Springfield for Washington in 1861.

Sketches from Frank Leslie's Illustrated Newspaper, *March 9, 1861*

THEIR DOORPLATE. It was in this house that three more boys were born to the Lincolns: Robert Todd was followed by Edward Baker in 1846; he died in 1850, the same year another boy, William Wallace, was born; Thomas (Tad), the youngest, was born in 1853.

arrived, he found Mary there among the guests, and as Mrs. Francis brought the estranged lovers together, she said to them: "Be friends again."

They were most willing to do so. They met often and in October Lincoln wrote Speed: "Are you now in *feeling* as well as *judgement*, glad you are married as you are?" He wanted a quick answer.

Speed must have said what Lincoln desired to hear, for early in the morning on November 4, Lincoln woke his friend James H. Matheny, asking him to be his best man, as he had decided to be married that very night.

PRACTICING LAW AND POLITICS

LINCOLN HAD three law partners. His first partnership, with John T. Stuart, Mary Todd's cousin, ended in the spring of 1841. At that time he became associated with Judge Stephen T. Logan, one of the best lawyers in the state. Logan was a studious man, metic-

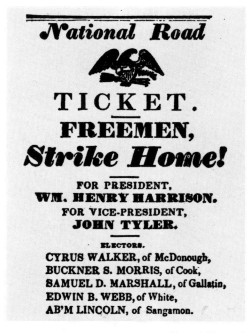

National Road

TICKET.
FREEMEN,
Strike Home!

FOR PRESIDENT,
WM. HENRY HARRISON.
FOR VICE-PRESIDENT,
JOHN TYLER.

ELECTORS.

CYRUS WALKER, of McDonough,
BUCKNER S. MORRIS, of Cook,
SAMUEL D. MARSHALL, of Gallatin,
EDWIN B. WEBB, of White,
AB'M LINCOLN, of Sangamon.

PRESIDENTIAL ELECTOR. In 1840 and 1844 Lincoln was chosen as a Whig elector, voting for Harrison and Clay respectively and campaigning actively for each man.

ulous and exact; he insisted that his partner prepare his cases carefully, consult the authorities, become less disorderly and slipshod, more thorough, precise and painstaking.

"I don't think he studied very much," recalled Logan later. "I think he learned his law more in the study of cases. He would work hard and learn all there was in a case he had in hand. He got to be a pretty good lawyer though his general knowledge of law was never formidable."

Their partnership terminated in 1844, when Logan desired to take his own son, David, into his office. At that time Lincoln asked his friend, twenty-six-year-old William H. Herndon, who had formerly worked in the Speed store and who now was in the Logan

office, whether he would not like to become his associate. Herndon was surprised. "I was young in the practice," he noted, "and was painfully aware of my want of ability and experience; but when he remarked in his earnest, honest way, 'Billy, I can trust you, if you can trust me,' I felt relieved, and accepted the generous proposal." Thus Lincoln's third and last partnership was formed.

A great deal of the time he traveled the Eighth Judicial Circuit, arguing cases, pleading, prosecuting, defending. Traveling on the circuit was not all law work; Lincoln used it to keep his political fences in order, to make new friends and prepare for the future.

Law was his profession, but his passion was politics. In 1843 he wrote: "Now if you should hear anyone say that Lincoln don't want to go to Congress, I wish you as a personal friend of mine, would tell him you have reason to believe he is mistaken. The truth is, I would like to go very much."

Still, when the Sangamon Whigs gathered in Springfield to name their

HIS POLITICAL RIVALS

candidate, their choice was not he, but Edward Dickinson Baker. The disappointed Lincoln was made only a delegate to the district convention to propose Baker's candidacy, about which he complained that he was "fixed a good deal like a fellow who made a groomsman to a man that has cut him out and is marrying his own dear 'gal.'" Baker's triumph, however, was short-lived; the district convention could not be swayed for him; it nominated John J. Hardin.

Hardin was elected, served one term in Congress, then was relieved by Baker, and there were rumors of an understanding whereby Baker would be followed by Lincoln.

Lincoln began the preparation for his candidacy in the summer of 1845, a full year before the congressional elections. In the fall circuit courts he was busy lining up the Whig leaders on his behalf. His opponents for the seat were the same men who had represented Illinois in Congress before, Edward D. Baker and John J. Hardin. Baker was ready to bow out and be

JOHN J. HARDIN became the candidate of the Illinois Whigs in 1843, thwarting Lincoln's aspirations. He was elected but remained in Congress for only a single term.

EDWARD D. BAKER followed Hardin as Congressman. He, too, served only one term —from 1845 to 1847—after which it was at last Lincoln's turn to go to Washington.

content with his one term, but Hardin would have liked to return to Washington once more. Lincoln wrote him: "If I am not (in services done the party and in capacity to serve in future) near enough your equal, when added to the fact of your having had a turn, to entitle me to the nomination, I scorn it on any and all grounds." With energy and resourcefulness Lincoln won his claim; the Whig convention nominated him by unanimous vote.

The ensuing campaign was hard fought. The Democrats opposed Lincoln with Peter Cartwright, the old Methodist preacher, a formidable vote-getter. He spoke well, he knew the people, he had many friends in the county.

Once during the canvass Lincoln walked into a religious meeting conducted by Cartwright. After a hell-raising sermon the preacher-politician cried out: "All who desire to lead a new life, to give their hearts to God, and to go to heaven, will stand." A few of the congregation got up. Then in a stern voice Cartwright asked: "All who do not wish to go to hell will stand." The rest of the men and women got up —all of them—save Lincoln.

Cartwright turned toward him. "May I inquire of you, Mr. Lincoln, where you are going?"

An imaginary representation by Jay Hambidge

HIS LAW OFFICE ON THE CIRCUIT was often under a shady tree outside the courthouse. Here he consulted with the local attorneys and listened to the stories of clients.

HIS LAW PARTNERS

STEPHEN T. LOGAN, one of the best lawyers of the state, took Lincoln in his office after the dissolution of the partnership between John T. Stuart and Lincoln in 1841.

WILLIAM H. HERNDON, nine years Lincoln's junior, became his law partner in December, 1844, when Lincoln gave up his three-year association with Judge Logan.

And Lincoln answered in his slow, drawling way: "If it is all the same to you—I am going to Congress."

In the election he defeated Cartwright by a comfortable margin, receiving 6,340 votes against his opponent's 4,829. But "being elected to Congress," so he wrote to Speed, "though I am grateful to our friends for having done it, has not pleased me as much as I have expected."

Of the $200 which his friends collected for his campaign expenses he returned $199.25, with the explanation: "I made the canvass on my own horse; my entertainment, being at the houses of friends cost me nothing; and my only outlay was 75 cents for a barrel of cider, which some farmhands insisted I should treat to."

CONGRESSMAN

LINCOLN TOOK his seat in Congress in December, 1847. Mary and the two children came with him to Washington, and the family took lodgings first at Brown's Hotel and then at Mrs. Sprigg's boarding house. But Mary was soon on her way back to Lexington; the life in Washington was not to her liking.

At the time Lincoln began his term, the war with Mexico was practically over, and the Whigs, bowing to public pressure, were willing to accept the annexation of California and New Mexico. In his message to Congress, President Polk reasserted that it was Mexico and not the United States which had started the war; it was Mexico that had struck the first blow and had shed the blood of Americans on American soil.

The Whigs held the President was not telling the truth. Lincoln submitted an eight-point resolution in which he asked the President to inform the House:

"*First*. Whether the *spot* on which the blood of our citizens was shed as in his messages declared was or was not within a territory of Spain, at least after the treaty of 1819, until the Mexican revolution.

"*Second*. Whether that spot is or is not within the territory which was wrested from Spain by the revolutionary government of Mexico.

"*Third*. Whether that spot is or is not within a settlement of people, which settlement has existed ever since long before the Texas revolution, and until its inhabitants fled before the approach of the United States Army."

Three weeks later the freshman Congressman from Illinois addressed the House, elaborating on his resolutions. In his speech Lincoln said: "The extent of our territory in that region depended not on any treaty-fixed boundary (for no treaty had attempted it), but on revolution. Any people anywhere being inclined and having the power have the right to rise up and shake off the existing government, and form a new one that suits them better. This is a most valuable, a most sacred right—a right which we hope and believe is to liberate the world. . . ." And he asked the President to answer him "fully, fairly, candidly" whether "the soil was ours where the first blood of the war was shed," whether it was within an inhabited country, and whether "the inhabitants had submitted themselves to the civil authority of Texas or of the United States." But if Polk could answer that question in

the affirmative, then he was wrong in ordering "General Taylor into the midst of a peaceful settlement purposely to bring on a war." Then—in Lincoln's opinion—the President is "a bewildered, confounded, and miserably perplexed man."

When his constituents back home read their Representative's speech, they became angry. They had not sent him to Congress to advocate such ideas; they did not share his antiwar stand. Friends wrote him, argued with him to change his mind, but Lincoln would not move; he stuck to his beliefs. He voted regularly on all resolutions designed to put the administration in the wrong on the origin of the war.

The opposition newspapers in his district were raging with fury. The Peoria *Democratic Press* called him a "second Benedict Arnold"; and the Springfield *Register* demanded: "Out damned spot." Soon the nickname stuck on him: "Spotty" Lincoln.

On other issues he was in step with his constituents, supporting every bill which was to prevent slavery in the territories acquired from Mexico. And though he thus declared himself for the Wilmot proviso, he opposed all unnecessary agitation on the slavery question.

During the year of 1848 Congress was preparing for the presidential election. Lincoln, realizing that Henry Clay, his "beau ideal of a statesman," could not win, rallied behind General Zachary Taylor, and when "Old Rough and Ready" became the Whig candidate, Lincoln traveled through New England campaigning in his behalf and making speeches on the slavery issue. His ideas are best shown in his Worcester address. Admitting that slavery was an evil, he told his audience that "we were not responsible for it and cannot affect it in states of this Union where we do not live. But the question of the *extension* of slavery to new territories of this country, is a part of our responsibility and care, and is under our control."

The election was won by the Whigs; Zachary Taylor became President, and Lincoln returned to the capital.

He spent the remainder of his term inconspicuously, and somewhat sadly, with the knowledge that for him there would be no other term; his spot resolutions barred his re-election.

He thought his political career was at an end; he believed that as a Congressman he was a failure.

54

HIS EARLIEST LIKENESS. A daguerreotype supposedly taken by Nicholas H. Shepherd toward the end of 1847 when the thirty-eight-year-old Lincoln was serving his solitary term in Congress.

Reproduced from the cleaned daguerreotype in the Library of Congress

HIS PATENT FOR AN "IMPROVED METHOD OF LIFTING VESSELS OVER SHOALS."

INVENTOR

EVER SINCE he had stranded with his flatboat on the New Salem dam, Lincoln had been thinking on a practical method of lifting vessels over shoals. At the end of his congressional term, he stayed on in Washington for a while, and it was then that he applied for a patent on a device which he had invented.

The idea of his invention came to him on a voyage from Buffalo to Chicago, when he saw that the captain of a grounded steamer told his men to collect all the loose planks, empty barrels and boxes, and force them under the sides of the boat. Lincoln watched the operation and was greatly impressed when the buoyant empty casks lifted the vessel, allowing the boat to clear the sand bar. Reaching home, he made a model of a vessel, to which he attached a kind of bellows just behind the water line on each side of the craft's hull. Whenever the keel would become stuck in the sand, the bellows were to be filled with air, buoyed up, and the boat would then float clear of the shoal.

His invention was never tested under real conditions. Lincoln was not unlike other amateur inventors who, after having the superb satisfaction of finding a solution to a problem and getting a patent for it, forgot all about it.

LINCOLN'S INVENTION. He whittled a model in his spare time, showing the device by which vessels could be lifted, then had a good one made by Walter Davis at the Hough Woodworking Shop in Springfield. The latter was sent to the patent office.

Springfield, Illinois. Sept. 27. 1849

Hon: J. M. Clayton
    Secretary of State
        Dear Sir:

Your letter of the 17th Inst. saying you had received no answer to yours in-forming me of my appointment as Secretary of Oregon, is received, and surprises me very much — I received that letter, accompanied by the commission, in due course of mail, and answered it two days after, declining the office, and warmly recommending Simeon Francis for, ~~the same office~~ — I have also written you several letters since, alluding to the same matter, all of which ought to have reached you before the date of your last letter —

        Your Obt. Servt.
            A. Lincoln —

HE WOULD NOT BECOME SECRETARY OF OREGON. Lincoln, urged to accept the appointment, said he would take the job if his wife consented. But Mary did not want to move to Oregon. Always a shrewd politician, she advised her husband to decline the offer.

OFFICE SEEKER

SHORTLY AFTER his return to Springfield from Washington, Lincoln became involved in a fight about a political plum—the Commissioner's job of the General Land Office, which had been promised to Illinois. At first there were two applicants, Cyrus Edwards, supported by Lincoln, and J. L. D. Morrison, the protégé of E. D. Baker, but when Justin Butterfield, a successful Chicago lawyer, made it known that he desired the office for himself, the excitement among the Springfield politicians mounted.

Lincoln, himself, was not averse to taking the appointment, if only Edwards and Morrison would withdraw. Morrison obliged, but Edwards, who

believed that Lincoln had betrayed him, decided to support Butterfield.

Lincoln worked hard to defeat his opponent and land the job. He circulated petitions, solicited signatures, and—as the date of the appointment neared—he rushed to Washington to influence the decision. He lost out; the office went to Butterfield.

On the way to the capital, Lincoln met a man from Kentucky in the stage, who offered him a chew, a smoke, and a drink. When his traveling companion refused to take any of them, the Kentuckian blurted out: "See here, stranger . . . my experience has taught me that a man who has no vices has damned few virtues."

HE DESIRED THE LAND OFFICE. Lincoln wrote Congressman Embree that to appoint Butterfield "will be an egregious political blunder," and asked that "either I, or the man I recommend should . . . be appointed . . . if any one from Illinois shall be."

Friday Morning Thar May 25th 1849

Dear Brother
            I hast to inform you
that father is yet a Live & that
is all & he Craves to See you all the
time & he wonts you to Come if
you are able to git hure, for
you are his only Child that
is of his own flush & blood
& it is nothing more than nature
for him to crave to See you, he
Says he has all most Despared
of Seeing you, & he wonts you
to prepare to meet him in the un
known world, or in heven, for he
thinks that ower Savour Savour
has a Crown of glory, prepared
for him I wright this with a
bursting hartt, I came to town
for the Docttor, & I won you to
Make an effort Come, if your
as able to get hure, & he wonts
me to tell your wife that he Loves
hure & wonts hur to prepare to meet
him at ower Savours feet, we are
all well, your Brother in hast
                    J, D, Johnston

HIS STEPBROTHER INFORMS LINCOLN that his father is very sick and "craves to see you. . . . for you are his only child that is of his own flesh & blood." John Johnston writes: "He has all most despared of seeing you, & he wonts you to prepare to meet him in the unknown world. . . . for he thinks that ower savour has a crown of glory, prepared for *him*."

FAMILY RELATIONS

BETWEEN HIM and his father there was no love lost. Thomas could never understand the ways of his son, why he read when he should have worked in the field, why he behaved as he did. He ruled him with a heavy hand, he was harsh and sometimes brutal to him. And Lincoln had not forgotten the many ugly scenes of his childhood.

Still, later when the old man was in trouble, the son was always ready with a helping hand. And Thomas was often in financial difficulties. In 1840 he bought three parcels of land of forty acres each, and this purchase became a continual worry for him. When his creditors threatened to foreclose, Lincoln came to his rescue, buying off one tract for $200 and allowing his father and stepmother the use of it till the end of their days.

At the time Lincoln served in Congress the old man once more turned to his son for help. John D. Johnston, his stepson, was in dire straits as well. While Thomas needed $20 to pay off a creditor who had obtained judgment and threatened to force a sale of the land, John asked Lincoln for $80. Both of them were desperate.

"I am dund and doged to death," wrote John to his stepbrother. "So I am most tired of living and I would all most Swop my Place in *Heaven* for that much money. I now you will think little of this for you never had the Tryal, but Abe, I would drother Live on bread and wotter than to have men allways duning me." John promised not only to pay interest on the money Lincoln would loan him, but to let his stepbrother have the land after his father had died.

Lincoln answered both his step-

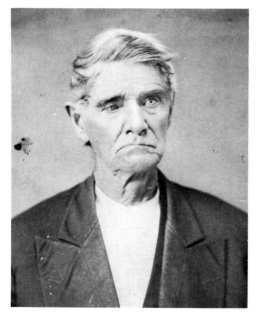

LINCOLN'S COUSIN, Dennis Hanks, who spent his childhood and early youth with him, and who married Lincoln's stepsister.

brother and father in the same letter. To his father he sent "very cheerfully" the twenty dollars which was necessary to save his land from sale, but to John's request he would not accede. Instead of money he gave him a lecture:

"At the various times when I have helped you a little, you have said to me, 'We can get along very well now' but in a short time I find you in the same difficulty again," he began. "Now this can only happen by some defect in your *conduct*. What that defect is, I think I know. You are not *lazy*, and still you *are* an *idler*. I doubt whether since I saw you, you have done a good whole day's work, in any one day. You do not very much dislike to work; and still you do not work very much, merely because it does not seem to you that you could get much for it. This habit of uselessly wasting time, is the whole difficulty; and it is vastly important to you, and still more so to your children that you should break this habit. It is more important to them, because they have longer to live, and can keep out of an idle habit before they are in it, easier than they can get out after they are in.

"You are now in need of some [ready?] money; and what I propose is, that you shall go to work, 'tooth

Dennis was a real character and story teller, "remembering" many episodes of Lincoln's early life which never actually happened.

WHEN HIS FATHER WAS DYING, Lincoln wrote this letter to his stepbrother. In it he told John that he could not come to see the old man, and asked Johnston to "Say to him that if we could meet now, it is doubtful whether it would not be more painful than pleasant; but that if it be his lot to go now, he will soon have a joyous meeting with many loved ones gone before; and where the rest of us, through the help of God, hope ere long to join them." Thomas Lincoln died five days after the letter was written.

always been [kind] to me, and I do not now mean to be unkind to you. On the contrary, if you will but follow my advice, you will find it worth more than eight times eighty dollars to you."

So Johnston had to do without his stepbrother's help. Whether he followed Lincoln's advice we don't know.

A year later he wrote to Lincoln, informing him that his father was sick and that his end seemed near. His note remained unanswered. Johnston mailed letter after letter asking him to come and say farewell to the old man. For a long while Lincoln remained silent, then he replied that the reason for not answering John's letters was not because he had "forgotten them, or been uninterested about them," but because it appeared to him that he could "write nothing which could do any good."

Then he went on: "I sincerely hope Father may yet recover his health; but at all events tell him to remember to call upon, and confide in, our great, and good, and merciful Maker, who will not turn away from him in any extremity. He notes the fall of a sparrow, and numbers the hairs of our heads; and He will not forget the dying man, who puts his trust in Him.

THE ONLY PHOTOGRAPH OF LINCOLN'S STEPMOTHER, TAKEN IN LATER LIFE. Sarah Bush Johnston understood her stepson, and loved him. Lincoln visited her for the last time not long before he left his home town, Springfield, for Washington.

and nail' for somebody who will give you money for it. Let father and your boys take charge of things at home— prepare for a crop, and make the crop; and you go to work for the best money wages, or in discharge of any debt you owe, that you can get. And to secure you a fair reward for your labor, I now promise you that for every dollar you will, between this and the first of next May, get for your own labor, either in money, or on your own indebtedness, I will then give you one other dollar. By this, if you hire yourself at ten dollars a month, from me you will get ten more, making twenty dollars a month for your work. In this, I do not mean you shall go off to St. Louis, or the lead mines, or the gold mines in Calif [ornia], but I [mean for you to go at it for the best wages you] can get close to home in Coles county. Now if you will do this, you will be soon out of debt, and what is better, you will have a habit that will keep you from getting in debt again. But if I should now clear you out, next year you would be just as deep in as ever. You say you would almost give your place in Heaven for $70 or $80. Then you value your place in Heaven very cheapl[y] for I am sure you can with the offer I make you get the seventy or eighty dollars for four or five months work. You say if I furnish you the money you will deed me the land, and, if you don't pay the money back, you will deliver possession. Nonsense! If you cant now live *with* the land, how will you then live without it? You have

THOMAS LINCOLN'S CABIN in Coles County, Illinois. Here Lincoln's father lived

Say to him that if we could meet now, it is doubtful whether it would not be more painful than pleasant; but that if it be his lot to go now, he will soon have a joyous [meeting] with many loved ones gone before; and where [the rest] of us, through the help of God, hope ere long [to join] them."

Five days after this note was written, Thomas Lincoln died and was buried near his cabin, his only son not being present at his funeral.

Lincoln's relationship to his stepmother was on a different plane. He was grateful for her love and everything she had done for him. And Sarah Bush Lincoln was devoted to her stepson. She said of him: "Abe was a good boy, and I can say what scarcely one woman, a mother, can say in a thousand and it is this: Abe never gave me a cross word or look and never refused in fact, or even in appearance, to do anything I requested him. I never gave him a cross word in all my life. He was kind to everybody and to everything and always accommodated others if he could, would do so willingly if he could. His mind and mine, what little I had, seemed to run together, more in the same channel."

from the year 1840 until death took him on January 17, 1851, at the age of 73.

TROUBLES WITH HIS STEPBROTHER. After his father died, Lincoln, as his heir, conveyed his interest in one part of the 120-acre farm (the west 80 acres) to his stepbrother, subject to Sarah Lincoln's dower right. But as the farm continued to be a source of difficulty, John desired to sell it and start his life afresh in Missouri. Lincoln objected. He told John that "Such a notion is utterly foolish. . . . Squirming and crawling about from place to place can do no good," and he made it clear that the east 40 acres he intended "to keep for mother while she lives. . . ." Johnston had previously persuaded his mother to relinquish her dower rights in the west 80 acres, and had sold them to John J. Hall, his brother-in-law, for $250. Now he urged his stepbrother to allow him to sell the remaining 40 acres. Lincoln answered John's proposal with this stinging rebuke.

RIDING THE CIRCUIT

WHEN HE returned to Springfield, Lincoln resumed his law practice, again riding through the fourteen counties in central and eastern Illinois—the Eighth Judicial District—spending a great part of the year away from home.

Life on the circuit was not an easy one. In the spring the roads were muddy; and when it rained there was no shelter from the elements, judge and lawyers were drenched to the bone. At times they had to drive or ride over unbroken prairie; at others, swollen streams had to be forded. Often they began their journey at dawn and traveled till nightfall, to be at the county seat in time for court. Even on a dry, sunny day when the roads were hard, the caravan of buggies with judge and lawyers never moved faster than four to five miles an hour. Thirty to forty miles were a good day's travel.

Court days were red-letter days in any community. People from neighboring places flocked to the county seats, filled the courtrooms, listened to the proceedings, enthralled by the legal battles.

Lawyers had little time to prepare their cases, and there were no books at hand to look up precedents. Their arguments were mainly based on common sense. Still, they had to work hard. In those secretaryless, typewriterless days they had to write out in longhand the pleadings, spending hours at such toil.

Abraham Lincoln was not considered an outstanding lawyer. "His knowledge of the law was acquired almost entirely by his own unaided study and by the practice of his profession," said a colleague of him. But "he always tried a case fairly and honestly. He never intentionally misrepresented the testimony of a witness or the arguments of an opponent. . . . He never misstated the law according to his own intelligent view of it." He could do little if he did not believe in a case. Some-

George W. Albin
vs
Thomas Bodine
} In Slander.

1st. Albin stole Blady's horse out of my pasture last night— He is a horsethief and that is what he came here for—

2nd. Albin stole that horse last night out of my pasture; and he is a horse thief, and I knew that was his business here—

3rd. He is a horse thief, and I always believed his business was horse stealing, and that is what brought him here—

4th. Albin stole Bradley's horse out of my pasture last night; and it is not the first horse he has stolen— He is a horse thief and follows that business—

5th. You stole that horse out of my pasture, and it is not the first one you have stolen—

6th. You know you stole that horse, and it is not the first horse you have stolen; and I believe you follow the business—

7th. You are a horse thief and you came here for that business— and I believe you came here for nothing else— You are a horse thief—

8th. He is a damn'd little thief, his business is horse stealing, and I can prove it—

LINCOLN'S BRIEF IN THE DEFENSE OF A SLANDERER. On May 15, 1850, at Paris, Illinois, George W. Albin's case against Thomas Bodine came up. Lincoln, together with Usher F. Linder, represented the defendant, whom the jury found not guilty as charged.

WHERE HE PRACTICED

COURTHOUSE AT PETERSBURG

times he withdrew from a trial when he found that his client had deceived him. Once he brought suit for a man to collect some money, and when the defendant in the case proved that he had already paid the sum for which he was being sued, Lincoln left the court-room, refusing to return. To the messenger who came to fetch him from the tavern he said: "Tell the Judge that I can't come—my hands are dirty and I came over to clean them."

He sided with the needy. A pension agent, named Wright, had charged the widow of a Revolutionary soldier half her pension of four hundred dollars for getting her claim allowed. The old woman, "crippled and bent with age," turned to the firm of Lincoln & Herndon.

Lincoln sued the agent, made an impassioned speech to the jury, recounting the horrors of Valley Forge, castigating mercilessly the robber of the widow. Herndon remembered that his law partner was never, either on the stump or on other occasions in court, so wrought up as over this injustice. And he not only won the case, charging nothing for it, but paid the old woman's hotel bill.

In his trials, like the other circuit lawyers, Lincoln depended little on precedents but argued from first principles. He invariably held the jury's attention, as he spoke the language of the people, with short, compact, and clear sentences. His delivery was distinct, and "he took pains that the jury never should be confused, never

Statue by Fred M. Torrey at Lincoln's Tomb

THE CIRCUIT RIDER. For twenty years Lincoln rode the circuit. The Eighth Judicial District of Illinois, where he practiced law, covered a vast territory. Traveling was arduous, whether on horseback or in carriage. In winter the roads were covered with ice; in summer the mud was knee deep. In fair weather, with the ground dry, one moved fast, making thirty or forty miles a day, but when it rained, a mile an hour was good going.

WHEN RIDING THE CIRCUIT

COURTHOUSE AT CLINTON

LOGAN COUNTY COURTHOUSE

COURTHOUSE AT METAMORA

63

HIS LAW ASSOCIATES

DAVID DAVIS
(1815-1886), Judge of the Eighth Judicial District, was more intimately associated with Lincoln than any other lawyer in Illinois, aiding greatly in securing his presidential nomination.

NATHANIEL POPE
(1784-1850), appointed a District Judge in March, 1819, presided on the bench of "Bankrupt Court" for thirteen months in 1841-42, the scene of much of the Logan and Lincoln practice.

SAMUEL H. TREAT
(1811-1887) was made a Supreme Court Judge in 1841, presiding also on the Eighth Circuit until his appointment to the bench in the Southern Illinois District in 1855.

JOSEPH GILLESPIE
(1809-1885), son of Irish immigrants, came to Illinois in 1819, settling in Edwardsville. A keen student, he was admitted to the bar in 1836, served with Lincoln in the Twelfth General Assembly.

LYMAN TRUMBULL
(1813-1896) came to Illinois in 1837 and began a law practice at Belleville. From 1841-43 he was Assistant Secretary of State, then he was elected to the U. S. Senate three times in a row.

CLIFTON MOORE
(1817-1886) came to Illinois from Ohio. He taught school for a while, then read law and was admitted to the bar in 1841. A 34-year land partnership with David Davis was ended by death.

ALBERT T. BLEDSOE
(1809-1877), a graduate of West Point and an ordained minister of the Episcopalian Church, practiced law in Springfield from 1840-1848. In the War he was a Confederate Cabinet member.

JAMES C. CONKLING
(1816-1899) who graduated from Princeton, had a fine law practice in Springfield. Lincoln often tried cases with him. Conkling married Mercy A. Levering, a girlhood friend of Mary Todd.

ASAHEL GRIDLEY
(1810-1881) came to Bloomington in 1831. He served in both Houses of the State Legislature. Clever both as a lawyer and businessman, he became Bloomington's first millionaire.

required to have in mind too many points." He won many more cases than he lost. But often he had runs of bad luck. Once he was beaten in every trial at every court held throughout the whole circuit—three months of continuous defeat.

While most of his cases were small, he had a big one for the Illinois Central Railroad, when McLean County demanded taxes on the company's property which lay within the boundary of the county. Lincoln was one of the lawyers for the railroad, losing the case in Circuit Court, but winning it before the Supreme Court. For his services he asked $5,000, which the company refused to pay. Lincoln sued, and collected the full amount just before the Panic of 1857 struck the country.

After the day's work in court was done, judge and lawyers sat down to dinner and "the hilarity went on till the early morning hours." Judge Davis —a huge Falstaff-like man—sat at the head of the table, the lawyers gathered around him talking philosophy, politics, economy, metaphysics—"the subjects of conversation ranged through the universe of thought and experience." Lincoln was the life and light of the company; his funny stories made Judge Davis laugh until he could hardly hold his 300 pounds; his repertoire was inexhaustible. A fellow lawyer recalled: "It was as a humorist that he towered above all other men it was ever my lot to meet." But while he could laugh at his own jokes as uproariously as any who listened to him, he had days when he was immersed in

WHERE HE STAYED NIGHTS

PIKE HOUSE IN BLOOMINGTON

64

a melancholy mood, and nothing could change it.

Often, when there were not enough rooms in the inns, the lawyers doubled up, sharing not only the same room but the same bed. The lawyer Henry C. Whitney remembered that Lincoln used to sleep "in a home made, flannel undershirt" which Herndon described as reaching "halfway between his knees and ankles." In this outfit—so an attorney remarked—he "was the ungodliest figure I ever saw."

During his leisure hours on the circuit, Lincoln studied algebra, was learning astronomy, and read Euclid, which he always carried with him. One of his law associates remembered: "I have seen him myself, upon the circuit, with 'a geometry,' or 'an astronomy' . . . working out propositions in moments of leisure."

The circuit calendar over, Lincoln returned to Springfield and to his law office. There he could be seen sitting with his legs stretched out upon another chair, working on a case. If anyone came in, he greeted the interrupter with a joke or anecdote. A student of his remembered that he heard him "relate the same story three times within as many hours to persons who came in at different periods, and every time he laughed as heartily and enjoyed it as if it were a new story. I had to laugh because I thought it funny that Mr. Lincoln enjoyed a story, so repeatedly told."

Yet, he took his profession seriously. When a young man asked his opinion on how to become a lawyer, Lincoln told him:

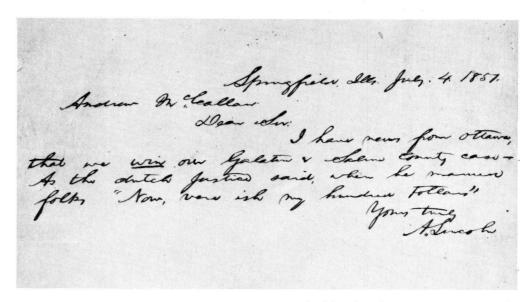

LINCOLN INSTRUCTS THE JURY as one of the lawyers for Ransom P. Adams, against whom Austin Richey brought a slander suit in the DeWitt County Court on May 16, 1854.

"NOW, VERE ISH MY HUNDRED TOLLARS?" asks Lincoln after winning a case. The humorous note was probably written in soothing vein to alleviate the pain of the high fee.

WHEN RIDING THE CIRCUIT

McCORMACK HOUSE IN DANVILLE

"If you are resolutely determined to make a lawyer of yourself, the thing is more than half done already. It is but a small matter whether you read with anybody or not. I did not read with anyone. Get the books and read and study them till you understand them in their principal features; and that is the main thing. It is of no consequence to be in a large town while you are reading. I read at New Salem, which never had three hundred people living in it. The books, and your capacity for understanding them, are just the same in all places. Always bear in mind that your own resolution to suceed is more important than any other one thing."

The years of law practice after his return from Washington were important ones for Lincoln. Senator Beveridge held that he needed "the invaluable discipline of defeat" just as much "as the hard schooling he already had received in humility and in respect for other men." From these years he emerged stronger "with the foundation of greatness firmly established and visible even to hostile eyes."

THE MAN WHO WAS THOROUGHLY AROUSED. The passing of the Kansas-Nebraska Act brought Lincoln back into the political arena. He made speeches, replying to Douglas, talking against the extension of slavery. Slowly he was making up his mind—in 1856 he joined the new Republican party and in a speech at Bloomington argued "the eternal right."

BACK IN THE POLITICAL ARENA

AT THE beginning of 1854 Stephen A. Douglas, chairman of the Senate's Committee on Territories, introduced a bill to organize the territories of Kansas and Nebraska. He suggested that slavery could be adopted or rejected by the people of the new territories, implying that no longer would it be prohibited north of the line of 36° 30′ as accepted by the Missouri Compromise.

The excitement about the Kansas-Nebraska Act created a tremendous stir in the country.

Lincoln, as he himself said, was aroused as he had never been before, though for the time being he remained silent. But in midsummer he began a speaking tour, voicing his disapproval of the Act, arguing against the extension of slavery. He stumped his state on behalf of his friend Richard Yates, who was running for re-election as Representative to Congress.

On October 3 Stephen A. Douglas came to Springfield, where he made a speech explaining his reasons for the introduction of the Kansas-Nebraska Act and defending his position. Next day Lincoln answered him. He reminded Douglas that as the question of slavery had been settled by the Missouri Compromise of 1820 and Clay's compromise measures of 1850, there was no justification for their repeal. He spoke of the aggressiveness of the slaveholding party and their attempt to acquire more slave territory. And while he admitted that the South had a constitutional right to hold slaves and was entitled to a fair fugitive slave law, he denied that because of this right, slavery should be extended to the new territories. In his opinion, slavery—though inherently wrong—had to be tolerated where it existed, but its further spread must be prevented.

Lincoln's speech made a profound impression; it marked the beginning of his renewed political career. A man who heard it thought it was "superior to Webster's reply to Hayne, because its theme is loftier and its scope wider."

The election in Illinois brought victory to the anti-Nebraska forces. Enough anti-Nebraska men were elected who, combined with the Whigs, constituted a majority in the Legislature; thus Lincoln's chances to be named for the Senate were promising. (At that time Senators were not elected by popular vote but by the Legislatures.) However, the anti-Nebraska men in the Legislature were not a coherent political group—Whigs, Democrats, and others who called themselves Republicans made up their ranks—

and they would not be united behind such an outspoken Whig as Lincoln was. After a bitter struggle lasting for ten ballots, Lincoln lost the fight.

The senatorial contest over, once more he immersed himself in his law practice.

The political situation of the country was in a state of flux, the controversy over slavery disrupting the parties. Both the Democrats and the Whigs were split into pro- and anti-slavery factions. Of the other two lesser political parties, the Know-Nothings were almost dead, while the new Republican party was considered a haven for the radical element.

Lincoln saw that a fresh political alliance comprising the anti-Nebraska forces from all parties was a necessity, but he also realized that the time had not yet come for it. He pondered what to do and concluded that the safest path was inaction. To Owen Lovejoy he wrote in the summer of 1855: "I fear to do anything lest I do wrong."

William Herndon, who was a strong abolitionist, had this to say about his law partner's dilemma:

"Finding himself drifting about with the disorganized elements that floated together after the angry political waters had subsided, it became apparent to Lincoln that if he expected to figure as a leader he must take a stand himself. Mere hatred of slavery and opposition to the injustice of the Kansas-Nebraska legislation were not all that was required of him. He must be a Democrat, Know-Nothing, Abolitionist, or Republican, or forever float about in the great political sea without compass, rudder, or sail."

Slowly, Lincoln's indecision vanished; he had made up his mind and was ready to act.

On May 29, 1856, an anti-Nebraska convention assembled at Bloomington, where the Republican party of Illinois officially came into being. At the end of the meeting, Lincoln—who now threw his lot with the new party—made a remarkable speech. Herndon, who was present, remembered:

"I have heard or read all of Mr. Lincoln's great speeches, and I give it as my opinion that the Bloomington

Probably a daguerreotype taken in 1854 or 1855

THE MAN WHO CREATED THE STORM. Stephen A. Douglas, Democratic Senator of Illinois, caused a furor such as seldom roused before, when he introduced his Kansas-Nebraska Act early in 1854, proposing that the slavery issue in the new territories should be decided by the people who lived there. This was a repudiation of the Missouri Compromise.

speech was the grand effort of this life. Heretofore he had simply argued the slavery question on grounds of policy—the statesman's grounds—never reaching the question of the radical and the eternal right. Now he was newly baptized and freshly born; he had the fervor of a new convert; the smothered flame broke out; enthusiasm unusual to him blazed up; his eyes were aglow with an inspiration; he felt justice; his heart was alive to the right; his sympathies, remarkably deep for him, burst forth, and he stood before the throne of the eternal Right. His speech was full of fire and energy and force; it was logic; it was pathos; it was enthusiasm; it was justice, equity, truth, and right set ablaze by the divine fires of a soul maddened by the wrong; it was hard, heavy, knotty, gnarly, backed with wrath. I attempted for about fifteen minutes as was usual with me then to take notes, but at the

states, adopted systems of emancipation at once; and it is a significant fact, that not a single state has done the like since—So far as peaceful, voluntary emancipation is concerned, the condition of the negro slave in America, scarcely less terrible to the contemplation of a free mind, is now as fixed, and hopeless of change for the better, as that of the lost souls of the finally impenitent— The Autocrat of all the Russias will ~~resign~~ resign his crown, and proclaim his subjects free republicans, sooner than will our American masters voluntarily give up their slaves—

Our political problem now is "Can we, as a nation, continue together permanently— forever— half slave, and half free?" The problem is too mighty for me— May God, in his mercy, superintend the solution—

Your much obliged friend, and humble servant

A. Lincoln—

PONDERING OVER SLAVERY: On August 15, 1855, Lincoln wrote to Judge George Robertson of Lexington, Kentucky, who was a member of the Sixteenth Congress when it had adopted the Missouri Compromise. At that time—so Lincoln reminded the Judge— Robertson had spoken of "the peaceful extinction of slavery," indicating his belief that sooner or later it would come to an end. "Since then we have had thirty-six years of experience," wrote Lincoln, "and this experience has demonstrated, I think, that there is no peaceful extinction of slavery in prospect for us." Then he continued: "When we were the political slaves of King George, and wanted to be free, we called the maxim, that "all men are created equal" a self-evident truth; but now when we have grown fat, and have lost all dread of being slaves ourselves, we have become so greedy to be *masters* that we call the same maxim "a self-evident lie."

Lincoln closed his letter with the pregnant question: "Can we, as a nation, continue together *permanently—forever*—half slave, and half free? The problem is too mighty for me. May God, in his mercy, superintend the solution."

end of that time I threw pen and paper away and lived only in the inspiration of the hour. If Mr. Lincoln was six feet, four inches high usually, at Bloomington that day he was seven feet, and inspired at that."

Not only Herndon was enraptured. Others felt like him; everybody was under Lincoln's spell—thus, no one recorded in full what he said. It became his "lost speech."

Two weeks later, on June 19, the Republican nominating convention met in Philadelphia, where in an informal ballot the delegates gave Lincoln 110 votes for the Vice-Presidency. Reading about it in the newspaper, he remarked: "I reckon that ain't me; there's another great man in Massachusetts named Lincoln, and I reckon it's him." However, in the final official ballot William L. Dayton was chosen as Frémont's running mate.

In the ensuing campaign Lincoln stumped for Frémont, the first Republican presidential candidate. And though the new party carried all but four of the Northern states, the occupant of the White House became a Democrat—James Buchanan.

Shortly after the new President's inauguration, the Supreme Court handed down its decision in the celebrated Dred Scott case. Roger B. Taney, the venerable Chief Justice, declared that a Negro could not be regarded as a citizen; that he was property, and if a slave owner took his property into a territory where slavery did not exist, the law of that territory could not take it away from him. This meant that Congress had no power to prohibit slavery in the territories.

When Douglas defended the Dred Scott decision in Springfield, Lincoln replied that the Supreme Court had often overruled its own decisions. "We shall do what we can to have it overrule this." He said that there had been days when the Declaration of Independence was held sacred. "But now, to aid in making the bondage of the negro universal and eternal, it is assailed and sneered at and construed, and hawked at and torn, till, if its framers could rise from their graves, they could not at all recognize it."

He challenged Douglas, who argued against the Republicans' insistence that the Declaration of Independence included all, black as well as white men, and that they do so "only because they want to vote, and eat, and sleep, and marry with negroes!"

Lincoln protested against such counterfeit logic which concluded that, "because I do not want a black woman for a *slave* I must necessarily want her for a *wife*. I need not have her for either, I can just leave her alone. In some respects she certainly is not my equal; but in her natural right to eat the bread she earns with her own hands without asking leave of any one else, she is my equal, and the equal of all others."

In his opinion both Douglas and Chief Justice Taney were doing "obvious violence to the plain, unmistakable language of the Declaration." As he saw it, "authors of that notable instrument intended to include *all* men, but they did not intend to declare all men equal *in all respects*. They did not mean to say all were equal in color, size, intellect, moral developments, or social capacity. They defined with tolerable distinctness, in what respects they did consider all men created equal—equal in certain inalienable rights, among which are life, liberty, and the pursuit of happiness. This they said, and this meant."

Answering Douglas "that slavery is the greatest source of amalgamation" he quoted the last census figures, which showed that in 1850 there were 405,751 mulattos in the country. "Nearly all have sprung from black slaves and white masters," he stated. And he laid the blame for slavery on the profit motive:

"The plainest print cannot be read through a gold eagle; and it will be ever hard to find many men who will send a slave to Liberia, and pay his passage, while they can send him to a new country, Kansas, for instance, and sell him for fifteen hundred dollars, and the rise."

Arguing the slavery issue, he clarified his mind. No longer was he doubtful what course he was to take. His future lay with the Republican party.

HIS STAND ON THE SLAVERY ISSUE IN 1855. In a lengthy letter to his friend Joshua Fry Speed, Lincoln wrote on August 24, 1855: "I do oppose the extension of slavery, because my judgment and feelings so prompt me; and I am under no obligation to the contrary." However, "if Kansas fairly votes herself a slave state, she must be admitted, or the Union must be dissolved." To Speed's inquiry about his position, Lincoln answered, "that is a disputed point—I think I am a whig; but others say there are no whigs, and that I am an abolitionist. When I was in Washington I voted for the Wilmot proviso as good as forty times, and I never heard of any one attempting to unwhig me for that. I now do no more than oppose the *extension* of slavery."

DEFENDING A FRIEND

DUFF ARMSTRONG, the son of Jack and Hannah Armstrong, Lincoln's friends at New Salem, was accused of murder. Lincoln defended him—and secured his acquittal.

ON THE morning of May 6, 1858, Abraham Lincoln threw a few things in his carpetbag, tucked some papers inside his stove-pipe hat, and set out from his Springfield home to make the forty-five-mile journey to Beardstown, where the following day he was to defend young Duff Armstrong on a charge of murder.

Duff Armstrong and James Norris, a friend of Duff's, were accused of the killing of James Metzker. There were many witnesses, and they all testified to that effect. One of them, the house-painter Charles Allen, swore that he saw Armstrong in the bright moonlight as he hit Metzker with a slung shot.

Lincoln listened to Allen patiently, cross-examined him, then turned to the jury: "Now I will show you that this man Allen's testimony is a pack of lies; that he never saw Armstrong strike Metzker with a slung shot; that he did not witness this fight by the light of the full moon, for the moon was not in the heavens that night!"

He asked the sheriff for an almanac and proved by it that at the hour of the brawl the moon was not bright, but setting, so Allen could not possibly have seen what he described.

With this and other evidence, all proving Duff's innocence, Lincoln went to the jury. It was a hot day, and he took off his coat and discarded his vest as he began to speak. Slowly and carefully he reviewed the testimony of the witnesses and picked it all to pieces. One of his suspenders fell from his shoulder—it was knitted of wool—but he didn't even notice. It remained hanging for the rest of the speech. He talked for more than an hour, ending his peroration on a personal note. "Gentlemen, I appear here without any reward for the benefit of that lady sitting there," said Lincoln, pointing to the crying Hannah, the mother of Duff, "who washed my dirty shirts when I had no money to pay her." He told the jury how he had arrived at New Salem as a young man and how he, a penniless stranger, had been given shelter and food by Duff's father and mother. He said that he did not believe that a son of such kindly people could be a murderer. And he pleaded for Duff Armstrong's life because God willed that this was a small way in which he could repay his debts to the friends who had been so kind to him in his youth.

Hannah Armstrong grabbed Lincoln's hand, overcome with emotion.

When the jury returned, its verdict was "Not Guilty." Lincoln turned to her with "What did I tell you?" and thoughtfully he added: "I pray to God that this lesson may prove in the end a good lesson to him and to all."

LINCOLN'S INSTRUCTIONS TO THE JURY, asking for Armstrong's acquittal. He handed it to the presiding justice, Judge James Harriott, who gave it to the jury without changing it.

AFTER DUFF ARMSTRONG WAS ACQUITTED, the photographer Abraham M. Byers stopped Lincoln on the street and asked him to his gallery. Lincoln, looking at his old Holland suit without any semblance of starch in it, protested, "These clothes are dirty and unfit for a picture." But Byers insisted, and Lincoln followed him to the studio where, on May 7, 1858, this ambrotype was taken.

NOMINATED FOR THE SENATE

DOUGLAS'S SENATORIAL term was to expire in 1858, and Lincoln was eager to enter the contest for the seat. When the "little giant" broke with the Administration, disagreeing with President Buchanan on the Lecompton Constitution, many Republicans advocated that the party in Illinois should support Douglas for re-election.

Lincoln went through anxious months. In his opinion, both Douglas and Buchanan were wrong, and the fact that the former might be "a little farther wrong of the two" was no reason for the Republicans to rally behind a Democrat and send him back to the Senate unopposed.

However, as election time neared, it became evident that the Republicans would not support Douglas. In May,

1858, Lincoln wrote a friend:

"I think our prospects gradually and steadily grow better, though we are not yet clear out of the woods by a great deal. There is still some effort to make trouble out of 'Americanism.'"

The senatorial campaign formally opened on June 16. On that day the Republican State Convention unanimously declared Lincoln to be its "first and only choice" for the Senate, a resolution intended against those party members who had tried to sway the Republicans behind Douglas.

Lincoln prepared a speech to accept the nomination and read it to his political friends. They listened to it critically and advised him against using the opening sentences, in which he said: "A house divided against itself

cannot stand. I believe this government cannot endure, permanently half *slave* and half *free*. . . . It will become *all* one thing, or *all* the other."

One of the Republican leaders said it was a "damned fool utterance"; another held the doctrine too much "ahead of its time." But Herndon urged: "Lincoln, deliver that speech as read and it will make you President."

Lincoln gave the address as he had written it.

Years later he said about it: "If I had to draw a pen across my record, and erase my whole life from sight, and I had one poor gift or choice left as to what I should save from the wreck, I should choose that speech and leave it to the world unerased."

ACCEPTING THE NOMINATION, Lincoln spoke to the Illinois Republican State Convention on June 16, 1858, in Springfield, declaring: "A house divided against itself cannot stand. I believe this

government cannot endure, permanently half *slave* and half *free*. . . . I do not expect the house to *fall*—but I *do* expect it will cease to be divided." This is how the *Illinois State Journal* reported it.

AT THE TIME OF THE SENATORIAL CONTEST. A daguerreotype taken on July 11, 1858, in Chicago, a day after Lincoln answered Douglas at the Tremont House. He is holding a copy of the Chicago *Press & Tribune*, the newspaper which backed him.

DEBATING WITH DOUGLAS

An imaginary rendering of the scene by Victor Perara

THE DEBATE AT GALESBURG on October 7, 1858. The platform on which Lincoln and Douglas spoke was erected at the end of Knox College and decorated by students with flags and streamers.

"OF ALL the damned Whig rascals about Springfield, Abe Lincoln is the ablest and the most honest," said Douglas when he heard that Lincoln would be his opponent in the senatorial contest. The "little giant" went with great confidence into the campaign. His star was shining brightly, he was the most popular political figure in his state; he had no fear of his antagonist, whom he was certain to defeat.

Lincoln's militant speech—"a house divided against itself cannot stand"—was the kind of talk Douglas liked to hear. Wherever he spoke, he quoted Lincoln's lines "I believe that this government cannot endure, permanently half *slave* and half *free*," asserting that his opponent was advocating war between North and South.

Painting by Robert Marshall Root in the Illinois State Capitol

THE DEBATE AT CHARLESTON on September 18, 1858. From l. to r.: Orlando B. Ficklin, Dr. W. M. Chambers, Stephen A. Douglas, Horace White, and Robert R. Hitt. On Lincoln's left: Henry Binmore of the Chicago *Times*, J. T. Cunningham, J. B. Sheridan of the Chicago *Times*, Usher F. Linder, Congressman H. P. H. Bromwell (with beard), Elisha Linder, and Richard J. Oglesby.

AUGUST 26, 1858, less than a week after the first debate with Douglas at Ottawa, and only a day before the famous discussion at Freeport, where Lincoln posed the question: "Can the people of the United States Territory, in any lawful way, against the wish of any citizen of the United States, exclude slavery from its limits prior to the formation of a state constitution?" Douglas answered that regardless of the Supreme Court decision it was for the majority of the people to introduce or exclude slavery from the territories.

OCTOBER 1, 1858, a week before the fifth debate at Galesburg. A fortnight later the humorist Petroleum V. Nasby (David R. Locke) came to see the Republican candidate in Quincy. Lincoln sat in his hotel room with his boots off. "I like to give my feet a chance to breathe," he said. His coat and vest on the chair, his necktie and collar off, at first glance he looked disheveled. But Locke cared little about the dress. He noted: "I never saw a more thoughtful face. I never saw a more dignified face. I never saw so sad a face."

The "little giant" opened his campaign in Chicago on July 9. Lincoln, who was in the city for the session of the U.S. District Court, answered him from the balcony of the Tremont House the next day, the Chicago *Press & Tribune* reporting that while his audience was only three fourths as large as Douglas's, "in point of enthusiasm, about four times as great."

After both of them spoke in Springfield, Lincoln challenged his opponent to a series of joint debates so they could discuss before the electorate their positions on the all-pervading issue of slavery. Douglas accepted the challenge, naming seven cities where neither candidate had spoken before and where he would be willing to appear.

A few days before the debates began, Lincoln met on the street Judge Beckwith, who was wondering whether his friend would be strong enough to stand up to Douglas. Lincoln asked him: "You have seen two men about to fight?" And when the Judge nodded, Lincoln continued:

"Well, one of them brags about what he means to do. He jumps high in the air, cracking his heels together, smites his fists, and wastes his breath trying to scare somebody. The other man says not a word. His arms are at his side, his fists doubled up, his head is drawn to the shoulder, and his teeth are set firm together. He is saving his wind for the fight, and as sure as it comes off he will win it, or die a-trying."

Their first encounter was at Ottawa on August 21. Carloads of men came from Chicago; others arrived in wagons, buggies, canal boats, on horses or afoot. Everyone in the town and its neighborhood took part in the excitement, waving flags, forming processions, cheering and marching. Many thousands squeezed before the platform, listening to the debaters, applauding and encouraging them. At the end, the enthusiastic Lincoln supporters carried their man on their shoulders. Gleefully, Douglas referred to this episode. "Lincoln was so used up in the discussion," he said in his subsequent speeches, "that his knees trembled, and he had to be carried from the platform."

Their second meeting was at Freeport on August 27. Here Lincoln posed the question: "Can the people of a United States Territory, in any lawful way, against the wish of any citizen of the United States, exclude slavery from its limits prior to the formation of a State Constitution?"

Douglas answered that popular sovereignty was not incompatible with the Dred Scott decision, arguing that it was for the people to introduce or exclude slavery from the territories. He held that if

5 FEET 4 INCHES TALL Stephen A. Douglas after serving two terms in the Senate was again candidate of the Illinois Democrats.

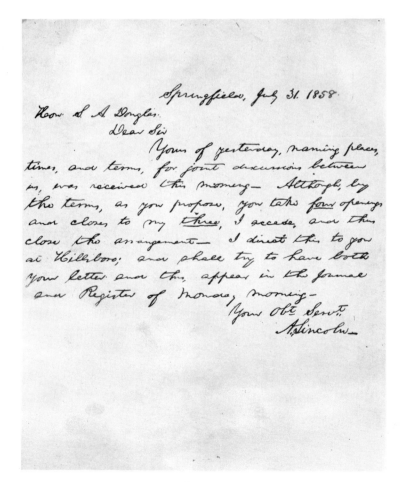

ACCEPTING THE TERMS. A week before Lincoln wrote this letter, he challenged Douglas to a series of joint debates. Douglas accepted, naming seven cities where he would be willing to speak.

the majority of them were opposed to slavery, their elected representatives would, "by unfriendly legislation, effectually prevent the introduction of it into their midst."

This answer—later known as the "Freeport Doctrine"—raised a storm of protest all over the land. Douglas was violently assailed by the extremists in the South, and was bitterly criticized by the moderates in the North. His answer widened the gap between the two opposing factions in the Democratic party, ultimately ending in their fatal schism.

The debates continued at Jonesboro, at Charleston, at Galesburg; and everywhere it was the same picture. At every place large crowds turned out to hear "the Tall Sucker and the Little Giant"; at every place there was the blaring sound of the brass bands; the cheering and hurrahing throughout the night; at every place the debate turned into a colorful spectacle, a sporting event of first magnitude.

In Quincy, the site of the sixth discussion, the popular German-American politician Carl Schurz saw Lincoln for the first time. And this is how he described him:

A PAGE FROM LINCOLN'S SCRAPBOOK, in which he carefully pasted the Chicago *Tribune's* reports of his own addresses and the *Times'* version of Douglas's speeches, to keep them for posterity.

6 FEET 4 INCHES TALL Abraham Lincoln was the nominee of the Illinois Republicans for the senatorial seat in opposition to Douglas.

"On his head he wore a somewhat battered stove-pipe hat. His neck emerged, long and sinewy, from a white collar turned down over a thin black necktie. His lank, ungainly body was clad in a rusty black dress coat with sleeves that should have been longer, but his arms appeared so long that the sleeves of a store coat could hardly be expected to cover them all the way down to the wrists. His black trousers, too, permitted a very full view of his large feet. On his left arm he carried a gray woolen shawl, which evidently served him for an overcoat in chilly weather. His left hand held a cotton umbrella of the bulging kind, and also a black satchel that bore the marks of long and hard usage."

The humorist David R. Locke, who wrote under the name of Petroleum V. Nasby, came for a visit as well, asking Lincoln whether he expected to defeat Douglas. No, he said, he did not expect to win be-cause of the gerrymandered districts, but he hoped to carry the state in the popular vote. "You can't overturn a pyramid, but you can undermine it; that's what I've been trying to do."

In their debates both Lincoln and Douglas touched on one single issue to the exclusion of any others—slavery. And while he discussed it, Lincoln's attitude softened. No longer did he hold that the government "cannot endure permanently half slave and half free," but declared that he had no intention of making the house all free by interfering with slavery in the states where it already existed. All he wished to accomplish was to reverse the trend. He said that if the people of the country would believe in the ultimate disappearance of slavery, agitation would cease and the Union would be safe.

Lincoln shifted ground on another point as well.

NOTES TO HIS LAST SPEECH in the senatorial campaign, which he delivered in Springfield on October 30, 1858. In his address Lincoln said: "Ambition has been ascribed to me. God knows how sincerely I prayed from the first that this field of ambition might not be opened. I claim no insensibility to political honors, but today could the Missouri restriction be restored, and the whole slavery question replaced on the old ground of 'toleration,' by *necessity* where it exists, with unyielding hostility to the spread of it, on principle, I would, in consideration, gladly agree, that Judge Douglas would never be *out*, and I never *in*, an office, so long as we both or either live." The night before he spoke, Lincoln and Henry Villard, reporter for the New York *Staats Zeitung*, had taken refuge from a storm in an empty boxcar while waiting for a train outside Springfield. There Lincoln reminisced and told that his wife insisted that he was going to be Senator and President too. "Just think of such a sucker as me as President," exclaimed Lincoln, laughing loudly.

BEFORE THE SIXTH DEBATE. An ambrotype by W. J. Thompson, taken at Monmouth on October 11, 1858, the day Lincoln spoke to a large audience for three hours.

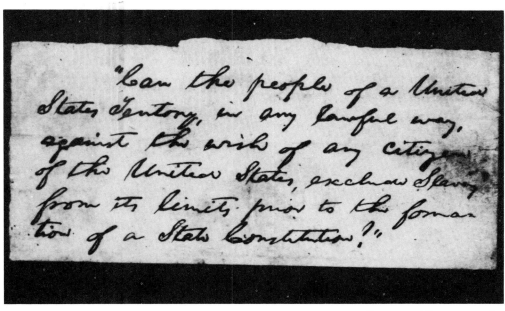

"Can the people of a United States Territory, in any lawful way, against the wish of any citizen of the United States, exclude Slavery from its limits prior to the formation of a State Constitution?"

LINCOLN'S FAMOUS QUESTION TO DOUGLAS—the Freeport Doctrine. The note in his own handwriting is in the collection of the Illinois State Historical Library, Springfield.

In his Chicago speech he argued on moral grounds that slavery was an evil, and based his contention largely on the words of the Declaration of Independence. At Charleston he retracted: "I am not, nor ever have been, in favor of bringing about in any way the social and political equality of the white and black races—that I am not, nor ever have been, in favor of making voters or jurors of negroes, nor of qualifying them to hold office, nor to intermarry with white people; and I will say in addition to this that there is a physical difference between the white and black races which I believe will forever forbid the two races living together on terms of social and political quality. And inasmuch as they cannot so live, while they do remain together there must be the position of superior and inferior, and I as much as any other man am in favor of having the superior position assigned to the white race."

Yet, he made it clear that both he and the Republican party believed slavery "a moral, a social and a political wrong."

He said at Quincy:

"Because we think it wrong, we propose a course of policy that shall deal with it as a wrong. We deal with it as with any other wrong, in so far as we can prevent its growing any larger, and so deal with it that in the run of time there may be some promise of an end to it."

The Republicans would not disturb slavery in the states where it was already in existence, said Lincoln, but "We insist on the policy that shall re-strict it to its present limits." Repeatedly he spoke out in opposition to the Dred Scott decision. "We propose so resisting it as to have it reversed if we can, and a new judicial rule established upon this subject."

Summing up the Republicans' policy, he said: "If there be any man who does not believe slavery is wrong . . . that man is misplaced and ought to leave us. While, on the other hand, if there be a man in the Republican party who is impatient over the necessity springing from its actual presence, and is impatient of the constitutional guarantees thrown around it, and would act in disregard of these, he too is misplaced, standing with us. He will find his place somewhere else; for we have a due regard, so far as we are capable of understanding them, for all these things. This . . . as well as I can give it, is a plain statement of our principles in all their enormity."

The election showed that Lincoln was the favorite of the people; his popular support was 4,085 votes larger than that of his opponent, but in the Legislature Douglas had the upper hand. "Glory to God and the Sucker Democracy, Douglas 54, Lincoln 41," read the telegram which informed the "little giant" in Washington that for six more years he was to represent the people of Illinois in the United States Senate.

And Lincoln, smarting under his defeat, said that he felt like the Kentucky boy who stubbed his toe. "I am too big to cry about it, but it hurts too awful bad to laugh!"

GROWING INTO A CANDIDATE

"I DO NOT THINK MYSELF FIT FOR THE PRESIDENCY," wrote Lincoln to the Rock Island editor Thomas J. Pickett on April 16, 1859, telling him that he thought "it best for our cause that no concerted effort, such as you suggest, should be made."

AFTER THE debates with Douglas, when his name became known far outside the boundaries of his own state Lincoln was urged to go after the presidential nomination. But he hesitated. To a newspaper editor eager to launch a boom for him, he wrote: "I must in candor say I do not think myself fit for the presidency."

Yet, as the summer months of 1859 waned and autumn came, Lincoln's mind, too, underwent a change. Between the lines of his letters written during this time one could perceive that he was no longer so hesitant; the presidential bug had bitten deep into his soul.

At the end of the year and in the early part of 1860 he was preparing his Cooper Union address, "and the final rounding-out of his anti-slavery argument." When that speech and his addresses in New England won widespread approval, he began openly to act as a candidate for the high office. He started a cautious letter-writing campaign, keeping in touch with politicians, asking their advice, and telling them of his position. To Samuel Galloway, a Republican lawyer in Columbus, Ohio, he wrote on March 24:

"My name is new in the field, and I suppose I am not the first choice of a very great many. Our policy, then, is to give no offence to others—leave them in a mood to come to us if they shall be compelled to give up their first love."

A month later, on April 29, he confided to an old

political associate that "the taste *is* in my mouth a little." He was now ready to fight. He advised Lyman Trumbull to be cautious. "You better write no letters which can possibly be distorted into opposition or quasi opposition to me," he wrote. "There are men on the constant watch for such things out of which to prejudice my peculiar friends against you. While I have no more suspicion of you than I have of my best friend living, I am kept in a constant struggle against suggestions of this sort. I have hesitated some to write this paragraph, lest you should suspect I do it for my own benefit, and not for yours; but on reflection I conclude you will not suspect me."

And he ended his letter by saying: "Let no eye but your own see this—not that there is anything wrong, or even ungenerous, in it; but it would be misconstrued."

"I HAVE ENLISTED," so he wrote to W. E. Frazer on November 11, 1859, "for the permanent success of the Republican cause; and for this object, I shall labor faithfully in the ranks, unless, as I think not probable, the judgment of the party shall assign me a different position."

In the six months since the Pickett letter Lincoln's mind had changed; he now saw that he might become his party's candidate.

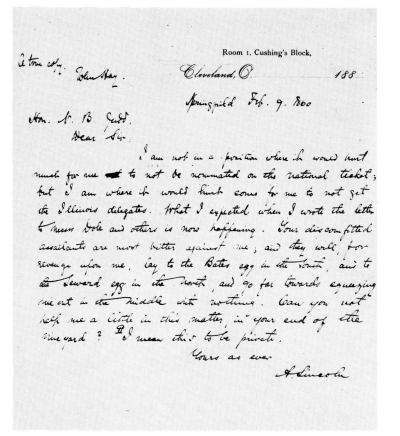

"I AM NOT IN A POSITION," wrote he on February 9, 1860, to Norman B. Judd, "where it would hurt much for me to not be nominated on the national ticket, but I am where it would hurt some for me to not get the Illinois delegates." This letter is in the handwriting of John Hay, who marked it as a copy of the original.

There could be no doubt any more that he was now an avowed candidate. He reviewed his competitors, analyzing their strengths and weaknesses. Of William H. Seward, the favorite Republican contender, who was known as a radical antislavery man, he thought that he "is the very best candidate we could have for the North of Illinois, and the very *worst* for the South of it." The chances of the former Ohio Governor, Salmon P. Chase, were not too good, he had not the unanimous support of his own state; John McLean, the Supreme Court Judge, happened to be too old; Edward Bates of Missouri would not be able to carry the German communities.

In going through the list, it must have dawned on Lincoln that he was the most "available" contender. He had many advantages over the others. He was known, and still not too well known; he had been in politics long enough, yet not long enough in national politics to make too many enemies; his origin and Southern birth assured him the votes of the moderates; he came from a "doubtful" Republican state, which he could win; he was well liked by the Germans; he was considered a moderate on the slavery issue. Thus he could look forward with some hope to the day when the Republican nominating convention was to meet in Chicago.

"THE TASTE *IS* IN MY MOUTH A LITTLE," wrote Lincoln to Lyman Trumbull on April 29, 1860. The nominating convention only a few weeks away, he was now in the race. Analyzing the chances of the other Republican contenders, he found that in the state of Illinois, Judge McLean was stronger than Seward or Bates.

A MONTH BEFORE THE CONVENTION, Lincoln was still undecided whether or not he would be able to go to the meeting at Chicago.

HE WRITES OUT
HIS
LIFE STORY

Photograph by Samuel M. Fassett, taken in Chicago on October 4, 1859

I was born Feb. 12, 1809, in Hardin County, Kentucky. My parents were both born in Virginia, of undistinguished families—second families, perhaps I should say. My mother, who died in my tenth year, was of a family of the name of Hanks, some of whom now reside in Adams, some others in Macon counties, Illinois. My paternal grandfather, Abraham Lincoln, emigrated from Rockingham County, Virginia, to Kentucky, about 1781 or 2, where, a year or two later, he was killed by indians, not in battle, but by stealth, when he was laboring to open a farm in the forest. His ancestors, who were quakers, went to Virginia from Berks County, Pennsylvania. An effort to identify them with the New England family of the same name ended in nothing more definite, than a similarity of christian names in both families, such as Enoch, Levi, Mordecai, Solomon, Abraham, and the like.

My father, at the death of his father, was but six years of age; and he grew up, litterally without education. He removed from Kentucky to what is now Spencer county, Indiana, in my eighth year. We reached our new home about the time the State came into the Union. It was a wild region, with many bears and other wild animals still in the woods. There I grew up. There were some schools, so called; but no qualification was ever required of a teacher, beyond "readin, writin, and cipherin" to the Rule of Three. If a straggler supposed to understand latin, happened to sojourn in

HIS AUTOBIOGRAPHICAL SKETCH, which Lincoln sent to Jesse W. Fell, then secretary of the Illinois State Central Committee in

ONE EVENING in Bloomington shortly after the 1858 senatorial contest, Jesse Fell, the secretary of the Illinois Republican State Central Committee, met Lincoln on the street and asked him to the law office of his brother. There Fell told Lincoln that wherever he traveled, people wanted to know more about the man who had challenged Douglas.

Fell suggested a newspaper article telling the country who Lincoln was and what he had done, thus preparing his candidacy for the Presidency. "I know your public life, and can furnish items that your modesty would forbid, but I don't know much about your private history," said Fell, "when you were born, and where, what were your opportunities for education, and so on. And I want you to give me these. Won't you do it?"

Lincoln answered: "Fell, I admit the force of much that you say, and I admit that I am ambitious and would like to be President. I am not insensible to the compliment you pay me, and the interest you manifest in the matter; but there is no such good luck in store for me as the Presidency of the United States; besides there is nothing in my early history that would interest you or anybody else; and, as Judge Davis says, 'It won't pay.'"

Yet, a year later, he had found that it might pay. By then he was an avowed presidential candidate—and such a newspaper article as Fell suggested could be very helpful to his cause. So he sat down and outlined his life story on three foolscap pages.

In the accompanying note Lincoln told Fell: "Herewith is a little sketch,

the neighborhood, he was looked upon as a wizzard— There was absolutely nothing to excite ambition for education. Of course when I came of age I did not know much— Still somehow I could read, write, and cipher to the Rule of Three; but that was all— I have not been to school since— The little advance I now have upon this store of education, I have picked up from time to time under the pressure of necessity—

I was raised to farm work which I continued till I was twentytwo— At twentyone I came to Illinois, and passed the first year in Illinois— Macon county— Then I got to New Salem (at that time in Sangamon, now in Menard county), where I remained a year as a sort of Clerk in a store— Then came the Black-Hawk war; and I was elected a Captain of Volunteers— a success which gave me more pleasure than any I have had since— I went the campaign, was elated, ran for the Legislature the same year (1832), and was beaten— the only time I ever have been beaten by the people— The next, and three succeeding biennial elections, I was elected to the Legislature— I was not a candidate afterwards. During this Legislative period I had studied law, and removed to Springfield to practice it— In 1846, I was once elected to the lower House of Congress— Was not a candidate for re-election— From 1849 to 1854, both

inclusive, practiced law more assiduously than ever before— Always a whig in politics, and generally on the whig electoral ticket, making active canvasses— I was losing interest in politics, when the repeal of the Missouri Compromise aroused me again— What I have done since then is pretty well known—

If any personal description of me is thought desirable, it may be said, I am, in height, six feet, four inches, nearly; lean in flesh, weighing on an average, one hundred and eighty pounds; dark complexion, with coarse black hair, and grey eyes— no other marks or brands recollected—

Hon J. W. Fell.   Yours very truly
                                    A. Lincoln

Springfield, Dec. 20. 1859
J. W. Fell, Esq
My dear Sir:
Herewith is a little sketch, as you requested— There is not much of it, for the reason, I suppose, that there is not much of me— If anything be made out of it, I wish it to be modest, and not to go beyond the materials— If it was thought necessary to incorporate any thing from any of my speeches, I suppose there would be no objection— Of course it must not appear to have been written by myself— Yours very truly
A. Lincoln

December, 1859. In the accompanying note he wrote: "Herewith a little sketch as you requested. There is not much of it, for the reason, I suppose, that there is not much of me." Joseph J. Lewis used the sketch for his essay which was printed in many papers.

as you requested. There is not much of it, for the reason, I suppose, that there is not much of me. If anything be made out of it, I wish it to be modest, and not to go beyond the materials. If it were thought necessary to incorporate any thing from any of my speeches, I suppose there would be no objection. Of course it must not appear to have been written by myself."

Fell sent the notes to Joseph J. Lewis, a prominent lawyer and essayist in Pennsylvania, who was to write the biography.

Lewis complained that the facts were "exceedingly meagre and few." He asked for more. "I want to know when he first began to speak. What was the success of his first efforts. Whether in the legislature he manifested his powers as a thinker and if so whether in his first or subsequent sessions. Whether he measured swords with Douglas when both were members. What his manner in speaking. What the character of his gesture—what his voice. Whether he controls juries—whether he is good at a law point. Whether as a lawyer he is

well and thoroughly read. Whether he is a good shot with the rifle—a good horseman—fond of the hunt—genial in manners—entertaining in conversation. From what I hear of him I can imagine some of these matters but I would like to have the actual fact."

But there was no more. Lincoln had put on paper all he wanted to say, for him the sketch of his life was there on the three sheets. And Lewis had to write his piece from those three pages. From his article the country learned for the first time the story of Lincoln's life.

SPEAKING IN NEW YORK

IN FEBRUARY, 1860, Lincoln journeyed to New York, where he was to speak before the "Young Men's Central Republican Union." The Democratic newspaper in his home town, the *Illinois State Register*, commented sarcastically on his trip: "Subject not known, consideration $200 and expenses. Object, presidential capital. Effect, disappointment."

On the day of his lecture a snowstorm had raged in the city; still, fifteen hundred people were present at Cooper Union when William Cullen Bryant, the poet-editor, introduced him. Lincoln began his speech by taking as his text a statement of Senator Douglas: "Our fathers, when they framed the Government under which we live, understood this question just as well, and even better, than we do now." He told his listeners that he was in complete agreement with Douglas. Examining in detail the background of the Constitution's thirty-nine signers, and elaborating on their attitudes on slavery, Lincoln advised: "Speak as they spoke and act as they acted upon it. This is all Republicans ask—all Republicans desire—in relation to slavery. As those fathers marked it, so let it be again marked, as an evil not to be extended, but to be tolerated and protected only because of and so far as its actual presence among us makes that toleration and protection a necessity. Let all the guaranties those fathers gave it, be, not grudgingly, but fully and fairly maintained. For this Republicans contend, and with this, so far as I know or believe, they will be content."

The audience liked the argument, it enjoyed listening to Lincoln's quaint dialect. "His voice was soft and sympathetic as a girl's," reported the newsman of the New York *World*.

In his speech Lincoln denied that the North was sectional, denied that the Republicans were associated with John Brown at Harper's Ferry or that they had any desire to stir up insurrections among the slaves. As he brought home his points, frequent applause interrupted his words.

"What will satisfy the South?" he asked. "Simply this: we must not only let them alone, but we must somehow convince them that we do let them alone." Then he proceeded: "Wrong as we think slavery is, we can yet afford to let it alone where it is, because that much is due to the necessity arising from its actual presence in the nation; but can we, while our votes will prevent it, allow it to spread into the national territories, and to overrun us here in these Free States? If our sense of duty forbids this, then let us stand by our duty, fearlessly and effectively."

At the end of the lecture a loud cheering rose in the hall. Noah Brooks of the *Tribune* exclaimed: "He's the greatest man since St. Paul," and he wrote for his paper: "No man ever before made such an impression on his first appeal to a New York audience."

The address over, some fellow Republicans asked Lincoln to the Athenaeum Club for supper. It was a small party, with politics the main topic of conversation. Then it was time for bed. The head of the lecture committee offered to take him to his hotel, so the two walked off to get a streetcar. Lincoln was limping. "Are you lame, Mr. Lincoln?" asked his companion. No, he was not lame, only the new boots which he wore were hurting his feet.

The streetcar came, they got on board and rode up on Broadway. At the Astor House Lincoln got out, a lonely, solitary figure in the snow as he walked through the door of his hotel. No one recognized him. He was a stranger in the great city.

TRIBUNE TRACTS.—No. 4.

National Politics.

SPEECH

OF

ABRAHAM LINCOLN,

OF ILLINOIS,

DELIVERED AT THE COOPER INSTITUTE, MONDAY, FEB. 27, 1860.

Mr. PRESIDENT AND FELLOW-CITIZENS OF NEW YORK: The facts with which I shall deal this evening are mainly old and familiar; nor is there anything new in the general use I shall make of them. If there shall be any novelty, it will be in the mode of presenting the facts, and the inferences and observations following that presentation.

In his speech last autumn, at Columbus, Ohio, as reported in "The New York Times," Senator Douglas said:

"Our fathers, when they framed the Government under which we live, understood this question just as well, and even better, than we do now."

I fully indorse this, and I adopt it as a text for this discourse. I so adopt it because it furnishes a precise and an agreed starting point for a discussion between Republicans and that wing of Democracy headed by Senator Douglas. It simply leaves the inquiry: "What was the understanding those fathers had of the question mentioned?"

What is the frame of Government under which we live?

The answer must be: "The Constitution of the United States." That Constitution consists of the original, framed in 1787 (and under which the present Government first went into operation), and twelve subsequently framed amendments, the first ten of which were framed in 1789.

Who were our fathers that framed the Constitution? I suppose the "thirty-nine" who signed the original instrument may be fairly called our fathers who framed that part of the present Government. It is almost exactly true to say they framed it, and it is altogether true to say they fairly represented the opinion and sentiment of the whole nation at that time. Their names, being familiar to nearly all, and accessible to quite all, need not now be repeated.

I take these "thirty-nine," for the present, as being "our fathers who framed the Government under which we live."

What is the question which, according to the text, those fathers understood just as well, and even better than we do now?

It is this: Does the proper division of local from federal authority, or anything in the Constitution, forbid our Federal Government to control as to slavery in our Federal Territories?

Upon this, Douglas holds the affirmative, and Republicans the negative. This affirma-

☞ FOR SALE AT THE OFFICE OF THE NEW YORK TRIBUNE. PRICE, PER SINGLE COPY, 4c. DOZEN COPIES, 25c.; PER HUNDRED, $1 25; PER THOUSAND, $10.

THE FIRST PUBLICATION OF THE COOPER UNION SPEECH.

84

THE DAY HE SPOKE AT COOPER UNIO
— on February 27, 1860 — Lincoln went Brady's Broadway studio to pose for this pictur
New print from George Eastman House

CAMPAIGNING IN NEW ENGLAND

ROBERT was going to school at Phillips Exeter Academy in New Hampshire, and Lincoln—on a trip to the East—planned to visit his son. On February 28—a day after his Cooper Union address—he left New York and, after a speech at Providence, went to Exeter.

If Lincoln had hoped for a peaceful and quiet visit, he was sadly mistaken. From everywhere the cry went up for speeches, Republican committeemen asking him to address their communities. He complied at Concord, Manchester, and Exeter.

The whole school at Exeter was present to listen to their schoolmate's father. And when Lincoln appeared on the platform, one of the boys, disappointed in his appearance, whispered to a friend: "Don't you feel kind of sorry for Bob?" And a girl burst out: "Isn't it too bad Bob's got such a homely father."

After a quiet Sabbath with Robert, Lincoln left Exeter for a speechmaking tour in Connecticut and Rhode Island. He gave addresses at Hartford, New Haven, Meriden, Norwich, Bridgeport, and Woonsocket.

In each town the halls were filled to capacity; he found cheering audiences wherever he spoke. For the main theme of his speeches he chose the property aspect of slavery. "One-sixth, and a little more, of the population of the United States are slaves, looked upon as property, as nothing but property," he said at Hartford. "The cash value of these slaves, at a moderate estimate, is two billion dollars. This amount of property value has a vast influence on the minds of its owners, very naturally. The same amount of property would have an equal influence upon us if owned in the North."

At New Haven he illustrated his point with the story of the dissenting minister who, arguing a theological question with his orthodox colleague, was always met by the reply: "I can't see it so." The dissenter opened the *Bible*, pointing out the passage; still his opponent replied: "I can't see it

NOTES TO HIS HARTFORD SPEECH, WHICH LINCOLN FORGETFULLY LEFT BEHIND HIM AT THE TABLE OF THE LECTURE HALL.

"LINCOLN IN NEW HAMPSHIRE" said the caption to this photograph, showing a bearded man with a top hat, seated on a slab of granite on the bank of New Hampshire's Contoocook River. Unfortunately, the figure at the river is not that of Lincoln. He was never in Peterborough (where the picture was taken), besides, when he visited New Hampshire in the early part of 1860 he was beardless.

so." The exasperated clergyman then pointed to a single word. "Can you see that?" "Yes, I see it," replied his orthodox colleague. So the dissenter laid a guinea over the word and asked him, "Do you see it now?"

"So here," said Lincoln, "whether the owners of this species of property do really see it as it is through two billions of dollars, and that is a pretty thick coating."

From the slavery issue he turned to the shoemaker's strike in Massachusetts, ridiculing Senator Stephen A. Douglas' idea that the strike arose from "this unfortunate sectional warfare."

"I am glad to see," he said, "that a system of labor prevails in New England under which laborers can strike when they want to; where they are not obliged to labor whether you pay them or not! I like the system which lets a man quit when he wants to, and wish it might prevail everywhere. One of the reasons why I am opposed to slavery is just here. What is the true condition of the laborer? I take it that it is the best for all to leave each man free to acquire property as fast as they can. Some will get wealthy. I don't believe in a law to prevent a man from getting rich; it would do more harm than good. So while we do not propose any war upon capital, we do wish to allow the humblest man an equal chance to get rich with everybody else. When one starts poor, as most do in the race of life, free society is such that he knows that there is no fixed condition of labor for his whole life."

He spoke every day at a different town, making eleven speeches in just as many days. "If I had foreseen it," he wrote to his wife, "I think I would not have come East at all."

THE REPUBLICANS CHOOSE
THEIR CANDIDATE

THE WHOLE country looked to Chicago, the seat of the Republican Convention.

The Democrats had already had their tumultuous convention session at Charleston, where the South presented an ultimatum directed to their Northern and Western brethren: "You must not apologize for slavery" was its gist. "You must declare it right; you must advocate its extension."

The great fight raged around the personality of Stephen A. Douglas. He was the pivot individual of the convention; the delegates were either wholeheartedly for or violently against him. The question was: Could he receive the two-thirds vote of the delegates necessary for the nomination? As the convention got under way, it became evident that he could not.

For the Douglas men, a solution of this predicament seemed a reduction of the hostile delegates. If a few of the ultra-Southern states—three or four at the utmost—would walk out, there would be enough supporters left in the rump convention to give Douglas the necessary two-thirds vote.

The break between the hostile groups came over the platform. Two proposals were before the convention. The majority report upheld the views of the Southern slaveholders and called for protection of slavery in the territories; the minority report was more conciliatory toward the demands of the North. After the supporters of Douglas secured the adoption of the minority report, forty-five Southern delegates left the convention in anger.

The rump convention was now ready to choose the presidential candidate. Douglas needed 202 votes. He started off with 145½ votes, which number during the fifty-seven ballots taken in the next two days did not increase materially. As his followers would not compromise on any other man, the convention adjourned, to meet again in Baltimore on June 18.

The Republican nominating convention assembled in Chicago on May 16, a date between the two Democratic conventions. A number of contenders vied for the nomination, and the favorite was William H. Seward, former Governor of New York, astutely managed by Thurlow Weed, New York's political boss. Seward's followers were so certain of his victory that they set up a cannon upon the lawn of his home at Auburn, to be fired as soon as the wire brought the news from Chicago.

But a candidate is not chosen till the last ballot.

The managers of Seward's competitors worked feverishly behind the scenes to wrest the nomination from

TWO MONTHS BEFORE THE REPUBLICAN CONVENTION—on March 16, 1860—Lincoln wrote to the Kansas politician Mark W. Delahay, promising him one hundred dollars "to bear the expences" (sic) if Delahay desired to take part in the proceedings at Chicago.

THE WEEK BEFORE THE STATE CONVENTION Lincoln was photographed Edward A. Barnwell at Decatur. The probable date of the sitting is May 8, 186

A new reproduction from the original; courtesy Decatur Public Library

In the Tarbell Collection, Allegheny College, Meadeville, Pa.

LINCOLN'S PROFILE, a photograph from 1860, found in Ida M. Tarbell's collection after her death. This unique, little-known picture is reproduced through the courtesy of Allegheny College, Miss Tarbell's alma mater and the recipient of her Lincoln collection.

the favorite. Edward Bates, a conservative, respectable jurist and a former Whig from Missouri, had the support of his home state as well as of Indiana, Maryland, and Delaware, and it was rumored that he was the second choice in a number of other states. Salmon P. Chase, Ohio's first Republican Governor, showed some strength, as did the old Supreme Court Justice John McLean. But most active were the man-

agers of candidate Abraham Lincoln.

Judge David Davis, with whom Lincoln had ridden circuit, established headquarters at his own expense at the Tremont House and was the head of the "Lincoln for President" group. He was helped by the lawyers Norman B. Judd and Leonard Swett and the newspapermen Joseph Medill and Charles H. Ray from the Chicago *Press & Tribune*. The strategy of this group

was to unite all anti-Seward forces and prove to them that Lincoln, who was neither a radical like Seward nor a conservative like Bates, and who "excited no hates anywhere" and "has made no records to be defended or explained," was the very candidate behind whom the convention could and should unite.

The Lincoln managers came to Chicago certain only of the Illinois votes. With great energy they went after the votes of the dubious states; they bargained, cajoled, courted, flattered, promised.

Lincoln sent a message to them: "Make no contracts that will bind me."

"Damn Lincoln!" cursed Dubois, one of his men. And they proceeded with their work. Indiana was won over by the promise to make Caleb B. Smith (the chairman of the Hoosier delegation) Secretary of the Interior and William P. Dole Commissioner of Indian Affairs. The Lincoln men pleaded so effectively with the New Jersey delegates, who were lined up behind the state's favorite son, Judge William L. Dayton, that they were confident New Jersey's second choice would be Lincoln and not Seward.

That Pennsylvania would vote on the first ballot for its favorite son, Simon Cameron, a rich machine politician, was certain, still Lincoln's managers hoped to gain the fifty-six votes of that state on the second trial.

Seward's strength lay in the East. His weakness was that the Eastern states would vote Republican regardless of the man, thus the personality of the candidate in those states was not so important. So it was pure common sense when John A. Andrew, chairman of the Massachusetts delegation, consulted with his colleagues from the doubtful states and told them: "You delegates all say that William H. Seward cannot carry the doubtful states. When we ask you who can, you from New Jersey give us the name of William L. Dayton, a most excellent and worthy man in every way, and entirely satisfactory to us; but when we go to Pennsylvania they name Simon Cameron; and Indiana and Illinois, Abraham Lincoln. Now it is impossible

Harper's Weekly, *May 12, 1860*

THE PROMINENT REPUBLICAN CANDIDATES, as pictured in *Harper's Weekly* before the convention assembled. In the center: William H. Seward, the favorite; top left: Edward Bates, conservative jurist from Missouri; top right: Nathaniel P. Banks, "favorite son" of Massachusetts. Middle row: William Pennington of New Jersey; Salmon P. Chase, Ohio's former governor; John McLean, Supreme Court Judge from Ohio; Simon Cameron, Pennsylvania's political boss. Bottom row: John C. Frémont, candidate of 1856; Lincoln; John Bell, who became the nominee of the Constitutional Union Party; Cassius M. Clay, the rabid Kentucky abolitionist.

to have all these three candidates, and unless you delegates from the four doubtful states can agree upon some one candidate, who you think can carry these states, we from New England will vote for our choice, William H. Seward of New York; but if you will unite upon some one candidate and present his name, we will give him enough votes to place him in nomination." But Andrew pleaded in vain.

On the day of the voting, Seward's managers were certain of New York, Michigan, and Minnesota, and had hopes of getting Maine. The news on

Photograph by Alexander Hesler in the Chicago Historical Society

THE WIGWAM, a temporary structure in Chicago, where on May 16, 1860, the Republican convention met to nominate their man.

Harper's Weekly, *May 19, 1860*

ON THE THIRD BALLOT the 10,000 excited spectators cramming the hall cheered themselves hoarse when Lincoln was chosen.

LINCOLN'S DRAFT AND THE FINAL NOTE TO GEORGE ASHMUN ON MAY 23, 1860, ACCEPTING THE REPUBLICAN NOMINATION.

the eve of the convention that the delegates of Rhode Island, Connecticut, and New Hampshire had decided not to support him because of his long anti-slavery record was not believed a serious obstacle.

On opening day ten thousand people filled the Wigwam, the hall of the convention. First the platform was presented. Horace Greeley, one of its drafters, was convinced that "An Antislavery man *per se* cannot be elected; but a tariff, River and Harbor, Pacific Railroad, Free Homestead man may succeed," so the platform comprised all these things.

And after it was adopted, an adjournment was motioned. Murat Halstead, the reporter of the Cincinnati *Commercial*, wrote for his paper: "So confident were the Seward men . . . of their ability to nominate their great leader, that they urged an immediate ballot and would have had it if the clerks had not reported that they were unprovided with tally-sheets."

During the night Lincoln's managers worked like beavers. They were determined to get the fifty-six votes of the Pennsylvania delegation. It was at midnight that Joseph Medill met David Davis in the hotel lobby just as the Judge was leaving the room where he had been conferring with the Pennsylvanians. "How will they vote?" Medill asked.

"Damned if we haven't got them."

"How did you get them?"

"By paying their price." (The price was that Pennsylvania's favorite son, Simon Cameron, was to become Secretary of the Treasury.)

"Good heavens! Give Cameron the Treasury Department? What will be left?" worried Medill.

"Oh, what's the difference?" replied Davis. "We are after a bigger thing than that; we want the Presidency, and the Treasury is not a great stake to pay for it."

Next morning the confident Seward men marched cockily through the streets of Chicago, certain of a Seward victory. Their band played and they cheered and marched, and marched a little bit too far. When they returned to the Wigwam, there was no place for them—all seats were occupied—the structure was filled to the last seat.

Vainly did they wave their tickets; they could not get in. They could not know that during the night the astute Lincoln managers had printed duplicate tickets and distributed them among the Lincoln supporters whom the Illinois railroads had brought to Chicago without charge.

The first ballot brought no great surprises. Calling the New England states first, Maine gave ten votes to Seward and six to Lincoln; Vermont was solidly behind its favorite son, Senator Collamer; Massachusetts cast twenty-one for Seward, four for Lincoln; Rhode Island's majority went to Judge McLean, Connecticut's to Bates. New York—as expected—cast all its seventy votes for Seward. New Jersey voted for Dayton, Pennsylvania's majority voted for Cameron, Maryland and Delaware for Bates. Virginia gave only eight to Seward and fourteen to Lincoln. Kentucky's vote was divided (between Seward, Lincoln, Chase,

McLean, and Charles Sumner); Ohio's majority went to Chase. Then came Indiana. A tumultuous shout broke loose when all of the Hoosier State votes—twenty-six of them—were given to Lincoln. Missouri cast its votes for Bates, Michigan for Seward—as did Wisconsin and the majority of Texas. Iowa was divided. California and Minnesota were behind Seward, and Oregon went for Bates. The territories of Kansas and Nebraska and the District of Columbia gave Seward ten out of a total of fourteen.

The result was 173½ for Seward, 102 for Lincoln, 50½ for Cameron, 49 for Chase, 48 for Bates, the other votes being divided among the lesser candidates.

The convention hall was bursting with excitement. Voices called impatiently: "Call the roll, call the roll."

On the second ballot Lincoln's support increased. New Hampshire gave him nine votes, Vermont ten, and he gained five in Rhode Island and Connecticut. The cheer was deafening when Pennsylvania changed, giving Lincoln all its support. At the end of the second ballot Seward had 184½ votes, while Lincoln's strength had increased to 181.

During the third ballot Lincoln got four more votes in Massachusetts, one in Rhode Island, eight in New Jersey, four in Pennsylvania, nine in Maryland. Murat Halstead reported the exciting scene:

"The number of votes necessary to a choice were 233, and I saw under my pencil as the Lincoln column was completed the figures 231½—one vote and a half to give him the nomination.

"There are always men anxious to distinguish themselves on such occasions. There is nothing that politicians like better than a crisis. I looked up to see who would be the man to give the decisive vote. In about ten ticks of a watch, Cartter of Ohio was up. I had imagined Ohio would be slippery enough for the crisis. And sure enough! Every eye was on Cartter, and everybody who understood the matter at all knew what he was about to do. He said: 'I rise (eh), Mr. Chairman (eh), to announce the change of five

Photograph by William Church (or William Marsh), taken on May 24, 1860

A WEEK AFTER HIS NOMINATION. A photograph taken at the request of John Henry Brown, the artist sent by Judge John H. Read to Springfield to paint Lincoln's portrait.

votes of Ohio from Mr. Chase to Mr. Lincoln.'

That made it. A secretary with a tally sheet in his hand shouted: "Fire the salute! Abe Lincoln is nominated."

A delegate wired to Springfield: "Abe, we did it. Glory to God!"

Lincoln waited in the *Journal* office for the news; when it came, people danced and sang, shouted and cheered.

"Gentlemen," said the newly named candidate, with a twinkle in his eye, "you had better come up and shake my hand while you can; honors elevate some men, you know." Then he said quietly: "Well, gentlemen, there is a little short woman at our house who is probably more interested in this dispatch than I am; and if you will excuse me, I will take it up and let her see it."

A LIFE MASK IS MADE

IN THE spring of 1860 while Lincoln was appearing in Chicago for William Jones and Sylvester Marsh in the famous sandbar litigation trial—involving valuable lake-front property created by accretion on the shores of Lake Michigan—the sculptor Leonard Wells Volk asked him to sit for a portrait bust.

"Mr. Volk, I have never sat before to sculptor or painter—only for daguerreotypes and photographs. What shall I do?"

Volk told him that he would take measurements of his head and shoulders, then a cast would be made of his face to save him a number of sittings.

At the studio while preparing for the casting, Volk put Lincoln at ease with the story of his Italian *formatore*, who once confided to him how he and a comrade of his were "doing"

Switzerland by hawking little images.

"One day, a Swiss gentleman asked him if he could make his likeness in plaster. 'Oh, yes, Signor; I am a sculptor!' said Matteo Mattei, who got some plaster, laid the big Swiss gentleman on his back, stuck a quill in each nostril for him to breathe through, and requested him to close his eyes. After pouring the soft plaster all over the man's face and forehead, he paused for reflection; as the plaster was beginning to set he became frightened, as he had never before undertaken such a job and had neglected to prepare the face properly, especially the gentleman's huge beard, mustache, and the hair about the temples and forehead, through which, of course, the plaster had run and become solid. Making an excuse to go outside the door, he told Volk, 'I run like . . .' "

"How did he get it off?" Lincoln wanted to know.

The sculptor answered that the Swiss gentleman probably had to break it off, and cut and pull out all the hair which the plaster touched.

Lincoln laughed heartily and held still as Volk put the plaster on his face.

"It was about an hour before the mold was ready to be removed," recalled Volk, "and being all in one piece, with both ears perfectly taken, it clung pretty hard, as the cheek-bones were higher than the jaws at the lobe of the ear. He bent his head low and took hold of the mold, and gradually worked it off without injury; it hurt a little, as a few hairs of the tender temples pulled out with the plaster and made his eyes water; but the remembrance of the poor Swiss gentleman evidently kept him in good mood."

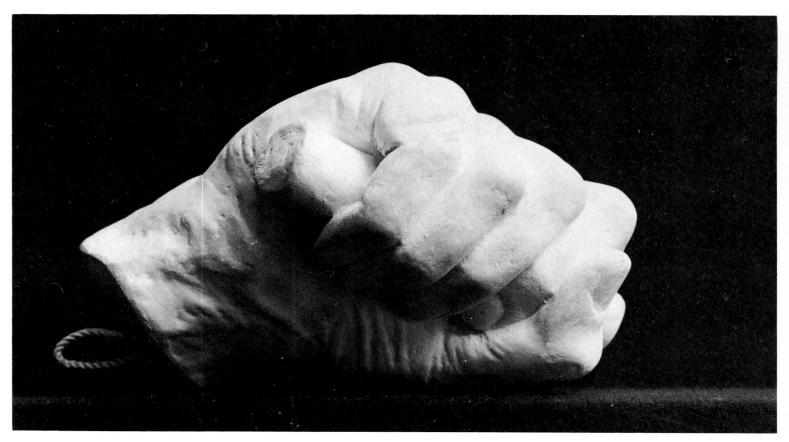

CAST OF HIS HAND, made by Leonard Wells Volk a day after Lincoln received formal notice of his nomination. The sculptor wanted him to hold something in his fist, so Lincoln went out in the woodshed and sawed off a piece of broom handle. As he was polishing the edges, Volk remarked that he need not whittle it off. "Oh well," said Lincoln, "I thought I would like to have it nice."

LIFE MASK, made by Volk in the spring of 1860, when Lincoln tried one of his famous law cases—Johnston v. Jones and Marsh—in Chicago. Between court sessions he went to the sculptor's studio, where Volk made a cast of his face. It was a cumbersome procedure; the mold was all in one piece and clung hard. When Lincoln first saw the cast, he burst out: "There is the animal himself."

95

SCULPTORS MODELED HIM

The first two sculptors who made busts of him were Leonard Wells Volk and Thomas D. Jones. After Volk completed his life mask Lincoln posed for a bust which was done even before he received the nomination. Jones finished his "mud head" in the summer of 1862.

The list of sculptors who followed Volk and Jones was a long one. On it are the names of two women, Sarah Fisher Ames, who modeled Lincoln from life in 1862, and Vinnie Ream, for whom the President sat in 1864.

Lincoln National Life Foundation

THE FIRST VOLK HEAD. Immediately after completing the life mask, sculptor Leonard Wells Volk began to work on a bust. To the austere features of the mask he added the eyes and the hair. Lincoln gave him some more sittings, and when he brought some friends to look at the completed work they all agreed that the clay model looked "just like him."

Lincoln National Life Foundation

THE BUST BY JONES was modeled in the early days of 1861 before Lincoln departed for Washington. The sculptor Thomas D. Jones (see his portrait on the opposite page) was commissioned by leading Republicans of Cincinnati to make a figure of the President-elect. He arrived in Springfield on Christmas Day, 1860, with an introductory letter from Ohio Governor Salmon P. Chase. Lincoln consented to sit for him one hour every day. Jones rented a room on the top floor of the St. Nicholas Hotel where the light was good, and it was here that he modeled the first bearded bust of Lincoln.

THE SHORT BUST. As the cost of the large bust (on the opposite page) in marble or bronze was high, Volk cut off the shoulders.

THE DRAPED LINCOLN. Volk sold the sculpture in several different sizes, the most popular one being thirty-two inches high.

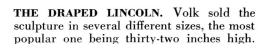

Photograph by John Carent taken in Volk's Chicago studio in 1868

AFTER THE SCULPTURED HEAD WAS FINISHED, Volk made further measurements for a bust. The last time Lincoln came to his studio was on April 5, 1860. By then the head was completed, but as Volk "desired to represent the breast and brawny shoulders as nature presented them," he asked his sitter to take off his clothes. In his reminiscences Volk said that Lincoln "stripped off his coat, waistcoat, shirt, cravat and collar, threw them on the chair, pulled his undershirt down a short distance, tying the sleeves behind him, and stood without a murmur for an hour or so."

When the sitting was over Volk thanked him, and Lincoln said he would gladly return if that would help. "No, I can do it better alone," answered Volk. Then Lincoln left. But a few minutes later he was back for help as he had forgotten to pull up his undershirt.

THE SCULPTOR THOMAS D. JONES (1811–81) painted by James H. Cafferty for the National Academy of Design.

AFTER THE
NOMINATION

He would not make any speeches; he would not make any new announcements. He felt he had made his position clear; he could add nothing to it. As he would not destroy southern institutions, the South had no reason to talk of secession.

The form letter which he mailed to those who asked about his political views said that they "were well known when he was nominated, and that he must not now embarrass the canvass by undertaking to shift or modify them."

Library of Congress

ONLY ONE PRINT REMAINED OF THIS PICTURE, and it had been pasted inside the covers of an 1860 political scrapbook by Lincoln's friend Nathaniel S. Wright of Canton, Illinois. The photographer was William S. Seavey, who may have taken it in the third week of June, 1860, and then presented a print of it to Wright. Before more pictures could be made—so the story goes—Seavey's gallery was gutted by fire and the original negative was lost.

ANOTHER PHOTOGRAPH FROM THIS PERIOD, taken in Springfield in June, 1860, by Joseph Hill, who recalled that Lincoln "had on white trousers, a sort of figured silk vest, and a long, black coat."

99

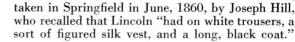

THE MELANCHOLY CANDIDATE, a photograph taken in Chicago either by William Shaw or by Samuel M. Fassett in the summer of 1860.

Chicago Historical Society

ARTISTS CAME TO PAINT HIS PORTRAIT

Chicago Historical Society

THE PAINTER THOMAS HICKS (1823–90) was the first of the dozen or more artists who came to Springfield to paint the Republican candidate's portrait and make his face known to the country. Sent by the New York firm of W. H. Schaus & Co., which used his finished painting (at left) for a lithograph (at right) drawn for them by Grozelier, Hicks brought a letter of introduction with him. It was from Horace Greeley's right-hand man on the New York *Tribune*, Charles A. Dana, and was addressed to Billy Herndon, Lincoln's law partner. Herndon obliged and took Hicks to Lincoln, and Lincoln expressed himself willing to pose for him in the morning from eight to nine. Hicks began his portrait on June 12, 1860, and finished it not long thereafter.

Lincoln had not sat for a painter before, as he readily admitted. "No, this is the first time I have had this specific sort of picture made, but I have had the sun pictures made several times."

A man from Massachusetts standing nearby pointed to a dark photograph with a light background hanging on the wall and remarked, "I see a photograph of you there, but it does not have any sun in it."

"No," Lincoln shot back. "Parson Brownlow says I am a nigger; and if he had judged alone from that picture, he would have had some ground for his assertion."

Lincoln found it more comfortable to be painted than to be photographed. He did not have to brace himself for a slow, motionless wait as he had done for the daguerreotypes and ambrotypes, and he could converse with the artist and anyone else who sauntered into the room.

He was curious to see how his face would come out. When Hicks finished his preliminary charcoal sketch Lincoln commented, "I see the likeness, sir." And when the painting emerged Lincoln was pleased. "It will give the people of the East a correct idea of how I look at home, and in fact, how I look in my office." And he added: "I think the picture has a somewhat pleasanter expression than I usually have, but that, perhaps, is not an objection."

Artists came with letters of recommendation, sent by politicians or publishers who wanted the paintings for exhibitions or as a model for their engravings. At first Lincoln sat for one, then for two; as time went on there were as many as half a dozen painters watching him as he opened his correspondence in the morning.

He was a difficult man to paint. His expression changed from one moment to the next. If he sat quietly he seemed listless, but when he told a tale his features came to life.

The painter Conant remembered: "I was much puzzled to decide what view of his face was most desirable for my purpose. His features were irregular and angular—the line of the nose was straight on one side and slightly curved on the other; the lower

(turn to page 102)

100

A lithograph drawn by J. E. Baker after the work of Charles A. Barry

DRAWING TEACHER CHARLES ALFRED BARRY (1830–92) arrived from Boston in June, 1860, with introductory letters from Massachusetts Governor Nathaniel Banks and other prominent political figures, to make a portrait of the candidate.

After reading the letters Lincoln told Barry: "They want my head, do they? Well, if you can get it, you may have it, that is, if you are able to take it off while I am on the jump; but don't fasten me into a chair. I don't suppose you Boston folks get up at cockcrowing as we do out here. I am an early riser and if you will come to my room at the State House on Monday at seven o'clock sharp, I will be there to let you in."

Barry was there at the appointed time that day and once more watched Lincoln reading his correspondence and answering letters.

Years afterward Barry recalled: "How vividly it all comes back to me—the lonely room, the great bony figure with its long arms and legs that seemed to be continually twisting themselves together; the long, wiry neck, the narrow chest, the uncombed hair; the cavernous sockets between the high forehead; the bushy eyebrows hanging like curtains over the bright, dreamy eyes, the awkward speech, the evident sincerity and patience."

Lincoln looked at the finished painting and commented: "Even my enemies must declare that to be a true likeness of Old Abe."

The painting is lost; when J. E. Baker drew it on stone he stylized Lincoln's features, making him resemble Lord Byron.

101

THE PAINTER JOHN HENRY BROWN (1818–91) was given instructions to "make him good looking" by Judge John Reed of Philadelphia. Reed intended to spend some three hundred dollars on the painting and he wanted Lincoln to look good.

Brown arrived in Springfield early Sunday morning, August 12, 1860. The next day he presented himself to Lincoln and was "favorably impressed" by the candidate. Lincoln was not ugly, as he had been told in the East. Instead of "making a picture," he would only have to "paint a portrait" to satisfy the Judge. Brown asked the candidate to accompany him to a photographer's gallery, and Lincoln acceded. They went to Preston Butler's establishment, where Brown ordered some ambrotypes which he was to use as models for his painting.

After five sittings the painting was completed (at left), and it pleased Lincoln. From Brown's ivory miniature Samuel Sartain made a mezzotint, but before his engraving (at right) could reach the public, Lincoln had grown a beard and the picture was outdated. So Sartain made a new engraving, adding the beard.

lip on the right side was fuller than on the left, as if swollen from a blow or the sting of an insect; while the lines of the lower part of his face met in sharp angles on each side. . . ."

Here are the impressions of two English journalists, giving diametrically opposite views of his features.

Edward Dicey, a special correspondent for the *Spectator*, wrote: "To say he is ugly is nothing; to add that his figure is grotesque is to convey no adequate impression. Fancy a man about six-foot high, and thin in proportion, with long bony arms and legs, which somehow seem always to be in the way; with great rugged furrowed hands, which grasp you like a vise when shaking yours; with a long scraggy neck and a chest too narrow for the great arms by his side. Add to this figure a head, cocoanut shaped and somewhat too small for such a stature, covered with rough, uncombed hair, that stands out in every direction at once; a face furrowed, wrinkled, and indented as though it had been scarred by vitriol; a high narrow forehead, sunk deep beneath bushy eyebrows, two bright, somewhat dreamy eyes that seem to gaze through you without looking at you; a few irregular blotches of black bristly hair in the place where beard and whiskers ought to grow; a

(turn to page 104)

Southern Illinois University

THE PAINTER ALBEN JASPER CONANT (1821–1915) had been sent by St. Louis businessman William M. McPherson. Conant tried to paint a Lincoln different from the melancholy, almost sinister expressions that he had seen in other pictures. He wanted to paint him as his friends knew him. During the sitting the painter inquired about the debates with Douglas to relax his sitter, and soon Lincoln was telling anecdotes. Now Conant had the expression he sought. When the painting was finished, Mrs. Lincoln admired it: "I hope he will look like that after the first of November."

A HITHERTO UNKNOWN PORTRAIT BY LEWIS PETER CLOVER (1819–96), painted from life in July, 1860. Clover was the rector of St. Paul's Episcopal Church in Springfield and a painter besides.

On August 3, 1860, the *Illinois State Journal* reported: "We took occasion yesterday to pay a visit to the studio of Rev. L. P. Clover, and examined a full size portrait of Mr. Lincoln (the result of four or five sittings), which is now receiving the finishing touches of the artist. We were much struck with the faithfulness of the picture, it will bear the closest inspection."

The painting has never been reproduced before.

103

Lithograph by C.H. Brainard

WAS THIS DRAWN FROM THE PAINTING OF THOMAS M. JOHNSTON? Did the twenty-four-year-old Johnston (1836–69), a Boston artist and the son of the famous illustrator David Claypoole Johnston, make a painting like this which lithographer Brainard transposed into the above lithograph?

Johnston began his portrait on July 20 "under the most favorable circumstances" and had about five sittings in all. After the first sitting he wrote to his father: "Mr. Lincoln is a very tall, awkward-looking man, but with a face and head that I really consider beautiful in the extreme, when compared with all the pictures that have been published over his name. . . . I had reason to expect

Lorant #13

to see a face that reminded one more of an over-sized pear than anything else."

A week later, on July 26, he informed Brainard: "The picture is a decided success." After Johnston delivered his painting, Brainard brought out a lithograph signed T.M.J. (on the left), but it is doubtful that Johnston had much to do with it. It rather seems that Brainard used a photograph as a model for the drawing, a photograph (on the right) which was taken by C. S. German in Springfield at the time Johnston was there.

No one knows what became of the original painting. Johnston died young in France in 1869—and the secret went with him.

close-set, thin-lipped, stern mouth, with two rows of large white teeth, and a nose and ears which have been taken by mistake from a head of twice the size."

But to William Howard Russell, the celebrated correspondent of the London *Times*, he looked different. Russell wrote: "The impression produced by the size of his extremities, and by his flapping and wide projecting ears, may be removed by the appearance of kindliness, sagacity, and the awkward bonhomie of his face; the mouth is absolutely prodigious; the lips, straggling and extending almost from one

line of black beard to the other, are only kept in order by two deep furrows from the nostrils to the chin; the nose itself—a prominent organ—stands out from the face with an inquiring, anxious air, as though it were sniffing for some good thing in the wind; the eyes dark, full, and deeply set, are penetrating, but full of an expression which almost amounts to tenderness; and above them projects the shaggy brow, running into the small hard frontal space, the development of which can scarcely be estimated exactly, owing to the irregular flocks of thick hair carelessly brushed across it."

Most artists had trouble with his eyes; they even disagreed as to their coloring. Conant said that they were "heavenly blue," while for the sculptor Volk they appeared "beaming dark dull."

To paint his skin was another problem. Herndon described his flesh as "coarse, pimply, dry, hard, harsh . . . no blood seemingly in it."

On his life mask not one but five moles are visible. In his youth he may have had acne which resulted in the pitting of his skin. And possibly this was the reason that he grew a beard—to hide the scars. Despite all jokes, he was vain about his appearance.

GEORGE FREDERICK WRIGHT (1828–81), a painter from Connecticut, had a broader background than most of the other artists who flocked to Springfield. He was commissioned to paint portraits of thirteen of Illinois's past governors and while working on his assignment he approached Lincoln and asked for a sitting.

Lincoln obliged and told him to come to the State House, where he could paint him while he was reading his mail.

Lincoln bought Wright's painting and presented it to his friend William Butler, one of his campaign managers. Staying for generations in the Butler family, it is now in the University of Chicago.

105

THE PRESIDENTIAL CAMPAIGN

A MONTH after the Republicans had chosen their candidate, the Democrats met again—this time at Baltimore. Many contested delegates from the South were present; for three full days nothing else was discussed but their admission. And when the Douglas factions from Alabama and Louisiana were admitted, all other anti-Douglas delegates from the South walked out; the chasm between the two sections of the party was as deep as ever.

On the first ballot of the rump convention Stephen A. Douglas received 173½ votes, James Guthrie ten, and John C. Breckinridge five. A resolution was then introduced to concede Douglas' nomination, as he had two thirds of the votes. But when objections were raised that Douglas had never received the two-thirds vote of *all* the Democratic delegates—only of those present—the suggestion was withdrawn. On the next trial Douglas controlled 187½ votes; Breckinridge,

7½; Guthrie, 5½. The renewed resolution to accept Douglas was passed, and thus the "little giant" at last became the candidate.

The Southern Democratic delegates who withdrew from the Charleston convention had already held a meeting in Richmond; now they met again in Charleston, joined by the seceding men of the Baltimore convention. There they adopted the rejected majority platform of Charleston, demanding the protection of slavery in all territories, and named John C. Breckinridge of Kentucky for the Presidency.

In this way the Democratic party had two sets of candidates; Douglas was the choice of the North, upholding popular sovereignty, and Breckinridge the proslavery nominee of the South.

The Republicans, certain to win the election because of the Democratic split, campaigned with the ardor of reformers. Companies of "Wide-Awakes" marched through the streets

in black circular capes and glazed military caps, carrying a rail with an oil lamp and a banner inscribed: "Lincoln and Hamlin." In Boston a giant rail-splitters' battalion held a demonstration—every one of the men stood at least six feet four inches in his stocking feet.

Lincoln set up his temporary office at the Springfield State House, receiving visitors and office seekers by the hundreds. Artists descended on him. Photographers came, painters, and sculptors. Friends asked for his picture; people wanted to know what he looked like. To the painter Alban Jasper Conant, who journeyed from St. Louis to make a likeness, Lincoln sounded like a "story-telling, whiskey-drinking, whiskey-selling country grocer"; it did not take him long to find out how wrong he was.

Conant entertained Lincoln with stories "to light up" his face. One of them—that about the slow horse—

THE CANDIDATES

JOHN BELL, the nominee of the Constitutional Union party, embodying conservative old men worried by the disruptive forces which were undermining the Union.

STEPHEN A. DOUGLAS, who split the Democratic ranks, became a candidate of the Northern and Western faction after the Southern delegates had withdrawn in protest.

JOHN C. BRECKINRIDGE, the candidate of the Southern Democrats, represented the slaveholding interest, supported by all party men who were against Douglas.

106

A FORTNIGHT AFTER HIS NOMINATION on June 3 the Chicago photographer Alexander Hesler came to Springfield to take the likeness of the "dressed up candidate"

Lincoln liked so well that he told it often. It went like this:

"A politician went to a livery stable to hire a horse, as he was in a hurry to drive sixteen miles to a convention where he desired the nomination for county judge. But on the way the horse broke down, the fellow could not make the convention, and lost the office. When the politician returned the horse to the stable he asked the liveryman why he did not tell him that he was training the horse to draw a hearse. The liveryman said he was not doing anything of the sort. 'Don't deny it,' the politician came back, 'for I know by his gait that you have spent a great deal of time training him to go before a hearse. But he will never do. He—is—so—slow—he could not get a corpse to the cemetery in time for the resurrection.' "

While the painter worked, Tad and Willie came to see what was going on. And as young boys will, they played with the paint, upset the furniture, exasperating the artist. Lincoln told them: "Boys, boys, you mustn't meddle! Now run home and have your face washed." Once Tad brought his friend to look at an unfinished portrait. "Come here, Jim," he shouted, "here's another Old Abe."

Lincoln, who made a resolution not to "write or speak anything upon doctrinal points" during the campaign, spent his days receiving visitors and writing letters. On political matters he kept his lips tight.

He was asked to say something to reassure the men "honestly alarmed" over the unrest in the South. "There are no such men," he answered. "It is the trick by which the South breaks down every Northern man. If I yielded to their entreaties I would go to Washington without the support of the men who now support me. I would be as powerless as a block of buckeye wood. The honest men—you are talking of honest men—will find in our platform everything I could say now, or which they would ask me to say."

He would say nothing which might be misconstrued, which might hurt his election. Rallies and political meetings were held almost every night in Springfield, but Lincoln would not at-

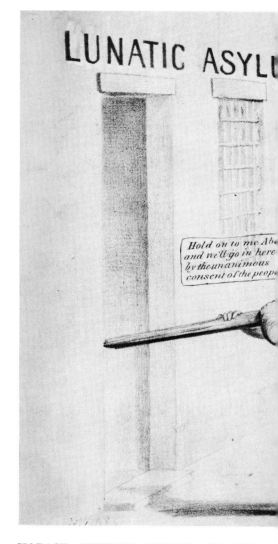

HORACE GREELEY, EDITOR OF THE

Drawn by Louis Maurer for Currier & Ives

THE RAIL CANDIDATE. A Negro and Horace Greeley carry Lincoln on a rail marked "Republican Platform." Lincoln comments wryly: "It is true I have split Rails, but I begin to feel as if this Rail would split me—it's the hardest stick I ever straddled."

tend them. Only when Carl Schurz came in midsummer to give an address did he make an exception. "I will go with you," he promised Schurz, "and hear what you have to say."

Schurz left for us vivid recollections of what took place. "The day was blazing hot," he wrote. "Mr. Lincoln expressed his regret that I had to exert myself in such a temperature, and suggested that I make myself comfortable. He indeed 'made himself comfortable' in a way which surprised me not a little, but which was thoroughly characteristic of his rustic habits. When he presented himself for the march to the Capitol grounds I observed that he had divested himself of his waistcoat and put on, as his sole garment, a linen duster, the back of which had been marked by repeated perspirations and looked somewhat like a rough map of

NEW YORK *TRIBUNE*, CARRIES THE CANDIDATE INTO THE LUNATIC ASYLUM AS LINCOLN MAKES PROMISES TO HIS FOLLOWERS.

the two hemispheres. On his head he wore a well-battered stovepipe hat which evidently had seen several years of hard service. In this attire he marched with me behind the brass band, after us the local campaign committee and the Wide-Awakes. Of course, he was utterly unconscious of his grotesque appearance. Nothing could have been farther from his mind than the thought that the world-conspicuous distinction bestowed upon him by his nomination for the presidency should have obliged him to 'put on dignity' among his neighbors. Those neighbors who, from the windows and the sidewalks on that hot afternoon, watched and cheered him as he walked by in the procession behind the brass band, may have regarded him, the future President, with a new feeling of reverential admiration, or

THE HELP WANTED SIGN IS TAKEN DOWN by Uncle Sam, who is advising the three other presidential candidates—Douglas, Breckinridge, and Bell—that he has concluded to "let Old Abe Lincoln have the place." In the White House, President Buchanan is packing.

109

awe; but he appeared before and among them entirely unconcerned, as if nothing had happened, and so he nodded to his acquaintances, as he recognized them in the crowd, with a 'How are you, Dan,' or 'Glad to see you, Ned!' or 'How d'ye do, Bill?' and so on—just as he had been accustomed to do. Having arrived at the place of meeting, he declined to sit on the platform, but took a seat in the front row of the audience. He did not join in the applause which from time to time rewarded me, but occasionally he gave me a nod and a broad smile. When I had finished, a few voices called upon Mr. Lincoln for a speech, but he simply shook his head, and the crowd instantly respected the proprieties of the situation, some even shouting: 'No, no!' at which he gratefully signified his assent."

While Lincoln remained silent, his chief Democratic opponent, Stephen A. Douglas, was campaigning vigorously. In speech after speech he reiterated that a Republican victory would mean secession and that "this country is in more danger now than at any moment since I have known anything of public life."

On election day Lincoln—who did not think it appropriate to vote for his own electors—was persuaded by his law partner to cast his vote for the rest of the Republican ticket, which he did. In the evening he went to the telegraph office to see the returns tap in. The special correspondent of the New York *Tribune* was there, and he reported to his newspaper:

"Mr. Lincoln sat or reclined upon a sofa, while his companions mostly stood clustering around him. . . .

Whenever the information was of a peculiarly gratifying character, as it often was, the documents would be taken out by some thoughtful friend of the populace outside, and read aloud in the State House, or elsewhere, to large crowds which had met and were enjoying celebrations on the strength of their own convictions that the expected news would be sure to justify them. Occasionally, a line or two would come with so much force of encouragement as to set the little group beside itself with elation." Lincoln was calmer than all the other men around him. Only once—during the night—did he show some excited emotions; that was when the news came that the Republican ticket had won in his own precinct, the "Fourth."

At last the result became known: the Republicans had won the election.

BEFORE HIS SPRINGFIELD HOME DURING THE CAMPAIGN. Surrounded by well-wishers, Lincoln (in a white suit) is standing in the doorway. Four years before—in 1856—while he was in Chicago, Mrs. Lincoln had remodeled the house with money received from the sale of some inherited land. The upper half story was made into a full story; the whole house was repainted and papered.

110

HE REMAINED SILENT and would not take a stand on "doctrinal points." It was about this time (on August 13, 1860) that the Springfield photographer Preston Butler took this ambrotype.

Springfield, May 26. 1860
Dear Judge—

The foregoing is the way of about such a letter as I think you should write— Of course you will put it in your own hand writing, prefixing proper heading; and adding at the bottom whatever assurances of your own you may think fit, that I will stand by my position.

Yours friend as ever
A. Lincoln

Since parting with you, I have had full and frequent conversation with Mr. Lincoln. The substance of what he says is that he neither is nor will be, in advance of the election, committed to any man, clique or faction; and that, in case the new administration shall devolve upon him, it will be his pleasure, and, in his view, the part of duty, and wisdom, to deal fairly with all— He thinks he will need the assistance of all; and that, even if he has friends to reward, or enemies to punish, as he has not, he could not afford to dispense with the best talent, nor to outrage the popular will in any locality—

(over)

Illinois State Historical Library

"WILL NOT BE COMMITTED TO ANY MAN, CLIQUE OR FACTION" wrote Lincoln in this recently discovered draft of his pre-convention plans which he sent to Judge David Davis.

From thousands of throats came a cheer. At the Springfield State House "men pushed each other, threw up their hats, hurrahed, cheered for Lincoln . . . and some actually laid down on the carpeted floor, and rolled over and over." On the streets men marched, singing and screaming and shouting: "Ain't I glad I've joined the Republicans!"

At Watson's confectionery the Republican women put on an oyster supper. Lincoln made his appearance, then he went home, where Mary with other ladies of Springfield served coffee and sandwiches to all who dropped in. "How do you do, Mr. President," was heard over and over again, and Lincoln smiled and shook hands and thanked everyone.

Harper's Weekly, *October 13, 1860*

THE REPUBLICAN "WIDE-AWAKES" in glazed black capes and military caps, carrying torches (made of rails with swinging oil lamps) and banners with the names of Lincoln and Hamlin, paraded in a great procession through the streets of New York.

112

From Frank Leslie's Illustrated Newspaper, *Nov. 24, 1860*

THE PRESIDENT-ELECT RECEIVES FRIENDS, WELL-WISHERS, AND OFFICE SEEKERS IN THE SPRINGFIELD STATE HOUSE.

The final returns showed that he had carried all the Northern states but one. In New Jersey the vote was so close that for days neither the Republicans nor the Democrats knew who was the winner. The final result gave Lincoln four votes and Douglas three. California's electoral votes went to Lincoln, though his popular majority in that state was only 657.

In the South eleven out of the fifteen slave states voted for Breckinridge, three states voted for the Bell-Everett ticket, and only one—Missouri—for Douglas. From that whole region Lincoln had not a single electoral vote. In the popular vote Lincoln got 1,866,452; Breckinridge, 849,781; Douglas, 1,376,957; Bell, 588,879. The figures proved that the majority of the country was for union and peace. Breckinridge, the only secession candidate, was backed by less than one-fifth of the electorate.

Smithsonian Institution

A LINCOLN BANNER WHICH WAS USED IN THE 1860 PRESIDENTIAL CAMPAIGN.

113

WHY A BEARD?

AFTER HIS election, Lincoln began to grow a beard. Tradition has it that he did this on the suggestion of an eleven-year-old child, and it is such a good story that one is reluctant to discard it.

Grace Bedell—that was the name of the little girl—wrote to him on October 15: "I have got four brothers and part of them will vote for you any way and if you will let your whiskers grow I will try and get the rest of them to vote for you; you would look a great deal better for your face is so thin."

The amused candidate answered that he had never worn any whiskers and asked Grace, "Do you not think people would call it a piece of silly affection if I were to begin it now?" Still, hardly a month later he was seen with stubble sprouting from his chin. Why? An astute scholar explains it this way: "Possibly Lincoln grew a beard because of his sense of history. The United States had never had a bearded President. . . . Republican rule, Republican policies, would inaugurate a new era. All men might know that, merely by observing the altered appearance of the Republican President. For a new life, he was producing a new profile. . . ."

GROW A BEARD—suggested an eleven-year-old girl—because "all the ladies like whiskers and they would tease their husbands to vote for you and then you would be President." To Grace Bedell's communication Lincoln replied with this delightfully human letter.

NOVEMBER 26, 1860: FIRST HIRSUTE PORTRAIT, after the election. A newspaper joked: "Old Abe is . . . puttin' on (h)airs!"

JANUARY 26, 1861: THE BEARD HAS GROWN SOME MORE, but does not yet fit his face. He still looks somewhat strange with it.

TWO DAYS BEFORE HIS DEPARTURE FROM SPRINGFIELD —on February 9, 1861—photographer Christopher S. German took this photograph, which showed for the first time the fully grown beard of the President-elect

HIS FAMILY. Mrs. Lincoln with Willie (left) and Tad poses for the daguerreotypist Preston Butler not long before they left for Washington. Mary Todd Lincoln bore her husband four children—all boys. Her eldest, Robert, born in 1843, was schooled at Exeter and Harvard and had a notable political and business career; he was Secretary of War in the Garfield-Arthur administration, Minister to England under Benjamin Harrison, then President of the Pullman Company of Chicago. He died in his eighty-third year in 1926. The second boy, Edward Baker, born in 1846, died four years later. Willie was born the same year Eddie died, in 1850; he lived for only twelve short years. Tad, the youngest and liveliest of the Lincoln children, was born in 1853 and died eighteen years later.

FAREWELL TO SPRINGFIELD

AFTER HIS nomination Lincoln established himself in the Governor's room of the State House. Politicians came, and office seekers, friends and strangers. The room was always full. Outside his house people were sleeping on the street to catch him in the morning and petition him for jobs. Dozens of others were waiting in his law office; everywhere he turned, he was surrounded by a demanding crowd.

The only place where he had peace, unmolested by people, was the improvised studio of Thomas D. Jones at the St. Nicholas Hotel. The sculptor started on his bust late in December, and while he was modeling on the "mud head," Lincoln read his mail, made notes, worked quietly.

Two great problems waited for solution. One: the composition of the Cabinet; the other: the formulation of a policy toward the South.

He suffered pressure from all quarters: Senators, Congressmen, Governors advised him—proposing and extolling the virtues of the men who should be called into the Cabinet. Visitors came by the hundreds, asking a thousand questions. The New York *Times* reporter was greatly impressed with Lincoln's ability to keep silent on vital matters without offending the questioners. "Now and then a blunt old farmer will blurt out something about the Cabinet, and perhaps suggest the difficulty of meeting the Secessionists. But the truly Republican President passes it off with a smile, and simply keeps mum. I never knew a public man who knew so well how to hold his tongue, and yet not offend his best friends."

At the end of January Mrs. Lincoln journeyed to New York to buy herself some dresses. And when Mary returned, Lincoln left for Farmington to visit his stepmother; he had not seen her for a long while, and he had never been to his father's grave.

Sarah Bush Lincoln was overjoyed to receive him. She laughed and cried, feeling that they would never meet again. "Something told me," she said later, "that something would befall Abe and that I should see him no more."

The two days in the country refreshed him from the bedlam of politicians and the office seekers.

Returning to Springfield he set to work on his inaugural speech in earnest. He locked himself up in a "dingy, dusty, and neglected back room" over his brother-in-law's store across the street south of the State House, and in this seclusion he composed his address. At his elbow he had his references, four in number—only

THE FUTURE TENANT OF THE WHITE HOUSE sells his old furniture. Late in January the President-elect advertised in the *Illinois State Journal*, offering for sale his furniture "consisting of Parlor and Chamber Sets, Carpets, Sofas, Chairs, Wardrobes, Bureaus, Bedsteads, Stoves, China, Queensware, Glass, Etc., etc." This receipt was given by Lincoln to the Springfield druggist, S. H. Melvin, who bought some of the household goods. However, most of the furniture was purchased by Lucian Tilton, head of the Great Western Railroad, who rented the house for $350 yearly. The Tiltons stayed in the Lincoln home until 1869, when they moved to Chicago, taking with them the Lincoln furniture. In the great fire of 1871 they lost all belongings, including those acquired from Lincoln.

HIS FAREWELL SPEECH—A Contemporary Representation. On February 11, 1861, Lincoln was leaving Springfield. From the back platform of his Washington-bound train, he made a short address. The words came slowly from his lips, sad words, filled with deep emotion. "No one, not in my situation can appreciate my feeling of sadness at this parting," he began. "To this place, and the kindness of these people, I owe everything. Here I have lived a quarter of a century, and have passed from a young to an old man. Here my children have been born, and one is buried. I now leave, not knowing when or whether ever I may return, with a task before me greater than that which rested upon Washington. Without the assistance of that Divine Being who ever attended him, I cannot succeed. With that assistance I cannot fail. Trusting in Him who can go with me, and remain with you, and be everywhere

four. One was Henry Clay's speech of 1850; another, Andrew Jackson's proclamation against nullification; the third, Webster's reply to Hayne; and the fourth, a copy of the Constitution.

When he finished with it, a compositor of the *Journal* set his writing in type and pulled a few proofs on eight pages. Lincoln revised the galleys, and another proof was made, this time on seven pages.

He was busy, he needed time to work and to think. He asked the *Journal* to print the notice: "The present week being the last that Mr. Lincoln remains in Springfield and it being indispensable that he should have a portion of his time to himself, he will see visitors, only at his office, No. 4 Johnson's building, from 3½ to 5 o'clock P.M. each day." But it was of no avail. People came just the same.

On February 6 he and Mrs. Lincoln gave a farewell party to their Springfield friends. The New York *Herald* said that "Seven hundred ladies and gentlemen came, composing the political elite of this state, and the beauty and fashion of this vicinity." It was a triumphant affair—a great night for Mary Lincoln, the new First Lady of the land, a fitting climax for her eighteen years of married life.

Contemporary woodcut by an unidentified artist

for good, let us confidently hope that all will yet be well. To His care commending you, as I hope in your prayers you will commend me, I bid you an affectionate farewell." The people who had come to see him off stood silent and weeping in the drizzling rain. It was good-by forever.

Sunday, February 10, was Lincoln's last day in Springfield. In the morning he had a long talk with Carl Schurz, whom he visited in his hotel and to whom he read his inaugural address, discussing it in great detail. In the afternoon he went to his office to speak about "unsettled and unfinished matters" with his law partner. After all this was disposed of, he "threw himself down on the old office sofa," lying there in meditation for a few moments.

"Billy, how long have we been together?" he asked Herndon.

"Over sixteen years," came the answer.

"We've never had a cross word during all the time, have we?"

"No indeed, we have not."

The two partners reminisced, recalling some incidents of their practice. Lincoln was in a cheerful mood. He gathered a bundle of papers and books which he was to take with him and started to go. Before leaving, he admonished Herndon not to take down their signboard.

"Let it hang there undisturbed," he said. "Give our clients to understand that the election of a President makes no change in the firm of Lincoln and Herndon. If I live I'm coming back some time, and then we'll go right on practicing law as if nothing had ever happened."

Early next morning—on February 11—hundreds of people were at the station to bid him farewell. Before the train pulled out, Lincoln appeared on the platform of the car and raised his hand to command attention. The multitude bared their heads in the drizzling rain, and standing thus, his neighbors heard his voice for the last time in the city of his home.

It was a sadly eloquent address. And when the last words were spoken, the train pulled out, taking him to Washington, never to return again.

THE FAREWELL ADDRESS. After Lincoln finished speaking, the train moved out of the station. The journalist Henry Villard walked into the President-elect's car, asking him for a copy of the address. Lincoln had none, but he was ready to write out the speech for Villard. He took paper and pencil and started to reconstruct what he had said, improving on the sentences as he went along. As the train rocked too hard, John Nicolay, his secretary, took over and continued with the writing, scrawling the words as Lincoln said them.

THE BALTIMORE PLOT

WHILE LINCOLN was traveling toward the capital, whispers of his assassination were rampant. It was rumored that he would meet his end at Baltimore, where secessionists were waiting to kill him.

On February 21, ten days after he set out from Springfield, he arrived at Philadelphia. In the evening of that day, Norman Judd had a visit in his hotel room from the detective Allan Pinkerton, "who had been employed for some days in Baltimore, watching and searching for suspicious persons there." Judd introduced the detective to Lincoln, and Pinkerton reported to the President-elect the story of an assassination plot, urging him not to pass through Baltimore—where the assassins were lying in wait for him.

The detective's report made little impression on Lincoln. He said that he had promised to raise the flag at Independence Hall and had accepted invitations at Harrisburg, and he would not break his engagements.

When he returned to his room after his talk with Pinkerton, another warning reached him. The son of William H. Seward had come posthaste from

AT SIX O'CLOCK IN THE MORNING of February 22, 1861, at Philadelphia's Independence Hall, Lincoln hoisted the new flag with a thirty-fourth star in honor of the newly admitted state of Kansas. In his speech the President-elect declared that if the country could not be saved without giving up the principle of equality as embodied in the Declaration of Independence, then—"I would rather be assassinated on this spot than surrender it."

HOW THE YOUNG THOMAS NAST DREW THE BALTIMORE SCENE—AND HOW THE *ILLUSTRATED NEWS* ALTERED THE DRAWING. Twenty-one-year-old Nast covered Lincoln's activities for the *Illustrated News*. He labored to get the details for his drawing (left). But his editors believed another story. Joseph Howard, Jr., a reporter for the New York *Times*, invented a tale from "the mys-terious death of his journalistic imagination," as he later admitted, in which Lincoln put on a plaid suit and a Scotch cap in Baltimore to disguise himself from would-be assassins. Thus the *News* showed Lincoln in the ridiculous attire in its wood engraving (right).

Washington with warning messages.

Still Lincoln would not change his plans. Early next morning he raised the flag in Philadelphia in honor of the newly admitted state of Kansas, then he left for Harrisburg.

If Lincoln was unperturbed, Judd and others in his party took the assassination rumors more seriously. During the night plans were changed; the President-elect was to slip away from Harrisburg accompanied only by Ward Hill Lamon and no one else. "A special car and engine was to be provided for him on the track outside the depot; all other trains on the road were to be sidetracked until this one had passed." Telegraph wires to Washington were to be cut until he had reached the city.

Lincoln—finally persuaded by his friends—put on a soft hat and an old overcoat to escape recognition. Reaching Philadelphia, he once more had a talk with the detective Pinkerton, who reported "that the conspirators had held their final meeting . . . and that it was doubtful whether they had the nerve to attempt the execution of their purpose." But he advised caution.

The new arrangements called for the detective to accompany Lincoln and act as his bodyguard. Pinkerton recorded: "We left the carriage at a dark spot a short distance from the depot, and Mr. Lamon keeping a little in the rear of Mr. Lincoln and myself, Mr. Lincoln leaning upon my arm and stooping a considerable [sic] for the purpose of disguising his height, we passed through the depot rapidly and entered the sleeping car." Instantly the train was set in motion and raced toward Baltimore, reaching it at half-past three in the morning. There the carriage was drawn through the streets of the city from one station to the other. No one knew that inside that horse-drawn, lonely car the President-elect was sleeping peacefully.

Early next morning the train reached Washington without any mishap. Pinkerton rushed to a telegraph office and reported: "PLUMS (meaning Lincoln) ARRIVED HERE WITH NUTS (the code name for Lamon) THIS MORNING—ALL RIGHT."

LINCOLN'S "DISGUISE" AT BALTIMORE gave cartoonists a Roman holiday. Like Adalbert Johann Volck in the above caricature, they showed Lincoln disguising himself in a Scotch cap and military cloak. Lincoln later told the historian Benjamin Lossing the reason for the story. "In New York some friend had given me a new beaver hat in a box, and in it had placed a soft wool hat. I had never worn one of the latter in my life. I had this box in my room. Having informed a very few friends of the secret of my new movements, and the cause, I put on an old overcoat that I had with me, and putting the soft hat in my pocket, I walked out of the house at a back door, bareheaded, without exciting any special curiosity. Then I put on the soft hat and joined my friends without being recognized by strangers, for I was not the same man."

As to the plot—Lincoln never believed in it. "I did not then," he told his friend Isaac Arnold, "believe I should have been assassinated had I gone through Baltimore as first contemplated, but I thought it wise to run no risk where no risk was necessary."

AT BRADY'S WASHINGTON GALLERY

It was probably the day after he arrived in Washington—a Sunday—that Lincoln walked over to Brady's Photographic Parlor on the corner of Pennsylvania Avenue and Seventh Street to have his picture taken. There was a great demand for his photograph; the country wanted to know what he looked like, especially since he had grown a beard.

He sat down at a table, deep in thought, waiting for the photographer's instructions. The portrait painter George H. Story, who was asked to assist, recalled that while Brady and Gardner were preparing the lighting—moving the overhead curtains with long poles—Lincoln sat silently, "seemed absolutely indifferent to all that was going on about him, and he gave the impression that he was a man who was overwhelmed with anxiety, and fatigue, and care."

Story was supposed to pose Lincoln in an artistic way, but he said, "Bring the camera and take your picture as he is," whereupon Gardner made five exposures with the multiple-lens camera.

Lost in his thoughts, Lincoln made an ideal sitter. He hardly moved during the procedure, keeping his left arm on the table and his right hand, somewhat swollen from shaking the hands of well-wishers during the journey, at the arm of his chair.

His face had a mystical quality; it was too elusive to capture on canvas or on a photographic plate. "None of the artists caught the deep though subtle and indirect expression of this man's face. They have only caught the surface. There is something else there," exclaimed the poet Walt Whitman.

What was this "something else"? John G. Nicolay, Lincoln's private secretary, pondered over it. He watched Lincoln's features in action, he observed them in repose. Why was it so difficult to catch the "something else" behind the lines and deep furrows? This was his explanation:

"Graphic art was powerless before a face that moved through a thousand delicate gradations of line and contour, light and shade, sparkle of the eye and curve of the lip, in the long gamut of expression from grave and gay and back again, from the rollicking jollity of laughter to that serious, faraway look which with prophetic intuitions beheld the awful panorama of war, and heard the cry of oppression and suffering. There are many pictures of Lincoln; there is no portrait of him."

THE DAY AFTER LINCOLN ARRIVED IN WASHINGTON— on February 24, 1861—he went to Mathew B. Brady's gallery. There were many requests for his photographs; newspapers and people wanted to know how he looked with his new beard. The painter George H. Story, who was present to pose him, recalled that Lincoln seemed to be worn down "with anxiety and fatigue and care."

THE INAUGURATION

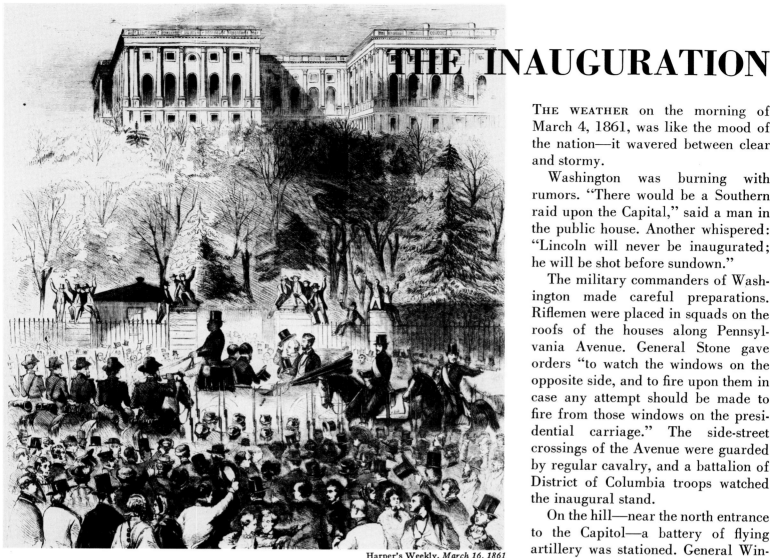

Harper's Weekly, *March 16, 1861*

ON THE WAY TO THE CAPITOL. President Buchanan with President-elect Lincoln rides in an open carriage along Pennsylvania Avenue, flanked by an entire squadron of cavalry.

Harper's Weekly, *March 16, 1861*

OUTGOING PRESIDENT BUCHANAN AND PRESIDENT-ELECT LINCOLN as they enter the Senate Chamber to witness the swearing-in of Hannibal Hamlin as the Vice-President.

THE WEATHER on the morning of March 4, 1861, was like the mood of the nation—it wavered between clear and stormy.

Washington was burning with rumors. "There would be a Southern raid upon the Capital," said a man in the public house. Another whispered: "Lincoln will never be inaugurated; he will be shot before sundown."

The military commanders of Washington made careful preparations. Riflemen were placed in squads on the roofs of the houses along Pennsylvania Avenue. General Stone gave orders "to watch the windows on the opposite side, and to fire upon them in case any attempt should be made to fire from those windows on the presidential carriage." The side-street crossings of the Avenue were guarded by regular cavalry, and a battalion of District of Columbia troops watched the inaugural stand.

On the hill—near the north entrance to the Capitol—a battery of flying artillery was stationed. General Winfield Scott was nearby, ready to take personal command in case of emergency.

And while the military trembled, Lincoln was calm. As the clock struck noon, President James Buchanan came for him at Willard's Hotel, and together they rode down Pennsylvania Avenue.

To the left and the right of the open carriage rode a squadron of cavalry; vigilant eyes watched the crowds from everywhere. Suddenly there was a commotion; a strange, popping, crackling noise was heard. The police were baffled, but their tension dissipated when they found that the noise came from the boots of the New England section marching behind the carriage. The New Englanders had come in their regular winter footgear, extra soles pegged on for heavy snows. The peg timber had shrunk in the warm Maryland sun, causing loud squeaks with

BEFORE THE UNFINISHED CAPITOL the people assembled to watch the inaugural ceremonies. Rumor reached General Scott's headquarters that Southern sympathizers would blow up the temporary platform erected at the east portico. So the General placed a guard under the floor of the stand and dispatched a battalion of District troops to take vigil around the foot of the steps. But the uneasiness of Scott did not seem to reach the crowd, who waited in the biting, gusty wind for Abraham Lincoln to appear.

125

Frank Leslie's Illustrated Newspaper, *March 16, 1861*

IN HIS INAUGURAL HE APPEALED TO THE SOUTH. "Physically speaking, we cannot separate," said the new President. "We cannot remove our respective sections from each other, nor build an impassable wall between them. A husband and wife may be divorced, and go out of the presence and beyond the reach of each other; but the different parts of our country cannot do this. They cannot but remain face to face, and intercourse, either amicable or hostile, must continue between them." The illustration is based on a photograph.

Lincoln National Life Foundation

LINCOLN INVITES BUCHANAN to attend the inaugural ball. A newly discovered letter.

every step, "noisy enough, in mass and in unison, to be heard for several blocks." The reporter of the *Evening Star*, paraphrasing Shakespeare, remarked: "Treasons and stratagems cannot be chargeable to men with so much music in their soles."

At Capitol Hill, Lincoln witnessed the swearing-in of his running mate, Hannibal Hamlin, then he proceeded to the portico, where Edward Dickinson Baker, his old Springfield friend, introduced him to the multitude.

The President-elect, in a shiny new hat and brand new suit, pushed his golden cane into a corner of the platform railing; he was looking for a place for his hat when—according to legend—Stephen A. Douglas took it and held it for him. Then Lincoln took from his pocket a sheaf of printed papers—the same set of proofs which the compositor back in Springfield had pulled for him, and which by now bore many written revisions—adjusted his spectacles and began to read his inaugural address.

He declared that he had no intention of interfering with the institution of slavery in the states where it already existed. He spoke out against secession, and affirmed that the government would "hold, occupy, and possess" its forts and property. In closing, he once more appealed to the South, holding out a peaceful hand.

His address lasted for half an hour, delivered in a clear and ringing voice. A listener wrote to his wife: "Old Abe delivered the greatest speech of the age. It is backbone all over."

And when he had finished, old and infirm Chief Justice Taney stepped forward and administered the oath.

126

The Chief Magistrate derives all his authority from the people, and they have con- ferred none upon him to fix terms for the separation of the States. The people them- selves can do this *also* if they choose; but the executive, as such, has nothing to do with it. His duty is to administer the present government, as it came to his hands, and to transmit it, unimpaired by him, to his successor.

Why should there not be a patient confidence in the ultimate justice of the people? Is there any better or equal hope, in the world? In our present differences, is either party without faith *of being* in the right? If the Almighty Ruler of nations, with his eternal truth and justice, be on ~~your side of the North, or on~~ *on your side of the North, or on yours of the South,* that truth, and that justice, will surely prevail, by the judgment of this great tribunal, the American people.

By the frame of the government under which we live, this same people have wisely given their public servants but little power for mischief; and have, with equal wisdom, provided for the return of that little to their own hands at very short intervals. While the people *retain their virtue, and vigilence, no administration* ~~~~ by any extreme of wickedness or folly, can very seriously injure the government, in the short space of four years.

☞ My countrymen, one and all, ~~~~ *think calmly and* ~~well,~~ upon this whole sub- ject. Nothing valuable can be lost by taking time. ~~~~ If there be an object to *hurry* any of you, in hot haste, to a step which you would never take *deliberately,* that object will be frustrated by taking time; but no good object can be frustrated by it. Such of you as are now dissatisfied, still have the old Constitution unimpaired, and, on the sensitive point, the laws of your own framing under it; while the new administration will have no imme- diate power, if it would, to change either. If it were admitted that you who are dissatisfied, hold the right side in the dispute, there still is no single good reason for precipitate action. Intelligence, patriotism, Christianity, and a firm reliance on Him, who has never yet forsaken this favored land, are still competent to adjust, in the best way, all our present difficulty.

In *your* hands, my dissatisfied fellow countrymen, and not in *mine,* is the moment- ous issue of civil war. The government will not assail *you.* ~~~~ You can have no conflict, without being yourselves the aggressors. *You* have no oath registered in Heaven to destroy the government, while *I* shall have the most solemn one to "preserve, protect and defend" it. ~~~~ ~~With~~ ~~~~

7744

☞ I am loth to close. We are not enemies, but friends— We must not be enemies. Though passion may have strained, it must not break our bonds of affection. The mystic chords of memory, streching from every battle- field, and patriot grave, to every living heart and hearth- stone, all over this broad land, will yet swell the cho- rus of the Union, when again touched, as surely they will be, by the better angels of our nature.

THE LAST PAGE OF THE INAUGURAL ADDRESS. It was put in type in Springfield, but since then Lincoln had revised many of its passages. William Seward, his Secretary of State, suggested a different ending. Lincoln took the idea, but rewrote Seward's draft.

FORMING THE CABINET

THE NIGHT after his election, so Lincoln told Gideon Welles, who was to become his Secretary of the Navy, "I went home, but not to get much sleep, for I then felt, as I never had before, the responsibility that was upon me. I began at once to feel that I needed support—others to share with me the burden. This was on Wednesday morning, and before the sun went down I had made up my Cabinet. It was almost the same that I finally appointed. One or two changes were made, and the particular position of one or two was unsettled."

The forming of the Cabinet was not as simple as all that. There were many obstacles to overcome. It had to have a geographical balance; each section, including the South, was to have its representation; and it had to respect the promises which Lincoln's managers had made at the convention.

The President-elect was anxious to quiet fears that extremists would dominate his Cabinet; newspapers buzzed with rumors that he would offer seats to three or four Southern Union men.

Lincoln discussed the composition of his official family with Hannibal Hamlin, the Vice-President-elect, when they met in Chicago late in November; then Thurlow Weed, the Republican boss, came at his invitation to Springfield and Lincoln told him that as he had never learned the trade of cabinetmaking, he wished the advice of one reputedly experienced in the trade. Far into the night the two men discussed names and personalities, David Davis and Leonard Swett listening and participating in the arguments.

About the two principal posts in the Cabinet they were in agreement; William H. Seward was to be chosen as Secretary of State, though Weed thought and Lincoln hoped that he would not accept that position, and Salmon P. Chase should be Secretary of the Treasury. Weed insisted that at least two Southerners should be included in the Cabinet. Lincoln revealed that he intended to invite Gideon Welles of Connecticut, Montgomery Blair of Maryland, Edward Bates of Missouri, and, as an obligation to Pennsylvania and Indiana, Simon Cameron and Caleb B. Smith respectively.

This brought up the question of party balance. Was it politic to include Chase, Cameron, Blair, and Welles—all of them former Democrats? asked Weed. Why give them a Cabinet majority? "You

WILLIAM HENRY SEWARD (1801-1872) became Secretary of State. After accepting the post, he wrote to his wife: "I will try to save freedom and my country."

SALMON P. CHASE (1808-1873), Ohio's former governor, became Lincoln's Secretary of the Treasury.

EDWARD BATES (1793-1869), a conservative Unionist from Missouri, became Attorney General.

CALEB BLOOD SMITH (1808-1864) of Indiana was promised the post of Secretary of the Interior.

SIMON CAMERON (1799-1889), Pennsylvania politician, became Secretary of War by convention trade.

GIDEON WELLES (1802-1878), a former Democrat from Connecticut became Secretary of Navy.

MONTGOMERY BLAIR (1813-1883), of the prominent political family, was made Postmaster General.

LINCOLN REBUKES HIS SECRETARY OF STATE. William H. Seward submitted to Lincoln his "Thoughts for the President's Consideration," proposing that "whatever policy we adopt, there must be an energetic prosecution of it. For this purpose it must be somebody's business to pursue and direct it incessantly." Seward, of course, believed that he should be the person to do this. In his reply Lincoln made it clear that it was the President's duty to run his administration; he would not give up his responsibilities.

seem to forget," said Lincoln, "that I expect to be there; and counting me as one, you see how nicely the Cabinet would be balanced and ballasted."

Weed was particularly against Welles. He told the President-elect that if he would purchase at some port city "an attractive figure head, to be adorned with an elaborate wig and luxuriant whiskers," it would make just as good a head for the Navy. To which Lincoln retorted: "Oh, 'wooden midshipmen' answer very well in novels, but we must have a live Secretary of the Navy."

After protracted arguments, weeks of negotiations, deliberations, considerations, the seven members of the President's official family emerged.

To William Cullen Bryant, editor of the New York *Post*, Lincoln confided: "As to the matter of the cabinet . . . I can only say I shall have a great deal of trouble, do the best I can."

THE CARTOONISTS COMMENT
ON THE NEW PRESIDENT

OUR PRESIDENTIAL MERRYMAN.

"The Presidential party was engaged in a lively exchange of wit and humor. The President Elect was the merriest among the merry, and kept those around him in a continual roar."—*Daily Paper*.

Harper's Weekly, *March 2, 1861*

TWO DAYS BEFORE THE INAUGURATION *Harper's Weekly* printed this unsigned cartoon about the "Presidential Merryman."

The new illustrated weeklies—*Frank Leslie's* began in 1855, *Harper's* in 1856, *Vanity Fair* in 1860—leaned heavily on political cartoons. And the new President, with or without a beard, offered an admirable subject.

Before his election, Currier & Ives and others issued cartoon posters against him, lampooning the gawky candidate and his rustic appearance.

Vanity Fair, which proclaimed a war on "political tricksters, venal editors, public charlatans," printed its first Lincoln cartoon on June 9, and *Harper's Weekly* ran its first one on August 25, 1860.

At the outset these cartoons were relatively mild, but after he became President the attacks on him sharpened; cartoonists assailed him brutally.

Frank Leslie's Illustrated Newspaper, *February 2, 1861*

"A JOB FOR THE NEW CABINET MAKER" read the caption under this friendly drawing in *Leslie's* a month before the inauguration.

Frank Leslie's Illustrated Newspaper, *March 2, 1861*

"A PRESIDENT-ELECT'S UNCOMFORTABLE SEAT" also appeared in *Leslie's*, exactly a month after the drawing shown on the left.

130

Vanity Fair, *March 16, 1861*

THE FIRST CARTOON COMMENTING ON LINCOLN'S GROWING A BEARD AND THUS SETTING A STYLE.

Vanity Fair, *May 4, 1861*

LINCOLN ASSURES COLUMBIA that the rare flowering plant "will bloom shortly and bear the Jeffersonia Davisiana."

Vanity Fair, *March 2, 1861*

TRUST US!—Thurlow Weed, the political boss, implores the President. And foremost of all, "Trust my friend Seward" (right).

Vanity Fair, *March 23, 1861*

WOULD IT BE FORT SUMTER OR PEACE? The caption under the drawing reads: "Prof. Lincoln in his great feat of balancing."

131

THE WAR BEGINS

At the time Lincoln took the oath, a Confederate government in the South under the presidency of Jefferson Davis, representing the states of South Carolina, Mississippi, Florida, Alabama, Louisiana, Georgia, and Texas, had been in operation for a month.

Great efforts were made to effect a last-minute compromise between the two sections. They all failed, as on the dominant issue the Republicans would not yield; they would not allow the extension of slavery.

In his inaugural address Lincoln told the South that it was in their hands, and not in his, "the momentous issue of civil war." He emphasized: "The government will not assail you. You can have no conflict without yourself being the aggressors. *You* have no oath registered in heaven to destroy the government, while *I* shall have the most solemn one to preserve, protect and defend it."

A day after his inauguration a report came to the President from Major Robert Anderson, the commandant of Fort Sumter in Charleston Harbor, that his provisions were running low and that after consultation with his officers on the prospects and possibilities of relief and reinforcement, he believed that the fort could only be effectively succored if a combined land and naval force would subdue the besieging Confederate batteries and hold the Secession militia at bay.

It was a grave problem which confronted Lincoln. Fort Sumter had provisions for less than a month. What to do then? Evacuate it? Send reinforcements and fight it out with the Confederate shore batteries?

Lincoln knew that if he were to make an aggressive move the lower South would retaliate and fight—and once the war started, the upper South might be lost to the Union. On the other hand, to withdraw the garrison and give up the fort would mean a tremendous loss of prestige for him and for his administration.

In his dilemma the President played for time. The counsels he got were contradictory. Some members of his Cabinet were for evacuation, others suggested a firm attitude and expeditions to reinforce the garrison.

The Secretary of State, who argued against initiating a war "to regain a useless and unnecessary position," communicated with the Confederate

Frank Leslie's Illustrated Newspaper, *December 1, 1860*

SECESSION MEETING IN SOUTH CAROLINA. The hotbed of secessionist sentiment was Charleston, where, in the latter part of 1860, many meetings were held advocating secession. On December 20 South Carolina withdrew from the Union—the first state to do so.

Frank Leslie's Illustrated Newspaper, *March 2, 1861*

THE FORMING OF THE CONFEDERACY. Early in 1861 seven Southern states seceded from the Union. In February of that year, delegates of the seceding states met at Montgomery, Alabama, drafted a constitution, and chose Jefferson Davis for their President.

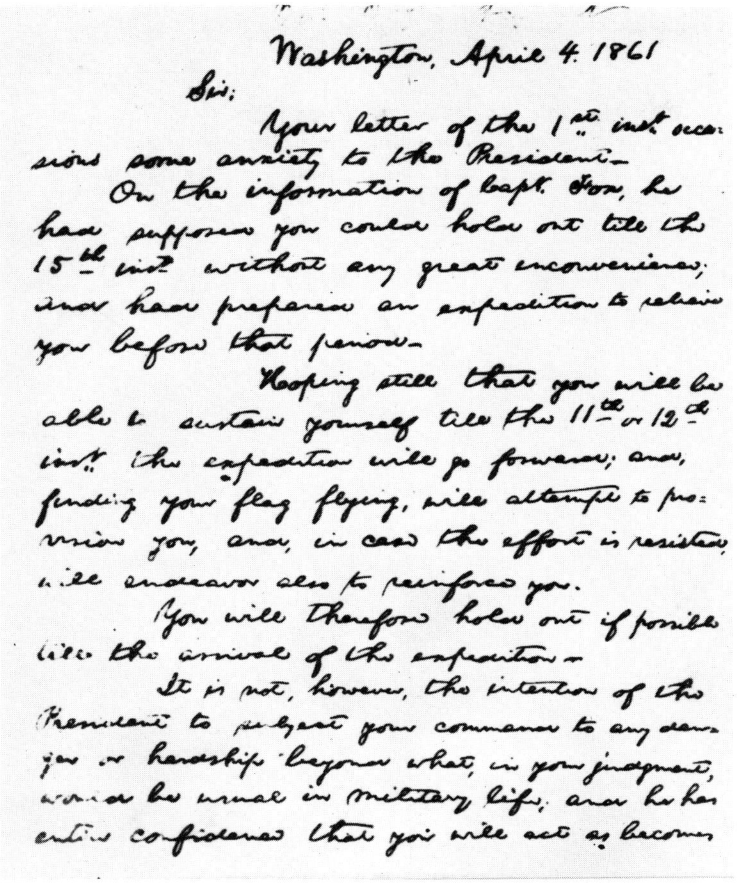

[Handwritten letter reproduced at top of page:]

Washington, April 4, 1861

Sir:

Your letter of the 1st inst. occasions some anxiety to the President.

On the information of Capt. Fox, he had supposed you could hold out till the 15th inst. without any great inconvenience; and had prepared an expedition to relieve you before that period.

Hoping still that you will be able to sustain yourself till the 11th or 12th inst. the expedition will go forward; and, finding your flag flying, will attempt to provision you, and, in case the effort is resisted, will endeavor also to reinforce you.

You will therefore hold out if possible till the arrival of the expedition.

It is not, however, the intention of the President to subject your command to any danger or hardship beyond what, in your judgment, would be usual in military life; and he has entire confidence that you will act as becomes

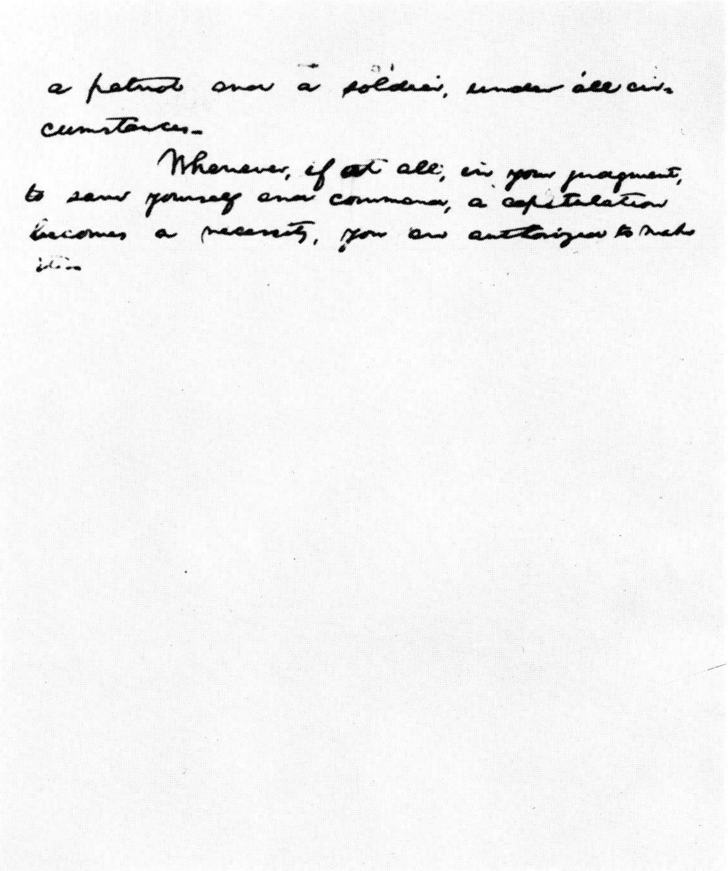

a patriot and a soldier, under all circumstances.

Whenever, if at all, in your judgment, to save yourself and command, a capitulation becomes a necessity, you are authorized to make it.

LINCOLN'S INSTRUCTIONS to the Commander of Fort Sumter, asking Major Robert Anderson to hold out if he can until reinforcements arrive. But the President emphasized that it was not his intention to subject the defenders of the fort "to any danger and hardship beyond what, in your judgment, would be usual in military life" and he ended his note: "Whenever, if at all, in your judgment, to save yourself and command, a capitulation becomes a necessity, you are authorized to make it." Ten days later Anderson surrendered.

commissioners in Washington. Lincoln was open to a bargain. He would be willing to evacuate the fort, if by that he could prevent the secession of Virginia. "A State for a fort," he was heard to say, "is no bad business." He sent his friend Ward Hill Lamon to South Carolina, where Lamon gave the impression that the fort would not be reinforced.

But as weeks passed, the President realized that evacuation of Fort Sumter would not satisfy the South; thus he made up his mind to supply it. He notified the Governor of South Carolina that a peaceful expedition would bring the garrison of Fort Sumter food and other necessities, but that neither men nor ammunition would be sent.

The Confederate government regarded this as a declaration of war. At 4:30 in the morning of April 12, 1861, General Beauregard's batteries at Charleston Harbor opened fire—the first shots in the Civil War.

AT THE OUTBREAK OF HOSTILITIES the army numbered about 16,000 men. Its officers were inexperienced, they had scant knowledge of staff work and administration. The troops had not enough guns, hardly any military maps, and no prepared plan of operation.

THE BOMBARDMENT OF FORT SUMTER. At 4:30 in the morning on April 12, 1861, the Confederate shore batteries at Charleston Harbor fired their first shell against Fort Sumter. With this the Civil War began. The shelling continued for a day and a half, when the exhausted defenders of the fort were forced to surrender. On Sunday, April 14, the Confederates hoisted their new flag over Fort Sumter.

ALL THE LADIES OF CHARLESTON were on the housetops watching the magnificent spectacle of Fort Sumter's bombardment. Shells were bursting in the night and there was a constant roar from the Confederate cannon. Everybody wondered why the guns from the fort did not reply.

For a day and a half the barrage continued; on April 13 the exhausted Union troops surrendered; on the 14th the Confederate flag was hoisted over the fort.

A day later, Lincoln issued a proclamation declaring that as the laws of the country were opposed in the seven Confederate states "by combinations too powerful to be suppressed by the course of judicial proceeding," he had called on the states of the Union for 75,000 troops of their militia "to suppress the said combinations." If Lincoln had asked ten times that number, the North would have responded. The firing on Fort Sumter closed the ranks in the free states; the people rallied behind the flag and their President. But his proclamation also drove four more slaveholding states —Virginia, North Carolina, Arkansas,

and Tennessee—into the Confederacy. Two other states—Kentucky and Missouri—were kept in the Union only with the greatest difficulty.

Not long thereafter, Lincoln reviewed the situation which had led to the war. In his Fourth of July message to Congress he said that "the assault upon and reduction of Fort Sumter was in no sense a matter of self defense on the part of the assailants. They well knew that the garrison in the fort could by no possibility commit aggression upon them. They knew—they were expressly notified— that the giving of bread to the few brave and hungry men of the garrison was all which would on that occasion be attempted, unless themselves, by resisting so much, should provoke more."

Lincoln made his position clear:

By the President of the United States
A proclamation
To the People of the United States of America.

Whereas the laws of the United States have been, for some time past, and now are, opposed, and the execution thereof obstructed, in the States of South Carolina, Georgia, Alabama, Florida, Mississippi, Louisiana, and Texas, by combinations too powerful to be suppressed by the ordinary course of judicial proceedings, or by the powers vested in the Marshals by law; therefore I, Abraham Lincoln, President of the United States, in virtue of the power in me vested by the Constitution and the laws, have thought fit to call forth, and hereby do call forth the militia of the several states of the Union, to the aggregate number of seventy-five thousand, in order to suppress said combinations, and to cause the laws to be duly executed. The details, for this object, will be immediately communicated to the State authorities, through the War Department.

I appeal to all loyal citizens to favor, facilitate, and aid this effort to maintain the honor, the integrity, and the existence of our National Union, and the perpetuity of popular government; and to redress wrongs already too long endured.

I deem it proper to say that the first service assigned to the forces hereby called forth will probably be to repossess the forts, places and property, which have been seized from the Union; and, in every event, the ut-

most care will be observed, consistly with the objects aforesaid, to avoid any devastation, any destruction of, or interference with, property, or any disturbance of peaceful citizens, in any part of the country.

And I hereby command the persons composing the combination aforesaid to disperse, and retire peaceably to their respective abodes, within twenty days from this date.

Deeming that the present condition of public affairs presents an extraordinary occasion, I do hereby, in virtue of the power in me vested by the Constitution, convene both Houses of Congress. Senators and Representatives are therefore summoned to assemble at their respective chambers, at 12 o'clock, noon, on Thursday, the fourth day of July next, then and there to consider, and determine, such measures as, in their wisdom, the public safety, and interest, may seem to demand.

DRAFT OF THE PRESIDENT'S PROCLAMATION, dated the day after Fort Sumter's evacuation, calling for 75,000 militia against "combinations too powerful to be suppressed by the ordinary course of judicial proceedings." The North responded willingly, but Lincoln's "war declaration" drove four more slave states—Virginia, North Carolina, Arkansas, and Tennessee—into the Confederacy.

"They knew that this Government desired to keep the garrison in the fort, not to assail them, but merely to maintain visible possession, and thus to preserve the Union from actual and immediate dissolution—trusting, as hereinbefore stated, to time, discussion, and the ballot-box, for final adjustment, and they assailed and reduced the fort for precisely the reverse object—to drive out the visible authority of the Federal Union and thus force it to immediate dissolution."

Eloquently the President laid his policy before the country, emphasizing that by the attack on the fort the South had "forced upon the country the distinct issue, immediate dissolution or blood.

"And this issue embraces more than the fate of these United States," he asserted. "It presents to the whole family of man the question, whether a constitutional republic or democracy —a Government of the people by the same people—can or cannot maintain its territorial integrity against its own domestic foes. It presents the question, whether discontented individuals, too few in numbers to control administration, according to organic law, in any case, can always, upon the pretenses made in this case, or on any other pretenses, or arbitrarily, without any pretense, break up their Government, and thus practically put an end to free government upon the earth. It forces us to ask: 'Is there, in all republics, this inherent and fatal weakness?' 'Must a Government, of necessity, be too *strong* for the liberties of its own people, or too *weak* to maintain its own existence?'

"So viewing the issue, no choice was left but to call out the war power of the Government; and so to resist force employed for its destruction, by force for its preservation."

135

WASHINGTON PREPARES FOR THE WORST

Frank Leslie's Illustrated Newspaper, *April 30, 1861*

THE FIRST UNION REGIMENT to reach the capital was the Sixth Massachusetts. Attacked by Rebel sympathizers in Baltimore, four soldiers were killed and many wounded.

A Brady photograph

AFTER THE OCCUPATION OF ALEXANDRIA, bulwarks were built to protect the machine shops and yard of the Orange & Alexandria Railroad from expected Confederate raids.

DEFENDERS OF WASHINGTON. One of the forts protecting the capital was Fort Corcoran at the approach to the Aqueduct south of the Potomac—named after the

VIRGINIA'S SECESSION placed the capital in great danger. If Maryland joined the South, Washington would be cut off; the only railroad to the North passed through Baltimore. The city had no military protection; troops from the North were anxiously awaited.

Word came that the Seventh New York Regiment had departed and was on its way to defend the capital, as was Governor Sprague with his Rhode Island regiment. But critical days passed

commander, Colonel Michael Corcoran (standing on the parapet) of the Sixty-Ninth New York Regiment. In the last week of May, Union troops crossed the Aqueduct Bridge at Georgetown and the Long Bridge at Washington, securing them against Confederate destruction. Soon the approaches to the bridges were fortified, eight-inch sea-coast howitzers, mounted on wooden carriages, were installed, and the grapeshot piled in the foreground was ready for the enemy. But there was no sight of them.

and there was still no sign of them. Would they arrive in time?

Lincoln paced the floor of his study, "stopped and gazed long and wistfully out of the window down the Potomac in the direction of the expected ships; and, unconscious of other presence in the room, at length broke out with irrepressible anguish in the repeated exclamation, Why don't they come! Why don't they come!"

The wounded soldiers of the Sixth Massachusetts—who a few days before had fought their way through Baltimore—came to pay their respects. For a while he talked to the soldiers warmly, thanking them for their bravery. "I begin to believe," said Lincoln bitterly to them, "that there is no North. The Seventh Regiment is a myth. Rhode Island is another. You are the only real thing."

At last—on April 25—the New Yorkers arrived. The regiment had marched the twenty miles from Annapolis to the junction, ready to battle any Rebel forces on the way. But there had been no Rebel force, and at the junction they found a train waiting for them to take them to the Capital.

When they arrived they were greeted with jubilation. The gloom lifted from the city as the troops marched with flying colors down Pennsylvania Avenue. The days of danger were gone. The Capital was safe.

137

A YOUNG HERO DIES

On May 24, twenty-four-year-old Elmer Ellsworth, Colonel of the picturesque Zouave regiment, led his men over the Aqueduct Bridge at Georgetown to secure the Virginia end of that vital artery. (Other regiments crossed the Long Bridge and the Chain Bridge, forestalling any Confederate attempt to destroy them.)

The Zouaves marched into Alexandria, and dashing young Ellsworth, perceiving the Rebel flag over the city's principal hotel, the Marshall House, climbed to the roof and brought the flag down with his own hands. The reporter of the New York *Tribune* went with him, and left his recollections of the event:

"We turned to descend," wrote E. H. Howe, "Corporal Brownell leading the way and Ellsworth immediately following with the flag. As Brownell reached the first landing-place . . . a man jumped from a dark passage and . . . leveled a double-barrelled gun square at the Colonel's breast." It was the proprietor of the hotel, and his bullets killed Ellsworth instantly. As he fell to the floor, his companion, Corporal Brownell, shot the assassin and in a temper of frenzy thrust his saber bayonet through and through the man's body.

The news of Ellsworth's death came to Lincoln while Senator Wilson of Massachusetts and a reporter from the New York *Tribune* were in his room. The President burst into tears and for a long while could not say a word. "I will make no apology, gentlemen, for my weakness," he said when he regained his composure, "but I knew poor Ellsworth well and held him in high regard."

In the evening he visited the navy yard, where Ellsworth's body lay in state. Looking at the young man's face, he moaned: "My boy! my boy! Was it necessary this sacrifice should be made?"

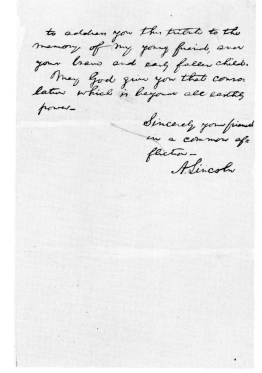

EPHRAIM ELMER ELLSWORTH, one of the first casualties of the war. Lincoln mourned the young man, once a student in his law office, as he would his own son.

THE DEEPLY MOVING LETTER OF SYMPATHY WHICH THE PRESIDENT SENT TO THE PARENTS OF EPHRAIM ELMER ELLSWORTH.

138

THE DEFEAT AT BULL RUN. The Union troops threw their arms away and fled in panic from the battlefield. "Turn back! Turn back! We are whipped!" they cried. In this first great encounter of the Civil War, General Irvin McDowell's 35,000 troops were defeated by an equal number of Confederate soldiers under the command of Beauregard and Johnston. It was the first of bad days for the Union.

THE FIRST BATTLE OF THE WAR

BEFORE A WAR, people always burst with self-confidence; before a war, people always think that their side is invincible. To the North the matter seemed quite simple. Attack the Confederates at Manassas, defeat them with a superior force, then move on to their capital and the war would end.

General Winfield Scott, the army's General in Chief, had a different proposal. He would establish a tight blockade of the Southern ports, then move an army down the Mississippi, hold the river from Cairo to the Gulf, thus sealing off the Confederacy from its supplies. Scott was against using arms against the South; he would rather wait till the blockade did its work.

To Lincoln the General's "Anaconda plan" seemed much too slow; the country grew impatient; it cried for a swift attack. He ordered General Irvin McDowell, the new commander of the troops, to move on without delay.

McDowell was prepared to take Manassas, but asked the President for a little time to organize his green troops. "You are green, it is true," replied Lincoln, "but they are green also; you are all green alike."

Thus, on a hot Sunday in the latter part of July, 35,000 Union troops crossed Bull Run to attack the Confederates under General Beauregard. At first, things went well, but when General Johnston's men from the Valley joined up with Beauregard, the Confederates counter-attacked, chasing the panicky Blues before them.

At Washington, Lincoln was awake the whole night, listening to the gloomy reports of the people who came from the battlefield.

The Union defeat at Bull Run turned out to be a greater disaster for the South than for the North. It made them overconfident. Instead of pursuing the Union army, they celebrated. Their soldiers sang:

> I come from old Manassas, with a
>   pocket full of fun—
> I killed forty Yankees with a
>   single-barrelled gun;
> It don't make a niff-a-stifference
>   to neither you nor I,
> Big Yankee, little Yankee, all run
>   or die.

Little did the happy Confederates realize that the war had just begun.

139

THE NEW COMMANDER

THE DEFEAT at Bull Run showed that it was not safe to leave McDowell in command of the army; thus Lincoln turned to General George B. McClellan, the only Union General who had been successful in the operations in western Virginia.

"Little Mac," as his men called him, was a complex personality; his name evokes controversy, even today. When he received the appointment as Commanding General of the army, he was thirty-five years old, but already

with a varied and successful military career behind him. He had studied at West Point, served in the Mexican War, then traveled in Europe, where he inspected military establishments. In 1857 he left the army to become chief engineer of the Illinois Central Railroad; before long he became president of the Eastern Division of the Ohio and Mississippi Railroad.

After the attack on Fort Sumter McClellan was commissioned as Major-General, commanding the Department

of the Ohio. His military successes in the early stages of the hostilities turned his head; he believed himself a military genius and was greatly pleased when newspaper writers referred to him as a second Napoleon.

Lincoln, looking for an energetic young war leader, hoped that McClellan would be the right one. As soon as the General took command, he was asked to prepare an all-round strategical plan. McClellan submitted a grandiose one which looked good

AFTER THE DEFEAT AT BULL RUN, Lincoln prepared this "memorandum of military policy" in which he suggested the strengthening of the army and the pushing forward of plans for making the blockade against the South more effective. In a postscript he added that "When the foregoing shall have been substantially attended to," two attacks should be launched, one against Manassas, and when done, "a joint movement from Cairo on Memphis and from Cincinnati on East Tennessee. From the earliest days of the war it was Lincoln who formulated the military strategy of the Union forces and mastered all the complicated problems.

on paper but took little cognizance of realities.

McClellan as a military leader had a great many faults but had one shining virtue—he was an excellent organizer. Students of his character, exasperated by his arrogance, hesitation, and procrastination, critical of his egotism and righteousness, doubtful of his grandiose military plans, have to admit that it was he who created the magnificent Army of the Potomac.

The country was impatient. Many weeks had passed since the defeat at Bull Run and nothing had happened. People were tired of hearing: "All quiet along the Potomac"; they asked for action, hoping that one great attack would break the Confederacy and end the war.

McClellan gave the impression that he wanted to fight, that he wanted to attack, that he wanted to move boldly against the South. But he implied that his hands were tied, as Scott, the General in Chief, had a defensive plan, hindering his offensive action at every point. Gradually "Little Mac" worked himself into a frenzy against "Old Fuss and Feathers"; in his mind Scott became an evil influence, and he used every means to have the old man removed from his post.

Seventy-five-year-old Scott, infirm with dropsy and vertigo, was tired of McClellan's brazenness; at the end of October he sent in his application for retirement. Lincoln regretfully accepted it, and on the first day of November he appointed McClellan as General in Chief of the Union forces.

The President paid a visit to the General's headquarters, trying to find out how McClellan felt about his new duties. "In addition to your present command, the supreme command of the Army will entail a vast labor upon you," Lincoln said in broaching the subject. "Little Mac" radiated supreme confidence. "I can do it all," said he firmly. The tremendous responsibilities did not make him humble; he felt that he was selected by the Divine Being to save the Union and that he was superior to anyone else in the land, including the President.

Lincoln was relieved to find such

LINCOLN'S CHOICE as new Commanding General of the army was George B. McClellan, who succeeded McDowell. McClellan was a brilliant organizer, the deviser of great strategical plans, but timid and hesitant when it came to leading his men into battle.

LINCOLN IN 1861—a photograph which he inscribed before giving it to the mother of his Springfield friend Joshua Fry Speed on October 3, 1861: "For Mrs. Lucy G. Speed, from whose pious hand I accepted the present of an Oxford Bible twenty years ago."

confidence in the man. He hoped that his new commander would be in agreement with his war policies, policies which were so simple that they could be expressed in a single sentence. The President fought for the restoration of the Union, and to achieve that aim it seemed to him that the objective of the Federal army was not the occupation of Southern territory, but the destruction of the Confederate fighting forces.

It was a fortnight after McClellan's appointment that the President, accompanied by Secretary Seward and John Hay, went over to the General's house

THE OLD GENERAL IN CHIEF OF THE ARMY, seventy-five-year-old Winfield Scott, the hero of the Mexican War, infirm with dropsy and vertigo and exasperated by McClellan's behavior toward him, sent Lincoln his resignation on the last day of October in 1861. On Scott's right is Henry van Rensselaer; on his left, Colonel E. D. Townsend, who later wrote the notable *Anecdotes of the Civil War*.

in Washington to discuss military matters with him. As McClellan was not at home, Lincoln decided to wait. His secretary noted in his diary that after Lincoln had waited about an hour, McClellan came in and, "without paying any particular attention to the porter, who told him the President was waiting to see him, went upstairs, passing the door of the room where the President and Secretary of State were seated. They waited about half an hour, and sent once more a servant to tell the General they were there, and the answer coolly came that the General had gone to bed."

The President returned to the White House, taking the rebuff humbly and telling his secretary that "it was better at this time not to be making points of etiquette and personal dignity." He needed McClellan and victories.

THE NEW GENERAL IN CHIEF OF THE ARMY, thirty-five-year-old George B. McClellan, proud of his resemblance to Napoleon, is standing between his aides-de-camp, Lieut. Col. A. V. Colburn and N. B. Sweitzer. Behind McClellan is the Prince of Joinville (wearing a felt hat), son of King Louis Philippe of France, and his nephew, the Comte de Paris (in the uniform of McClellan's staff), author of the compendious *History of the Civil War*.

TROUBLES
IN THE WEST

As his chief of the newly created Western Department—composed of Illinois and the states and territories west of the Mississippi to the Rockies—Lincoln selected John C. Frémont, the Republican presidential candidate of 1856. The forty-eight-year-old "Pathfinder of the West" was to set up his headquarters at St. Louis, raise an army and move it down the Mississippi toward Memphis.

At his farewell visit in Washington, Frémont asked the President whether he had any further instructions for him. "No," said Lincoln, "I have

THE COMMANDER OF THE WESTERN ARMIES, forty-eight-year-old John C. Frémont, appointed on July 3, 1861. He was an inefficient and fumbling General, making embarrassing political decisions. Lincoln removed him from his command in October.

LINCOLN WROTE FRÉMONT on September 2, asking him to modify his proclamation in which Frémont—taking on preroga-

HENRY W. HALLECK succeeding Frémont, was to restore order from the chaos left by his predecessor and concentrate his army by the Mississippi.

DON CARLOS BUELL as Commander of the newly organized Department of the Ohio was ordered to hold Kentucky and move into eastern Tennessee.

tives which belonged to the President—freed the slaves of all persons resisting the government. Frémont refused to obey.

AFTER FRÉMONT REFUSED to modify his proclamation, Lincoln ordered him to do so. There could not be two heads of government.

given you *carte blanche*, you must use your own judgment and do the best you can." Frémont badly misunderstood Lincoln's answer; he felt that he was entitled to make every decision—even political ones—without consulting the President. Thus, a month after his arrival in Missouri, and without further consultation, he issued a proclamation freeing the slaves of all persons resisting the government.

The President wrote the General that he must modify his proclamation, as the official policy of the government was that the war was being fought for the restoration of the Union and not for the abolition of slavery. Frémont remonstrated that his attack on slavery was as much a military movement as a battle, and he would rescind his proclamation only if the President commanded him to do so. This Lincoln did "cheerfully."

His slavery proclamation was not Frémont's only blunder. He failed as an organizer; in his department inefficiency and graft were rampant; and he failed as a commander. When, in October, the Confederates in Missouri overwhelmed a Federal garrison at Lexington, Lincoln finally removed him from his post.

McClellan, who became General in Chief of the army at the time Frémont was relieved, reorganized the Western command, making two departments where one had been before; to Frémont's old department he added the western part of Kentucky, while the new Department of the Ohio was to consist of the rest of Kentucky and Tennessee. General Henry W. Halleck was to become Frémont's successor, and the Department of the Ohio was to be commanded by Don Carlos Buell. Lincoln hoped that these plans would work out.

ORDERING AN OFFENSIVE

BEFORE HE became the Commanding General of the Army, McClellan was an advocate of offensive action. But after his appointment his ardor cooled; he vacillated and hesitated, he procrastinated and postponed. Thinking himself greatly outnumbered by the enemy, he asked Lincoln for more troops and pleaded for more time to prepare his army.

The President beseeched him to move against the Confederates before the winter weather would stop operations. He sent the General a plan suggesting a continued frontal and flank attack at Manassas. Lincoln knew that to restore the Union by force— as was his government's policy—the North must wage an offensive and destroy the Rebel army.

To Lincoln's proposal McClellan replied that he had a different plan, but he was unwilling to reveal —even to his Commander in Chief—what his strategy was to be. The General had the strange notion that Lincoln would not be able to keep the secret. But to a fellow officer McClellan confided that he was preparing to transport his army down the Potomac, land it at Urbana on the southern bank of the Rappahannock, from where he planned to march it to Richmond and take the Rebel capital.

The idea might have worked if prosecuted quickly and vigorously. But "Little Mac" spent so much time in preparing the move that, by the time he was ready, winter had set in, bringing with it rain and muddy roads. The offensive had to be postponed until spring, and the great Army of the Potomac sat it out in winter quarters, doing nothing.

The beginning of the year 1862 found Lincoln in an exasperated mood. In the West the two commanders, Buell and Halleck, were at loggerheads in co-ordinating their operations; in the East the army idled in camp, and to top it all, the General in Chief became ill with typhoid fever. "The bottom is out of the tub," complained the President to his Quartermaster General.

General William B. Franklin and General Irvin McDowell, who served under McClellan, were asked to Washington to make preparations in case McClellan had to be replaced on account of his illness. When "Little Mac" heard of the proposed meeting, he believed it was a plot to ease him out of his command, so he got out of his bed and went himself to the White House, proving that he was well and able enough to hold the reins of his armies. There was no need for his replacement.

Throughout the North the agitation for an offensive grew. Bending to pressure, Lincoln wrote out an order—marked General War Order No. 1—in which he directed McClellan (who in the meantime had recovered) to move the army toward Manassas, seize a point on the railroad southwest of that place, and to begin operations not later than February 22.

It was an unusual procedure to set the date of the offensive for all the world to know, but Lincoln's purpose in issuing it was to prod his General into action. McClellan—as usual—argued against the President's plan, and offered a scheme of his own. While the merits and faults of the plans were discussed, the date for the offensive passed; General War Order No. 1, though never revoked, was forgotten.

TO PROD McCLELLAN INTO ACTION Lincoln issued his General War Order No. 1, directing the General in Chief to begin not later than February 22, 1862, to move his army toward Manassas.

WILLIE (William Wallace) was his father's favorite. Born a year after Eddie's death, he grew into a gifted boy, "thoughtful, grave beyond his years." When he died of pneumonia at the age of twelve his father was desolate. On Thursdays, the day of Willie's death, he would not eat, and he wanted to make all Thursdays into days of national mourning for the boys who lost their lives in the war.

WILLIE DIES

Early in 1862, twelve-year-old Willie Lincoln caught a cold; within a few days he died.

His parents were prostrate with grief. The mulatto seamstress, Elizabeth Keckley, was preparing the boy's body for the last rites when Lincoln came into the room, gazed at the face of his beloved son long and earnestly. Mrs. Keckley heard him murmur: "My poor boy, he was too good for this earth. God has called him home. I know that he is much better off in heaven, but then we loved him so. It is hard, hard to have him die." Then he gave his tears free rein; "he buried his head in his hands, and his tall frame was convulsed with emotion. . . ."

Shutting himself away from his family, Lincoln abandoned himself to his pain. On Thursdays—the day of Willie's death—he fasted, and he wanted to set aside each Thursday as a day of national mourning for the families who had lost sons in the war.

Mary feared that he would lose his sanity. She begged the Reverend Francis Vinton of New York's Trinity Church, who happened to be visiting the capital, to speak sense to him, and Vinton had a long talk with him. He admonished Lincoln that his indulgence in his grief was sinful and unworthy of one who believed in the Christian religion. "Your son," he said, "is *alive*, in Paradise. Do you remember that passage in the Gospels: 'God is not the God of the *dead*, but of the living, for *all* live unto him'?"

(turn to page 149)

THE TWO YOUNGER LINCOLN BOYS, Willie and Tad, with Lockwood Todd, a nephew of Mrs. Lincoln. The pro-slavery Democrat Lockwood Todd was no great admirer of his famous relative. During the presidential campaign of 1860 he was heard to say that Lincoln's connection with the Todd family was a disgrace and that he "would not vote for him to save him from hell." But after the election he accepted a Custom House appointment in San Francisco, and later in the war he marched with Sherman "to the sea."

THOMAS (OR TAD), the youngest of the boys, was a tense child with a slight speech impediment. His marks in school were low.

MARY was a good mother, she loved her children dearly. When Willie died, she mourned excessively and tried to communicate with her dead son through spiritual mediums "by means of scratches on the wainscoting and taps on the walls and furniture." To a friend she wrote: "When I can bring myself to realize that he has indeed passed away, my question to myself is, can life be endured?"

ROBERT, the eldest son, had the least knowledge of his father. He was away at school most of the time, first at Phillips Exeter, then at Harvard, and spent little time at home with his parents.

At the same time, Mary Lincoln mourned no less than her husband. Willie was the second son taken from her by death. Wild in her grief, she screamed and moaned and behaved as if she were losing her mind. After one of these attacks, her husband took her by the arm, led her to the window and, pointing in the direction of the insane asylum, he said:

"Mother, do you see that large white building on the hill yonder? Try and control your grief, or it will drive you mad, and we may have to send you there."

But it was two years before Mary took off her black dress, before she gave up mourning for her beloved son.

THE SECOND BRADY SITTING

There are so many pictures of Lincoln taken during his four presidential years that one wonders how he found the time to visit the photographers so often. Actually he went to them seldom. In 1861 and 1862 he visited Brady only once in each year. In 1863 Gardner photographed him on two occasions; in 1864 Brady's assistant took his picture once in the gallery and twice in the White House. And in 1865, just a few days before his death, he sat for Gardner. But each time he was posed in half a dozen or more attitudes, and thus the impression is given that he was a much-photographed man.

Sitting before the camera he always put on his "photographer's face," as Mary teasingly called it. But as soon as he began to talk "the dull, listless features dropped like a mask. The melancholy shadow disappeared in a twinkling. The eye began to sparkle, the mouth to smile, the whole countenance was wreathed in animation so that a stranger would have said, 'Why, this man, so angular and somber a moment ago, is really handsome.' " Billy Herndon expressed it even better when he said: "Sometimes it appeared to me that Lincoln's face was just fresh from the presence of its Creator."

EVERY TIME LINCOLN WENT TO BRADY'S GALLERY ON PENNSYLVANIA AVENUE HE POSED FOR MANY DIFFERENT PICTURES.

THE DATE OF THIS SITTING IS NOT CERTAIN. The photographs may have been taken in late 1862 or in the spring of 1863. There is no contemporary evidence about their exact date.

The print on the opposite page was made directly from the oversized original plate in the National Archives. Such "imperial photographs," as they were called, measured 17 x 21 inches; they were enlarged with a Woodward solar camera (David Woodward of Baltimore patented his enlarger in 1857).

About the time these photographs were taken, Nathaniel Hawthorne gave this description of Lincoln: "His hair was black, still unmixed with gray, stiff, somewhat bushy, and had apparently been acquainted with neither brush nor comb. . . . His complexion is dark and sallow, betokening, I fear, an insalubrious atmosphere around the White House."

"THE CHEESEBOX ON A RAFT"—as the new Northern ironclad, *Monitor*, was nicknamed —had its historic encounter with the Confederate *Merrimac* on March 9, 1862, at Newport News, ending the threat to the transport of General McClellan's troops to the Peninsula.

BESIEGING THE ENEMY. The Army of the Potomac slowly moved up the Peninsula, building heavily fortified positions, in preparation for an all-out drive on Richmond.

TRYING OUT A NEW IDEA: IN HIS

THE PENINSULAR CAMPAIGN

ALMOST A YEAR had gone by since the fall of Fort Sumter, and the armies in the East had hardly seen any battles. The President demanded action. Mc-Clellan suggested—instead of moving toward Manassas as Lincoln proposed—taking the army to Urbana and marching it from there to Richmond.

Lincoln was not convinced of the soundness of such strategy, but as eight of McClellan's division commanders voted in favor of it, he was ready to sanction it. He asked only that enough troops be left behind for the defense of Washington and that the move should start not later than the middle of March.

INFLATING BALLOON "INTREPID" PROFESSOR LOWE RECONNOITERS FOR THE UNION THE POSITION OF THE CONFEDERATES.

Yet, before McClellan was ready to move, the Confederates evacuated their lines around Manassas and took up new positions behind the Rappahannock. This frustrated "Little Mac's" strategy, which was based on the assumption that the Rebel army would stay in northern Virginia while he would march between it and Richmond.

McClellan now decided to take the army to the lower Chesapeake by boat, landing at Fortress Monroe, and moving up the region between the York and

James rivers known as the Peninsula, attacking and capturing the Confederate capital.

Lincoln endorsed the changed strategy; thus, on the first day of April, the Union forces began to land at Fortress Monroe and started their march toward Richmond. Before Yorktown their advance bogged down, McClellan complaining that he had not enough men. Angry at Lincoln, who had retained McDowell's corps for the defense of the capital, he moved slowly and cautiously. A whole

153

month had passed before Yorktown fell, and during this time the Confederates had ample opportunity to concentrate their forces.

A day after the Confederates evacuated the defenses of Yorktown—General Johnston taking his troops back to fight the battle for Richmond nearer the city—Lincoln arrived at Fortress Monroe, accompanied by his Secretaries Stanton and Chase. McClellan implored the President to let him have more troops, as in his mind the Rebel army greatly outnumbered him. Lincoln promised to dispatch McDowell with reinforcements from Washington, but when "Stonewall" Jackson moved up the Valley, threatening the safety of the capital, Lincoln changed his mind. "The President is not willing to uncover the Capital entirely," wired the Secretary of War to McClellan.

On May 26 McClellan was within five miles of Richmond. It was on this day that Lincoln wired him: "I think the time is near when you must either attack Richmond or give up the job and come to the defense of Washington." That day "Stonewall" Jackson was driving the Union forces under General Banks before him in the Valley, menacing the capital.

When McClellan was ready to move against Richmond, luck was against him. On the night of May 30 a heavy rainstorm flooded the low grounds

of the Chickahominy, threatening the military bridges and isolating the two wings of his army. General Joseph E. Johnston, the Confederate commander, realizing his advantage, ordered an attack; on May 31 and on the day following, 60,000 men in gray moved through the mud and fought the Federals between Fair Oaks and Seven Pines.

It was the first great bloody encounter for the reorganized Army of the Potomac, and McClellan was desperate to see so many of his troops perish. Six thousand of his men were killed, and the Confederate losses ran even higher. General Johnston, the head of the Rebel forces, was severely wounded in the shoulder and had to relinquish his command. In his place Jefferson Davis named Robert E. Lee, who was to lead the newly baptized "Army of Northern Virginia" against the Army of the Potomac.

The greatly outnumbered Lee was determined to take the initiative and drive McClellan off the Peninsula. On June 26 he began his attacks. For a whole week the armies fought a series of engagements—which became known as the Battles of the Seven Days. At Mechanicsville and at Gaines's Mill the Confederates well-nigh smashed the Union, but McClellan was able to extricate his army; he shifted his base from White House on the Pamunkey to Harrison's Landing on the James. Lee harassed him

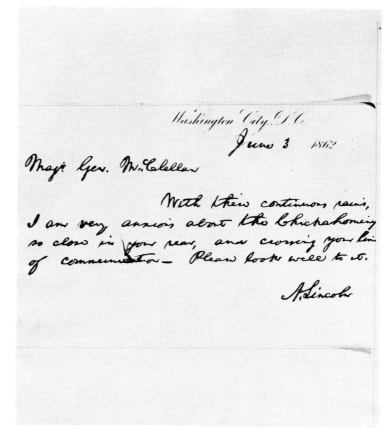

DURING THE BATTLES, PRESIDENT LINCOLN KEPT IN CLOSE TOUCH WITH GENERAL McCLELLAN, COMMANDER OF THE ARMIES.

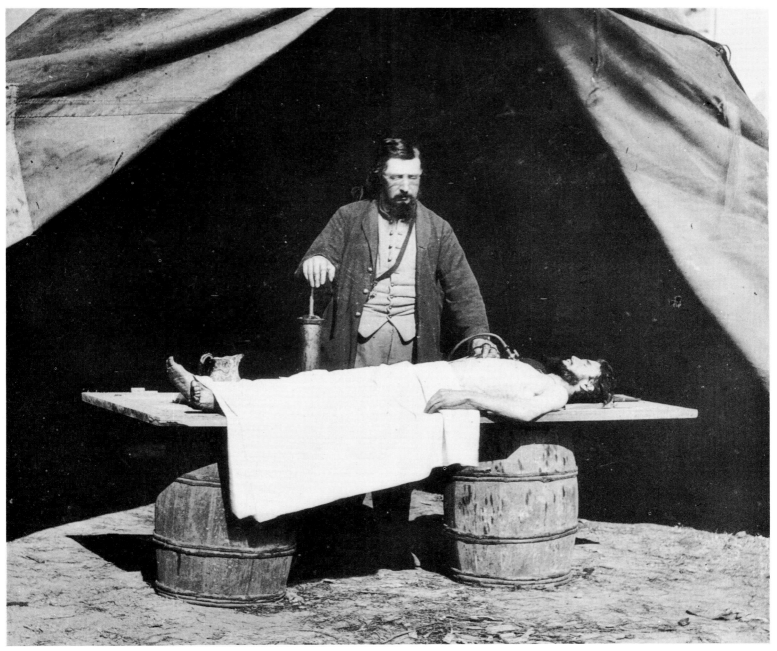

AN ARMY SURGEON EMBALMS THE BODY OF A DEAD SOLDIER, WHICH WILL BE SENT TO THE FAMILY OF THE FALLEN MAN.

at Savage's Station and Frayser's Farm and then, in the last Battle of the Seven Days, at Malvern Hill.

If McClellan had counterattacked at Malvern Hill, he might have taken Richmond. But instead of boldly moving against Lee, he took his army from the field to its new base. He charged Lincoln with the responsibility for the defeat, accusing him of withholding the promised reinforcements. On June 28—after the second of the Seven Days battles—he wrote to Edwin Stanton, who had earlier in the year replaced Cameron as Secretary of War: "If I save this army now, I tell you plainly that I owe no thanks to you or to any other persons in Washington. You have done your best to sacrifice this army."

That very day an anxious Lincoln wired Mc-

Clellan: "Save your Army, at all events. Will send re-inforcements as fast as we can." But on July 1 in another telegram Lincoln told the General that "It is impossible to re-inforce you for your present emergency. If we had a million of men we could not get them to you in time. We have not the men to send. If you are not strong enough to face the enemy you must find a place of security, and wait, rest, and repair. Maintain your ground if you can; but save the Army at all events, even if you fall back to Fortress Monroe. We still have strength enough in the country, and will bring it out."

But when McClellan remonstrated, asking for 50,000 men, Lincoln simply told him that the North had not, "outside of your Army, seventy-five thou-

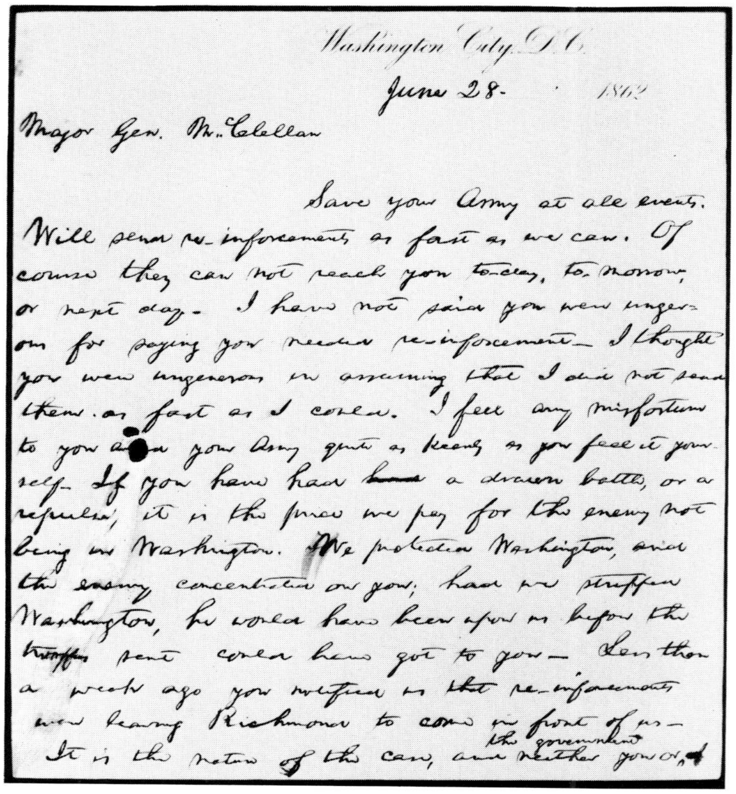

Washington City, D.C.
June 28. 1862

Major Gen. McClellan

Save your Army at all events. Will send re-inforcements as fast as we can. Of course they can not reach you to-day, to-morrow, or next day. I have not said you were ungenerous for saying you needed re-inforcement. I thought you were ungenerous in assuming that I did not send them as fast as I could. I feel any misfortune to you and your Army quite as keenly as you feel it yourself. If you have had a drawn battle, or a repulse, it is the price we pay for the enemy not being in Washington. We protected Washington, and the enemy concentrated on you; had we stripped Washington, he would have been upon us before the troops sent could have got to you. Less than a week ago you notified us that re-inforcements were leaving Richmond to come in front of us. It is the nature of the case, and neither you or the government

"SAVE YOUR ARMY AT ALL EVENTS" wrote Lincoln to McClellan, after Gaines's Mill. "Will send re-inforcements as fast as we can. . . . I have not said you were ungenerous for saying you needed re-inforcements. I thought you were ungenerous in assuming that I did not send them as fast as I could. I feel any misfortune to you and your Army quite as keenly as you feel it yourself."

sand men East of the mountains. Thus, the idea of sending you fifty thousand, or any other considerable force promptly is simply absurd."

A little while after the Seven Days Battles Lincoln went to Harrison's Landing to see McClellan and discuss future plans with him. The General handed Lincoln a letter stating his political ideas and offering the President advice as to how to handle the slavery issue.

On his return to Washington, Lincoln appointed General Henry W. Halleck as General in Chief, and after careful consultation with the military advisers, ordered McClellan to move the Army of the Potomac to a position south of the capital. Thus, operations on the Peninsula came to an end.

The losses in the peninsular campaign were extremely heavy; Lincoln appealed to the states for 300,000 more soldiers. In response to this request James Sloan Gibbons wrote the famous lines:

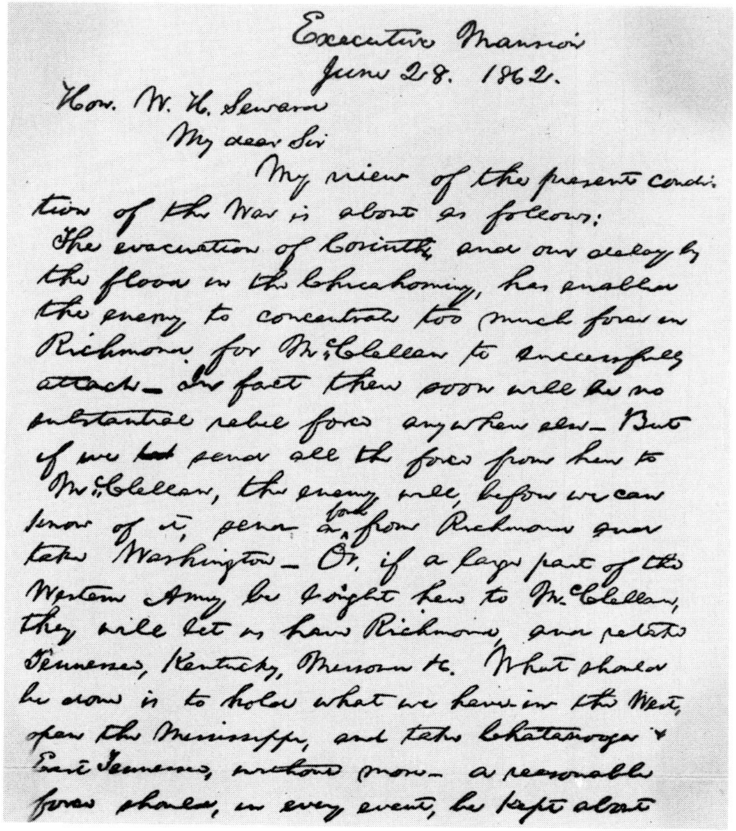

We are coming, Father Abraham, three hundred thousand more,
From Mississippi's winding stream and from New England's shore;
We leave our ploughs and workshops, our wives and children dear,
With hearts too full for utterance, with but a silent tear;
We dare not look behind us, but steadfastly before:
We are coming, Father Abraham, three hundred thousand more!

Executive Mansion
June 28. 1862.

Hon. W. H. Seward
My dear Sir

My view of the present condition of the War is about as follows:

The evacuation of Corinth, and our delay by the flood in the Chicahominy, has enabled the enemy to concentrate too much force in Richmond for McClellan to successfully attack. In fact there soon will be no substantial rebel force anywhere else. But if we send all the force from here to McClellan, the enemy will, before we can know of it, send a force from Richmond and take Washington. Or, if a large part of the Western Army be brought here to McClellan, they will let us have Richmond, and retake Tennessee, Kentucky, Missouri &c. What should be done is to hold what we have in the West, open the Mississippi, and take Chattanooga & East Tennessee, without more. A reasonable force should, in every event, be kept about

Washington for its protection. Then let the country give us a hundred thousand new troops in the shortest possible time, which added to McClellan, directly or indirectly, will take Richmond, without endangering any other place which we now hold, and will substantially end the war. I expect to maintain this contest until successful, or till I die, or am conquered, or my term expires, or Congress or the country forsakes me; and I would publicly appeal to the country for this new force were it not that I fear a general panic and stampede would follow. So hard is it to have a thing understood as it really is. I think the new force should be all, or nearly all infantry, principally because such can be raised most cheaply and quickly.

Yours very truly
A. Lincoln

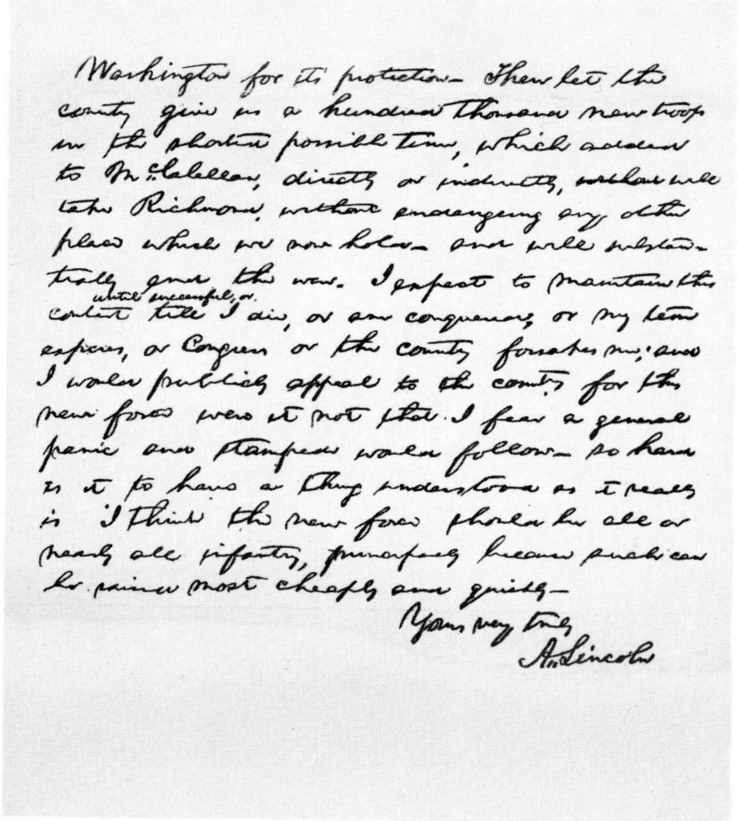

LINCOLN THE STRATEGIST gives his opinion about the military situation to the Secretary. With McClellan checked on the Peninsula, he hoped "to hold what we have in the West, open the Mississippi, and take Chattanooga and East Tennessee." Firmly he said: "I expect to maintain this contest until successful, or till I die, or am conquered, or my term expires, or Congress or the Country forsake me."

PINKERTON MEN WATCHED THE BRIDGES—many of them shaky and makeshift—over which supplies went to the front. With each advance, each retreat, some were destroyed; each time the engineers had to rebuild them. Alert detectives were everywhere.

157

HORACE GREELEY

HORACE GREELEY, the erratic editor of the New York *Tribune,* was impatient with the President's conciliatory attitude toward slavery. In an open letter printed in his paper on August 19, 1862; under the headline "The Prayer of Twenty Millions," he attacked Lincoln because he did not fight "Slavery with Liberty," accusing him of being "strangely and disastrously remiss" in his duty.

In August, 1862, Horace Greeley, the editor of the New York *Tribune* wrote to Senator Charles Sumner of Massachusetts: "Do you remember that old theological book containing this: 'Chapter One—Hell; Chapter Two—Hell Continued.' Well, that gives a hint of the way Old Abe *ought to be* talked to in this Crisis of the Nation's destiny."

Greeley was wrought up about Lincoln, who would not act to free the slaves. At the end of March he received a letter from the President in which Lincoln said that "compensated" emancipation, as proposed by Congress, and buying out all slaveholders in the border slave states should be urged "persuasively, and not menacingly upon the South."

Through his grapevine in the White House Greeley had been informed that the President had some kind of a new plan about the slaves—some-

thing different from his former policy of non-interference—but what this new policy might be, Greeley could not learn.

An intermediary reported to Lincoln that Greeley was angry about the slow progress of the war and especially about the President's neglect to make a direct attack upon slavery.

"Why does he not come here and have a talk with me?" asked Lincoln. Greeley had no desire to do that. He did not want to give the impression that he and his paper were influenced by the President.

Before the go-between reached New York to tell Greeley about the Emancipation Proclamation, the editor's open letter under the title "The Prayer of Twenty Millions" appeared in the *Tribune.*

In his letter Greeley accused the President of letting himself be influenced by certain fossil bor-

LINCOLN'S ANSWER TO GREELEY at the time when he had already decided on the Emancipation Proclamation but would not talk of it. The President, in his famous reply, wrote: "My paramount object in this struggle *is* to save the Union, and is *not* either to save or destroy slavery. If I could save the Union without freeing *any* slaves I would do it, and if I could save it by freeing *all* the slaves I would

der-state politicians, who wanted him to forget that "slavery is everywhere the inciting cause and sustaining base of treason." Greeley berated Lincoln, saying "that a great proportion of those who triumphed in your election . . . are sorely disappointed and deeply pained by the policy you seem to be pursuing with regard to the slaves of Rebels" and that the people of the country "require of you, as the first servant of the Republic . . . that you EXECUTE THE LAWS." Greeley further declared that the President was "strangely and disastrously remiss" in his duties "with regard to the emancipating provisions of the Confiscation Act," which were designed "to fight Slavery with Liberty."

It was a forceful attack which Lincoln could easily have refuted. All he had to do was to refer to the Emancipation Proclamation, which at that time was already written, reposing in his drawer.

But strangely, he remained silent about it. He wrote Greeley, defending his position, a position which he no longer held.

Lincoln had changed his mind about the slavery issue because of military and political reasons. The military consideration was to enroll the colored men in the Federal army, while the political one was that once the slaves were freed, neither England nor France could recognize the Confederacy.

Greeley complained to a friend that Lincoln had "added insult to injury by answering my 'Prayer of Twenty Millions,' which asked only for the honest enforcement of an existing law, as if it had been a demand for the abolition of slavery; thus adroitly using me to feel the public pulse, and making me appear as an officious meddler in affairs that properly belong to the government. No, I can't trust your 'honest Old Abe.' He is too smart for me."

do it; and if I could save it by freeing some and leaving others alone I would also do that. What I do about slavery, and the colored race, I do because I believe it helps to save the Union; and what I forbear, I forbear because I do *not* believe it would help to save the Union. I shall do *less* whenever I shall believe what I am doing hurts the cause, and I shall do *more* whenever I shall believe doing more will help the cause. I shall try to correct errors when shown to be errors; and I shall adopt new views so fast as they shall appear to be true views.

"I have here stated my purpose according to my view of *official* duty; and I intend no modification of my oft expressed *personal* wish that all men everywhere could be free."

THE BATTLE

OF

ANTIETAM

WHILE MCCLELLAN edged his way up the Peninsula, Lincoln created the Army of Virginia and placed all the forces around the capital under the command of John Pope. McClellan was relieved as General in Chief so he could concentrate entirely on the movement of the Army of the Potomac. But after Pope suffered a crushing defeat at Manassas on August 29 and 30, Lincoln once more asked "Little Mac" to take over the supreme command. The President told his Cabinet that he would take the sole responsibility for his decision.

Lincoln had no illusions about McClellan. He knew his shortcomings. He knew that "to attack or advance with energy and power is not in him;

to fight is not his forte," but he was aware also that in defensive operations no other General could match him. Besides, he needed McClellan so he told his Secretary of the Navy, Gideon Welles, "to reorganize the army and bring it out of chaos." Thus, early one morning, he drove to "Little Mac's" house and told him: "General, you will take command of the forces in the field."

McClellan was greatly pleased. He wrote to his wife: "Again I have been called upon to save the country. The case is desperate, but with God's help I will try unselfishly to do my best, and, if He wills it, accomplish the salvation of the nation."

In the next weeks the General cer-

SEPTEMBER 17, 1862, THE RAIL FENCE ON

tainly needed "God's help." Lee had started out with his army and invaded Maryland, and McClellan was to stop him. This time luck was on his side. An order of Lee's was found revealing the disposition of the Confederate troops, making McClellan jubilant. "Here is a paper with which if I cannot

Photograph by Alexander Gardner

THE BRIDGE AT ANTIETAM, captured by Federal cavalry on the night of September 16. In the ensuing battle, Union casualties mounted to 14,000 killed and wounded; Confederate losses were more than 11,000. Lee held his lines and moved back to northern Virginia.

THE HAGERSTOWN PIKE WHERE HOOKER'S BATTERIES ALMOST ANNIHILATED STONEWALL JACKSON'S CONFEDERATE TROOPS.

whip 'Bobbie Lee,' I will be willing to go home," he said, and wrote Lincoln that he was confident of success. The President replied tersely: "Destroy the rebel army if possible."

The great clash between the two armies came at Antietam in one of the bloodiest battles of the war.

The Union forces were doing well all along the line. If McClellan had been daring, he could have smashed the Confederate forces and the war would have come to an end. But, as always, he was cautious. He kept a whole corps in reserve and did not order them into battle. He allowed Lee to withdraw and

retreat into Virginia without pursuing him—thus forsaking a decisive victory.

To his superiors in Washington, the General reported complete success. To Lincoln such a dispatch meant that McClellan was pursuing Lee. But, alas, he was to learn better.

161

EMANCIPATION PROCLAMATION

SINCE EARLY June, 1862, the President—while waiting in the telegraph office for news from the battlefronts—had been working on a document. The superintendent of the office recalled that Lincoln "would look out of the window a while and then put his pen to paper, but he did not write much at once. He would study between times and when he had made up his mind he would put down a line or two, and then sit quiet for a few minutes. After a time, he would resume his writing, only to stop again at intervals to make some remark to me or to one of the cipher operators as a fresh dispatch from the front was handed to him."

He never did more than a single sheet a day, and each day he would read over all the pages, then revise them, carefully studying each sentence. In this way the Emancipation Proclamation was drafted.

In midsummer, 1862, Lincoln called a Cabinet meeting, and it was then that he revealed to his Secretaries that he was determined upon the adoption of the emancipation policy, as he felt that "the end of the rope on the plan of operations we had been pursuing" was reached, "and [we] must change our tactics, or lose the game!"

He emphasized that he had not called them together to ask their advice, "but to lay the subject-matter of a proclamation before them."

There was considerable discussion. Lincoln later told the painter Carpenter: "Various suggestions were offered. Secretary Chase wished the language stronger in reference to the arming of the blacks. Mr. Blair . . . deprecated the policy, on the ground that it would cost the Administration the fall elections. Nothing, however, was offered that I had not already fully anticipated and settled in my own mind, until Secretary Seward spoke. He said in substance: 'Mr. President, I approve of the proclamation, but I question the expediency of its issue at this juncture. The depression of the public mind, consequent upon our repeated reverses, is so great that I fear the effect of so important a step. It may be viewed as the last measure of an exhausted government, a cry for help; the government stretching forth its hands to Ethiopia, instead of Ethiopia stretching forth her hands to the gov-

THE CABINET LISTENS TO THE PRESIDENT as he reads the Emancipation Proclamation. This is one of the original sketches of the artist Francis B. Carpenter from which the famous painting now hanging in the Capitol at Washington was made.

CARPENTER'S PAINTING, 14 feet, 6 inches long, and 9 feet in height. L. to r.: Sec. of War Stanton; Sec. of Treasury Chase; the President; Sec. of Navy Welles; Sec. of State Seward; Sec. of Interior Smith; Postmaster General Blair; Attorney General Bates.

162

ernment!' " Seward said that the proclamation might be considered by many as the government's last *shriek.* " 'Now,' continued Seward, 'while I approve the measure, I suggest, sir, that you postpone its issue, until you can give it to the country supported by military success, instead of issuing it, as would be the case now, upon the greatest disasters of the war!' "

Seward's view struck the President "with very great force." It was an aspect of the case that, as he confessed, he had entirely overlooked. Thus, he put the draft of the proclamation aside, waiting for victory.

After the battle of Antietam, Lincoln "determined to wait no longer." He completed the second draft of the preliminary proclamation, and on the 22nd of September he called the Cabinet together. "Gentlemen," he said after reading a funny chapter from

MODELING FOR THE PAINTING. The painter, Francis B. Carpenter, sat for a photographer in the very position in which Secretary of State William H. Seward was to be portrayed. The artist also used the chair at right and books on the floor as models.

LINCOLN SITS FOR A PAINTING. Carpenter, the artist, took a photographer to the White House and posed the President as he was to appear in the Emancipation Proclamation painting. The author of this volume found this photograph among the Carpenter papers and published it first in the July 19, 1947, issue of the *Saturday Evening Post.*

STUDIES FOR THE PAINTING. These drawings from Carpenter's sketchbook, which Stefan Lorant unearthed in 1947, reveal the artist's meticulousness. Carpenter made many sketches of his subjects and details around them, both from life and from photographs.

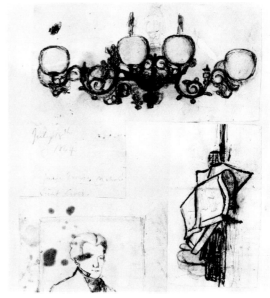

CARPENTER'S STUDIES OF THE DRAPERIES, DESK, CANDELABRA, PAINTING ON THE WALL AND PAPERS ON THE TABLE.

FACSIMILE OF PRESIDENT LINCOLN'S DRAFT OF THE PRELIMINARY EMANCIPATION PROCLAMATION, WHICH WAS ISSUED

the humorist Artemus Ward's latest book, "I have, as you are aware, thought a great deal about the relation of this war to slavery; and you all remember that, several weeks ago, I read to you an order I had prepared on this subject, which, on account of objections made by some of you, was not issued. Ever since then, my mind has been much occupied with this subject, and I have thought all along that the time for acting on it might very probably come. I think the time has come now. I wish it were a better time. I wish that we were in a better condition. The action of the army against the rebels has not been quite what I should have best liked. But they have been driven out of Maryland, and Pennsylvania is no longer in danger of invasion. When the rebel army was at Frederick, I determined, as soon as it should be driven out of Maryland, to issue a Proclamation of Emancipation such as I thought most likely to be useful. I said nothing to any one; but I made the promise to myself, and (hesitating a little)—to my Maker. The rebel army is now driven out, and I am going to fulfill that promise. I have got you together to hear what I have written down. I do not wish your advice about the main matter—for that I have determined for myself. This I say without intending anything but respect for any one of you. But I already know the views of each on this question. They have been heretofore expressed, and I have considered them as thoroughly and carefully as I can. What I have written is that which my reflections have determined me to say. If there is anything in the expressions I use, or in any other minor matter, which any one of you thinks had best be changed, I shall be glad to receive the suggestions. One other observation I will make. I know very well that many others might, in this matter, as in others, do better than I can; and if I were satisfied that the public confidence was more fully possessed by any one of them than by me, and knew

166

qualified voters of such state shall have participated, shall, in the absence of strong countervailing testimony, be deemed conclusive evidence that such state and the people thereof, are not then in rebellion against the United States.

That attention is hereby called to an Act of Congress entitled "An Act to make an additional Article of War" approved March 13, 1862, and which act is in the words and figure following:

> Be it enacted by the Senate and House of Representatives of the United States of America in Congress assembled, That hereafter the following shall be promulgated as an additional article of war for the government of the army of the United States, and shall be obeyed and observed as such:
> Article — All officers or persons in the military or naval service of the United States are prohibited from employing any of the forces under their respective commands for the purpose of returning fugitives from service or labor, who may have escaped from any persons to whom such service or labor is claimed to be due, and any officer who shall be found guilty by a court-martial of violating this article shall be dismissed from the service.
> SEC. 2. And be it further enacted, That this act shall take effect from and after its passage.

Also to the ninth and tenth sections of an act entitled "An Act to suppress Insurrection, to punish Treason and Rebellion, to seize and confiscate property of rebels, and for other purposes," approved July 17, 1862, and which sections are in the words and figure following:

> SEC. 9. And be it further enacted, That all slaves of persons who shall hereafter be engaged in rebellion against the government of the United States, or who shall in any way give aid or comfort thereto escaping from such persons and taking refuge within the lines of the army; and all slaves captured from such persons or deserted by them and coming under the control of the government of the United States; and all slaves of such persons found on [or] being within any place occupied by rebel forces and afterwards occupied by the forces of the United States, shall be deemed captives of war, and shall be forever free of their servitude, and not again held as slaves.
> SEC. 10. And be it further enacted, That no slave escaping into any State, Territory, or the District of Columbia, from any other State, shall be delivered up, or in any way impeded or hindered of his liberty, except for crime, or some offence against the laws, unless the person claiming said fugitive shall first make oath that the person to whom the labor or service of such fugitive is alleged to be due is his lawful owner, and has not borne arms against the United States in the present rebellion, nor in any way given aid and comfort thereto; and no person engaged in the military or naval service of the United States shall, under any pretence whatever, assume to decide on the validity of the claim of any person to the service or labor of any other person, or surrender up any such person to the claimant, on pain of being dismissed from the service.

And I do hereby enjoin upon and order all persons engaged in the military and naval service of the United States to observe, obey, and enforce, within their respective spheres of service, the act and sections above recited.

And the executive will in due time recommend that all citizens of the United States who shall have remained loyal thereto throughout the rebellion, shall (upon the restoration of the constitutional relation between the United States, and their respective states, and people, if that relation shall have been suspended or disturbed) be compensated for all losses by acts of the United States, including the loss of slaves.

In witness whereof, I have hereunto set my hand, and caused the seal of the United States to be affixed.

Done at the City of Washington, this twenty second day of September, in the year of our Lord, one thousand, eight hundred, and sixty two, and of the Independence of the United States, the eighty seventh.

Abraham Lincoln

By the President:
William H. Seward,
Secretary of State

ON SEPTEMBER 22, 1862. THE FINAL PARAGRAPH AND THE PRESIDENT'S SIGNATURE ARE IN THE CLERK'S HANDWRITING.

of any Constitutional way in which he could be put in my place, he should have it. I would gladly yield it to him. But though I believe that I have not so much of the confidence of the people as I had some time since, I do not know that, all things considered, any other person has more; and, however this may be, there is no way in which I can have any other man put where I am. I am here. I must do the best I can, and bear the responsibility of taking the course which I feel I ought to take."

The Cabinet agreed with the President's proposal.

The Secretary of State made a relevant suggestion. When Lincoln read the passage "That, on the first day of January, in the year of our Lord one thousand eight hundred and sixty-three, all persons held as slaves within any State or designated part of a State, the people whereof shall then be in rebellion against the United States, shall be then, thenceforward, and forever FREE; and the Executive Government of the United States, including the military and naval authority thereof, will *recognize* the freedom of such persons, and will do no act or acts to repress such persons, or any of them in any efforts they may make for their actual freedom," Seward interrupted the reading.

"I think, Mr. President, that you should insert after the word '*recognize*,' in that sentence, the words '*and maintain*.'" Lincoln replied that he had already considered that expression but had not introduced it because it was not his way to promise what he was not entirely *sure* that he could perform. But Seward insisted, and the words were added.

That very day the preliminary Emancipation Proclamation was made public, declaring that if the states then in rebellion did not return to their allegiance by January 1, 1863, the President would issue another proclamation whereby the slaves in those states would become "forever free."

A SAVAGE ATTACK ON LINCOLN drawn by Dr. Adalbert Volck shows Lincoln writing the Emancipation Proclamation with the devil holding the inkstand. The paintings on the wall depict the massacre at San Domingo after the abolition of slavery, and John Brown with a halo—"St. Ossawatomie." In the corner of the room the Statue of Liberty wears a baboon head; the curtain is fastened by a vulture.

"WORSHIP OF THE NORTH," AN ENGRAVING BY DR. VOLCK.

THE ATTACKS OF A BALTIMORE DENTIST

The German-born Adalbert Johann Volck (1828–1912) came to America in 1848 to escape military service in his homeland. In the new world he started out as an artist, then became a dentist.

In the early months of the Civil War he made a series of etchings assailing General Benjamin F. Butler ("Bombastes Furioso Buncombe"), who had moved with his troops into Maryland. In eight of his plates Dr. Volck lampooned the President, which he recanted in his later years. "I feel the greatest regret ever to have aimed ridicule at that great and good Lincoln," he wrote.

DON QUIXOTE AND SANCHO PANZA. Abraham Lincoln and his political general Benjamin F. Butler, "the Beast of New Orleans." A cartoon etching by Dr. Adalbert Johann Volck, the German-born Baltimore dentist, which was suppressed by the Federal government.

"GREAT AMERICAN TRAGEDIANS, comedians, clowns" entitled Volck this sketch.

LINCOLN AS NEGRO CHIEF, a Volck drawing based on a rumor circulated in the South.

"THE KNIGHT of the rueful countenance" —another Volck drawing against Lincoln.

LINCOLN VISITS ANTIETAM

FOR LINCOLN it was nothing new to go to headquarters near the battlefield and to encourage and boost his commanders into activity. On October 1 he went to General McClellan's camp and stayed there for several days.

The General's hesitancy depressed the President. One morning, while out for a walk, he asked his companion whether he knew what the sight before them was—the sight of the hundreds of army tents. The friend answered that it was the Army of the Potomac, to which Lincoln remarked bitterly: "So it is called, but that is a mistake; it is only McClellan's bodyguard."

After Lincoln returned to the capital, McClellan was given explicit orders to cross the Potomac while the roads were passable and give battle to

Lee. To do this he was promised liberal reinforcements.

But precious days passed, and the Army of the Potomac was still in camp. The General in his dispatches to Washington asked for more horses, more supplies, more of everything. Lincoln lost his patience—in a strong note he told McClellan that he must advance.

Once more McClellan asked for more cavalry; he argued with Halleck, telling the General in Chief why he could not start his move. At last November 1 was agreed upon as the date when the Army of the Potomac would go into action. Still McClellan went on with his complaints. When in a dispatch he wailed about his fatigued horses, Lincoln sent him a sarcastic

note asking what his horses had done since the battle of Antietam that made them so fatigued. The President would not accept any more excuses; either McClellan would take the offensive or he would be removed.

When McClellan did cross the Potomac, advancing cautiously, Lincoln saw that he would never be fast enough to catch up with Lee. So, in an order signed on the 5th of November, McClellan was relieved from his command—ending his military career. To the politician Frank Blair, who intervened on the General's behalf, Lincoln answered:

"I said I would remove him if he let Lee's army get away from him, and I must do so. He has got the 'slows.'"

OF LINCOLN'S COMING TO ANTIETAM, General McClellan wrote to his wife: "I incline to think that the real purpose of his visit is to push me into a premature advance into Virginia. I may be mistaken, but I think not." "Little Mac" faces the President; others, from l. to r.: Col. D. B. Sacket, Capt. G. Montieth, Lt. Col. N. B. Sweitzer, Col. G. W. Morrell, Col. A. S. Webb, Scout Adams, Dr. J. Letterman, and perhaps Capt. H. Loeb. Behind the President: Gen. Henry J. Hunt, Gen. Fitz-John Porter, Col. F. T. Locke, Gen. A. A. Humphreys, and at the right is Col. G. A. Batchelder. The identity of the top-hatted man inside the tent is unknown.

OCTOBER 3, 1862: LINCOLN IN McCLELLAN'S TENT. The President came to urge his hesitant General to make use of his Antietam victory, and go after Lee. But McClellan asked for time to reorganize his troops, asked for more supplies, asked for more horses. When Lincoln saw that McClellan's hesitation had allowed Lee's army to escape, he removed "Little Mac" from his command.

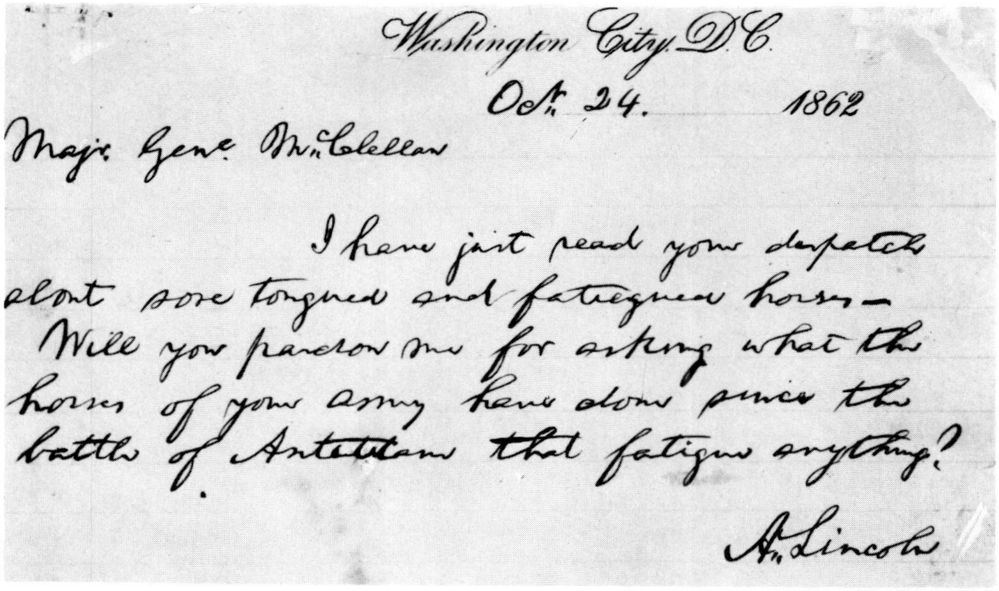

Washington City D.C.
Oct. 24. 1862

Maj. Gen. McClellan

I have just read your despatch about sore tongued and fatigued horses — Will you pardon me for asking what the horses of your army have done since the battle of Antietam that fatigue anything?

A. Lincoln

AN ANGRY LINCOLN sent this dispatch after McClellan—instead of pursuing Lee—complained of "sore tongued and fatigued horses." The President sarcastically asked "what the horses of your army have done since the battle of Antietam that fatigues anything?"

BURNSIDE SUCCEEDS McCLELLAN

"IN THE course of the 7th of Nov.," General McClellan recalled, "I heard incidentally that a special train had brought out from Washington Gen. Buckingham, who had left the railway very near our camp, and, without coming to see me, had proceeded

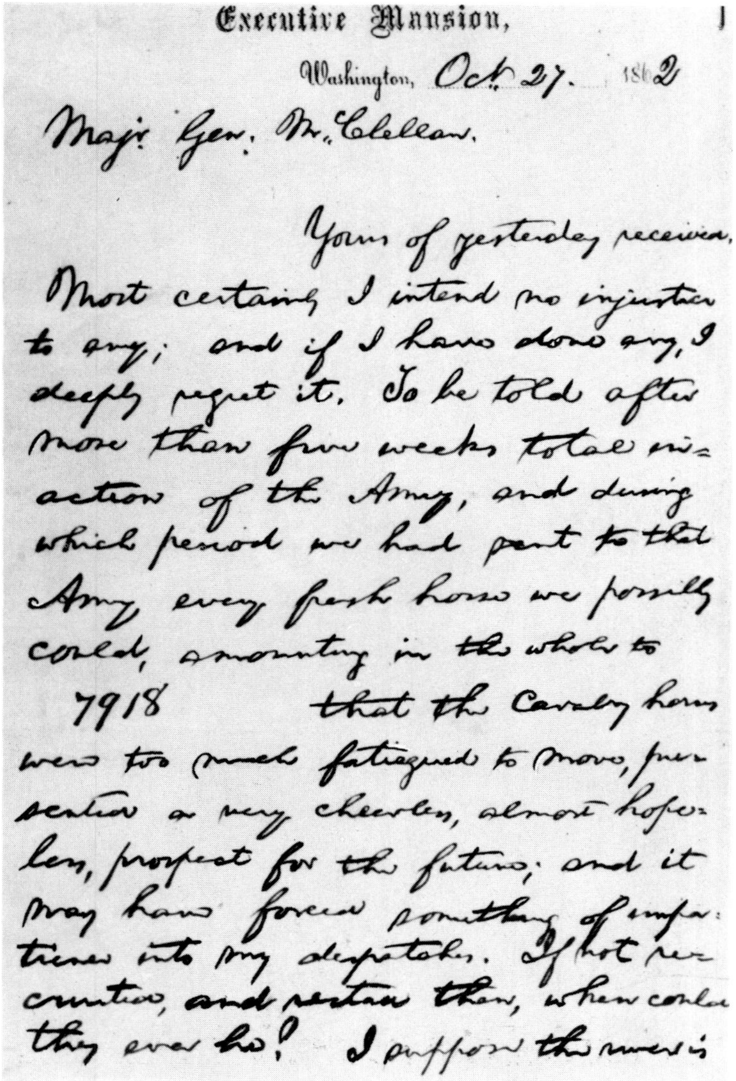

Executive Mansion,
Washington, Oct. 27. 1862

Maj. Gen. McClellan.

Yours of yesterday received. Most certainly I intend no injustice to any; and if I have done any, I deeply regret it. To be told after more than five weeks total inaction of the Army, and during which period we had sent to that Army, every fresh horse we possibly could, amounting in the whole to 7918 that the Cavalry horses were too much fatigued to move, presented a very cheerless, almost hopeless, prospect for the future; and it may have forced something of impatience into my despatches. If not recruited, and rested then, when could they ever be? I suppose the river is

rising, and I am glad to believe you are crossing.

A. Lincoln

A HUMBLE LINCOLN apologized to McClellan for sending the dispatch three days before. But "to be told after more than five weeks total inaction of the Army . . . that the Cavalry horses were too much fatigued to move, presented a very cheerless, almost hopeless prospect for the future." This was one of Lincoln's last communications to his General; nine days later McClellan was removed.

through a driving snow storm, several miles to Burnside's camp. I at once suspected that he brought the order relieving me from command, but kept my own counsel. Late at night I was sitting alone in my tent, writing to my wife. All the staff were asleep. Suddenly some one knocked upon the tent-pole, and, upon my invitation to enter, there appeared Burnside and Buckingham, both looking very solemn. I received them kindly and commenced conversation upon general subjects in the most unconcerned manner possible. After a few moments Buckingham said to Burnside: 'Well, General, I think we had better tell Gen. McClellan the object of our visit.' I very pleasantly said that I should be glad to learn it. Whereupon Buckingham handed me two orders of which he was the bearer."

The orders directed McClellan to turn over his command to Major General Burnside immediately. McClellan read the papers with a smile; then said: "Well, Burnside, I turn the command over to you."

The embarrassed Burnside, near tears, asked "Little Mac" to keep his command for a day or two until he could study the situation.

Poor Burnside! He was a friend of McClellan, he admired him and was indebted to him. Before the war, when he had failed in business, it was McClellan—then with the Illinois Central Railroad—who had procured for him a position with that company.

Burnside had no desire to take over the command. It had been offered him twice before, and twice he had declined, feeling that he was not competent for it. But now he could no longer refuse. He knew that if he would not take it, another corps general, Joseph Hooker, would be appointed, whom Burnside disliked.

Lincoln had chosen Burnside not only because he was successful in the North Carolina campaign, but because he needed an aggressive general who was willing to attack. Realizing the weakness of the Confederate position, he felt that if the Army of the Potomac would force Lee to battle, the war might come to an end.

GENERAL AMBROSE E. BURNSIDE, a handsome, dashing and brave soldier, succeeded McClellan as commander of the Army of the Potomac. A critic commented: "You have to know Burnside some time before you realize there is not much behind the showy front."

173

THE CAMPAIGN IN THE WEST

ONE DID not have to be a great military strategist to realize that to win the fight over the Confederacy, the Union must aim at two primary objectives —one, the capture of Richmond; the other, the opening of the Mississippi.

Lincoln, whose strategical thinking was far above that of his Generals, saw clearly why the opening of the Mississippi was such a vital part of Northern operations. The Confederacy received supplies from the West, from the states beyond the river, and all these goods were transported by the railroads which connected the Mississippi Valley with the East. Corinth, in northern Mississippi, and Chattanooga, in eastern Tennessee, were important railway junctions. If the Union could capture them, the Confederate armies in northern Virginia would be in dire peril.

The first important victories in the Western theater—the capture of Fort Henry on the Tennessee and Fort Donelson on the Cumberland River, in February, 1862—were won by an unknown commander, Ulysses S. Grant.

A short, stocky, silent man, forty-year-old Grant was not a success in life. He was graduated from West Point, where he was in the middle of his class; had taken part in the Mexican War, and after the war he had been ordered to the Pacific Coast, where he spent dreary years at Fort Vancouver and at the small frontier settlement of Humboldt Bay in California. With nothing much to do, with wife and children thousands of miles away, Grant took to the bottle, and drank more than was good for him. He was warned by his commanding officer—and finally he resigned.

After eleven years in the army he was out of the service. Penniless, he went to St. Louis to join his family.

Six dismal years followed. He tried to earn his living as a farmer, as a real estate agent, as a clerk in a customhouse. At last he became a clerk in his father's leather store at Galena.

After Fort Sumter, Grant tried to land a military appointment. In June, Governor Yates appointed him as Colonel of the 21st Illinois Volunteers, and a month later he was ordered to Mexico, Mo., where he was made brigadier general. Later, Frémont placed him in charge of a district with headquarters at Cairo, Illinois.

Grant's success at Fort Henry and Fort Donelson made his name popular all over the country.

But when in April in the bloody battle at Shiloh, he suffered tremendous losses in men and material, public opinion turned against him. He was accused of reckless exposure of the army and denounced as unfit "by both habit and temperament" for an important military command. The President was urged to remove the general "as an imperious necessity to sustain himself," but Lincoln said: "I can't spare this man—he fights."

After Shiloh, the bulk of the western forces under General Halleck moved cautiously against Corinth; when that city fell and Fort Pillow and Memphis were abandoned, the Mississippi was opened up as far as Vicksburg.

To occupy the Mississippi line, Lincoln selected two political generals— both greatly incompetent in war leadership—Nathaniel P. Banks of Massachusetts, and John A. McClernand of Illinois. Strangely, the President made no use of Grant. The best general in the West was left to guard communications near the river. Why did Lincoln act as he did? Professor T. Harry Williams gives this explanation: "The autumn of 1862 was simply a period when Lincoln's powers of human evaluation were not as sharp as usual. It was his bad time, his time to pick poor Generals."

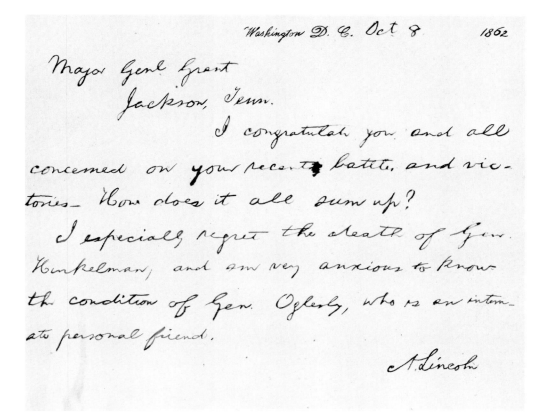

A CONGRATULATORY NOTE TO GRANT, written the very day when the Union forces under General Buell met the Confederates under General Bragg at Perryville. In his dispatch Lincoln inquires about Richard Oglesby, an old friend from his circuit-riding days.

This photographic print was made from an original Brady plate, showing that Brady used a four-lens camera, getting his subject four times on a single plate with one exposure. Thus, when cartes de visites were printed, one operation yielded not less than four pictures.

A GREAT GENERAL, Ulysses Simpson Grant, Brigadier General of the 21st Illinois Volunteers. He took Fort Henry on the Tennessee and Fort Donelson on the Cumberland River in February, 1862, victories which were jubilantly acclaimed in the North. But when, two months later, his forces were decimated in the battle of Shiloh, the outcry against him was so formidable that his career hung by a hair. Still, Lincoln stood by him.

OBERON AND TITANIA.

Oberon (Mr. President Lincoln). "I DO BUT BEG A LITTLE **NIGGER** BOY,
TO BE MY HENCHMAN."

Titania (Miss Virginia). "SET YOUR HEART AT REST.
THE **NORTHERN** LAND BUYS NOT THE CHILD OF ME."

ONE GOOD TURN DESERVES ANOTHER.

Old Abe. "WHY I DU DECLARE IT'S MY DEAR OLD FRIEND SAMBO! COURSE YOU'LL FIGHT FOR
US, SAMBO. LEND US A HAND, OLD HOSS, DU!"

A TENNIEL CARTOON in *Punch* (April 5, 1862) mirrors the reactionary attitude of the British ruling class. It lampoons Lincoln's suggestion to make financial compensation to the slave holders, and pay a fair and equitable price for their human properties.

RIDICULING LINCOLN'S EFFORT to enlist Negroes as soldiers, this Tenniel cartoon (*Punch*, August 9, 1862) was wide of the mark. From the time of their emancipation till the end of the Civil War, more than 180,000 former slaves enlisted under the Union flag.

"UP A TREE."
Colonel Bull and the Yankee 'Coon.
Coon. "AIR YOU IN ARNEST, COLONEL?"
Colonel Bull. "I AM."
Coon. "DON'T FIRE—I'LL COME DOWN."

CRITICIZING LINCOLN'S APOLOGY for the arrest of the Confederate Commissioners, Mason and Slidell. (*Punch*, Jan. 11, 1862).

AN ENGLISH WEEKLY

From the time of his election to the Presidency Lincoln faced the hostility of the English ruling class. They scorned his background, they laughed at his appearance, and they ridiculed his political philosophy. For them he seemed a buffoon, a simpleton.

Businessmen hate nothing more than to lose money, and the English manufacturers and merchants suffered heavy losses because the Northern blockade made it hard to British ships to carry goods to or from their customers in the southern part of the United States. Commerce with the Confederacy was hurt, the English merchants blamed Lincoln for it, and they hoped for a Confederate victory. Lincoln needed all his political sagacity to keep the mother country on the sidelines.

English anti-Lincoln sentiment found graphic expression in the Empire's leading satirical weekly, *Punch*. In its pages, the most celebrated Victorian cartoonist, one-eyed John Tenniel (1820–1914), who joined the weekly a decade before the Civil War and remained its chief contributor until the first world war some sixty years later, assailed the American President and the Union with merciless fervor. His political "big-cuts" were savage attacks.

His first drawing in *Punch*, "The American Difficulty," appeared on

PUNCH, OR THE LONDON CHARIVARI.—August 23, 1862.

LINCOLN'S TWO DIFFICULTIES.

Lin. "WHAT? NO MONEY! NO MEN!"

ENLARGING ON LINCOLN'S TROUBLES, this *Punch* cartoon (August 23, 1862) overstates the President's difficulties. True, the Union needed money; true, the Union needed soldiers, but true also that the North was determined to win the struggle it began.

PUNCH, OR THE LONDON CHARIVARI.—September 27, 1862.

THE OVERDUE BILL.

Mr. South to Mr. North:—"YOUR 'NINETY DAYS' PROMISSORY NOTE ISN'T TAKEN UP YET, SIRREE!"

CHIDING THE PRESIDENT for his Secretary of State's predictions that the war would end within three months, this cartoon appeared in *Punch's* issue of Sept. 27, 1862, barely five days after Lincoln announced to the country his preliminary Emancipation Proclamation.

FIGHTS LINCOLN

May 11, 1861; it shows a beardless Lincoln (the artist seemed unaware that Lincoln had grown a beard since his election) sitting before a fireplace holding a poker and exclaiming: "What a nice White House this would be, were it not for the Blacks."

From then on until February, 1865, when his last anti-Lincoln drawing appeared, Tenniel drew some twenty cartoons against the American President. Most of these were grossly unfair, cruelly misrepresenting the Northern position. Otherwise a mild and gentle man (he later became famous as the illustrator of Lewis Carroll's *Alice*), Tenniel turned into a ranting fanatic

on the subject of Lincoln.

Not until Lincoln's death did *Punch* change its tune. On May 6, 1865, shortly after the assassination, there appeared a large drawing by Tenniel: the mourning figure of Britannia laying a wreath on Lincoln's bier (see page 334); Columbia, prostrate with grief, kneels on one side of the bier, and on the other side kneels a freed Negro slave. It was Tenniel's and *Punch's* way of making amends for all the unjust criticism of Lincoln during the preceding four years. *Punch*, at last, at the somber moment of Lincoln's death, repented the savagery of its attacks on the American President.

PUNCH, OR THE LONDON CHARIVARI.—July 26, 1862.

THE LATEST FROM AMERICA;

BARTENDER LINCOLN works on a brew (*Punch*, July 26, 1862) with Bunkum, Bosh, Brag, Soft Sawder and Treacle.

177

THE BATTLE
OF
FREDERICKSBURG

THE CITY WAS WITHIN SIGHT. The Union forces under General Burnside were separated from Fredericksburg by the Rappahannock River. In this picture, taken of the city from the Union side of the river, a group of Confederate soldiers stand on the destroyed bridge.

BEFORE FREDERICKSBURG: FEDERAL

THE ARMY WAITED. As the pontoons on which they were to cross the Rappahannock had not arrived, Gen. Burnside halted his men. And while the Army of the Potomac waited by the river, the Confederates took up strong positions in the heights around Fredericksburg.

BURNSIDE WORKED hard, turning night into day, preparing his strategy. He knew that the President expected him to move fast, and he was determined not to fail him. Already on the 9th of November, only two days after his appointment, he had submitted to Lincoln his scheme, suggested moving the army to Fredericksburg and from there on to Richmond.

Neither Lincoln nor General in Chief Halleck was impressed with his plan. Halleck went to see Burnside and argued with him for its modification, but Burnside would not hear of this; his mind was set on moving down the Rappahannock, and he asked Halleck for pontoon bridges on which the army could cross to Fredericksburg. When the General in Chief returned

ARTILLERY IS READY FOR ACTION TO SUPPORT THE ADVANCE OF ITS TROOPS ACROSS THE RAPPAHANNOCK RIVER.

to Washington, he reported to the President, after which he wired Burnside: "The President has just assented your plan. He thinks it will succeed if you move rapidly, otherwise not."

Burnside started out with great confidence. He moved to Falmouth and might have taken Fredericksburg, but when he arrived at the Rappahannock and found that the pontoon bridges for which he had asked were not there, he gave orders to halt.

For a whole week the army was at a standstill, waiting for the bridges, giving Lee time to rush Longstreet to Fredericksburg; thus, before the pontoons arrived, Confederate troops were in entrenched positions at the heights of the city.

Burnside's bogging down worried

Lincoln; he traveled to Aquia Creek, spoke to him and urged him to move forward speedily. The President feared that Lee might endanger the Federals' crossing of the river, and suggested a diversified attack on several points. Burnside was against this; he was confident that he could cross the Rappahannock without any mishap. This he did, after the pontoons arrived.

On December 13 the Union forces moved against the fortified Confederate positions in a daring, frontal charge. The result was disastrous. As they marched forward, the Confederate guns opened up, mowing down their lines. Before nightfall the losses of the Union mounted to 12,000 men.

In his tent Burnside cried hysterically: "Oh! oh those men! Oh, those

men!" repeating the words over and over again. Realizing the disaster, he spoke of leading his reserve in a suicidal attack against the Confederate entrenchments, and had it not been for his officers, who restrained him from such an ill-considered move, he would have done it.

Fredericksburg was one of the worst reverses the North suffered—and a weeping Burnside took his troops back over the river. He offered no excuses; he took the blame for the debacle. To Halleck he wrote: "The fact that I decided to move to Warrenton on this line, rather against the opinion of the President, Secretary of War, and yourself, and that you left the whole movement in my hands, without giving me orders, makes me responsible."

Photograph by Capt. A. J. Russell

WHERE BURNSIDE LAUNCHED HIS ATTACK. At the southern end of Marye's Heights, outside Fredericksburg, ran a sunken road with a stone wall; behind this, Confederate infantry took up its position. "Seven assaults were made on the stone fence during the day," wrote one Confederate soldier, "and five thousand men were sent to eternity before Burnside convinced himself that the position was impregnable." This dramatic photograph was taken when the second attack of the road was made on May 3, 1863.

People in the North became despondent when they learned of the new defeat. Newspapers blamed Burnside for the terrible losses; his own officers implored the President to remove the General and not to leave the army under his command.

Burnside, too, went to Washington to see Lincoln. He proposed that he cross the Rappahannock once more and try the attack again, but the President cautioned him to wait.

The General kept on remonstrating with Lincoln, arguing for his plan. He told the President that regardless of his division commanders' opposition to his strategy, he wanted to carry it out. But if his resignation was desired, he would be ready to offer it, as nothing was further from his mind than to embarrass the President.

After some hesitation, Lincoln gave in; Burnside ordered the advance, and the troops went forward. However, by then the weather had become so adverse, raining without letup, that the move had to be halted.

Some of the high-ranking officers—General Hooker, General Brooks, General Newton, and others—were bitter about the "mud march" and were openly critical of the Commanding General's tactics. Hearing of this, the enraged Burnside prepared an order—the celebrated Order No. 8—dismissing the officers from the army. Henry J. Raymond, the publisher of the New York *Times*, happened to visit the headquarters while the excitement was at its height. The General showed him the order, and the worried Raymond rushed to Washington to tell Lincoln about it.

On January 24 Burnside once more journeyed to Washington and told Lincoln that he must either approve his order dismissing the officers or accept his resignation. It had to be one or the other. After such a peremptory request, Lincoln had no other choice but to relieve the General of his command.

Troubles never come singly. To military troubles were added political ones. While Lincoln tried to straighten things out in the command of the Army of the Potomac, he also had to fight a serious political battle. A cabal of Senators from his own party tried to force the reconstruction of the Cabinet. The President fought back with firmness, but in a desperate mood. To a friend he confided: "We are on the brink of destruction. It appears to me the Almighty is against us and I can hardly see a ray of hope."

LINCOLN'S THANKS to the Army of the Potomac after the Fredericksburg defeat.

A photograph by Mathew Brady or one of his assistants

AFTER THE BATTLE OF FREDERICKSBURG the Sixth Maine Infantry forms ranks. Young boys stand next to veterans; everyone who could handle a rifle was welcome. The death toll had been heavy; Union casualties amounted to more than 12,000.

THE BUTT OF RIDICULE

AFTER THE DRAFT RIOTS IN NEW YORK
this cartoon comment appeared in *Leslie's.*

Frank Leslie's Illustrated Newspaper, *August 29, 1863*

THE NAUGHTY BOY GOTHAM, WHO WOULD NOT TAKE THE DRAFT.
MAMMY LINCOLN—"*There now, you bad boy, acting that way, when your little sister Penn takes hers like a lady!*"

When Lincoln was riding with him on the way to his inauguration, President Buchanan had said: "If you are as happy, my dear sir, on entering this house as I am on leaving it and returning home, you are the happiest man in the country." The new President soon found himself treated more harshly than his predecessor had been.

The cartoonists, both at home and abroad, tore into him with merciless fervor. They drew him as a boorish clod; they pictured him as a bewildered simpleton. Frank Bellew assailed him in *Frank Leslie's Illustrated Newspaper* and unsigned cartoons lampooned him in *Harper's Weekly*, but the most violent attacks appeared in the English weeklies, with John Tenniel supplying the drawings for *Punch* and Matt Morgan for *London Fun.*

He was repeatedly caricatured with his military leaders—with General Halleck, with General Burnside—and with the egotistic General McClellan, and he was ridiculed with members of his Cabinet—Seward, Welles, and Stanton.

Lincoln withstood the attacks forthrightly, without a complaint. He bowed to the cartoonist's right of criticism, however cruel and unjust they were.

A practical reminder. 1862

Chicago Historical Society

TWO SKETCHES by Colonel David H. Strother, who drew under the pseudonym "Porte Crayon" for *Harper's New Monthly Maga-* zine. Both are from 1862 and both comment on difficulties with Army Chief McClellan, who was hesitant in taking Richmond.

Harper's Weekly, *January 31, 1863*

MANAGER LINCOLN, a *Harper's Weekly* cartoon published on January 31, 1863, at the time General Hooker took over the command of the army. The lengthy caption under the cartoon reads: "Ladies and Gentlemen, I regret to say that the Tragedy, entitled The Army of the Potomac, has been withdrawn on account of Quarrels among the leading Performers, and I have substituted three new and strik- ing Farces or Burlesques, one, entitled *The Repulse of Vicksburg,* by the well-known popular favorite E. M. Stanton, Esq., and the others, *The Loss of the Harriet Lane,* and *The Exploits of the Alabama*—a very sweet thing in Farces, I assure you—by the Veteran composer Gideon Welles (Unbounded applause by the COPPERHEADS)" The President was not popular with cartoonists.

Executive Mansion,

Washington, January 26, 1863.

Major General Hooker:

General.

I have placed you at the head of the Army of the Potomac. Of course I have done this upon what appear to me to be sufficient reasons. And yet I think it best for you to know that there are some things in regard to which, I am not quite satisfied with you. I believe you to be a brave and a skilful soldier, which, of course, I like. I also believe you do not mix politics with your profession, in which you are right. You have confidence in yourself, which is a valuable, if not an indispensable quality. You are ambitious, which, within reasonable bounds, does good rather than harm. But I think that during Gen. Burnside's command of the Army, you have taken counsel of your ambition, and thwarted him as much as you could, in which you did a great wrong to the country, and to a most meritorious and honorable brother officer. I have heard, in such way as to believe it, of your recent...

ON JANUARY 26, 1863, THE DAY AFTER GENERAL HOOKER WAS APPOINTED TO

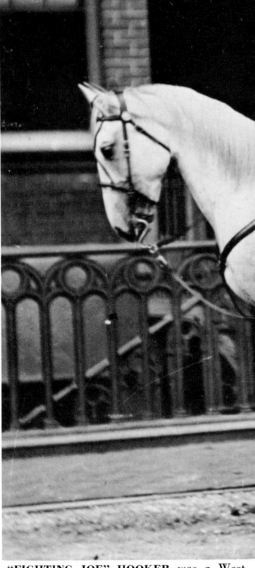

"FIGHTING JOE" HOOKER was a West Point graduate, had distinguished himself in the Mexican War, and was known as an

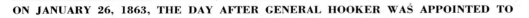

HOOKER SUCCEEDS BURNSIDE

THE MAN who replaced Burnside was handsome Joseph Hooker, "a gay cavalier, alert and confident, overflowing with animal spirits, and as cheery as a boy." The journalist Noah Brooks, who went with Lincoln in April, 1863, to visit Hooker in his camp on Falmouth Heights, opposite Fredericksburg, described him as "tall, shapely, well-dressed, though not natty in appearance, his fair red and white complexion glowing with health, his bright blue eyes sparkling with intelligence and animation, and his auburn hair tossed back upon his well-shaped head. His nose was aquiline, and the expression of his somewhat small mouth was one of much sweetness though rather irresolute, it seemed to me."

Hooker liked to talk, liked to boast, liked to intrigue. As soon as he got the appointment, he bragged of his perfect plans and exclaimed: "May God have mercy on General Lee for I will have none." Lincoln, noting this, said to Brooks with a sigh: "That is the most depressing thing about Hooker. It seems to me that he is overconfident."

The President asked the General to Washington, and the two had a protracted conversation, during which Hooker unburdened his soul against Halleck and asked for permission to report directly to the President. (Lincoln assented to this request, and

184

ly saying that both the Army and the Government needed a Dictator. Of course it was not for this, but in spite of it, that I have given you the command. Only those generals who gain successes, can set up dictators. What I now ask of you is military success, and I will risk the dictatorship. The government will support you to the utmost of its ability, which is neither more nor less than it has done and will do for all commanders. I much fear that the spirit which you have aided to infuse into the Army, of criticising their Commander, and withholding confidence from him, will now turn upon you. I shall assist you as far as I can, to put it down. Neither you, nor Napoleon, if he were alive again, could get any good out of an army, while such a spirit prevails in it.

And now, beware of rashness. Beware of rashness, but with energy, and sleepless vigilance, go forward, and give us victories.

Yours very truly
A. Lincoln

aggressive fighter. But he was prone to boast and brag and talk against his superiors. And he much liked his liquor.

COMMAND THE ARMY OF THE POTOMAC, LINCOLN HANDED HIM THIS LETTER.

for the next few months the General gave his reports to and received orders from the President. Halleck—the General in Chief—was not taken into their confidence; he had hardly any knowledge of what the President and his General were planning.)

At the end of their interview, Lincoln handed Hooker a letter, a note of warning and advice. In it he told the new head of the Army of the Potomac that he thought him "a brave and skilful soldier," but that during General Burnside's command of the army "you have taken counsel of your ambition, and thwarted him as much as you could, in which you did a great wrong to the country, and to a most meritorious and honorable brother officer."

Lincoln let Hooker understand that he was aware of his loose talk "that both the Army and the Gov-

ernment needed a Dictator. Of course it was not *for* this, but in spite of it, that I have given you the command. Only those generals who gain successes, can set up dictators. What I now ask of you is military success, and I will risk the dictatorship." He ended it with the famous and beautifully written sentences: "And now, beware of rashness. Beware of rashness, but with energy, and sleepless vigilance, go forward, and give us victories."

Some months later, Hooker, who always carried the President's letter in his pocket, read it in camp to Noah Brooks, commenting, "That is just such a letter as a father might write to his son. It is a beautiful letter, and, although I think he was harder on me than I deserved, I will say that I love the man who wrote it."

Harper's Weekly, *January 3, 1863*

AFTER THE DISASTROUS DEFEAT of General Burnside at Fredericksburg, the President was the target of violent newspaper attacks. In this unsigned *Harper's Weekly* cartoon, Columbia asks him: "Where are my 15,000 sons—murdered at Fredericksburg?" Lincoln: "This reminds me of a little joke . . . " Columbia: "Go tell your joke at SPRINGFIELD!!"

CROSSING THE RAPPAHANNOCK. Russell's brigade, the first division of the Sixth

HOOKER'S DEFEAT AT CHANCELLORSVILLE

DURING THE winter months of 1863, Hooker prepared the Army of the Potomac for the offensive, hoping to accomplish what Burnside had failed to do. In April, Lincoln came for a visit and was much impressed by what he saw. He took a review, and a journalist present reported that "it was noticeable that the President merely touched his hat in return salute to the officers, but uncovered to the men in the ranks."

While riding in an ambulance to see the First Corps, the President's vehicle passed over a rough road and the ambulance driver cussed loudly at his wild team of six mules. Lincoln touched the man on the shoulder:

"Excuse me, my friend, are you an Episcopalian?"

"No, Mr. President; I am a Methodist."

"Well," said Lincoln, "I thought you must be an Episcopalian, because you swear just like Governor Seward, who is a church warden."

Hooker had submitted a plan for Lincoln's approval. His strategy was to have the army cross above Fredericksburg, then send the cavalry to the rear of the Confederates to destroy their supply lines. This done, the infantry would start its attack, and Lee's army—caught between the cavalry and the infantry—would be destroyed.

All this sounded good on paper, but when it came to its execution, the cavalry moved so slowly that the rainy period began, and the offensive had to be stopped. Hooker had to wait till the weather would permit operations.

With the coming of spring the offensive started; by the end of April the Army of the Potomac had crossed the Rappahannock, and on the 1st of May it was moving toward Fredericksburg.

THE BATTLE OF CHANCELLORSVILLE. On May 2, 1863, General Couch's corps formed a line covering the retreat of the

Lee's army attacked the Union's advance units and Hooker had to fall back in a defensive position around the village of Chancellorsville.

The battle went against the Union, even though the Confederates lost more than 11,000 men. Stonewall Jackson, the South's most able General, was one of the casualties; he was

Harper's Weekly, *May 16, 1863*
Army Corps, goes over the river to storm the Confederate works on the opposite side.

Harper's Weekly, *May 2, 1863*
LINCOLN REVIEWS THE ARMY OF THE POTOMAC. On April 9 the President visited General Hooker and, with him, and other officers and their wives, took part in a grand review of the army. At the end of the month "Fighting Joe" Hooker led the army into battle; the Union forces were beaten by General Lee in the bloody encounter at Chancellorsville.

Harper's Weekly, *May 23, 1863*
Eleventh Army Corps. This sketch of the battlefield was made by A. R. Waud, the famous war artist for *Harper's Weekly*.

fired upon by his own men by mistake and died a week later from his wound. Hooker, who on the day of the battle was hurt by a falling pillar, his head and side injured, ordered the return of the army to the north side of the Rappahannock.

Lincoln was deeply disturbed. It had been arranged that, for security reasons, Hooker would not send him reports while the fighting was in progress. The dismal news that the army had once more to cross the river in retreat reached him three days after the event. Noah Brooks, who was at the White House when the dispatch arrived, noted that the appearance of the President as he read the telegram was piteous, his face "was ashen in hue" and he was a picture of despair. "Clasping his hands behind his back, he walked up and down the room, saying, 'My God! My God! What will the country say! What will the country say!'"

That same afternoon, Lincoln left for Hooker's headquarters. He asked the General about his intentions, and Hooker replied that he would continue his operations on the Rappahannock. Lincoln cautioned him to stay on the defense and take his time.

Early in June, Lee invaded Pennsylvania. Hooker suggested the same old plan—to cross the Rappahannock and attack the rear of the Confederate army at Fredericksburg.

Lincoln would not hear of it. In a telegram on June 5 he told Hooker: "I would not take any risk of being entangled upon the river, like an ox jumped half over a fence, and liable to be torn by dogs, front and rear, without a fair chance to gore one way or kick the other. If Lee would come to my side of the river, I would keep on the same side & fight him, or act on the defence, according as might be my estimate of his strength relatively [sic] to my own."

As Lee was marching northward, the President finally persuaded Hooker to follow the Confederate army and pull away from the Rappahannock. Lincoln revealed himself as a master of military strategy. "If the head of Lee's army is at Martinsburg and the tail of it on the plank road between Fredericksburg and Chancellorsville, the animal must be very slim somewhere. Could you not break him?" he asked his General.

But "Fighting Joe" seemed to have lost his fighting spirit. He acted like McClellan, asking for more troops, demanding more supplies, exaggerating the numbers of the enemy, and complaining against "Old Brains," General in Chief Halleck.

Exasperated, Lincoln relieved him from his command on June 28, appointing in his stead General Meade.

THE BATTLEFIELD OF GETTYSBURG WITH LITTLE ROUND TOP IN THE DISTANCE.

FIELD TELEGRAPHERS POSE FOR THE

Painting by Paul Philippoteaux for the Cyclorama at Gettysburg

ON JULY 3 GENERAL PICKETT LED HIS CHARGE AGAINST THE UNION POSITIONS.

A MEMORABLE PHOTOGRAPH FROM

THE BATTLE OF GETTYSBURG

"FIGHTING JOE" Hooker was succeeded by George Gordon Meade, the "old snapping turtle," who wanted to force Lee to a battle at Pipe Creek in Maryland, just south of the Pennsylvania border. But when the Confederates advanced toward Gettysburg, he had to change his plans. It was there that the two armies clashed in the greatest single battle of the Civil War. After fearful losses, the Union forces won, and Lee had to withdraw.

Lincoln hoped that Meade would use his advantage, pursue Lee, and destroy the Confederate army. But when he read Meade's congratulations to his troops, in which the General declared that the Union army must "drive from our soil every vestige of the presence of the invader," Lincoln said dejectedly: "Drive the invader from our soil. My God! Is that all?"

Through the General in Chief, "Old Brains" Halleck, he urged Meade to attack Lee before the Confederate army could cross the Potomac and escape to safety. But Meade hesitated.

Lincoln remarked bitterly that Meade would "be ready to fight a magnificent battle when there is no enemy to fight." He was right. While Meade procrastinated, the high waters of the Potomac receded and Lee

PHOTOGRAPHER AFTER THE FIGHTING.

GATEWAY TO THE CEMETERY—WHERE THE BATTLE RAGED MOST FIERCELY.

Photograph by Alexander Gardner

GETTYSBURG—TAKEN ON JULY 3, 1863.

Painting by Paul Philippoteaux for the Cyclorama at Gettysburg

THE BADLY BATTERED HEADQUARTERS OF GENERAL MEADE AT CULP'S HILL.

crossed the river, taking his army back to Virginia. Lincoln said in exasperation: "We had them within our grasp. We had only to stretch forth our hands and they were ours."

Halleck informed Meade that "the escape of Lee's army without another battle has created great dissatisfaction in the mind of the President, and it will require an active and energetic pursuit on your part to remove the impression that it [sic] has not been sufficiently active heretofore."

Meade read the note with fury and

asked to be relieved. Now Lincoln sat down and wrote a long and bitter letter —which he never sent. In it he said that he was deeply sorry when his words caused the General "the slightest pain." But he also told Meade of the fateful error which he had committed. "I do not believe you appreciate the magnitude of the misfortune involved in Lee's escape." The President could not understand why—so he continued—when Lee was blocked by the high water, Meade "stood and let the flood run down, bridges be built,

and the enemy move away at his leisure without attacking him." After all, he had twenty thousand veteran troops with him besides the army which had fought at Gettysburg, while Lee could not receive a single additional recruit. Lincoln was immeasurably distressed to see such a golden opportunity passed by. "He was within your easy grasp, and to have closed upon him would, in connection with our other late successes, have ended the war. As it is, the war will be prolonged indefinitely."

A HITHERTO UNKNOWN PHOTOGRAPH
AND
A BIT OF DOGGEREL IN HIS OWN HAND

That more than a century after his death an unknown photograph of Lincoln and an important manuscript in his own handwriting should come to light is just short of a miracle. Sleuths have searched every nook and corner and every attic for Lincoln material, and it was believed that they had brought to the surface everything worth saving. And yet here is the first publication of a hitherto unknown photograph, taken on Sunday, August 9, 1863, in the gallery of Alexander Gardner in Washington.

The story of the picture is a simple one. Lincoln presented the sepia-toned oval Imperial photograph (measuring 13 x 16 inches) to his secretary, John Hay, who hung it in his house. Before his death in 1905 he presented the picture to his son, Clarence L. Hay, and when Clarence died in the early part of 1969, his son, the noted naturalist, another John Hay, inherited it. It is through his courtesy that it is published here for the first time.

And here also is the long-lost doggerel which Lincoln penned some two weeks after the battle of Gettysburg and about three weeks before the photograph on the left was taken.

On July 19, 1863, John Hay wrote in his diary: "The Tycoon was in very good humour. Early in the morning he scribbled this doggerel & gave it to me." When Hay's diary was published in 1939, Tyler Dennett, its editor, noted: "Doggerel not in the diary."

But recently when David A. Jonah, the eminent librarian of Brown University, was scanning the Hay papers he came upon it in a folder labeled "Miscellaneous." It is through his courtesy that a reproduction of the original is printed on this page.

A DOGGEREL IN LINCOLN'S HAND, PENNED ON JULY 19, 1863:
Gen. Lee's invasion of the North, written by himself—
"In eighteen sixty three, with pomp, and mighty swell,
Me and Jeff's Confederacy went forth to sack Phil-del.
The Yankees they got arter us, and gin us partic'lar h-ll,
And we skedaddled back again, and didn't sack Phil-del."

A NEWLY DISCOVERED LINCOLN PHOTOGRAPH taken by Alexander Gardner in August, 1863, and presented by Lincoln to John Hay. It is reproduced here for the first time through the courtesy of John Hay's grandson.
Reproduced directly from the original

THE GUNS AT MORRIS ISLAND, S. C., were besieging Fort Wagner. On August 29 Lincoln telegraphed to his wife: "All quite well. Fort Sumpter [sic] is certainly battered down, and utterly useless to the enemy, and it is *believed* here . . . that both Sumpter and Fort Wagner are occupied by our forces. It is also certain that Gen. Gilmore has thrown some shot into . . . Charleston."

HIS FOURTH OF JULY MESSAGE. President Lincoln cautiously tells the country that news from the Army of the Potomac promises a great success. By then the Battle of Gettysburg was already won.

VICTORIES AT LAST

IF MEADE had pressed the Confederates after Gettysburg, he might have won a final victory. But even though Lee escaped, the tide for the Union had turned at last. A day after Gettysburg, General Grant had captured the fortified city of Vicksburg after a siege of many months, and once more the Father of Waters could flow "unvexed to the sea." In the West the picture looked brighter as well; Rosecrans' victories in Tennessee held hopeful promise for the future.

Lincoln told an officer before Grant captured Vicksburg that if the general were successful in taking the city, he "is my man and I am his the rest of the war."

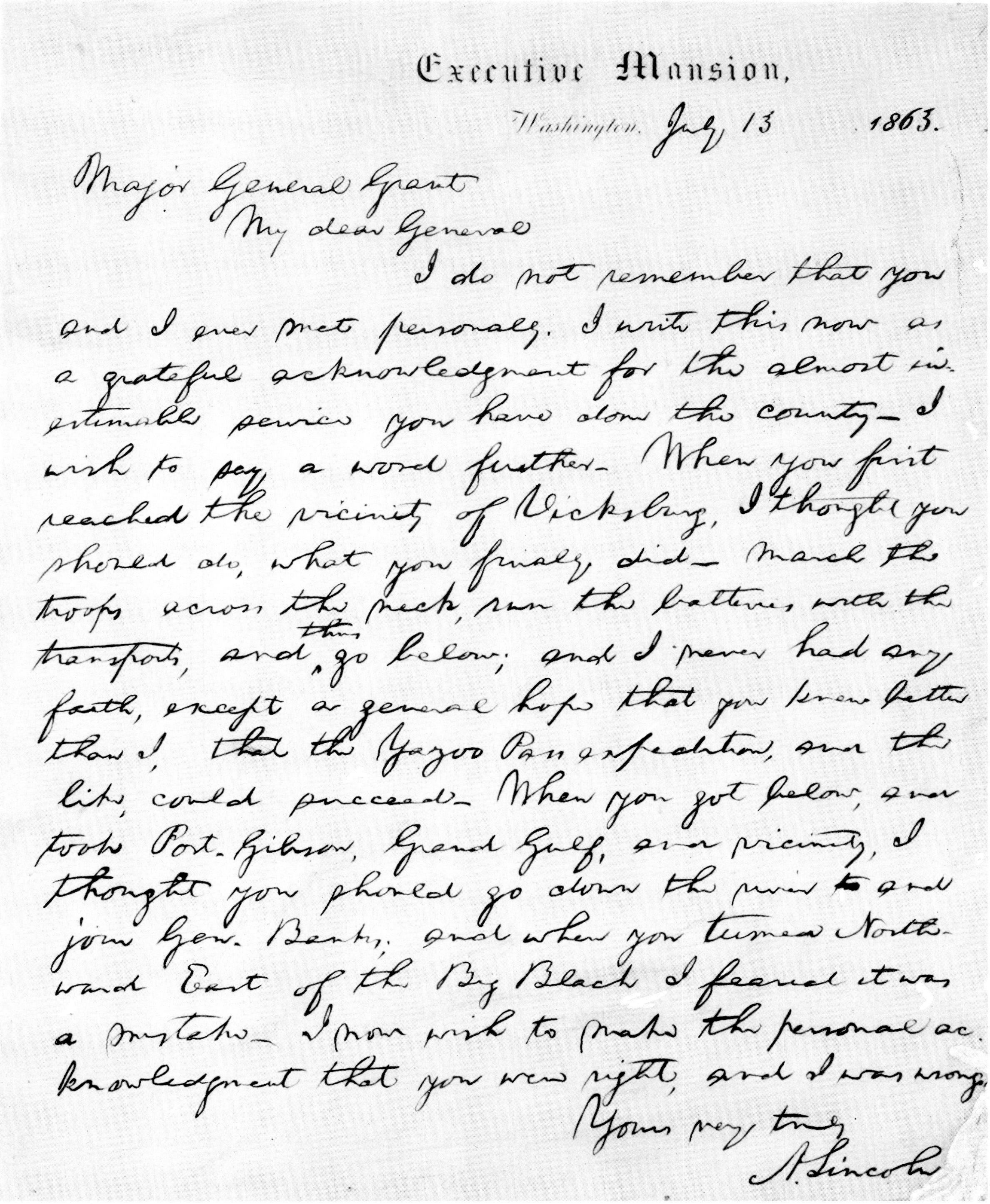

Executive Mansion,

Washington, July 13 1863.

Major General Grant

My dear General

I do not remember that you
and I ever met personally. I write this now as
a grateful acknowledgment for the almost in-
estimable service you have done the country— I
wish to say a word further. When you first
reached the vicinity of Vicksburg, I thought you
should do, what you finally did— march the
troops across the neck, run the batteries with the
transports, and thus go below; and I never had any
faith, except a general hope that you knew better
than I, that the Yazoo Pass expedition, and the
like, could succeed. When you got below, and
took Port-Gibson, Grand Gulf, and vicinity, I
thought you should go down the river and
join Gen. Banks; and when you turned Northward
East of the Big Black, I feared it was
a mistake— I now wish to make the personal acknowledgment that you were right, and I was wrong.

Yours very truly

A. Lincoln

THE PRESIDENT'S "THANK YOU" NOTE to Grant after the fall of Vicksburg. In it Lincoln humbly admitted that he had been critical of the General's strategy; however: "I now wish to make the personal acknowledgment that you were right, and I was wrong."

193

HUSBAND AND WIFE

A DAY AFTER HE WROTE of "Nanny Goat" he sat for this photograph with the Washington *Sunday Morning Chronicle*.

"MY WIFE is as handsome as when she was a girl," said Lincoln to a man during a reception, "and I a poor nobody then fell in love with her and what is more, I have never fallen out."

He loved her, there is no doubt of that; his letters which escaped destruction are proof of his devotion. When she was away from home, he felt miserable. Once when Mary was in New York shopping, Lincoln wired her: "The air is so clear and cool, and apparently healthy, that I would be glad for you to come. Nothing very particular, but I would be glad to see you and Tad." And when they quarreled, he had the blues. To a member of his Cabinet Lincoln said one morning gloomily that they must settle the case of a lieutenant for whom Mary had interfered, for "Mrs. Lincoln has for three nights slept in a separate apartment."

Their married life had probably no more disagreements than that of other married couples who have lived together for more than two decades.

She was jealous of him. There is an amusing conversation which Elizabeth Keckley, the mulatto seamstress, overheard while she was dressing Mary for a reception:

"Well, Mother, who must I talk with to-night—shall it be Mrs. D?" asked Lincoln with a merry twinkle in his eye.

"That deceitful woman! No, you shall not listen to her flattery."

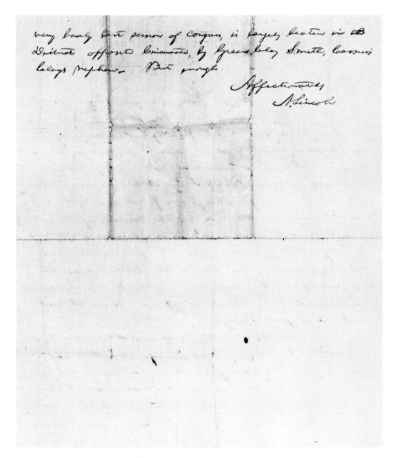

"TELL DEAR TAD POOR 'NANNY GOAT' IS LOST" wrote Lincoln to his wife, "and Mrs. Cuthbert and I are in distress about it." And this is how it happened. "The day you left, Nanny was found resting herself and chewing her little cud on the middle of Tad's bed; but now she's gone! The gardener kept complaining that she destroyed the flowers, till it was concluded to bring her down to the White House . . . the second day she had disappeared and has not been heard of since. This is the last we know of poor 'Nanny.' "

Executive Mansion,

Washington. June 9. 1863.

Mrs Lincoln

Philadelphia. Pa,

Think you better put "Tad's" pistol away — I had an ugly dream about him.

A. Lincoln

ON JUNE 9 he wired Mary at Philadelphia: "Think you better put 'Tad's' pistol away—I had an ugly dream about him." This is one of a series of dispatches from 1863. Copies of them, in Lincoln's writing, were found in the War Department's telegraph office.

"Well, then, what do you say to Miss C? She is too young and handsome to practice deceit."

"Young and handsome, you call her? You should not judge beauty for me. No, she is in the league with Mrs. D. and you shall not talk with her."

"Well, Mother, I must talk with some one. Is there any one that you do not object to?" trying to button his glove, with a mock expression of gravity.

"I don't know as it is necessary that you should talk to anyone in particular. You know well enough, Mr. Lincoln, that I do not approve of your flirtations with silly women, just as if you were a beardless boy, fresh from school."

"But, Mother, I insist that I must talk to somebody. I can't stand around like a simpleton, and say nothing. If you will not tell me who I may talk with, please tell me who I may *not* talk with." She told him, and the two went down happily to the reception.

Mary had many faults; she was high-strung, irrational, went into debt for clothes, was often tactless, meddling in affairs which were none of her business, but she was always a good mother, a loyal, faithful and loving wife.

Dated, June 15, 1863.

Mrs Lincoln

Philadelphia. Pa.

Tolerably well — Have not rode out much yet, but have at last got new tires on the carriage wheels, & perhaps, shall ride out soon.

A. Lincoln

ON JUNE 15 LINCOLN REPORTS BUYING TIRES FOR THE CARRIAGE WHEELS.

Washington. D. C. Sept. 21, " 1862

Mrs A Lincoln

Fifth Avenue Hotel

New, York

The air is so clear and cool, and apparently healthy, that I would be glad for you to come. Nothing very particular, but I would be glad see you and Tad,

A. Lincoln

ON SEPTEMBER 21 MARY WAS TOLD THAT HE WOULD BE GLAD TO SEE HER.

THE GETTYSBURG ADDRESS

AFTER THE battle of Gettysburg, thousands of dead Blues and Grays lay on the fields, united in their stillness, to be dug into the earth wherever they had fallen.

The people of Gettysburg were greatly disturbed by the conditions. They felt that the fallen soldiers ought to be gathered from their temporary interment and buried at a spot designated for that purpose.

The Governor of Pennsylvania asked one of Gettysburg's leading citizens, David Wills, to make a report on the matter, and Wills suggested the creation of a national soldiers' ceme-

tery, to be maintained by the states whose sons had fallen in the battle. His idea was accepted. Seventeen acres of land were bought in the name of Pennsylvania; the cost of the ground and the burials was apportioned among the states in the ratio of their congressional representation. Illinois, who had only six soldiers buried in Gettysburg, paid $12,000, yet there was no dissent.

The work of removal and reinterment of the bodies began on October 27, 1863, and was completed six months later. The total number of reinterments at that time numbered 3,512.

Before the work began, elaborate

preparations were made to dedicate the burial ground with imposing ceremonies.

October 23, 1863, was the date set, and Edward Everett, one of the country's foremost orators, was invited to deliver the principal address. Everett was willing to speak, if only the time to prepare his speech were not so short. He suggested a later date. The committee agreed, and postponed the ceremonies to Thursday, November 19.

Invitations were sent out to the President, members of the Cabinet, high-ranking military officers, and other distinguished persons to take

JUST BEFORE GOING TO GETTYSBURG Lincoln visited Gardner's photographic parlor in Washington on Seventh Street to have his picture taken. Noah Brooks, the journalist, later remembered that as they were going down the stairs of the White House the President

rushed back and returned with a large envelope containing the advance copy of Everett's oration, a one-page supplement to a Boston newspaper. Lincoln wanted to read it between sittings, but he became "engaged in talk" and left it lying on the little table.

196

THE PRESIDENT WITH HIS TWO SECRETARIES, John G. Nicolay and John Hay (standing); a photograph taken by Alexander Gardner. On Sunday, November 8, 1863, John Hay wrote in his diary: "Went with Mrs. Ames to Gardner's Gallery & were soon joined by Nico and the Prest. We had a great many pictures taken. Some of the Prest, the best I have seen. Nico & I immortalized ourselves done in group with Prest." Nicolay thought the background too bare, so he had the President's White House room painted in.

"A FEW APPROPRIATE REMARKS"

THE FIRST DRAFT OF THE GETTYSBURG ADDRESS; the first page in ink, the second in pencil. Of the address, Lincoln made at least six copies. The first draft was probably written in Washington, the second one in David Wills' house at Gettysburg the morning he delivered the address; the third was written out a few days later at the request of Wills, the fourth at the request of Edward Everett, the fifth for the historian and diplomat George Bancroft, and the sixth for the autographed leaves which were to be sold at the Soldiers' and Sailors' Fair in Baltimore, April 1864.

Students who analyzed the Gettysburg address found that it had 272 words (there are that many in the fifth and sixth drafts, while the first draft had but 239), of which five were one-letter words (the article "a"), forty-six were of two letters, forty-four of three letters, fifty-six of four letters, thirty of five letters, twenty-five of six, thirteen of seven, and the rest of eight or more. Lincoln liked to use short words. Of his address, 204 were a single syllable each, 50 of two syllables, and only 18 of three or more. In his speech not once did he employ the pronoun "I."

part at the consecration ceremony.

Lincoln was not asked to make a speech. As one of the committee members said, it was not thought that the President would be able "to speak upon such a great and solemn occasion as that of the memorial services." But, as Lincoln—much to the surprise of the committee—had accepted the invitation, he was asked "to set apart formally these grounds to their sacred use by a few appropriate remarks."

Lincoln was to leave Washington for Gettysburg on Wednesday, the 18th, accompanied by Secretary of State William H. Seward, his Secretary of the Interior, John Palmer Usher, and Montgomery Blair, his Postmaster General.

General James B. Fry, from the War Department, was his special escort, and when he came to the White House, urging him to hurry or they would miss the train, the President told the story of the man in Illinois who was being conveyed to the gallows. As the spectators were hurrying past his cart, he called out: "Boys, you needn't be in such a hurry; there won't be any fun till I get there."

The presidential train reached Gettysburg in the evening, and Lincoln was escorted to David Wills' house, where he was to stay the night. After dinner a band came to serenade him and he was called upon for a speech. He told the crowd that as he had no speech to make, he wanted only to thank them for the compliment. "In my position it is sometimes important that I should not say any foolish things," he said, when someone inter-

ONE OF HIS BEST-KNOWN LIKENESSES. It was taken by Alexander Gardner, probably on November 8, 1863, eleven days before Lincoln delivered the Gettysburg Address.

rupted: "If you can help it." There was laughter and Lincoln replied: "It very often happens that the only way to help it is to say nothing at all."

Then he went to his room, laid out his papers and began to write. About eleven o'clock William, his colored servant, came down in search of Mr. Wills. Lincoln asked his host where he could find Seward, as he desired to talk with him. Wills was ready to fetch the Secretary of State from the Harper house next door, but Lincoln demurred. "No, I will go and see him." The two went out together, the President carrying the sheets of paper on which he had been writing. For half an hour he remained with Seward, discussing his address.

The story that Lincoln wrote his speech on the train from Washington to Gettysburg has nothing to it. It is possible that he looked at it, penciling some alterations on the pages while he traveled, but as to the writing—this was first done in Washington.

His draft needed two sheets of the Executive Mansion letter paper. On the first there were nineteen lines written carefully with ink; the second one was written with pencil. There is the probability that Lincoln had discarded the first draft of the second page. Perhaps he was not pleased with the ending and rewrote it in Gettysburg at the Wills' house, and when it was ready, he took it to Seward to ask his opinion of it.

Next morning, after breakfast, John G. Nicolay, his private secretary, found him copying the address on the same kind of paper which he had used for the penciled first draft of his second page.

THE BIG DAY AT GETTYSBURG. Union troops are marching through the village; other thousands of people are waiting at the cemetery to take part in the consecration ceremonies.

THE ONLY PHOTOGRAPH WHICH SHOWS

Josephine Cobb, the eminent iconographer of the National Archives, found the negative of this photograph, the only one in which the platform can be clearly seen in the distance. After the blocked-out area was enlarged many hundreds of times, the figure

200

LINCOLN AT THE CONSECRATION CEREMONIES HELD AT THE GETTYSBURG NATIONAL CEMETERY ON NOVEMBER 18, 1863.

of Lincoln sitting at the platform became visible (as is shown on the next page). The conventional story about the Gettysburg photograph, which was believed by everyone until the discovery of this picture, was that a photographer had placed himself before the platform with his camera to take the President as he delivered his oration. But before he had time to uncap the lens to expose the unwieldy wet plate negative, Lincoln had finished his speech (it took him scarcely more than two minutes to deliver his 239-word-long address). Thus it was thought that no photograph existed of Lincoln at Gettysburg. Fortunately, as this picture proves, another photographer was there. He stood farther away and made his exposure picturing Lincoln on the platform.

201

LINCOLN AT GETTYSBURG. The enlarged section of the view on the previous page with Lincoln on the platform. It was only a short time before that he had dismounted from the horse that carried him in the colorful procession to the cemetery. But it was some three hours more before his turn would come and the man at his right, his friend, Ward Hill Lamon, introduced him to the assemblage.

The new draft, written in ink, covering again two pages and without erasure, was the one which he held in his hand while he delivered his speech in the afternoon.

The ceremonies began at ten o'clock in the morning. The band played, and through the streets of Gettysburg the procession moved toward the cemetery. Lincoln, dressed in black and wearing his tall hat and white gauntlets, rode in the midst of it.

Arriving at the cemetery, the military and civic bodies took up their positions; a prayer was said, and then Edward Everett began his oration, lasting for about two hours.

"He spoke without reference to his manuscript or consultation of any notes. He had gone carefully over his address as written and had timed it and marked in the margin just what portion he would omit. His mind and utterance moved from paragraph to paragraph with shrewd tread. His sentences were perfectly balanced. Even his gestures appeared to have been, and probably had been, rehearsed and were faultless. It was oratory at its classic best."

When Everett finished, a hymn was sung, and then Ward Hill Lamon introduced the President of the United States.

Lincoln appeared to be uneasy. While Everett was speaking, he drew out his manuscript, adjusted his spectacles, and read it over once more. And as he stood up, he held his pages firmly in both of his hands. His voice was thin and high; he always began in that way when he spoke out of doors. According to the Associated Press reporter, his words were frequently interrupted by applause, but others who were present did not recall that the audience acclaimed his words.

Lincoln was on his feet less than three minutes; after the two-hour oratory his address did not sound like much. The audience felt disappointed. He himself thought that the speech did not "scour" and that it was a "flat failure." Talking to Lamon about it later, he said: "I tell you, Hill, that speech fell on the audience like a wet blanket. I am distressed about it. I ought to have prepared it with more care."

"On the platform from which Mr. Lincoln delivered his address, and only a moment after it was concluded, Mr. Seward turned to Mr. Everett and asked him what he thought of the President's speech. Mr. Everett replied, 'It is not what I expected from

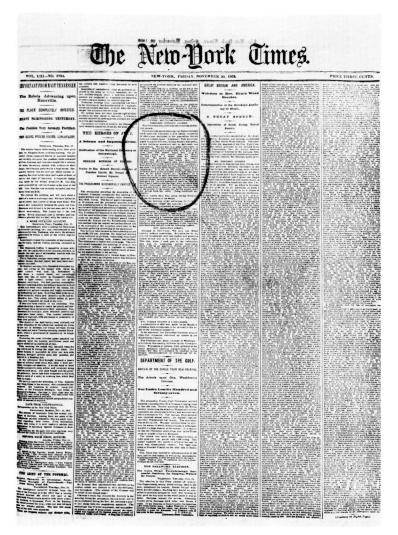
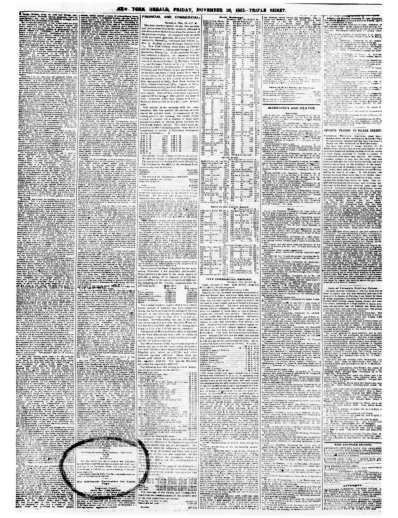

HOW THE NEWSPAPERS REPORTED THE SPEECH. The New York *Times* printed it in full, though without editorial comment; the New York *Herald* mentioned it only as "Dedicatory remarks of the President of the United States" without reporting what he said.

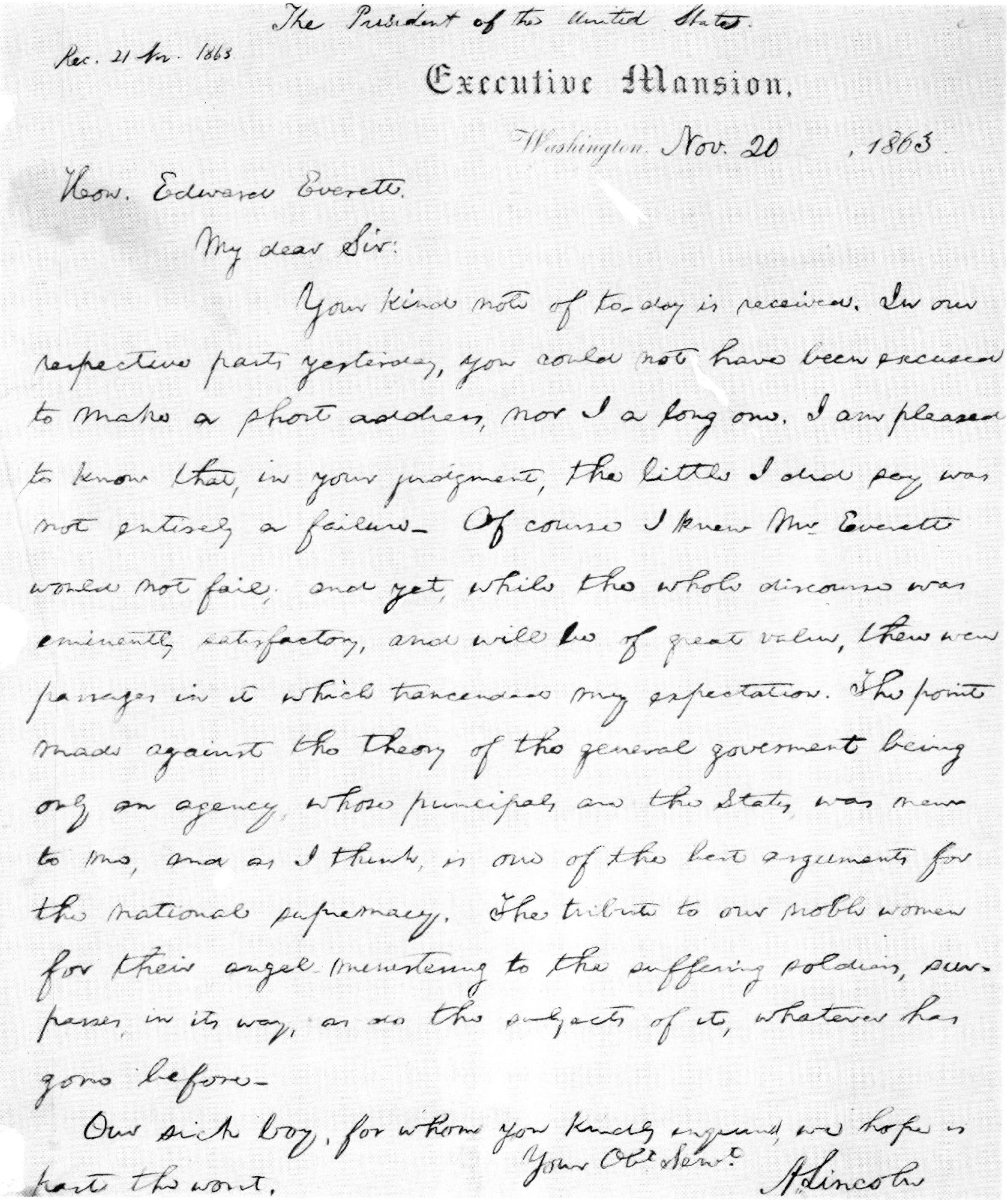

The President of the United States.

Executive Mansion,

Washington, Nov. 20 , 1863.

Hon. Edward Everett.

My dear Sir:

Your kind note of to-day is received. In our respective parts yesterday, you could not have been excused to make a short address, nor I a long one. I am pleased to know that, in your judgment, the little I did say was not entirely a failure. Of course I knew Mr. Everett would not fail; and yet, while the whole discourse was eminently satisfactory, and will be of great value, there were passages in it which transcended my expectation. The point made against the theory of the general government being only an agency, whose principals are the States, was new to me, and as I think, is one of the best arguments for the national supremacy. The tribute to our noble women for their angel-ministering to the suffering soldiers, surpasses, in its way, as do the subjects of it, whatever has gone before.

Our sick boy, for whom you kindly inquire, we hope is past the worst,

Your Obt. Servt.

A. Lincoln

"I AM PLEASED TO KNOW," wrote Lincoln to Edward Everett, the principal speaker at the Gettysburg ceremonies, who congratulated him a day after the event, "that in your judgement the *little* I did say was not entirely a failure." Lincoln valued Everett's opinion; he admired him as a great orator, and said that he had never received a compliment he prized more highly than that of Everett.

him. I am disappointed.' Then in his turn Mr. Everett asked, 'What do you think of it, Mr. Seward?' The response was, 'He has made a failure, and I am sorry for it. His speech was not equal to him.' Mr. Seward then turned to me and asked, 'Mr. Marshal, what do you think of it?' I answered, 'I am sorry to say that it does not impress me as one of his great speeches.' "

About three o'clock in the afternoon Lincoln got back to the Wills' house. His duties were not yet done. People came to shake his hand at a reception, and then he had to walk over to the Presbyterian Church, where a patriotic meeting had been announced for five o'clock.

He marched through the streets with John Burns, cobbler and constable of the village, who had distinguished himself in the battle of his home town.

When it was time to leave for the station, Joseph L. Gilbert, the reporter for the Associated Press, stepped up to the President, asking him for the manuscript of his speech to compare it with his own shorthand notes. Lincoln handed it to him, and Gilbert hastily compared it with his own transcript.

On the journey back to Washington, the President was in low spirits. He talked little. He lay down on one of the side seats of the carriage with a wet towel across his forehead.

Next day he was not feeling well, still he got out of bed to see a woman whose husband had been sentenced to be shot. Lincoln wired General Meade asking him to suspend the execution.

As it turned out, the President suffered from smallpox. Though most of the time he had to stay in bed, this did not frighten office seekers away. "Come in," called he cheerfully from his bed. "I have something now that I can give to everybody."

His address at Gettysburg was still on his mind. He was curious to see what the newspapers would say about it. But most of them were silent. The larger papers did not comment on it editorially. Neither Horace Greeley in the *Tribune* nor Henry J. Raymond in the *Times* nor James Gordon Bennett in the *Herald* mentioned it. And those who took notice of it charged that

Executive Mansion,
Washington, Nov. 20 . 1863.

Major Gen. Meade
Army of Potomac

An intelligent woman deep distress, called this morning, saying her husband, a Lieutenant in the A. P., was to be shot next Monday for desertion; and putting a letter in my hand, upon which I relied for particulars, she left without mentioning a name, or other particular by which to identify the case. On opening the letter I found it equally vague, having nothing to identify by, except her own signature, which seems to be "Mrs" "Anna S. King" I could not again find her. If you have a case which you shall think is probably the one intended, please apply my despatch of this morning to it.

A. Lincoln

A DAY AFTER THE GETTYSBURG ADDRESS Lincoln went about his business as usual, though he was not feeling well. It soon turned out that he had the smallpox. On November 20 the President saw "an intelligent woman in deep distress," who begged him to interfere on behalf of her husband, who "was to be shot next Monday for desertion." Lincoln promised to help, which was made difficult as "she left without mentioning a name." Still, he sent General Meade a dispatch, and followed it up by an explanatory letter.

Lincoln had desecrated the graves of Union soldiers by making a stump speech in a national cemetery.

The *Patriot and Union* of Harrisburg, Pennsylvania, wrote: "We pass over the silly remarks of the President; for the credit of the nation we are willing that the veil of oblivion shall be dropped over them and that they shall no more be repeated or thought of." The Chicago *Times* and the Springfield *Register* were equally caustic.

The first favorable comment came from the correspondent of the Chicago *Tribune*, who held that "The dedicatory remarks by President Lincoln will live among the annals of man." This sentiment was not shared by the London *Times*. That newspaper wrote: "The ceremony was rendered ludicrous by some of the sallies of that poor President Lincoln, who seems determined to play, in this great American union, the part of the famous Governor of Barataria. Anything more dull and commonplace it wouldn't be easy to produce."

The first long and appreciative report appeared in Massachusetts. The Springfield *Republican* recognized the greatness of the speech and advised its readers: "Turn back and read it over, it will repay study as a model speech. Strong feelings and a large brain were its parents—a little painstaking, its accoucheur."

1861   **"THE FATE OF THE RAILSPLITTER,"** a crudely done Southern drawing, lacks craftsmanship and imagination. It was published in Richmond in October.

SOUTHERN THRUSTS

"Abraham Lincoln got elected!/Bigger fool than we expected!" wrote a versifier in the *Southern Confederacy* in 1861. The press in the South was venomous in its attacks on Lincoln; for Southern newspapermen he was the devil incarnate, the cause of all trouble, a despot who trampled on the Constitution.

The Richmond *Enquirer* described him on the very day of his inauguration as the "delightful combination of a Western country lawyer with a Yankee Bar-Keeper" whose speeches consisted of "condensed lumps of imbecility, buffoonery, and vulgar malignity."

The cartoons against him were crude and simplistic. Most Southern papers did not use illustrations, but two of them—the *Southern Punch* and *The Southern Illustrated News*—did, and here is what they printed.

THE SOUTHERN ILLUSTRATED NEWS.

MASKS AND FACES.

1862   **KING ABRAHAM BEFORE AND AFTER** issuing the Emancipation Proclamation. The scroll reads Jan. 1, 1863, the date of freedom for the slaves. A woodcut in the November 8, 1862, issue of *The Southern Illustrated News.*

Abduction of the Yankee Goddess of Liberty.
THE PRINCE OF DARKNESS (ABRAHAM LINCOLN) BEARS HER AWAY TO HIS INFERNAL REGIONS.

GODDESS—Monster of Perdition, let me go !
ABRAHAM—Never ! You have been preaching about the Constitution too long already. I was the first to rebel against constituted authority. "Hell is murky !" You go thither !

1863   **LINCOLN AS SATAN**—a drawing in the November 14, 1863 number of *Southern Punch.*

1863 **"MASTER ABRAHAM GETS A NEW TOY"** is the title of this drawing from *The Southern Illustrated News* of February 21, 1863. The President plays with his new general, "Fighting Joe" Hooker. Lincoln's other military leaders—seven of them—lie broken and discarded upon the table and on the shelves.

1864 **"I WISH I WAS IN DIXIE"** sings Lincoln the troubadour. Other cartoonists in the North and in England also caricatured him as a singer of plaintive songs.

1863 **"SCHOOLMASTER LINCOLN AND HIS BOYS"**—the badly mauled generals McClellan, Pope, Banks, and Burnside. He threatens to spank the "worthless set."

ON FEBRUARY 9, 1864, LINCOLN VISITED BRADY'S GALLERY, where he was photographed in various poses. Some memorable pictures—like the one on the opposite page showing him with his son —were made that day. The photographer who took them was not actually Brady, to whom they were formerly attributed, but one of his camera operators, Anthony Berger.

The profile (left), which is used on our penny, and the portrait (right), which adorns our five-dollar bill, were made on this date.

BRADY PHOTOGRAPHS LINCOLN, an imaginary rendition by C. C. Beall which he painted for the Lincoln National Life Insurance Company, Fort Wayne, Indiana.

A BRADY SITTING

One day in 1863 a young lieutenant and his two friends were in Brady's Gallery to have their pictures taken when John Nicolay, Lincoln's secretary, entered with the message that the President was downstairs in his carriage. The young men relinquished their turn and watched with awe as Lincoln was photographed.

Twenty-year-old Lieutenant John L. Cunningham recalled that the President was in a jovial mood and bantered with the photographer, the Frenchman Thomas Le Mere. When Le Mere said that because of the great demand for a full-length portrait he would like to try one, Lincoln put on his pixie look. Could that be done on a single negative? he asked impishly. "You see, I'm six feet four in my stockings." Le Mere reassured him and went on with the posing. Lincoln suggested raising his arms as if addressing a jury, but the operator wanted a calmer attitude. He adjusted the President's coat and showed Lincoln how to hold his arms. "Just look natural," he coached.

"That is what I would like to avoid," came the reply.

The picture-taking over, Lincoln told

(turn to page 211)

208

LINCOLN AND HIS SON TAD at Brady's studio. Of this photograph, taken February 9, 1864, the journalist Noah Brooks wrote: "Lincoln explained to me that he was afraid that this picture was a species of false pretense. Most people, he thought, would suppose the book a large clasped Bible, whereas it was a big photograph album which the photographer, posing the father and son, had hit upon as a good device . . . to bring the two sitters together. Lincoln's anxiety lest somebody should think he was 'making believe read the Bible to Tad,' was illustrative of his scrupulous honesty." This print was widely circulated, had its place in many homes.

PIECES OF A NEGATIVE TAKEN BY THE MULTIPLE-LENS CAMERA ON FEBRUARY 9, 1864, IN BRADY'S WASHINGTON GALLERY.
Whether the camera on this occasion provided three, four, or eight likenesses on the same wet plate glass negative we do not know. Four variants of the same pose, which were all taken at the same time, have come down to us—three in a row and a broken plate.

young Cunningham and the other two the story of the farmer who brought a big oak log to the mill to have it sawed into planks. The miller did the best he could, until a hidden iron spike embedded in the log broke his saw. A big commotion followed. The miller was at sixes and sevens over losing his precious saw, but all the farmer cared about was that nothing should happen

to his log. "That camera man," concluded Lincoln, "seemed anxious about the picture; but boys, I didn't know what might happen to the camera."

A sitting at Brady's gallery did not mean that Brady himself worked the camera. As early as 1851, long before his name became associated with that of Lincoln, the *Photographic Art Journal* noted that Brady's "failing eyesight

precluded the possibility of his using the camera with any certainty." But he posed and directed his sitter and arranged the lighting.

One of the most elaborate sittings was on February 9, 1864, when Anthony Berger, another of Brady's assistants, took the pictures. The memorable photographs on this and the following pages were made on that day.

211

PRINT MADE DIRECTLY FROM THE ORIGINAL NEGATIVE,
ken by Anthony Berger, Brady's assistant, on February 9, 1864.

THE ANSWER TO CHASE'S OFFER TO RESIGN. When the "secret" Pomeroy circular was printed in the newspaper, the Secretary of the Treasury told Lincoln that he would be ready to resign if the President desired it. After a week, Lincoln sent Chase this reply.

THE POMEROY CIRCULAR

SALMON P. CHASE, the Secretary of the Treasury, had presidential aspirations. He believed that "a man of different qualities from those of the President will be needed for the next four years," and assuming that he was just this kind of a man, he allowed his friends to organize a movement on his behalf.

When Lincoln heard of it, he was somewhat disturbed; he would not have liked to see the dissatisfied element of the party rallying behind Chase, a key dispenser of patronage. But he had not lost his humor and he would do nothing against Chase. He wanted a strong and vigorous Treasury Department, and Chase's "mad hunt for the Presidency" reminded him of an incident of his youth when he and his stepbrother were plowing corn. At that time Lincoln was driving the horse while his brother was holding the plow. "The horse was lazy," recalled the President, "but on one occasion rushed across the field so that I, with my long legs, could scarcely keep pace with him. On reaching the end of the furrow, I found an enormous *chin fly* fastened upon him, and knocked him off. My brother asked me what I did that for. I told him I did not want the old horse bitten in that way. 'Why,' said my brother, 'that's all that made him go.'

"Now," Lincoln ended his story, "if Mr. Chase has a presidential *chin fly* biting him, I'm not going to knock him off, if it will only make his department *go*."

Early in 1864 Senator Pomeroy of Kansas, assisted by other Republican radicals, issued a circular in which it was argued that Lincoln could not be re-elected, therefore the candidacy of Chase was proposed. The circular was prepared for private and confidential distribution but soon was printed in the newspapers. Chase wrote the President that he "had no knowledge of the existence of this letter" and was ready to resign. Lincoln thought about it for a week, then wrote: "Whether you shall remain at the head of the Treasury Department is a question which I will not allow myself to consider from any standpoint other than my judgment of the public service, and, in that view, I do not perceive occasion for a change."

The boom for Chase was of short duration; as the date of the convention approached, one state after the other declared to support Lincoln for a second term. His renomination was not in doubt; all efforts to replace him failed.

213

E OF HIS FULL-LENGTH PHOTOGRAPHS—there are only three
ers; this one was taken on February 9, 1864, in Brady's Gallery.

LINCOLN FINDS HIS GENERAL

THE NEW COMMANDER OF THE ARMIES. In March, 1864, forty-two-year-old Ulysses S. Grant was made Lieutenant General of the Army, a rank held heretofore only by George Washington. In him Lincoln had at last found the man who was to subdue the South and bring the war to an end. His make-up was entirely different from that of Lee. Professor T. Harry Williams puts it this way: "Lee thought of war in the old way as a conflict between armies and refused to view it for what it had become—a struggle between societies. To him, economic war was needless cruelty to civilians. Lee was the last of the great old-fashioned generals, Grant the first of the great moderns." *(Mathew B. Brady made this photograph in 1864 at Cold Harbor; the print used here was done directly from the original glass negative in the possession of the National Archives in Washington, D. C.)*

"Do YOU know, General, what your attitude towards Lee for a week after the battle reminded me of?" asked Lincoln of General Meade when they met in Washington. "No, Mr. President, what is it?" replied Meade. "I'll be hanged if I could think of anything else," said Lincoln, "than an old woman trying to shoo her geese across a creek."

The President was greatly disappointed that Meade did not pursue Lee after Gettysburg, and that he had made Richmond, and not the Confederate army, his objective—an idea which Lincoln had been "trying to repudiate for quite a year."

While Meade rested his men in winter quarters, the armies in the West under Grant won notable victories. Bragg was beaten at Chattanooga and retired into Georgia, and Longstreet took his men back to the Virginia border.

After these successes Grant's star shone brightly; in January, 1864, most of the forces west of the Mississippi were placed under him, and the cry increased that he should be made General in Chief.

When, in February, Congress passed a bill reviving the rank of Lieutenant General, the President—as was expected of him—promptly appointed him to the post.

Grant set up headquarters with the Army of the Potomac, giving Meade the short command: "Wherever Lee goes, there you will go also." There would be no more shilly-shallying, no more hesitation. Grant was preparing an offensive: Meade would go after Lee from the north, Butler was to move against Richmond from the south; Sherman in the West would harass the Confederates in northern Georgia, while Banks would advance from New Orleans to Mobile. Thus all the Union armies would converge—as Grant put it—"toward a common center."

Lincoln liked the plan; he believed in its success.

Frank Leslie's Illustrated Newspaper, *March 6, 1864*

MR. LINCOLN FINDS A BROOM TO HIS LIKING. In this cartoon from *Leslie's* on March 7, 1864, the broom labeled "Grant" re- places the worn-out brooms of McClellan, Hooker and Pope after Grant's victories had made it clear he should be the Union leader.

Currier & Ives lithograph from October 1864

THE OLD BULL ON THE RIGHT TRACK. Bulldog Grant is watching Richmond at the end of the dog track. "I am bound to take it." But the dogs—labeled Davis, Lee and Beauregard—retort: "You ain't got this kennel yet, old fellow!"

215

GRANT AND HIS OFFICERS at Massaponax Church, Virginia, on May 21, 1864. Sitting on the bench, facing the camera, are General Horace Porter reading a newspaper, General Grant, General Rawlins, Colonel Ely S. Parker. On the far end of the left bench is General Meade. It is the last day of "trench warfare" at Spotsylvania; for two weeks the Union armies

THE CAMPAIGN IN THE WILDERNESS

AT THE beginning of May, 1864, Grant was ready to move after Lee. To Lincoln's encouraging note he replied: "Should my success be less than I desire, and expect, the least I can say is, the fault is not with you."

The President was confident of his new chief of the army. At their first interview he told Grant "that he had never professed to be a military man or to know how campaigns should be conducted, and never wanted to interfere in them: but that procrastination on the part of commanders, and pressure from the people at the North and Congress, which was always with him, forced him into issuing his series of 'Military orders'—one, two, three,

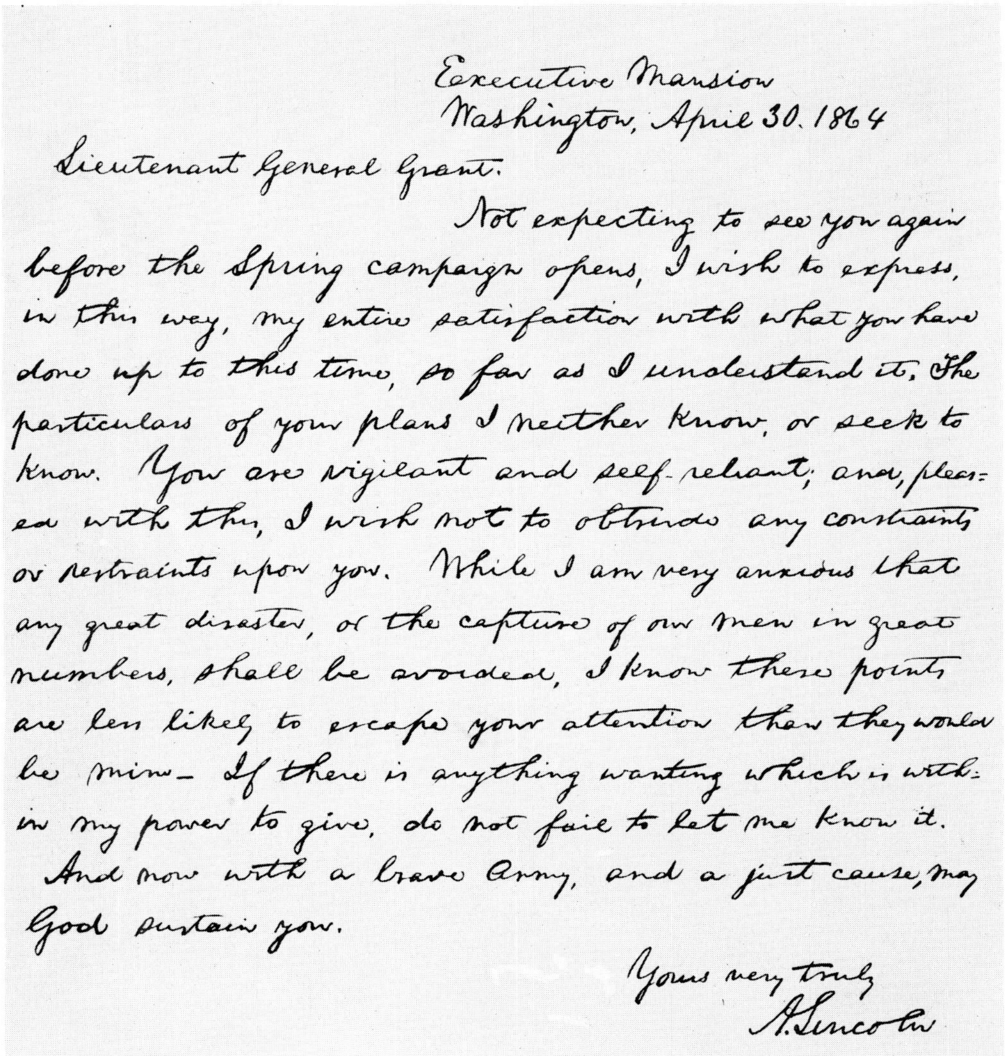

*Executive Mansion
Washington, April 30. 1864*

Lieutenant General Grant.

Not expecting to see you again before the Spring campaign opens, I wish to express, in this way, my entire satisfaction with what you have done up to this time, so far as I understand it. The particulars of your plans I neither know, or seek to know. You are vigilant and self-reliant; and, pleased with this, I wish not to obtrude any constraints or restraints upon you. While I am very anxious that any great disaster, or the capture of our men in great numbers, shall be avoided, I know these points are less likely to escape your attention than they would be mine— If there is anything wanting which is within my power to give, do not fail to let me know it.

And now with a brave Army, and a just cause, may God sustain you.

*Yours very truly
A. Lincoln*

A NOTE FROM LINCOLN TO GRANT BEFORE THE START OF THE SPRING CAMPAIGN.

maneuvered, marched and fought with thousands of wounded lying on the fields uncared for. But Grant would not let up.

etc. He did not know but they were all wrong, and did know that some of them were. All he wanted or had ever wanted was some one who would take the responsibility and act, and call on him for all the assistance needed, pledging himself to the use of all the power of the Government in rendering such assistance." Grant reassured him that he would do his utmost and avoid annoying him or the War Department.

But however hard Grant tried, and he certainly did try hard, sacrificing thousands and thousands of his men's lives, he could not smash Lee, who parried every Union attack and evaded every enveloping movement.

The fighting in the Wilderness (as the region south of the Rapidan was called) lasted for months. Grant, at the outskirts of Richmond, could not force Lee to an open battle. The Union casualties reached the staggering total of over 50,000; still the Confederate capital could not be taken.

When Grant realized that his plan did not work, he boldly shifted strategy. Marching his troops from the vicinity of Richmond, he came up from the south on the Peninsula, moving toward Petersburg, trying to cut the lines which connected the capital with the other parts of the Confederacy.

Lincoln wired him: "I begin to see it; you will succeed. God bless you all."

Lee stopped the Union forces before Petersburg. Grant was willing to make a "desperate effort" to take the city, but Lincoln warned him: "Pressed as we are by lapse of time, I am glad to hear you say this; and yet I do hope you may find a way that the effort shall not be desperate in the sense of great loss of life."

Thus the siege at Richmond began. The Federal troops dug in before the city. A few weeks before, on May 11, while his men were gathering at Spotsylvania, Grant had written to Halleck that he would fight it out on this line "if it takes all summer." It certainly did take all summer, and the winter as well. Grant's forces were in their trenches for almost ten months.

In the meanwhile, the Departments of Washington, the Susquehanna, West Virginia, and the Middle Department were merged into one division under the command of the brilliant cavalry leader Philip H. Sheridan.

A Confederate raiding party under Jubal Early almost got into Washington on July 11 and 12, scaring the city's populace. Lincoln insisted that Grant should visit Monocacy, where the Union forces waited for a renewed

THE SIEGE OF PETERSBURG. The heavy long-range guns of the Fort Brady battery

Confederate attack in the Valley. Grant went, gave orders, then saw Lincoln in the capital, conferring with him and Halleck.

The rift between Grant and Halleck, the General in Chief, developed into

THE HARVEST OF DEATH. Within an hour 7,000 Union men were killed at Cold Harbor on June 3 when Grant made a frontal attack on Lee's fortified positions. In the Wilderness campaign Grant's army lost about 56,000 men, the number of Lee's original forces.

fired at a range of five miles, pounded the Rebel works and threw shells into its

enmity; Grant believed that Halleck hated him and was not willing to cooperate. When "Old Brains" proposed that Grant withdraw a part of his army to put down draft riots, Grant bluntly refused, and Lincoln, who read the

troops. Grant made up his mind to "fight it out on this line if it takes all sum-

General's protests, wrote him on August 17:

"I have seen your despatch expressing your unwillingness to break your hold where you are. Neither am I willing. Hold on with a bulldog grip,

mer." For ten months his army was in the trenches—all summer and all winter, too.

and chew and choke as much as possible."

Though July and August were the darkest months of his Presidency, Lincoln did not lose his head; he was confident of victory.

HIS DAILY ROUTINE

LINCOLN WAS a light sleeper and rose early. In the summer, when he lived outside of Washington at the Soldiers' Home, he breakfasted on a cup of coffee and an egg, then he drove to his office so he would be there at eight o'clock. Arriving at the White House, he looked at his mail, read the dispatches from the war theater, then at ten he began to receive visitors, who for long hours had been waiting for him.

On Tuesdays and Fridays he held Cabinet meetings, beginning at noon. On other days the door of his office was usually thrown open at that time, allowing the crowd to rush in *en masse*. Some came to show him inventions, others to get appointments, but most of them came to ask for reprieves and pardons.

Women were there accompanied by their Congressmen seeking reprieves for their husbands, sons or brothers. One morning Thaddeus Stevens brought a lady with him whose son had been court-martialed and was to be shot. After listening to her story, Lincoln wrote out a pardon. The lady burst out: "I knew it was a Copperhead lie! They told me he was an ugly looking man, but he is the handsomest man I ever saw in my life."

Another time a Congressman argued for the life of a neighbor of his who was going to be executed. Lincoln said: "Well, I don't believe *shooting* him will do him any good. Give me that pen," and with that he wrote out a pardon.

The morning appointments over, he joined his family for lunch, "running the gantlet through the crowds who filled the corridors between his office and the rooms at the west end of the house occupied by the family." He ate a biscuit, a glass of milk and some fruit.

In the afternoon he was back again at his desk; then he went for an hour's drive. At six o'clock he dined.

The evenings he spent mostly in his office, talking to friends or reading to them poetry of Shakespeare or Burns. He liked music if it was sad and sentimental, and he enjoyed going to the theatre. But he never read an entire novel in his whole life.

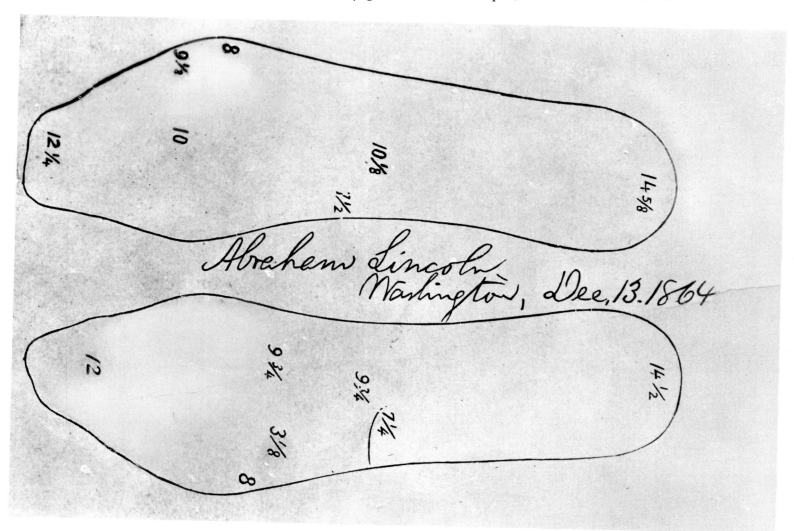

HIS FEET TROUBLED HIM. He discovered a clever shoemaker in New York City who could make boots which did not hurt. So he stood on a paper, marked the outlines of his feet, and ordered a pair of shoes by mail. Chiropodists, like a Dr. Zacharie, came to the White House and, as Lincoln said in a testimonial, "operated on my feet with great success, and considerable addition to my comfort."

THE "BROKEN PLATE" LINCOLN, discovered by the author of this volume in 1947, is the work of Anthony Berger, one of Brady's assistants, who took the picture in the Cabinet Room of the White House on April 20, 1864.

A FRENCH MERCHANT DRAWS LINCOLN

The Frenchman Pierre Morand, a counting-room clerk in a Paris export firm, came to America for the first time around 1840. Apparently he liked what he saw, because he came back and finally settled. For a period he stayed in New York, then in Cincinnati. Around 1846 he became the agent for the French syndicate of the Swan Lands in Virginia. He moved to the outskirts of Clarksburg, living there to 1861.

After the outbreak of the Civil War he went often to Washington, where he became acquainted with Lincoln and made sketches of him. It is obvious that his drawings are not the work of a professional; yet in their amateurish simplicity they seem authentic. They show Lincoln as he really looked.

In his later years Morand fell on bad days, losing his money in an oil lands speculation. In 1902—he was then eighty-two—he offered to the St. Louis lawyer Frederick W. Lehman, an avid bibliophile, the drawings which he had made of Charles Dickens when they both sailed on the same boat to America in 1842. He asked $3 to $10 for each of the drawings, and Lehman purchased not only the Dickens sketches but twenty-three additional ones as well, among them the seven of Abraham Lincoln printed on these pages.

The Lehman family presented the Morand sketches to the Missouri Historical Society

LINCOLN TELLS A STORY, relaxing from the rigors of the Presidency. A drawing made by Pierre Morand in 1864.

LINCOLN IN UNUSUAL ATTIRE at his summer residence at the Soldiers' Home in Washington, where the family stayed during the hot months.

LINCOLN STANDS ON THE SIDEWALK outside the Sickles House in Washington in October, 1864. General Sickles' name became well known after his part in the battle of Gettysburg.

THE PRESIDENT WALKS WITH SENATOR VAN WINKLE on a hot summer day. Lincoln kept prodding the perspiring little man to keep ahead of Kansas Senator Lane, who wanted to catch up with them.

ABRAHAM LINCOLN AS PIERRE MORAND OBSERVED HIM IN THE CAPITAL IN THE SUMMER MONTHS OF 1864.

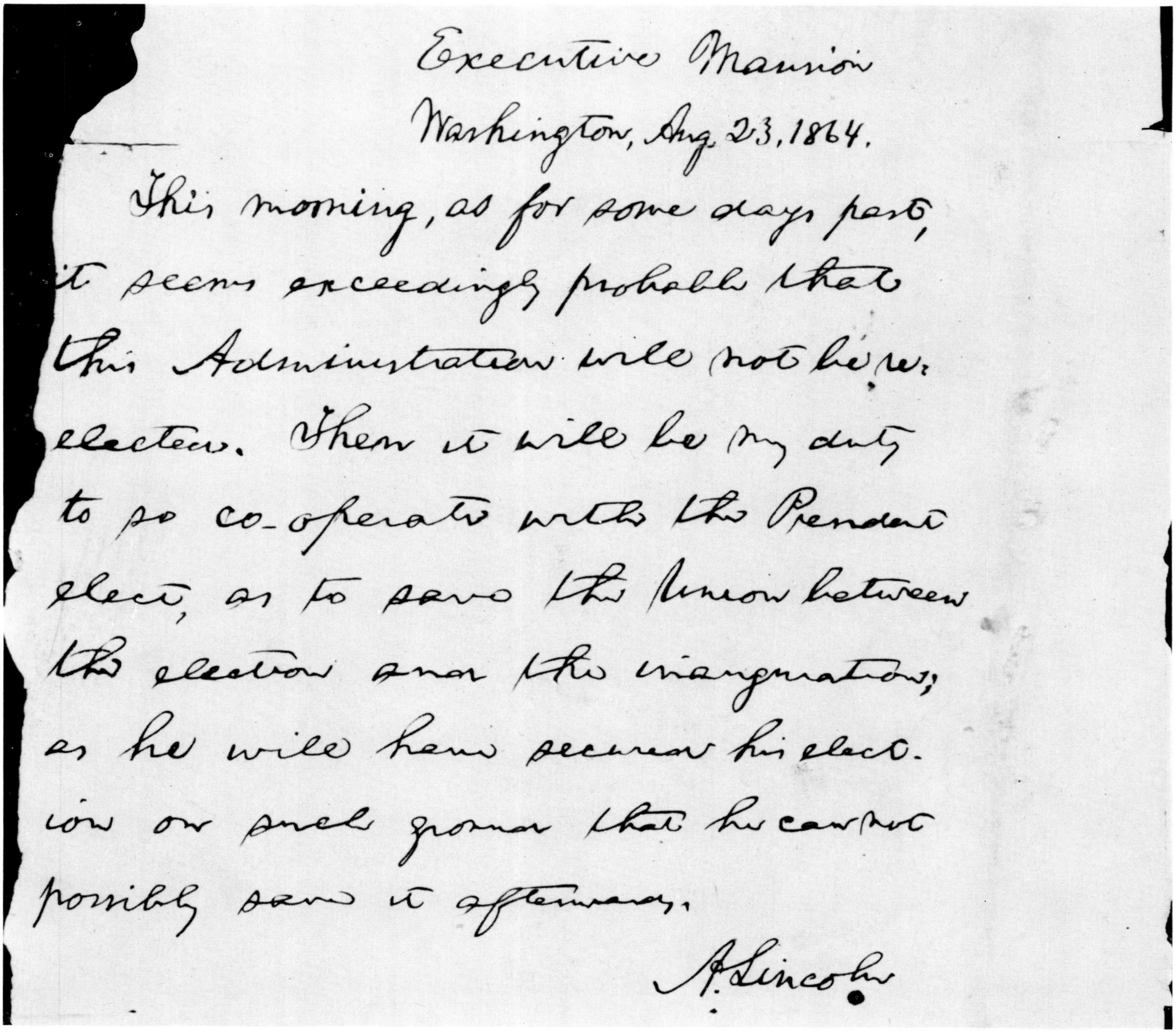

Executive Mansion

Washington, Aug. 23, 1864.

This morning, as for some days past, it seems exceedingly probable that this Administration will not be re-elected. Then it will be my duty to so co-operate with the President elect, as to save the Union between the election and the inauguration; as he will have secured his election on such ground that he cannot possibly save it afterwards.

A. Lincoln

WHEN LINCOLN THOUGHT HE COULD NOT BE RE-ELECTED. On August 23, a week before the Democratic convention assembled in Chicago to select its nominee (which was certain to be General George B. McClellan), the President wrote out the above document.

SIGNED UNSEEN

IN THE summer of 1864 the military situation was bad and the political was even worse. Grant's tremendous casualties in the Wilderness campaign had hit many homes; the cry for peace grew. The Army of the Potomac was bogged down before Richmond, and Sherman was still before Atlanta.

In Congress the radicals in the President's own party, using the general dissatisfaction, tried to ease Lincoln out of office. They passed a bill nullifying Lincoln's Amnesty and Reconstruction plan, which the President had issued in a proclamation earlier that year. In it Lincoln proposed that as soon as ten per cent of the voters of 1860 in any of the seceded states should form a loyal government, that government would be recognized as legal. The bill of the radical Republicans, however, declared that not ten per cent but a majority of the voters must declare themselves loyal to the Union before their state would be taken back into the fold; furthermore, that the new state constitution must prohibit slavery.

Lincoln pocketed the radicals' bill, and explained his own position. Whereupon, two of the radicals, Wade and Davis, issued a manifesto denouncing the President's reconstruction policies.

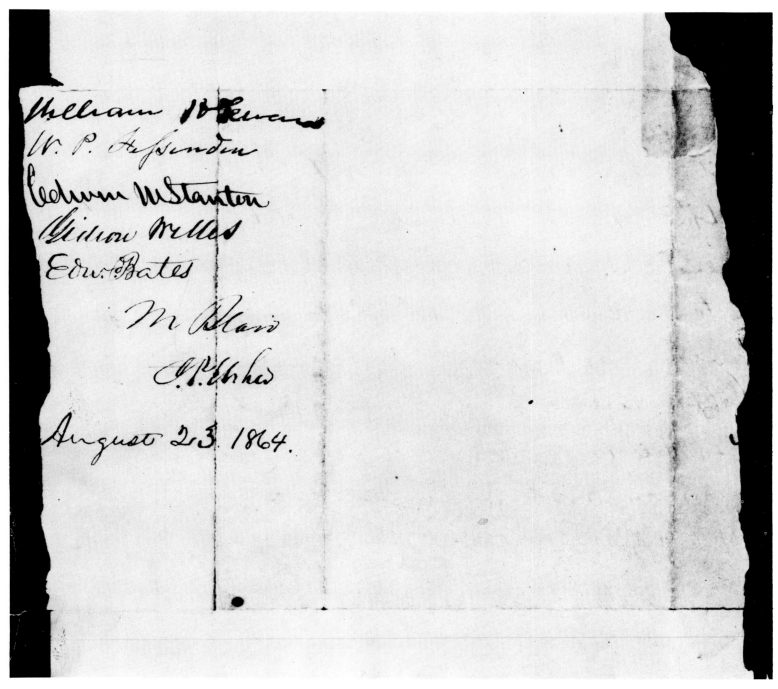

William H Seward
W. P. Fessenden
Edwin M Stanton
Gideon Welles
Edw. Bates
M Blair
J P Usher

August 23 1864.

Without letting his Cabinet see it, he asked the members of his political family to sign it on the reverse side of the sheet. They did so without asking any questions, finding out only after the President was successfully re-elected just what it was that they had endorsed.

The break between the President and his adversaries was complete, and it seemed as if Lincoln could not win his re-election. It was then that he asked his Cabinet to sign the above document.

After his re-election he showed the paper to his official family, telling them:

"You will remember that this was written at a time six days before the Chicago nominating convention, when as yet we had no adversary, and seemed to have no friends. I then solemnly resolved on the course of action indicated above. I resolved, in case of the election of General McClellan, being certain that he would be the candidate, that I would see him and talk matters over with him. I would say, 'General, the election has demonstrated that you are stronger, have more influence with the American people than I. Now let us together—you with your influence and I with all the executive power of the Government—try to save the country. You raise as many troops as you possibly can for this final trial, and I will devote all my energy to assisting and finishing the war.' "

The Secretary of State interrupted: "And the General would answer you, 'Yes, yes,' and the next day when you saw him again and pressed these views upon him, he would say, 'Yes, yes,' and so on forever, and would have done nothing at all."

"At least," said Lincoln, "I should have done my duty and have stood clear before my own conscience."

UNCLE SAM REVIEWS THE 1864 PRESIDENTIAL CANDIDATES; ON THE LEFT, NEXT TO LINCOLN, IS THE CANDIDATE OF THE

In the summer of 1864 Lincoln's popularity was at a low ebb. Horace Greeley, writing in his New York *Tribune*, declared that not only Chase, but Frémont, Butler or Grant would make as good a President as Lincoln. He suggested nominating one of these men to preserve "the salutary one-term principle" of the last three decades.

The radical wing of the party, strongly opposing Lincoln, named John C. Frémont as their candidate.

Yet, when the regular Republican convention met, it was Lincoln again on the first ballot. Every state with the exception of Missouri voted for him. For the second place, the convention named Andrew Johnson, a Democrat from the border states. Why Johnson? asked Thaddeus Stevens, the leader of the Radicals. Couldn't the party find a candidate "without going down into one of those d——d rebel provinces to pick one up?"

To the congratulations of the National Union League the President answered: "I do not allow myself to suppose that either the convention or the League have concluded to decide that I am either the greatest or best man in America, but rather they have concluded it is not best to swap horses while crossing the river, and have further concluded that I am not so poor a horse that they might not make a botch of it in trying to swap."

226

CAMPAIGN CARTOONS ASSAIL LINCOLN

"I KNEW HIM, HORATIO; A FELLOW OF INFINITE JEST. * * * WHERE BE YOUR GIBES NOW?—*Hamlet, Act IV, Scene 1.*

Drawn by J. H. Howard in 1864

THE CANDIDATE OF THE DEMOCRATS, General George B. McClellan, pictured as Hamlet, is looking at Lincoln's head as he repeats the famous lines of Shakespeare about Yorick.

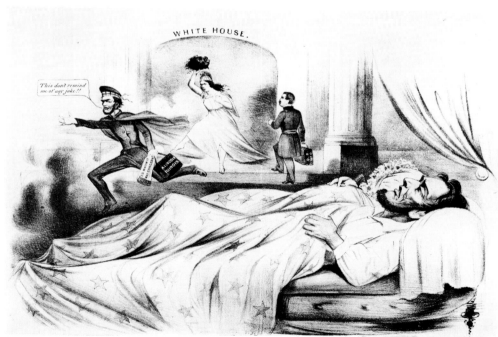

Currier & Ives lithograph from October 1864

ANOTHER ANTI-LINCOLN CARTOON, recalling the story of his passing through Baltimore in 1861 in a Scotch cap, shows **the Democratic candidate moving into the White House.**

An 1864 cartoon by an unidentified artist

CRATS—**GENERAL GEORGE B. McCLELLAN.**

After his nomination Lincoln lived through anxious weeks. The Army of the Potomac was exhausted and the country yearned for peace. "I know," wrote Horace Greeley to the President, "that nine-tenths of the whole American people, North and South, are anxious for peace—peace on almost any terms—and utterly sick of human slaughter and devastation. . . . I firmly believe that, were the election to take place tomorrow, the Demo-

227

Currier & Ives lithograph

IN THIS CAMPAIGN CARTOON distributed by Currier and Ives (August, 1864) the newly nominated Democratic candidate, General McClellan, is shown trying to save the Union, which Lincoln and Jeff Davis are tearing apart. "Peace" was to be his platform.

An anti-Lincoln cartoon of unknown origin

THE KING OF THE CANNIBALS. This crudely drawn cartoon was made in 1864 during the second presidential campaign. It presents Lincoln as a savage chief with his advisers

cratic majority in this State [New York], and Pennsylvania would amount to 100,000 and that we should lose Connecticut also. Now if the Rebellion can be crushed before November, it will do to go on; if not, we are rushing on certain ruin. . . ." And Greeley concluded: "I beg you, implore you, to inaugurate or invite proposals for peace forthwith. And in case peace cannot now be made, consent to an *armistice for one year*, each party to retain, unmolested, all it now holds, but the rebel ports to be opened. Meantime, let a national convention be held, and there will surely be no more war at all events."

Other politicians thought along the same lines. A call was issued for another convention to Cincinnati, to nom-

The COMMANDER-IN-CHIEF conciliating the SOLDIER'S VOTES on the Battle Field.

Now, Marshal, sing us 'Picayune Butler,' or something else that's funny.

An 1864 pen drawing by an unidentified artist

IN A PRESIDENTIAL CAMPAIGN ANYTHING GOES. A slanderous cartoon of Lincoln on the battlefield of Antietam where, according to a newspaper story, the President asked his friend Lamon to sing a funny song. Though false, the accusation was often repeated.

inate, if necessary, a new candidate for the Presidency.

In the newspapers, correspondents and editorial writers were asking for the withdrawal of both Lincoln and Frémont from the Presidential race, and "the nomination of a man that would improve confidence and infuse life into our ranks."

This was the picture when the Democratic convention met in Chicago. The platform declared that "after four years of failure to restore the Union by experiment of war . . . the public welfare demands that immediate efforts be made for a cessation of hostilities. . . ." They nominated George B. McClellan, who accepted the nomination but refused the platform as "No peace can be permanent without Union."

A contemporary print

A PLEA FOR FRÉMONT'S CANDIDACY. The Pathfinder in this cartoon is a man of Justice and Principles; Lincoln, one of Expediency; McClellan, a master of Defeat and Retreat.

229

HARDIN COUNTY, KENTUCKY.

THE SOARING EAGLE, NOT REPLYING.

CAPTAIN LINCOLN, ON DECK.

AN ANTI-LINCOLN BIOGRAPHY

DURING 1864, Lincoln was violently attacked in newspapers and pamphlets. One such missile was a burlesque campaign biography, the fictitious story of Lincoln's life. Starting with his birth, it described his early childhood, talked of his years at Indiana. "Here in the solitude of Nature," wrote the anonymous pamphlet writer, "Abraham began to feel a yearning for wisdom, and was shocked one day by meeting a free nigger who knew more

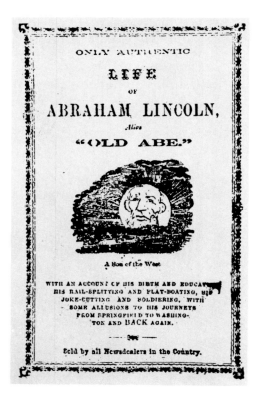

TITLE PAGE of an anti-Lincoln pamphlet, containing a satirical account of his life, with drawings reproduced on these pages.

than he himself. This gave him a love of liberty and a horror of slavery. From that sentiment, so early inspired, resulted the Famous Emancipation Proclamation."

Then the pamphleteer spoke of Lincoln's flatboat trip to New Orleans, his participation in the Black Hawk War, his turning into a lawyer, his campaigns for the Legislature and the Senate.

After this he went on:

"It was now determined that Mr. James Buchanan had been long enough in office, and that he was getting soiled, so the nation prepared to put on a clean President.

"Abraham, though quite as modest as he was honest, thought this a good chance to make twenty-five thousand a year, so he went to New York and advocated his claims to the position, in a speech at Cooper Institute, charging two shillings admission fee. The Republicans admired his cheek, and nominated him at the Chicago Convention of 1860. He accepted, in a letter, in which he said he almost wished they had chosen a statesman instead. The whole country has wished so, since.

"In one time, Abraham was elected. There were two other candidates, and more people voted against Lincoln than voted for him. He was therefore made President."

The biography ended with a description of President Lincoln's personal appearance and habits.

"Mr. Lincoln stands six feet twelve in his socks, which he changes once every ten days. His anatomy is composed mostly of bones, and when walking he resembles the offspring of a happy marriage between a derrick and a windmill.

"When speaking he reminds one of the old signal-telegraph that used to stand on Staten Island. His head is shaped something like a ruta-bago, and his complexion is that of a Saratoga trunk. His hands and feet are plenty large enough, and in society he has the air of having too many of them.

"In his habits he is by no means foppish, though he brushes his air sometimes, and is said to wash. He swears fluently. A strict temperance man himself, he does not object to another man's being pretty drunk, especially when he is about to make a bargain with him. He is fond of fried liver and onions, and is a member of the church. He can hardly be called handsome, though he is certainly much better looking since he had the smallpox. As a public speaker he differs considerably from Daniel Webster and Artemus Ward. He is hospitable, bilious, and writes a good hand. Mrs. Lincoln thinks well of him. He is 107 years old.

"Such is Abraham Lincoln. Take him at his best he is much better than those think him who underrate his virtues. For his friends, who like his administration, he would make a better candidate for re-election than some man they do not like so well. With others, it is different."

230

LINCOLN SPLITTING RAILS, IN SANGAMON.

LINCOLN TELLING LITTLE STORIES, IN CAMP.

LINCOLN SPEAKING AT COOPER INSTITUTE.

LINCOLN WRITING HIS LETTER OF ACCEPTANCE.

LINCOLN PASSING BALTIMORE.

LINCOLN ASSUMING COMMAND OF THE ARMY AND NAVY.

A GOOD GOVERNMENT BARGAIN.

LINCOLN AND HIS CABINET.

SECRETARY SEWARD AND HIS LITTLE BELL.

CONSCRIPTS IN THE FIELD.

LINCOLN OUT WALKING.

THE END.

SHERMAN TAKES ATLANTA

WHILE GRANT'S armies were hammering against the Confederate capital, General Sherman was pushing the Confederates back to Atlanta.

Sherman described vividly the Atlanta campaign: "We were generally in a wooded country," he wrote, "and though our lines were deployed according to tactics, the men generally fought in strong skirmish-lines, taking advantage of the shape of the ground and of every cover. We were generally the assailants, and in wooded and broken countries the 'defensive' had a positive advantage over us, for they were always ready, had cover, and always knew the ground to their immediate front; whereas we, their assailants, had to grope our way over unknown ground, and generally found a cleared field or prepared entanglements that held us for a time under a close and withering fire. Rarely did the opposing lines in compact order come into actual contact, but when, as at Peachtree Creek and Atlanta, the lines did become commingled, the men fought individually in every possible style, more frequently with the musket clubbed than with the bayonet, and in some instances the men clinched like wrestlers, and went to the ground together."

The battle for Atlanta was fought a mile and a half outside the city, both the Union and Confederate forces suffering severe losses (Union 9,719; Confederates 10,841). On September 2 the city was occupied and a few days later General Sherman himself arrived. He noted in his diary:

"Hundreds of sutlers and traders were waiting at Nashville and Chattanooga, greedy to reach Atlanta with their wares and goods, with which to drive a profitable trade with the inhabitants. I gave positive orders that none of these traders, except three (one

GENERAL SHERMAN (LEANING ON THE

for each separate army), should be permitted to come nearer than Chattanooga; and, moreover, I peremptorily required that all the citizens and families resident in Atlanta should go away, giving to each the option to go south or north, as their interests or feelings dictated. I was resolved to

AFTER ATLANTA'S CAPTURE, General Sherman's army moved into the abandoned Confederate fortifications. To Sherman's message "Let us fight it out like men," General Hood, the Confederate commander, replied: "We will fight you to the death! Better die a thousand deaths than to submit to live under you or your Government and your Negro allies!"

GUN) POSES FOR THE PHOTOGRAPHER DURING THE ATLANTA CAMPAIGN WHICH WAS TO SEAL OFF THE CONFEDERACY.

make Atlanta a pure military garrison or depot, with no civil population to influence military measures. I had seen Memphis, Vicksburg, Natchez, and New Orleans, all captured from the enemy, and each at once was garrisoned by a full division of troops, if not more; so that success was actually

crippling our armies in the field by detachments to guard and protect the interests of a hostile population."

Sherman knew that he "would be strongly criticized," but he desired to show the South that: "one, we were in earnest; and the other, if they were sincere in their common and popular

clamor 'to die in the last ditch,' that the opportunity would soon come."

To General Halleck he wrote: "If the people raise a howl against my barbarity and cruelty, I will answer that war is war, and not popularity seeking." They were tough words, different from the feeling in his heart.

233

CALCULATING THE ELECTORAL VOTE. After Lincoln learned the outcome of the state elections in Pennsylvania, Ohio, and Indiana, he tried to figure out his strength. On a sheet of paper he wrote out the number of electors from the different states.

AN ANTI-LINCOLN CAMPAIGN CARD, alluding to his remark that he was nominated because the convention "concluded it is not best to swap horses while crossing the river."

THE 1864

THE DEMOCRATS had chosen as their presidential candidate the former General in Chief of the army, George B. McClellan, to oppose Lincoln. Their platform stated that "after four years of failure to restore the Union by the experiment of war . . . during which . . . the Constitution itself has been disregarded in every part . . . the public welfare demands that immediate efforts be made for a cessation of hostilities . . . to the end that, at the earliest practicable moment, peace may be restored on the basis of the Federal Union of the States."

But "Little Mac" would not accept such a platform. "I could not look in the face of my gallant comrades of the army and navy," wrote he, "who have survived so many bloody battles, and tell them that their labors and the sacrifices of so many of our slain and wounded brethren had been in vain; that we had abandoned that Union for which we have so often perilled our lives."

Events soon proved that the Democratic platform makers were far from the truth. The war a failure? McClellan had hardly time to accept the nomination, when the news of Sherman's victory at Atlanta and Farragut's triumph at Mobile Bay became known. Secretary of State Seward declared: "Sherman and Farragut have knocked the bottom out of the Chicago nominations."

Now that the tide ran in his favor, Lincoln was willing to make a bargain with the radicals in his party, who had rallied behind General Frémont as presidential candidate. If Frémont would withdraw, Lincoln was ready to drop Montgomery Blair from the Cabinet, a move so vociferously demanded by the radicals. On September 22 Frémont obliged, and a day later Lincoln accepted Blair's resignation. Through this deal the President reunited his party for the ensuing campaign, silencing Wade and Davis.

234

CAMPAIGN

On October 2, Salmon P. Chase, who was no longer Secretary of the Treasury, wrote: "There is not now, the slightest uncertainty about the re-election of Mr. Lincoln. The only question is by what popular and electoral majority. God grant that both may be so decisive as to turn every hope of rebellion to despair!"

McClellan waged a losing battle from the beginning. The Democrats used shopworn campaign charges, attacking the "ignorance, incompetency, and corruption of Mr. Lincoln's administration." The New York *World* asked: "Mr. Lincoln, has he or has he not an interest in the profits of public contracts?" and answered that it could be proven that the President had succumbed to opportunities and temptations of his office. " 'Honest old Abe' has few honest men to defend his honesty," said the newspaper.

The election favored Lincoln. The President won with 2,213,665 popular votes against McClellan's 1,802,237. Two hundred and twelve Lincoln electors were chosen against twenty-one for McClellan—those of New Jersey, Delaware and Kentucky. The ballots of the soldiers—counted separately—gave the President 116,877 votes against McClellan's 33,748.

"I give you joy of the election," wrote Ralph Waldo Emerson to a friend. "Seldom in history was so much staked on a popular vote. I suppose never in history."

The result proved that in spite of the long and bloody war, the people of the country were resolved to finish the work they had begun. They elected a Congress with enough Republican members to insure the passage of a constitutional amendment abolishing slavery.

Replying to a serenade after the voting, Lincoln said that the election "has demonstrated that a people's government can sustain a national election in the midst of a great civil war."

COMPARING THE 1860 AND 1864 VOTES. Lincoln, like all presidential candidates, made calculations of the outcome. The result turned out even better than he had anticipated.

Cartoon by John Tenniel in the London Punch, Sept. 24, 1864

MRS. NORTH AND HER ATTORNEY. The lady tells Lincoln: "You see . . . we have failed utterly in our course of action. I want peace, and so, if you cannot effect an amicable arrangement, I must put the case in other hands."

Executive Mansion
Washington, Nov 21. 1864

To Mrs Bixby, Boston. Mass,

Dear Madam,

I have been shown in the files of the War Department a statement of the Adjutant General of Massachusetts that you are the mother of five sons who have died gloriously on the field of battle. I feel how weak and fruitless must be any word of mine which should attempt to beguile you from the grief of a loss so overwhelming. But I cannot refrain from tendering you the consolation that may be found in the thanks of the republic they died to save. I pray that our Heavenly Father may assuage the anguish of your bereavement, and leave you only the cherished memory of the loved and lost, and the solemn pride that must be yours to have laid so costly a sacrifice upon the altar of freedom.

Yours very sincerely and respectfully,

A. Lincoln.

THE LETTER TO LYDIA BIXBY bears all the earmarks of Lincoln's compassion and of his style. There was a heated debate among scholars whether Lincoln really wrote it or whether it was penned by his secretary, John Hay. But there was no doubt in their minds that the alleged facsimile (reproduced above) was a forgery. The original letter has never been found.

THE LETTER AS WRITTEN BY LINCOLN was first reported and quoted in full in the Boston *Transcript* on November 25, 1864.

THE BIXBY LETTER— A FORGERY?

Mrs. Lydia Bixby (1801–78) of Boston had five sons, who all served with the Union Army and by 1864—so she believed—were killed in battle. (In reality only two of them died on the battlefield, and a third in a Confederate prison. The fourth son was captured, while the fifth deserted and died forty-five years later in Chicago.

William Schouler, adjutant general of Massachusetts, told Governor Andrew of her case and the Governor suggested that President Lincoln should send his personal condolence to her "such as the noble mother of five dead heroes so well deserves." Lincoln wrote the letter, Schouler delivered it, and it was made public when the Boston *Transcript* printed it soon thereafter.

Though the original in Lincoln's handwriting disappeared, twenty-seven years later facsimiles appeared and sold for $2 apiece. Where these facsimiles really copied from Lincoln's original, or were they forgeries? When John Hay was asked, he said: "The letter of Mr. Lincoln to Mrs. Bixby is genuine . . . but the engraved copy of Mr. Lincoln's alleged manuscript is, in my opinion, a very ingenious forgery."

RE-ELECTED

On November 8, 1864, the voters of the North gave their confidence to the President. The cartoon by Frank Bellew in *Harper's Weekly* (on the right) printed a day before the election was prophetic: it was Lincoln for four more years.

On the evening of the great day Lincoln waited for the results in Edwin Stanton's office. The figures were brought to him as soon as they reached the telegraph department of the War Office. At one time—during a lull in the returns—Lincoln began to read a piece by his favorite humorist, Petroleum V. Nasby, and Charles A. Dana, Assistant Secretary of War, had to listen to it. "Mr. Stanton viewed these proceedings with great impatience," recalled Dana later, "but Mr. Lincoln paid no attention to that. He would read a page or a story, pause to consider a new election telegram, and go ahead with a new passage." Stanton was indignant. How could Lincoln behave in such a way? How could he amuse himself, be flippant and frivolous when his and the nation's fate was at stake? The Secretary of War had not the imagination to understand, so Dana recorded, that it was Abraham Lincoln's way to relieve the strain on his mind and to maintain "the safety and sanity of his intelligence."

Long Abraham Lincoln a Little Longer.

Harper's Weekly, *November 26, 1864*

THE CARTOON OF LONG ABRAHAM in *Harper's Weekly* shortly after the election.

Frank Leslie's Illustrated Newspaper, *December 3, 1864*

JEFF DAVIS'S NIGHTMARE, a cartoon in *Frank Leslie's Illustrated Newspaper* soon after Lincoln's reelection. Later Southern and Northern representatives met at Hampton Roads.

LINCOLN'S SUPREME COURT

THE HEAD of the Court, eighty-four-year-old Roger B. Taney, a Democrat serving since the Jackson era, was hostile to Lincoln, who openly defied and denounced his Dred Scott decision. And two other Justices—Nelson and Clifford—felt like Taney.

Soon after the war began, the Chief Justice challenged the President's use of arbitrary power. When John Merryman, an active Secessionist sympathizer, was arrested, Taney branded Lincoln: "He certainly does not faithfully execute the laws, if he takes upon himself legislative power . . . by arresting and imprisoning a person without due process of law."

The President in an effort to ensure the administration's policies offered a plan for a revision of the judiciary system. Congress adopted such a plan and increased the number of Justices to ten. This gave Lincoln the margin of safety.

The important issue before the Court involved foreign vessels that were seized for violation of the blockade. Lincoln always maintained that the conflict between North and South was not a war but an insurrection. Thus, the Confederacy could not be acknowledged by foreign nations as a sovereign and independent state. But if it was insurrection then the seizure of foreign vessels was illegal. The Court of ten Justices—four of them appointed by Lincoln—upheld the North's right to blockade the Southern ports, as "the conflict was insurrection *and* war; the Southerners were traitors *and* enemies."

On October 12, 1864, Chief Justice Taney died and Lincoln named Salmon P. Chase to succeed him. From then on the Court was in reality Lincoln's Supreme Court.

LINCOLN'S SUPREME COURT at the beginning of the year 1865, when the number of Supreme Court Justices was increased to ten. A dramatic and little-known photograph by Mathew B. Brady. From left to right: Associate Justice David Davis of Illinois, Lincoln's long-time friend and manager in the 1860 Republican Convention; Associate Justice Noah Haynes Swayne of Ohio, who was sworn in three years earlier; Robert Cooper Grier of Pennsylvania; James Morse Wayne of Georgia, longest-serving member

of the Court; Chief Justice Salmon P. Chase of Ohio, who was appointed by President Lincoln a few weeks before—Dec. 6, 1864; Samuel Nelson of New York; Nathan Clifford of Maine; Samuel Freeman Miller of Iowa; and Stephen Johnson Field of California. The tenth Justice, John Catron of Tennessee, is not in the picture. Of the ten Justices, no fewer than five were Lincoln appointees. Swayne, Miller and Davis were named to the Court in 1862, Field in 1863 and Chase in 1864. Of the other five Justices, Wayne received his appointment by President Jackson in 1835, Catron by President Van Buren in 1837, Nelson by President Tyler in 1845, Grier by President Polk in 1846, and Clifford by President Buchanan in 1858.

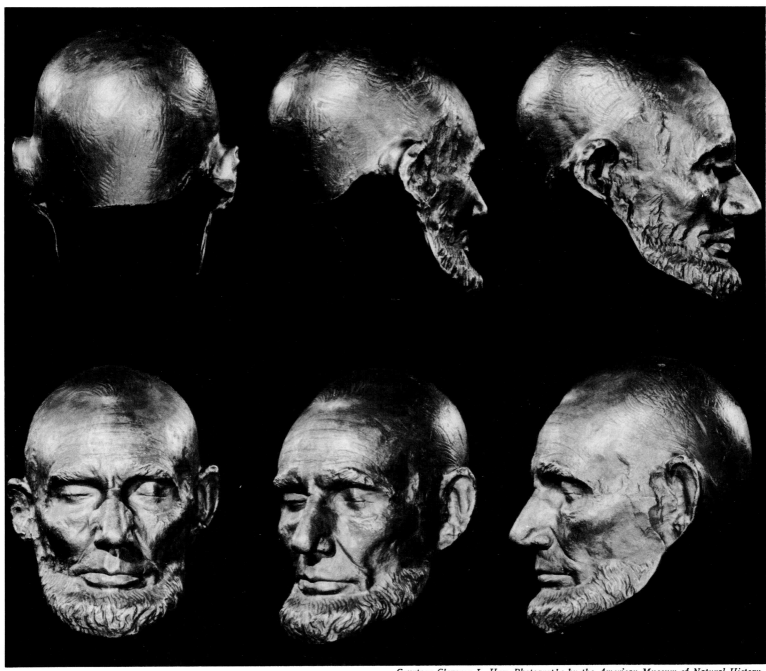

Courtesy Clarence L. Hay. Photographs by the American Museum of Natural History

THE ANATOMY OF LINCOLN'S HEAD. Rotating views of a life mask taken by the sculptor Clark Mills in Washington probably the second week of February, 1865. At that time Lincoln was 56 years old almost to the day. He had sixty more days to live.

ANOTHER LIFE MASK IS TAKEN

LINCOLN WAS 56 years old when the sculptor Clark Mills took his life mask. Mills—according to a description of his method—encased Lincoln's head in a tight cap and then spread the plaster over the face, leaving only a small space open under the nostrils. When the plaster hardened he asked the President to twitch his face muscles, which made the plaster fall off from the skin. The whole procedure lasted less than fifteen minutes.

The anthropologist Harry L. Shapiro, in examining the mask, pointed out that the prominent feature of Lincoln's face was its "great breadth, emphasized by the jutting arch of his cheek bones." It was because of this that his cheeks below seemed to look hollow, giving him a cadaverous look.

Lincoln's face was described by his law partner–biographer William Herndon in this way: "The cheek bones were high, sharp and prominent; his jaws were long, upcurved and massive, looked solid, heavy and strong; nose large, long and blunt, a little awry toward the right eye; chin, long sharp and uncurved; face long, narrow, sallow and cadaverous . . . ears large and jutting; lower lip thick, hanging under-curved or down-curved; little gray eyes." A graphic description.

241

MARCHING THROUGH GEORGIA

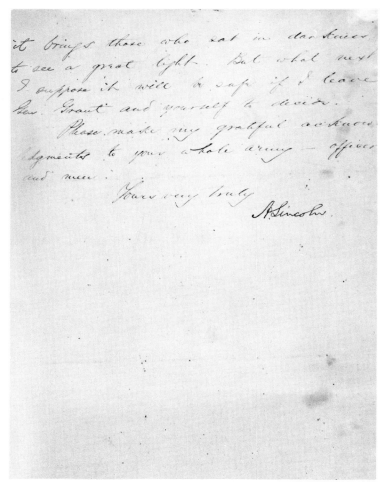

BEFORE General Sherman left Atlanta on his march to the sea, he wrecked everything of military value in the city. As his army moved across Georgia, ransacking the land, cutting a swath of devastation sixty miles wide, and making the state "an example to rebels." Railroads were torn up, public buildings and machine shops burned, cotton made useless, mules and horses taken. Sherman later said: "The burning of the private dwellings, though never designed by me, was a trifling matter compared with the manifold results that soon followed. . . . I have never shed many tears over the event, because I believe it hastened what we all fought for, the end of the war."

By Christmas he took the city of Savannah.

GENERAL SHERMAN WITH HIS OFFICERS. When Lincoln met the General at City Point late in March, 1865, he said to him: "Sherman, do you know why I took a shine to Grant and you?" "I don't know, Mr. Lincoln, you have been extremely kind to me, far more than my deserts." "Well, you never found fault with me."

LINCOLN'S REPLY TO SHERMAN'S FAMOUS DISPATCH. On December 22 the General wired to the President: "I beg to present you as a Christmas-gift the city of Savannah." Lincoln thanked him: "Now, the undertaking being a success, the honor is all yours."

Frank Leslie's Illustrated Newspaper, *February 18, 1865*

A WILDLY APPLAUDING AND HURRAHING CONGRESS GAVE ITS BLESSING TO THE PASSING OF THE 13TH AMENDMENT.

THE 13TH AMENDMENT

THOUGH SLAVERY was virtually dead, it was not yet legally abolished. The President asked Congress to pass a Constitutional amendment to that effect, and Congress responded with great willingness.

The amendment, finally voted by both Houses and passed on January 31, 1865, provided that "neither slavery nor involuntary servitude, except as a punishment for crime, whereof the party shall have been duly convicted, shall exist within the United States or any other place subject to their jurisdiction."

When it was ratified by three-fourths of the states and became the supreme law of the land—on December 18, 1865—Lincoln had been dead for more than eight months.

243

THE SECOND INAUGURAL

MARCH FOURTH was a somber and drizzly day, the roads covered with mud, a cold, gusty wind blowing. Lincoln had been since early morning at the Capitol, signing bills passed by Congress at the session to end at noon.

When the galleries of the Senate Chamber were opened, they were soon filled with pretty women in lovely crinolines and with costly jewelry on their bare necks. The journalist Noah Brooks noted that "they chattered and clattered like zephyrs among the reeds of a waterside."

At the beginning of the ceremonies, the President took his place in the center of the front row; at his left were the Supreme Court Justices, at his right, the members of his Cabinet.

On the stroke of twelve the outgoing and incoming Vice-Presidents entered the hall arm in arm. They sat down on the dais of the presiding officer; then Hannibal Hamlin, the outgoing man,

WASHINGTON, MARCH 4, 1865: Lincoln reads the last sentences of his immortal second inaugural: "With malice toward none; with charity for all; with firmness in the right, as God gives us to see the right, let us strive on to finish the work we are in." As he spoke the words, noon has long

A NOTE OF THANKS to the Republican boss, Thurlow Weed, for his congratulations on the second inaugural address. Lincoln wrote: "I expect the latter to wear as well as—perhaps better than—any thing I have produced; but I believe it is not immediately popular."

passed, and his listeners are getting restless. Already Vice-President Johnson (sitting next to Lincoln's empty chair) is putting on his hat; next to him with bowed head is his predecessor, Hannibal Hamlin. The Justices of the Supreme Court are on Lincoln's left: Chase, Nelson, Clifford, Swayne, Miller, Field. They are fidgeting in their seats; a missed lunch is not conducive to good humor. Among the others in the picture, Frederick Meserve seemed to recognize John Wilkes Booth in a top hat before the taller statue, and others of the conspirators just below the speaker's table. It is another of those amusing hypotheses which unfortunately cannot be proven. Any person in a multitude with a beard and a hat looks like any other person with a beard and hat. A resemblance, and there is some, does not prove that this man is Booth, nor that one is Paine or Atzerodt or Spangler or Herold.

THE SECOND INAUGURAL ADDRESS IN ABRAHAM LINCOLN'S OWN HANDWRITING. IT COVERED ONLY FOUR PAGES OF FOOLSCAP.

rose and made a little speech, thanking the Senators for the kindnesses bestowed on him. After he finished, he called on Andrew Johnson to take the oath as Vice-President.

Before he came to the Chamber, Johnson was not feeling well; he had just recovered from an attack of typhoid fever. To overcome his indisposition he drank a tumbler of whiskey, as he felt he needed all his strength for the occasion.

The alcohol showed its ill-effect. Johnson rose to say a few words, but he wandered into a lengthy stump speech, creating a painful scene.

"Johnson is either drunk or crazy," whispered Gideon Welles into Stanton's ear. Lincoln lowered his head, looking down in deep humiliation.

At last Johnson came to the end of his tirade, repeated the oath, and, taking his Bible in his hand, spoke with dramatic gestures: "I kiss this Book in the face of my nation of the United States."

As Lincoln walked toward the eastern portico, he was heard to tell an official: "Do not let Johnson speak outside."

The multitude "in the great plaza in front of the Capitol, as far as the eye could reach, and breaking in waves along its outer edges among the budding foliage of the grounds beyond" greeted the President with a tremendous shout. And when the cheering subsided, the tall figure of Lincoln stepped forward and began to read his inaugural address, printed in two broad columns upon a single page of large paper.

It was received in most profound silence. A journalist who was on the platform, reported that: "Every word was clear and audible as the ringing and somewhat shrill tones of Lincoln's voice sounded over the vast concourse.

the cause of the conflict might cease with, or even before, the conflict itself should cease. Each looked for an easier triumph, and a result less fundamental and astounding. Both read the same Bible, and pray to the same God; and each invokes His aid against the other. It may seem strange that any men should dare to ask a just God's assistance in wringing their bread from the sweat of other men's faces; but let us judge not that we be not judged. The prayers of both could not be answered; that of neither has been answered fully. The Almighty has His own purposes. "Woe unto the world because of offences! for it must needs be that offences come; but woe to that man by whom the offence cometh!" If we shall suppose that American Slavery is one of those offences which, in the providence of God, must needs come, but which, having continued through His appointed time, He now wills to remove, and that He gives to both North and South, this terrible war, as the woe due to those

by whom the offence came, shall we discern therein any departure from those divine attributes which the believers in a Living God always ascribe to Him? Fondly do we hope — fervently do we pray — that this mighty scourge of war may speedily pass away. Yet, if God wills that it continue, until all the wealth piled by the bond-man's two hundred and fifty years of unrequited toil shall be sunk, and until every drop of blood drawn with the lash, shall be paid by another drawn with the sword, as was said three thousand years ago, so still it must be said "the judgments of the Lord, are true and righteous altogether."

With malice toward none; with charity for all; with firmness in the right, as God gives us to see the right, let us strive on to finish the work we are in; to bind up the nation's wounds; to care for him who shall have borne the battle, and for his widow, and his orphan — to do all which may achieve and cherish a just, and a lasting peace, among ourselves, and with all nations.

LINCOLN DID NOT READ THE ADDRESS FROM THIS MANUSCRIPT BUT FROM A PRINTED GALLEY OF TWO BROAD COLUMNS.

There was applause, however, at the words 'both parties deprecated war, but one of them would *make* war rather than let the nation survive, and the other would *accept* war rather than let it perish'; and the cheer that followed these words lasted long enough to make a considerable pause before he added sententiously 'and the war came.' There were occasional spurts of applause, too, at other points along this wonderful address. . . ."

During the President's speech, the sun broke through the clouds; superstitious people looked upon it as a good omen for the future.

Harper's Weekly, *March 18, 1865, after a photograph by Gardner*

TAKING THE OATH from Salmon P. Chase, whom the President had made Chief Justice only three months before. Lincoln's lips touched the page of the fifth chapter of Isaiah.

FROM EIGHT TO ELEVEN the President shook hands with more than six thousand people. In this picture most of the notable figures may be seen. In the group at left is General Sherman with Senator

A lithograph by Major & Knapp, published and copyrighted by Frank Leslie in 1865
Sumner; behind them, Admiral Farragut, General Meade, General Hooker and other military men; on the right of Lincoln is Vice-President Johnson and General Grant, behind him his cabinet.

THE INAUGURAL BALL

ON THE evening of March 4 the President gave a reception to the public which was attended by many thousands. During these hours Lincoln shook hands, according to newspaper accounts, with more than six thousand persons. But there were many more who could not get near the President. One of them, the poet Walt Whitman, reported that he was "in the rush inside with the crowd—surged along the passage-ways, the blue and other rooms, and through the great east room. Crowds of country people, some very funny. Fine music from the Marine Band, off in a side place. I saw Mr. Lincoln, drest all in black, with white kid gloves and a claw-hammer coat, receiving as in duty bound, shaking hands, looking very disconsolate, and as if he would give anything to be somewhere else."

Frederick Douglass, the Negro leader, was detained by the policemen at the door. But Lincoln sent out for him and shook his hand cordially. "Douglass, I saw you in the crowd today listening to my inaugural address. There is no man's opinion that I value more than yours; what do you think of it?" Douglass told him: "Mr. Lincoln, it was a sacred effort." And Lincoln smiled: "I am glad you liked it."

One of the men in the receiving line was a young lieutenant who had lost his leg in the war. As soon as Lincoln saw him hobbling along on his crutches, he moved toward him, and taking the lad's hand in his own, he said: "God bless you, my boy!" For the lieutenant it was an unforgettable moment. "Oh! I'd lose another leg for a man like that!" he whispered to his companion.

248

MARY LINCOLN'S DRESSES WERE GREATLY ADMIRED. She spent thousands of dollars for the imported fabrics, went deep into debt for her clothes, believing that as First Lady her duty was to be better dressed and more elegant than any other woman in the land.

PREPARING THE FINAL BLOW

ENTRENCHMENT IN CHARLESTON, S. C.

THE CITY AFTER ITS EVACUATION.

THE ADVENT of spring brought good tidings for the North. Lee's army was exhausted; the Union forces outnumbered it by two to one.

In March, Grant asked the President to visit his headquarters, as he desired to confer with him; besides "the rest would do you good."

Lincoln, too, wanted to see the commander of the army and to talk to him about the surrender terms. He boarded the *River Queen* and, accompanied by Mrs. Lincoln and his son

THE DICTATOR, the new great 17,000-pound mortar, is moved to the Petersburg front. When the gun was first fired, the flatcar on which it was mounted broke down—the detonation was too much. The big mortar took an effective part in the Battle of the Crater.

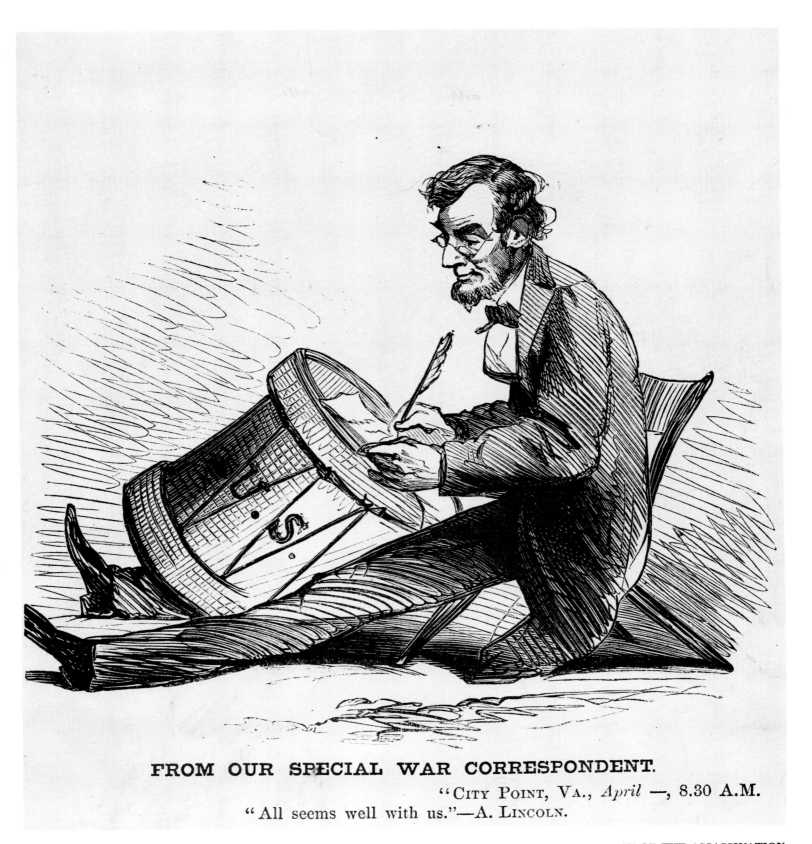

FROM OUR SPECIAL WAR CORRESPONDENT.

"CITY POINT, VA., *April* —, 8.30 A.M.

"All seems well with us."—A. LINCOLN.

A CARTOON BY THOMAS NAST WHICH HAPPENED TO COME OUT IN *HARPER'S WEEKLY* ON THE DAY OF THE ASSASSINATION.

Tad, arrived at City Point on March 23, about nine o'clock in the evening. That night General Grant came to pay his respects, and next morning the President traveled in a railway coach to the front.

Mrs. Lincoln followed him in an ambulance with Mrs. Grant and Colonel Badeau. In the conversation Badeau mentioned that all the wives of the officers had been ordered to the rear except Mrs. Griffin, the wife of

General Griffin. Jealous Mary Lincoln's temper snapped: "Let me out of this carriage at once. I will ask the President if he saw that woman alone." It took quite a while before she could be smoothed down.

IN THE TRENCHES before Petersburg. For ten long months the city was besieged.

During the summer the two armies stood in their entrenchments, broiling in the hot sun.

Occasionally they shot at each other, occasionally there was a battle, but mostly they

Later in the day Lincoln rode with General Meade to a high slope, surveying the battlefield. He saw the dead bodies lying on the field, he watched the burial squads, he saw the doctors helping the wounded, he saw the sad faces of prisoners. With a worn and haggard countenance he said that he hoped this was the beginning of the end, and that there would be no more bloodshed. And when an officer told him that he had seen a young Confederate soldier—just a boy—moaning for his mother and then dying, "Mr.

Lincoln's eyes filled with tears and his voice was choked as he repeated the familiar phrase 'robbing the cradle and the grave.' "

In the evening he sat a while at the headquarters campfire, reminiscing. Grant asked him: "Mr. President, did you at any time doubt the final success of the cause?" and Lincoln answered emphatically: "Never for a moment."

The following day the *River Queen* moved down the James, while on the banks of the river, cheering soldiers greeted their Commander in Chief. At

Aiken's Landing, General Sheridan came on board. Lincoln shook his hands: "General Sheridan, when this peculiar war began I thought cavalrymen should be at least six feet four high, but"—and he looked down at Sheridan—"I have changed my mind —five feet four will do in a pinch."

In the afternoon a review of the Army of the James was planned, Lincoln riding with Grant and General Ord over two miles to the reviewing ground, Mrs. Lincoln and Mrs. Grant following their husbands in an ambu-

THE DEFENDERS OF "FORT HELL," as the Rebel soldiers named Fort Sedgwick. In front of this Federal picket post lay "Fort Damnation," the Confederate Fort Mahone.

"bore it as a Christ might have done."

On March 27 General Sherman arrived at City Point and in the evening, with Grant and Admiral Porter, he saw the President. The four men talked till late at night, and the next day they continued their conference. The theme of their talk was the ending of the war. Grant and Sherman believed

that there had to be one more battle— the last. Lincoln hoped that it could be avoided, as "there had been blood enough shed." The Generals told him that this depended mainly on Lee's attitude.

Then they spoke about the surrender terms and about the future of the South. Lincoln pronounced that he was

waited. The Confederate defenses were formidable; they could not be penetrated.

lance. When Mrs. Lincoln saw that Mrs. Ord, the wife of the General, was near the President, she fumed: "What does this woman mean by riding by the side of the President and ahead of me? Does she suppose that *he* wants *her* by the side of *him*?" And as soon as the review was over, she gave Mrs. Ord a terrible tongue-lashing.

A member of Grant's party recalled that during her visit Mrs. Lincoln "repeatedly attacked her husband in the presence of officers because of Mrs. Griffin and Mrs. Ord" and that Lincoln

Painting by G. P. A. Healy in the White House

THE MEETING ON THE RIVER QUEEN. Lincoln confers with General Sherman, General Grant, and Admiral Porter on surrender terms and how to treat the South after the war ended.

A CHARCOAL SKETCH FROM LIFE, drawn by Albert Hunt at City Point on March 27, 1865. The artist handed the drawing to Mr. Lincoln, who gave it to his wife, and Mary in turn—probably not liking it—presented it to the Negro coachman—who treasured it.

ready—once the Rebel forces laid down their arms—to guarantee Southern inhabitants all the rights as citizens of a common country.

On the 29th the President accompanied Grant and his staff to the railway station; the General was leaving for the Petersburg front to direct operations. Lincoln shook his hands and those of his officers. "Good-by, gentlemen. God bless you all! Remember, your success is my success!"

On April 1 Grant crashed around Lee's right; with only one railroad connecting Richmond with the lower South, the Confederates were compelled to give up Petersburg. On the 2nd, the city was evacuated; the next day Richmond was given up. Jefferson Davis and his cabinet fled.

On April 3 Lincoln came to Petersburg. Overjoyed, he said to Grant: "Do you know, General, that I have had a sort of sneaking idea for some days that you intended to do something like this."

Returning to City Point, he wired his Secretary of War: "Stayed with General Grant an hour and a half and returned here. It is certain now that

AFTER THE CONFEDERATE GOVERNMENT LEFT RICHMOND, arsenals, warehouses, bridges were burned and dynamited by the retreating Rebel army, making everything of military value unusable to Grant. It was a useless measure, too late to stop Union forces.

Contemporary sketch by J. Becker in Frank Leslie's Illustrated Newspaper, *April 22, 1865*

IN RICHMOND, "Dar come Marse Linkum, de Sabior ob de lan'— we so glad to see him," came the greeting from the Negroes as the President, almost unattended, drove into the former capital of the Confederacy on the fourth of April, 1865. But a colored man in the crowd said: "Go 'way, dat ain' no Fadder Abraham. Why, dat man look lak a 'onery ol' famah, he do," and shook his head sadly.

Richmond is in our hands, and I think I will go there to-morrow."

Stanton begged him to be cautious, and Lincoln replied: "I will take care of myself."

Next day the President almost unguarded went to the captured Confederate capital. "Bress de Lawd, dere is de great Messiah!" cried out an old Negro when he recognized Lincoln. "I knowed him as soon as I seed him. He's bin in my heart fo' long yeahs. Glory, hallelujah!" With this he fell on his knees. But Lincoln told him: "Don't kneel to me. You must kneel to God only and thank him for your freedom."

He drove to the Executive Mansion where, a short while before, Jefferson Davis had conducted affairs; an observer who saw him remarked that he looked "pale, and haggard, utterly worn out."

After lunch there was an informal reception, attended by Union officers. General Weitzel asked Lincoln what he should do with the conquered people. "If I were in your place, I'd let 'em up easy, let 'em up easy," the President was heard to answer.

255

LEE SURRENDERS

To FIGHT longer did not make sense. Lee realized it. He had hardly more than 10,000 rifle-bearing men. He was outnumbered five to one, his supply lines had been cut, his soldiers had very little to eat.

The two armies raced westward. When Lee reached Amelia Court House he hoped to find supplies there, but there were none. His army was in a sorry plight—no shoes, many barefoot, their uniforms ragged, hardly any ammunition left.

On April 8, while Lincoln was on his way to Washington, Grant wrote notes to Lee, demanding his surrender.

Next morning, Sunday, April 9, Lee found Sheridan's cavalry in front of him and behind them were troops of Ord and Griffin—a forest of infantry.

"There is nothing left for me to do but to go and see General Grant, and I would rather die a thousand deaths," said Lee. There was no more hope of joining up with General Johnston's forces in North Carolina and continuing the fight.

He sent a note to Grant asking for an interview "with reference to the surrender of this army." Grant, who had nursed a sick headache for a day, named the place—on the edge of Appomattox Village at the McLean house.

Lee came in resplendent uniform, Grant in mudsplashed clothes.

"I met you once before, General Lee," said Grant, "while we were serving in Mexico." Lee, too, had remembered the occasion, but had forgotten what Grant looked like. Then he came to the point of the matter.

"I suppose, General Grant, that the object of our present meeting is fully understood. I asked to see you to ascertain upon what terms you would re-

AFTER THE CONFEDERATES GAVE UP PETERSBURG, Grant and Sheridan pursued Lee's troops vigorously. On April 6 Grant relayed Sheridan's message to Lincoln, which reported the capture of seven thousand prisoners and a great amount of war equipment, the dispatch ending: "If the thing is pressed I think that Lee will surrender." The following day Lincoln answered with this telegram.

Painting by Alonzo Chappell

THE SURRENDER AT APPOMATTOX. On April 9, 1865, General Lee met with General Grant to hear his terms. The Union Commander demanded "the officers and men surrendered to be paroled and disqualified from taking up arms again until properly exchanged, and all arms and munitions and supplies to be delivered up as captured property." Lee had agreed, and thus the war ended.

ceive the surrender of my army."

Grant replied that the terms were the same as those he mentioned in his communication the day before—that all "officers and men surrendered to be paroled and disqualified from taking up arms again until properly exchanged, and all arms, ammunition and supplies to be delivered up as captured property."

Lee nodded in acceptance. Grant wrote out the agreement but forgot to put in the word "exchanged." Lee pointed this out and marked the place where "exchanged" should be put in.

Grant asked whether Lee had any request. Yes, he had. As the cavalrymen and artillerists in his army owned their own horses, they should be allowed to keep them as they would be

sorely needed for the spring plowing.

So Grant agreed to "let all the men who claim to own a horse or mule take the animals home with them to work their little farms."

Lee made a grateful acknowledgment. He said: "This will have the best possible effect upon the men. It will be very gratifying and will do much toward conciliating our people."

The last bloody battle, which Lincoln so dreaded, was avoided. The war came to an end; the Union was safe.

Grant, in keeping with Lincoln's spirit, asked his men to refrain from all celebration. He said: "The war is over; the rebels are our countrymen again; and the best sign of rejoicing after the victory will be to abstain from all demonstrations in the field."

THE END OF THE WAR as announced in an extra edition of the *St. Louis Dispatch*.

THE LAST DAYS

AT 4:30 in the afternoon on April 9, 1865 — Palm Sunday — Grant telegraphed from Appomattox: "General Lee surrendered the Army of Northern Virginia this afternoon on terms proposed by myself. The accompanying additional correspondence will show the conditions fully."

When two days later the President spoke to a large crowd from the balcony of the White House, he explained his future policies toward the South.

"We all agree that the seceded states, so-called, are out of their practical relation with the Union, and that the sole object of the government, civil and military, in regard to those states, is to again get them into that proper practical relation. I believe that it is not only possible, but in fact easier, to do this without deciding or even considering whether those states have ever been out of the Union, than with it. Finding themselves safely at home, it would be utterly immaterial whether they had ever been abroad."

His son Tad listened to his speech and listened to Senator Harlan who posed the question: "What shall we do with the rebels?"

When the crowd shouted, "Hang them," Tad turned to his father: "No, no, papa. Not hang them. Hang on to them!" Lincoln cried out happily: "That's it—Tad has got it. We must hang on to them!"

And he told a Southerner who came to see him: "I love the Southern people more than they love me. My desire is to restore the Union. I do not intend to hurt the hair of the head of a single man in the South if it can possibly be avoided."

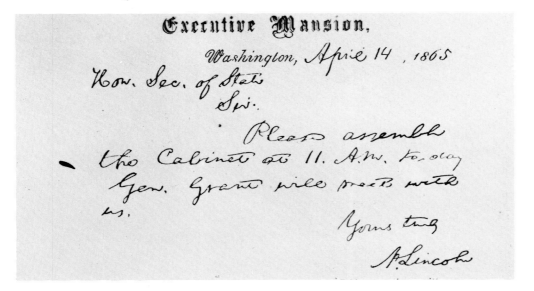

ON THE DAY HE WAS ASSASSINATED, Lincoln asked Seward to assemble the Cabinet for 11 o'clock in the morning to meet with the victorious General of the Armies, U. S. Grant.

HIS LAST PHOTOGRAPH, taken by Alexander Gard on April 10, 1865, four days before Lincoln's de

GOOD FRIDAY, APRIL 14, 1865

THE SECOND week of April the President had a strange dream. He was used to dreams, but this time the dream seemed to be weirder than any of the ones before. He related it to Mary.

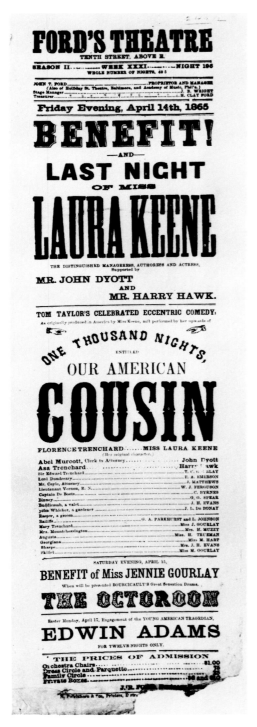

THE PLAYBILL of Ford's Theatre for April 14, 1865—Good Friday—announcing the appearance of Laura Keene, the popular actress, in "Our American Cousin."

"About ten days ago," he said, "I retired very late. I had been up waiting for important dispatches from the front. I could not have been long in bed when I fell into a slumber, for I was weary. I soon began to dream. There seemed to be a death-like stillness about me. Then I heard subdued sobs, as if a number of people were weeping. I thought I left my bed and wandered downstairs. There the silence was broken by the same pitiful sobbing, but the mourners were invisible. I went from room to room; no living person was in sight, but the same mournful sounds of distress met me as I passed along. I saw light in all the rooms; every object was familiar to me; but where were all the people who were grieving as if their hearts would break? I was puzzled and alarmed. What could be the meaning of all this? Determined to find the cause of a state of things so mysterious and so shocking, I kept on until I arrived at the East Room, which I entered. There I met with a sickening surprise. Before me was a catafalque, on which rested a corpse wrapped in funeral vestments.

Around it were stationed soldiers who were acting as guards; and there was a throng of people, gazing mournfully upon the corpse, whose face was covered, others weeping pitifully. 'Who is dead in the White House?' I demanded of one of the soldiers, 'The President,' was his answer; 'he was killed by an assassin.' Then came a loud burst of grief from the crowd, which awoke me from my dream. I slept no more that night; and although it was only a dream, I have been strangely annoyed by it ever since."

Mary was horrified when she heard about the dream. "I wish you had not told it. I am glad I don't believe in dreams, or I should be in terror from this time forth."

"Well," answered Lincoln, "it is only a dream, Mary. Let us say no more about it, and try to forget it."

His political friends worried about him; there were anonymous letters, threatening to kill the President.

"What does anybody want to assassinate me for?" asked Lincoln. "If anyone wants to do so, he can do it any day or night, if he is ready to give his

A CONTEMPORARY SKETCH OF THE BOX by Alfred R. Waud of *Harper's Weekly*.

FORD'S THEATRE IN WASHINGTON, where Booth shot Lincoln. On April 14, 1865, the President entered through the second door from the right—the main entrance. The first door led to the gallery, while the other three doors served as exits. In the saloon of Peter Taltavul (the two-story building adjoining the theater) Booth waited, drinking his whiskey before committing the deed.

life for mine. It is nonsense." He did not believe "that any human being lives" who would do him any harm.

April the fourteenth was Good Friday. On that day Major General Robert Anderson, who four years before had surrendered Fort Sumter, sent up the Union flag to wave once more over the fort. On that day General Ulysses S. Grant arrived in Washington. On that day Edwin Stanton, the Secretary of War, announced that all further drafting and recruiting would be stopped. On that day Lincoln wrote to General Van Alen that his effort was "to restore the Union, so as to make it, to use your language, a Union of hearts and hands as well as of States."

For Lincoln, the day began as usual. He arose at seven, worked in his office for a while, then took his breakfast. The morning hours were given over to interviews. People came with requests, they came for help. He listened to

261

them, listened to their problems, listened to their worries. One of the callers was John A. J. Creswell, of Maryland. Lincoln greeted him, "Creswell, old fellow, everything is bright this morning. The war is over. . . . We are going to have good times now, and a united country." The dark clouds of the past years were lifting; the future looked bright.

Always keen for news, he walked over to the War Department. But there was no word from Sherman, no word of his army.

At eleven the Cabinet met. Before the meeting Lincoln chatted with the secretaries. The Postmaster General inquired whether the President would be sorry if the Southern leaders would escape. "Well," said Lincoln slowly, "I should not be sorry to have them out of the country; but I should be for fol-lowing them up pretty close, to make sure of their going." Everyone laughed and Lincoln joined in the merriment.

He expected to hear from Sherman soon, he told his political family, and he expected good news. For the night before he had had a dream, one he had dreamed often before. He saw himself in a strange vessel moving swiftly toward a dark and unknown shore. Each time before, this dream had been followed up by an important event.

General Grant arrived and he was greeted with cordiality. Lincoln asked the General, who told of Lee's surrender, "What terms did you make for the common soldiers?" And Grant answered, "I told them to go back to their homes, and they would not be molested, if they did nothing more." This pleased the President.

At the meeting the problems of re-construction were discussed. Lincoln spoke out the hope that the Southern state governments would soon be working in an orderly way. "We can't undertake to run state governments in all these Southern states. The people must do that—though I reckon that at first some of them may do it badly." He pleaded for a forgiving attitude toward those who took part in the rebellion. "We must," he said, "extinguish our resentments if we expect harmony and union."

The discussion over, the President was in no rush to leave. He exchanged pleasantries with General Grant, who apologized that he could not go with the President that night to the theatre as planned. It was around two o'clock when the two men parted.

For Lincoln there was a hurried luncheon, then more work, and more

IN THE PRESIDENT'S BOX ON THE FATAL NIGHT

MAJOR HENRY REED RATHBONE, an attaché of the War Office, who accompanied the President to the theatre, after some others— among them General Grant and his wife—turned down the invitation. When Booth fired the fatal shot, Rathbone jumped at the attacker. But by then the actor had thrown away his pistol and drawn a dagger. In the short scuffle Rathbone was wounded in the arm.

CLARA HARRIS, the daughter of Senator Ira T. Harris of New York, and the stepsister and future wife of Major Rathbone was another occupant of the box. She was attractive, well liked by Washington society—as elegant as she was witty. The Lincolns picked up Miss Harris and Major Rathbone at Senator Harris's residence at Fifteenth and H Street and together they drove to the theatre.

Drawn by Albert Berghaus for Frank Leslie's Illustrated Newspaper, *April 29, 1865*

JOHN WILKES BOOTH ENTERS BOX 7 AND SHOOTS LINCOLN. AT THE PRESIDENT'S RIGHT, CLARA HARRIS AND MAJOR RATHBONE.

signing of papers. Putting his signature under the pardon of a deserter he made the remark, long remembered, "Well, I think the boy can do us more good above ground than underground."

DIAGRAM OF THE BOX. The letter O marks the dark corridor which led from the dress circle to the box of the President. H is the entrance to the corridor; I is the bar which Booth used to prevent entrance to the box, while F denotes the open door to the box. The chairs where the President and Mrs. Lincoln watched the performance are marked A and B; the sofa and chairs where Clara Harris and Major Rathbone sat are C, D — and J is the dress circle; K the parquette; L the footlights; and M the stage. The letter N marks the spot where Booth jumped over the balustrade of the President's box and onto the stage.

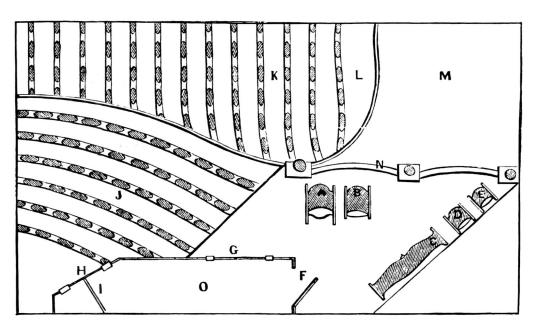

By three o'clock the presidential carriage was at the gate to take him and Mary to the Navy Yard. As the President walked down the steps, a colored woman—Nancy Bushrod—approached him with a petition for her soldier-husband's pay. Lincoln told her to return the next day when the necessary papers would be ready.

"My good woman, perhaps you'll see many a day when all the food in the house is a single loaf of bread. Even so, give every child a slice and send your children off to school." With that he bowed before her—as Nancy Bushrod told later—"lak I wuz a natchral bawn lady."

There was another incident. A one-armed soldier, waiting to catch sight of Lincoln, called out, "I would almost give my other hand if I could shake that of Abraham Lincoln." The President, hearing the remark, walked to-

BOX 7 IN FORD'S THEATRE, as it looked the night of Lincoln's assassination. A contemporary photograph from a War Department photographer two days after the event. The box was decorated with flags, an engraved portrait of George Washington and, in the center, the blue-and-gold flag of the U.S. Treasury Guard. When Booth jumped he caught the spur of his right boot in this flag, fell on the stage, eleven feet below, and broke his left leg.

BOOTH'S DERRINGER PISTOL with which he killed Lincoln was small, only six inches long and weighing half a pound.

THE BLACK-WALNUT ROCKER, put in the box for the President's comfort for the evening was upholstered in red damask.

264

Drawn by Albert Berghaus for Frank Leslie's Illustrated Newspaper, *May 20, 1865*

"THE SOUTH IS AVENGED!" cried John Wilkes Booth—or so people heard him say—after he jumped to the stage. Actor Henry Hawk, who played the part of Asa Trenchard in the play, stood stunned, unable to move. Booth escaped before the pandemonium.

ward the soldier and grabbed his hand. "You shall do that and it shall cost you nothing."

The drive to the Navy Yard was a short one. Arriving there the Lincolns inspected the ironclad *Montauk*, fresh from the engagement at Fort Fisher.

On the way home the President was in an elated mood; he was spinning plans for the future. "We have had a hard time since we came to Washing-

ton," he said to Mary, "but the war is over, and with God's blessing we may hope for four years of peace and happiness, and then we will go back to Illinois and pass the rest of our lives in quiet. We have laid by some money, but shall not have enough to support us. We will go back to Illinois. I will open a law office in Springfield or Chicago and practice law, and at least do enough to help give us a livelihood."

As the carriage came to a halt before the White House, Lincoln spotted two of his old friends from Illinois who were just leaving the mansion— General Isham N. Haynie and Governor Richard Oglesby. He asked them to return and settled down with them in the reception room. Relaxed, he read to the friends no less than four chapters of his favorite humorist, Petroleum V. Nasby's *Letters*. Only when

265

Sketch by Albert Berghaus in Frank Leslie's Illustrated Newspaper, *May 13, 1865*

THE FATALLY WOUNDED PRESIDENT could not be taken too far. The doctors searched for a bed near by. Lincoln was carried across Tenth Street to the house of W. Petersen.

dinner was announced at six o'clock did the visitors leave.

After the meal, Lincoln once more walked over to the War Department. His special guard, William H. Crook, accompanied him. Outside the White House some rough-looking men looked darkly at the President. "Crook, do you know, I believe there are men who want to take my life," mused Lincoln. "And I have no doubt they will do it." Crook thought it strange that he should talk in this way; he had never spoken in such a manner before. "Why do you

ON THE NIGHT OF APRIL 14, 1865: THE Doctors, Cabinet members, military leaders crowded the room. Sitting at the end of the bed are Secretary of the Navy Welles and

think so, Mr. President?" Lincoln answered, "Other men have been assassinated," adding after a pause, "I have perfect confidence in those who are around me. . . . I know no one could do it and escape alive. But if it is to be done, it is impossible to prevent it."

Arriving at the War Office, he joked about the strength of Major Eckert, the Chief of the Telegraph Department. "I have seen Eckert break five pokers," he said to the Secretary of War, "one

Sketch by Albert Berghaus in Frank Leslie's Illustrated Newspaper, *May 20, 1865*

THE PETERSEN HOUSE, opposite Ford's Theatre, where Lincoln was laid on the bed of roomer William T. Clark. It was here that the President died at 7:22 the next morning.

Harper's Weekly, *May 16, 1865*

LITTLE ROOM OF THE PETERSEN HOUSE WHERE ABRAHAM LINCOLN BREATHED HIS LAST AT 7:22 THE FOLLOWING MORNING.

Secretary of War Stanton; on the bed, Dr. Robert K. Stone, the Lincolns' family physician. In the group at the head (l. to r.) are: Postmaster General William Dennison; the Senator from Massachusetts, Charles Sumner; Surgeon-General Joseph Barnes; Robert T. Lincoln; General Henry Halleck; John Hay, the President's secretary; and Quartermaster General Montgomery Meigs.

after the other, over his arm, and I'm thinking he would be the kind of man to go with me this evening. May I take him?" Stanton was opposed to Lincoln's going to the theatre. But the President had promised Mary and it was now too late to cancel it. The Secretary would not release Eckert— he needed him for urgent work. When Crook heard this, he offered his services, but Lincoln would not hear of it. "No, Crook, you've had a long, hard day's work, and must go home."

Back in the White House, Lincoln worked at his desk, and he saw some more people. At half past seven, as he was ready to leave for the theatre, Schuyler Colfax, the Speaker of the House, arrived with George Ashmun of Massachusetts, the man who five years before had brought him the official news of his nomination. Ashmun asked for an interview the following day, and Lincoln obligingly wrote out a card which was to admit him to his office—his last written words.

About a quarter past eight the Lincolns were on their way. A few minutes later they stopped at Senator Ira T. Harris's residence at Fifteenth and H Street, where the Senator's daughter and her fiancé joined them, the party reaching Ford's Theatre about eight thirty. As the President entered his box, the audience rose to its feet, shouting and applauding, and the orchestra

(turn to page 270)

267

HOW ARTISTS DREW THE DEATH SCENE. Hermann Faber, a hospital steward, was sent to the room by the Surgeon General's office. After making a rough sketch, he turned to a new sheet for this finished drawing.

JOHN H. LITTLEFIELD'S PAINTING shows no less than twenty-four people around the dying Lincoln. In this work the little chamber of ten by fifteen feet had grown to an enormous room, large enough to fit into a royal palace.

A. H. RITCHIE'S ENGRAVING portrays twenty-six people who were supposed to be present in the tiny space when the President died in the Petersen house. Of course this is an exaggeration of the artist, and a fanciful one, too.

ALONZO CHAPPEL'S PAINTING has forty-six persons around Lincoln. In it the tiny

THE ROOM WHERE LINCOLN DIED. It measured ten by fifteen feet, and was furnished only with a bureau, a table, a few chairs and a bed. This is a reconstruction.

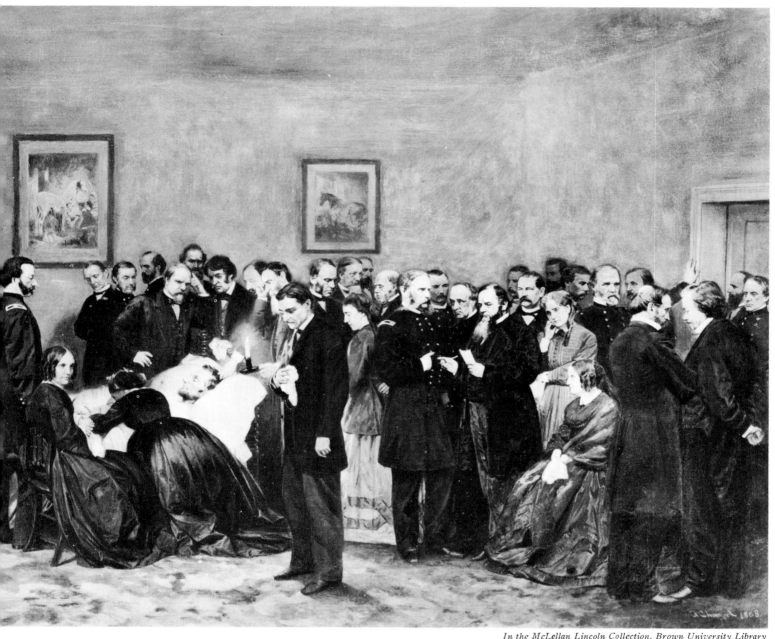

room had grown to a palace chamber. The design for the painting was made by F. B. Batchelder, who commissioned Photographer Brady to take pictures of the people in the exact poses they were to assume in the painting. From these Brady photographs Alonzo Chappel then made the painting, including everyone who came to the Petersen house that night. In the group on the left the dominant figure sitting in the chair is Vice-President Andrew Johnson. The people standing from left to right are: Major Henry Rathbone, who was in the box with the Lincolns; Congressman Isaac N. Arnold from Illinois; Postmaster General William Dennison; Secretary of the Navy Gideon Welles (with beard); Attorney General James Speed; Dr. J. C. Hall; Dr. C. H. Liebermann; Secretary of Interior John P. Usher; Secretary of Treasury Hugh McCulloch; Governor R. J. Oglesby of Illinois; Speaker of the House Schuyler Colfax; Dr. E. King Stone; Surgeon General Joseph K. Barnes (at the bed). The two ladies in the foreground: Mrs. Lincoln (weeping on the bed) and the wife of Senator Dixon. Standing in the large group on the right: Dr. Lyman Beecher Todd; Assistant Surgeon Charles A. Leale; Assistant Acting Surgeon Dr. Charles

S. Taft; Assistant Secretary of the Interior William T. Otto; Congressman John F. Farnsworth of Illinois; Senator Charles Sumner of Massachusetts; Assistant Surgeon General Charles H. Crane; the delegate from Dakota Territory, John B. S. Todd. The figure standing in the foreground is Robert T. Lincoln, the President's eldest son. Behind him, his head turned toward the right, is the Reverend Dr. Phineas Gurley. Then follow: Assistant Secretary of the Treasury Maunsell B. Field; Isham N. Hayne, Adj. General of Illinois; Benjamin Brown French of New Hampshire; General Christopher C. Auger (in front); Brigadier General Thomas M. Vincent; General Henry W. Halleck; Secretary of War Edwin M. Stanton; Brig. General George V. Rutherford; Assistant Secretary of War Thomas T. Eckert; Brig. General Louis H. Pelouse; John Hay; Quartermaster General Montgomery C. Meigs; Major Almon F. Rockwell; Leonard J. Farwell, the former Governor of Wisconsin; David K. Cartter, the Chief Justice of the District of Columbia; Congressman Edward H. Rollins; Congressman Gilman Martson. The ladies on the right: Mrs. Mary C. Kinney (sitting), her daughter Constance Kinney (standing), in the center, Clara Harris.

The artist Albert Berghaus described the room: "The walls are covered with a brownish paper, figured with a white design. Its dimensions are about ten by fifteen feet. Some engravings and a photograph hang upon the walls. . . . The only furniture in the room was a bureau covered with crochet, a table, eight or nine plain chairs, and the bed upon which Mr. Lincoln lay when his spirit took its flight. The bedstead was a low walnut, with headboard from two to three feet high. The floor was carpeted with Brussels, considerably worn. Everything on the bed was stained with . . . blood . . ."

269

HIGHLY IMPORTANT!

The President Shot!

Secretary Seward Attacked.

FIRST DISPATCH.

To the Associated Press.

WASHINGTON, Friday, April 14, 1865.

The President was shot in a theater to-night, and perhaps mortally wounded.

SECOND DISPATCH.

To EDITORS: Our Washington agent orders the dispatch about the President "stopped." Nothing is said about the truth or falsity of the dispatch.

THIRD DISPATCH.

Special Dispatch to The N. Y. Tribune.

The President was just shot at Ford's Theater. The ball entered his neck. It is not known whether the wound is mortal. Intense excitement.

FOURTH DISPATCH.

Special Dispatch to The N. Y. Tribune.

The President expired at a quarter to twelve.

FIFTH DISPATCH.

To the Associated Press.

WASHINGTON, April 15—12:30 a. m.

The President was shot in a theater to-night, and is perhaps mortally wounded.

The President is not expected to live through the night. He was shot at a theater.

Secretary Seward was also assassinated.

No arteries were cut.

Particulars soon.

SIXTH DISPATCH.

Special Dispatch to The N. Y. Tribune.

WASHINGTON, Friday, April 14, 1865.

Like a clap of thunder out of clear sky spread the announcement that President

We give the above dispatches in the order in which they reached us, the first having been received a little before midnight, for we know that every line, every letter will be read with the intensest interest. In the sudden shock of a calamity so appalling we can do little else than give such details of the murder of the President as have reached us. Sudden death is always overwhelming; assassination of the humblest of men is always frightfully startling; when the head of thirty millions of people is hurried into eternity by the hand of a murderer—that head a man so good, so wise, so noble as ABRAHAM LINCOLN, the Chief Magistrate of a nation in the condition of ours at this moment,—the sorrow and the shock are too great for many words. There are none in all this broad land to-day who love their country, who wish well to their race, that will not bow down in profound grief at the event it has brought upon us. For once all party rancor will be forgotten, and no right-thinking man can hear of Mr. Lincoln's death without accepting it as a national calamity. We can give in these its first moments, no thought of the future. God, in his inscrutable Providence, has thus visited the Nation; the future we must leave to Him.

Later.—The accounts are confused and contradictory. One dispatch announces that the President died at 12½ p. m. Another, an hour later, states that he is still living, but dying slowly. We go to press without knowing the exact truth, but presume there is not the slightest ground for hope. Mr. Seward and his son are both seriously wounded, but were not killed. But there can be little hope that the Secretary can rally with this additional and frightful wound.

AT FIRST, NEWSPAPERS WERE NOT ALLOWED TO REVEAL THE ASSASSIN'S NAME.

played "Hail to the Chief." Lincoln acknowledged the ovation, then sat down in the large rocking chair which was put into the box for his comfort. Mary was next to him, Clara Harris and Major Rathbone were sitting at their right. The show continued. It was a comedy, _Our American Cousin,_ written by Tom Taylor. Lincoln had seen it before, but did not seem bored by seeing it again.

He reached out for Mary's hand. "What will Miss Harris think of my hanging on to you so?" she whispered, and he answered, holding on to her, "She won't think anything about it." He enjoyed the show, laughed at the familiar lines, was amused by the situations. The time passed pleasantly.

At half past nine a dark-haired man with a black mustache and black felt hat dismounted his horse at the rear of the theatre. He was a familiar figure at the stage door—John Wilkes Booth, the renowned member of the celebrated theatrical family, the son of Junius Booth and the brother of Edwin, two of the great performers of their time.

Twenty-six-year-old John Wilkes Booth, whose name was ever to be linked to that of Abraham Lincoln, was a curious and strange person, tense, restless, excitable. What he wanted most from life was fame. He wanted to be known, he wanted to be liked, he wanted to be admired. He searched for love, restlessly moving from one woman to the other, never finding peace. He desired more than was given to him. His egomania, his

Harper's Weekly, _April 29, 1865_

AFTER HIS DEED, John Wilkes Booth leaped to the stage, and shouting "_Sic semper tyrannis_" (Ever thus to tyrants), he escaped.

Frank Leslie's Illustrated Newspaper, _May 13, 1865_

AT THE STAGE DOOR the assassin jumped on his waiting horse, held by the slow-witted chore boy "Peanuts John," and galloped off.

feeling of self-importance, was of monumental proportion. He wanted his name to be known a "thousand years afterward." He sympathized with the South, though he never took up arms to fight for the Confederacy. And he loathed Lincoln, violently and unreasonably, believing him to be the root of all evil. He had heard him at the White House three nights before, when the President had spoken out the hope that the emancipated slaves of Louisiana would be allowed to vote. Booth fumed with anger at such a proposition. "That means nigger citizenship," he had muttered. If Lincoln advocated such policies, he ought to be put away. If no one would do it, he, Booth, would be the instrument of fate. He began to see himself as the avenger.

Ever since last September he had been thinking of a scheme to abduct Lincoln, take him to Richmond, hand him over to the Confederate government, which in turn would exchange him for Confederate soldiers who were captured by Union forces.

Lincoln was to be overpowered in a theatre—where else? Booth was first and last an actor. The scene must have dramatic value—it had to be played with spectators present. At first it was not in the actor's mind to harm the President. But when the abduction plan came to naught, he thought of more desperate means. Under the date of April 13 he wrote in his diary: "Until today, nothing was ever thought of sacrificing to our country's wrong. For six months we had worked to capture, but

(turn to page 277)

War Department, Washington, April 20, 1865,

$100,000 REWARD!

THE MURDERER

Of our late beloved President, ABRAHAM LINCOLN,

IS STILL AT LARGE.

$50,000 REWARD!

will be paid by this Department for his apprehension, in addition to any reward offered by Municipal Authorities or State Executives.

$25,000 REWARD!

will be paid for the apprehension of JOHN H. SURRATT, one of Booth's accomplices.

$25,000 REWARD!

will be paid for the apprehension of DANIEL C. HARROLD, another of Booth's accomplices.

LIBERAL REWARDS will be paid for any information that shall conduce to the arrest of either of the above-named criminals, or their accomplices.

All persons harboring or secreting the said persons, or either of them, or aiding or assisting their concealment or escape, will be treated as accomplices in the murder of the President and the attempted assassination of the Secretary of State, and shall be subject to trial before a Military Commission and the punishment of DEATH.

Let the stain of innocent blood be removed from the land by the arrest and punishment of the murderers.

All good citizens are exhorted to aid public justice on this occasion. Every man should consider his own conscience charged with this solemn duty, and rest neither night nor day until it be accomplished.

EDWIN M. STANTON, *Secretary of War.*

DESCRIPTIONS.—BOOTH is 5 feet 7 or 8 inches high, slender build, high forehead, black hair, black eyes, and wears a heavy black moustache. JOHN H. SURRATT is about 5 feet 9 inches. Hair rather thin and dark; eyes rather light; no beard. Would weigh 145 or 160 pounds. Complexion rather pale and clear with color in his cheeks. Wore light clothes of fine quality. Shoulders square; check bones rather prominent; chin narrow; ears projecting at the top; forehead rather low and square, but broad. Parts his hair on the right side; neck rather long. His lips are firmly set. A slim man. DANIEL C. HARROLD is 23 years of age, 5 feet 6 or 7 inches high, rather broad shouldered, otherwise light built; dark hair, little (if any) moustache; dark eyes; weighs about 140 pounds.

GEO. F NESBITT & CO., Printers and Stationers, cor. Pearl and Pine Streets, N. Y.

THE POSTER OF THE WAR DEPARTMENT. The reward was high, and when distributed was split in thirty-four parts. Lieutenant Colonel E. J. Conger, who led the chase after John Wilkes Booth, was awarded $15,000—the largest amount received by any one person.

Harper's Weekly, May 13, 1865

BOOTH TOOK HIS LAST REFUGE in a barn. As he would not surrender to the cavalry who found him, the building was set afire.

Frank Leslie's Illustrated Newspaper, May 13, 1865

BOOTH WAS STILL ALIVE when the soldiers dragged him out of the burning barn at Garrett's farm near Port Royal, Virginia.

271

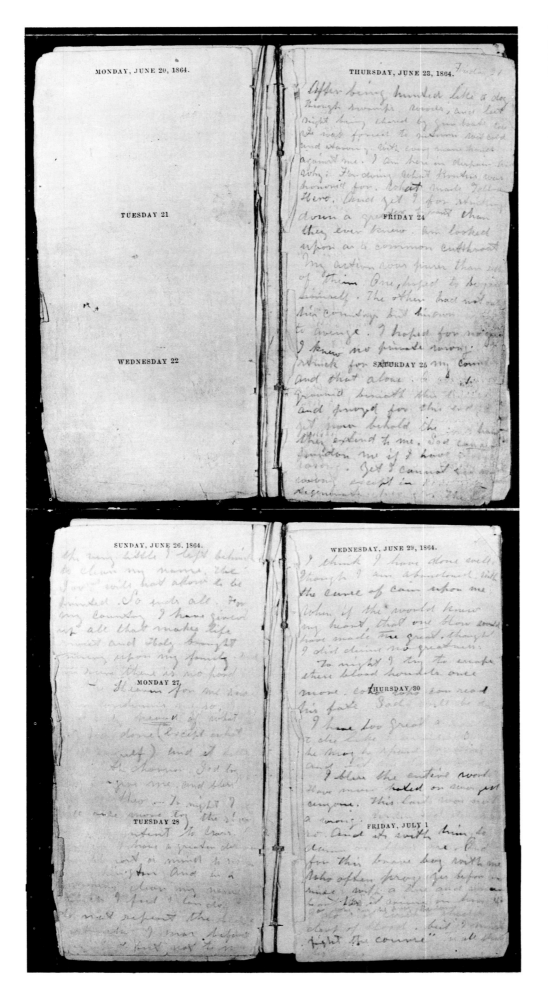

THE ASSASSIN'S DIARY. Booth kept a record, written in mental anguish at hurried moments during his flight. The diary, found on his body, was taken by the War Department and kept a secret. Two years after Booth's death President Johnson ordered the Secretary of War to produce it—but Stanton was hesitant. When at last the diary came to light, eighteen pages preceding the date of the assassination were missing. And they are missing until this day. The illustration on the left shows Booth's entry in his notebook on Friday, April 21, 1865 (written on pages for June 23 to June 29, 1864), not long before he met his end. *"After being hunted like a dog through swamps, woods, and last night being chased by gunboats till I was forced to return wet, cold, and starving, with every man's hand against me, I am here in despair. And why? For doing what Brutus was honored for. What made Tell a Hero. And yet I, for striking down a greater tyrant than they ever knew, am looked upon as a common cutthroat. My action was purer than either of theirs. One hoped to be great himself. The other had not only his country's but his own, wrongs to avenge. I hoped for no gain. I knew no private wrong. I struck for my country and that alone. A country that groaned beneath this tyranny, and prayed for this end, and yet now behold the cold hands they extend to me. God* cannot *pardon me if I have done wrong.* Yet *I cannot see my wrong, except in serving a degenerate people. The little, the very little, I left behind to clear my name, the Government will not allow to be printed. So ends all. For my country I have given up all that makes life sweet and holy, brought misery upon my family, and am sure there is no pardon in the Heaven for me, since man condemns me so. I have only* heard *of what has been done (except what* I *did myself), and it fills me with horror. God, try and forgive me, and bless my mother. Tonight I will once more try the river with the intent to cross. Though I have a greater desire and almost a mind to return to Washington, and in a measure clear my name—which I feel I can do. I do not repent the blow I struck. I may before my God, but not to man. I think I have done well. Though I am abandoned, with the curse of Cain upon me, when, if the world knew my heart, that one blow would have made me great, though I did desire no greatness. Tonight I try to escape these bloodhounds once more. Who, who can read his fate? God's will be done. I have too great a soul to die like a criminal. Oh, may He, may He spare me that, and let me die bravely. I bless the entire world. Have never hated or wronged anyone. This last was not a wrong, unless God deems it so, and it's with Him to damn or bless me. As for this brave boy with me, who often prays (yes, before and since) with a true and sincere heart—was it crime in him? If so, why can he pray the same?*

I do not wish to shed a drop of blood, but 'I must fight the course.' 'Tis all that's left to me."

THE MAN WHO KILLED LINCOLN: JOHN WILKES BOOTH. His description on the reward posters read: 26 years old, 5 feet, 7 or 8 inches tall, slender build, weighing 160 pounds, with black hair, black eyes, and a heavy black mustache. Booth—one of the most celebrated actors of his time—was a ladies' man. When he was captured, the photographs of five women were found in his wallet.

THE ONLY PHOTOGRAPH OF ABRAHAM LINCOLN IN HIS COFFIN—PUBLISHED HERE FOR THE FIRST TIME. While Lincoln's body lay in state in New York's City Hall before the busts of Jackson and Webster, the photographer Jeremiah Gurney, Jr., received permission to photograph it. As soon as Secretary of War Edwin Stanton learned about this in Washington, he wired to Adjutant General E. D. Townsend (at the foot of the coffin opposite Admiral Charles A. Davis), and ordered him to seize and destroy the plates and any proofs made from them. On April 29, 1865, General John A. Dix, commanding the Department of the East, reported to Stanton that he had destroyed the larger plate and its print, while of the smaller plate he enclosed a proof. He wrote to the Secretary of War that "Mr. Gurney is desirous that the plate should be preserved, and thinks Mr. Lincoln's family, when they see the proof, will be willing to have it returned to him." But Stanton replied that "the family will not consent to the publication," therefore "you will . . . destroy the plate as heretofore directed and any copies that may be printed as heretofore ordered." Eighty-seven years later the single print, which Stanton retained, turned up in the papers of John G. Nicolay, Lincoln's private secretary—to whom Stanton's son sent it after his father's death. It was found in the Illinois State Historical Library in Springfield, Illinois, by Donald Rietveld, a fifteen-year-old schoolboy from Des Moines, Iowa.

A FUTURE PRESIDENT WATCHES LINCOLN'S FUNERAL, on April 25, 1865, from the window of his grandfather's house in New York City. The little boy in the second-story window (see arrow) on Broadway and Fourteenth Street is six-and-one-half-year-old Theodore Roosevelt, who, with his brother Elliot (the father of Eleanor Roosevelt), was looking at the funeral. The house belonged to grandfather Van Schaack Roosevelt.

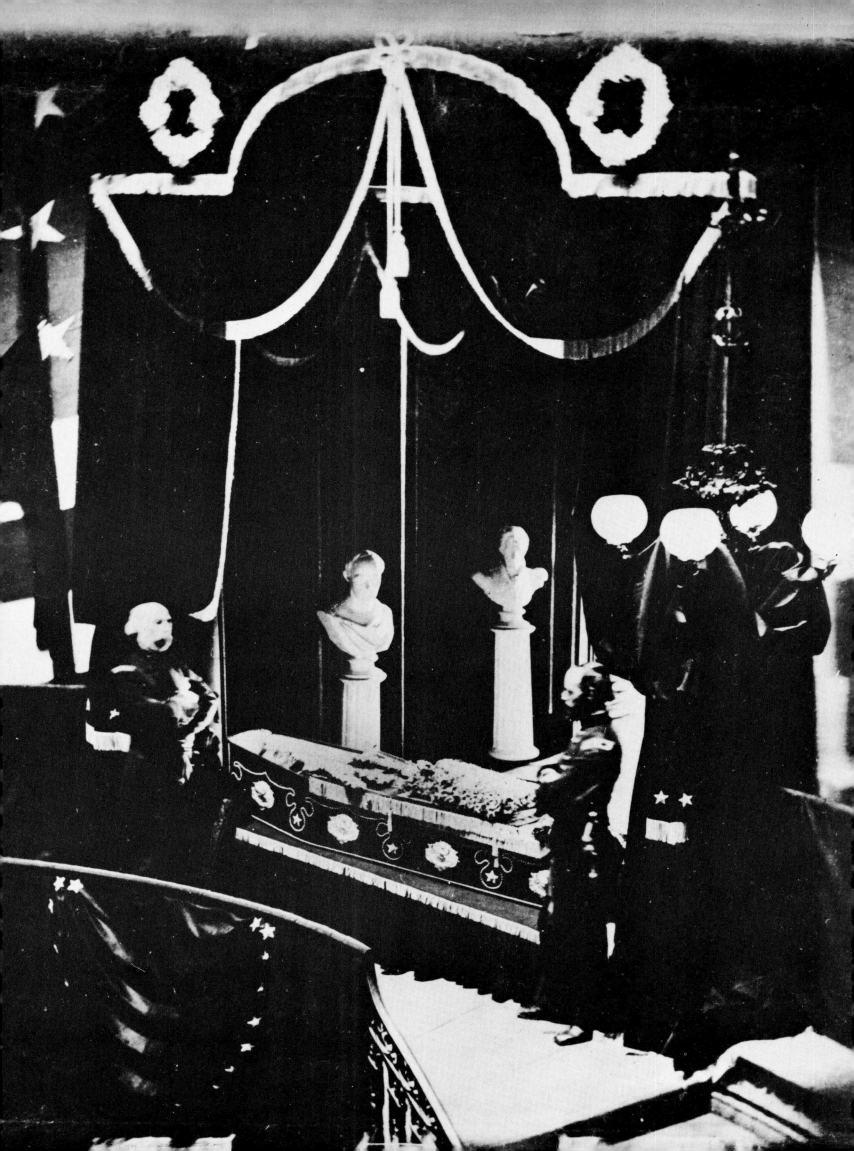

Harper's Weekly, *May 6, 1865*

THE SOMBER FUNERAL SERVICE IN THE WHITE HOUSE.

Harper's Weekly, *May 13, 1865*

THE CORTEGE WHICH CARRIED THE PRESIDENT'S BODY.

Frank Leslie's Illustrated Newspaper, *May 13, 1865*

THE ORNATE COFFIN OF ABRAHAM LINCOLN

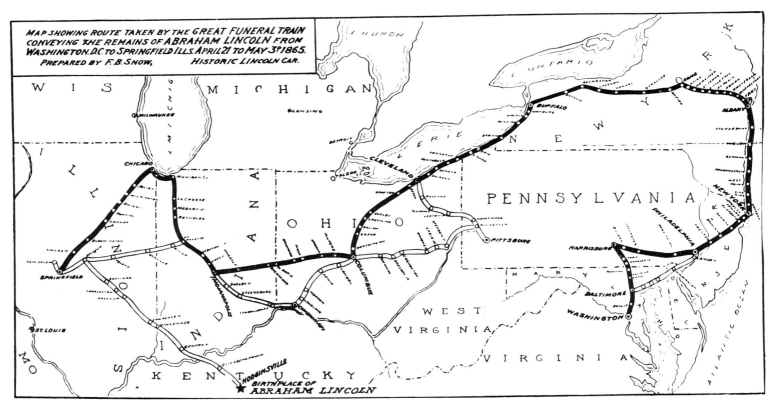

THE ROUTE OF THE FUNERAL TRAIN. The remains of the President left Washington on April 21 and reached Springfield on May 3. The train took a circuitous route, touching on many cities on the way, giving citizens a chance to take their farewell. The cities of Harrisburg, Philadelphia, New York, Albany, Buffalo, Cleveland, Columbus, Indianapolis and Chicago were stations on the route.

THE PEOPLE OF SPRINGFIELD SAY FAREWELL. Lincoln's body lay in state on May 3rd and 4th in Springfield. Men and women of his home town, light and dark alike, as seen in the picture, came to the State House to pay homage to their beloved President.

our cause being almost lost, something decisive and great must be done."

Thus, on this evening of April 14, with a small pistol and a dagger, he walked toward the President's box. Booth had had little sleep during the past twenty-four hours. His day had been busy, rushing from one place to the other, making final preparations for the deed which was to make his name "famous" forever. He attended to every detail. He engaged a horse at a livery stable, he bored a hole in the door of the President's box, so he could observe Lincoln from the outside, and he had a final meeting with his fellow conspirators. At this meeting George Atzerodt, who was to kill the Vice-President, told Booth that he could not do such a deed, he could not be a murderer. Booth replied that he was a fool and that he would be hanged in any case.

The clock showed nine thirty when Booth walked into the theatre. He had left his horse in the care of Edman Spangler, the stagehand, who in turn handed the reins to "Peanuts" Burrough, the stage doorkeeper. Once more the actor had walked up to Taltavul's saloon, asked for a whiskey and washed it down with a chaser. By then the third act of the play was in full swing. Outside the presidential box, John F. Parker, the President's special guard, had become bored, left his place and was stilling his thirst in a nearby drinking spot, leaving the President without guard.

As Booth entered the foyer he caught the eye of Jennie Gourlay, the actress, and she recalled later that he seemed pale and ill, distraught and strange, with "a wild look in his eyes."

By then it was thirteen minutes past ten, or a little later. On the stage Mrs. Montchessington upbraided Asa Trenchard, the play's chief character: "I am aware, Mr. Trenchard, that you are not used to the manner of good society, and that alone will excuse the impertinence of which you have been guilty." With this she left the scene.

Booth was now at the door of the presidential box, peering through the little hole he had bored that afternoon. Noiselessly he opened the door and entered the box.

On the stage Asa Trenchard soliloquized: "Don't know the manners of good society, eh? Wal, I guess I know enough to turn you inside out, old gal—you sockdologizing old mantrap."

At this moment a sharp sound was heard—the report of a pistol. Then voices from the President's box and a shout: "The President is shot!"

Major Rathbone threw himself at the stranger, who now had dropped his deringer and drew his dagger. The two wrestled, and Booth's knife cut deep into Major Rathbone's arm. Freeing himself, the assassin was the actor again. Crying out, "*Sic semper tyrannis*" (Ever thus to tyrants), he leaped onto the stage some eleven feet below. As he jumped his spur caught in the flag of the Treasury Guard, throwing him hard on his leg. He had foreseen everything but this—the obstacle of the flag, the injury to his leg. But he was up in a moment, and ran across the stage and to the alley where "Peanuts" John Burrough was holding his horse. The assassin mounted the horse in a fury and galloped away.

All this happened with the speed of lightning. The shooting of Lincoln, the escape of the assassin had taken but seconds. Booth left the theatre about twenty minutes after ten. It was about fifteen minutes later that he crossed the

THE END OF THE JOURNEY. At last the funeral train reached Springfield, Lincoln's home town. And, after the long journey across country, at last his remains were laid to rest at a temporary vault in Oak Ridge Cemetery with thousands of mourners watching it.

THE TEMPORARY RESTING PLACE. Soldiers guard the vault at Oak Ridge Cemetery in the Illinois Capital, where President Lincoln's body was temporarily placed. This photograph was taken a short time after the funeral ceremonies in May, 1865.

Anacostia Bridge.

In the box the fatally wounded President slumped forward in his chair. An army surgeon climbed to the box from the stage. "Oh, Doctor! Is he dead?" moaned Mary. "Will you take charge of him? Do what you can for him. Oh, my dear husband! My dear husband!"

The young physician, twenty-three-year-old Dr. Charles Leale, looked somber. He saw that the wound was mortal. The bullet of the deringer had hit Lincoln at the back of his head. A later examination proved the course of it "was obliquely forward toward the right eye, crossing the brain in an oblique manner and lodging a few inches behind that eye. In the track of the wound were found fragments of bone, which had been driven forward by the ball, which was embedded in the anterior lobe of the left hemisphere of the brain."

During the night the President struggled with death in a little room across the street from the theatre. By early morning all was over. At 7:22 A.M. he breathed his last. And a voice called out: "Now he belongs to the ages!"

GEORGE ATZERODT, 33, a carriage painter of German extraction from Port Tobacco on the Potomac, was to kill Vice-President Johnson. The military tribunal sentenced him to die on the gallows.

LEWIS PAINE, 20, the son of a Baptist minister, whose part in the plot was to murder Secretary of State Seward. The dull-witted Paine was one of the four conspirators who were condemned to hang.

THE CONS

AND THE

SAMUEL B. ARNOLD, 28, a friend of Booth since school days, who joined the actor in his mad scheme, was given a life sentence.

EDMAN SPANGLER, a middle-aged widower, a stagehand at Ford's Theatre, helped Booth escape. His sentence was six years.

THE PLOT against Abraham Lincoln began in September, 1864. It was in that month that John Wilkes Booth approached two of his boyhood friends—Samuel Arnold and Michael O'Laughlin—asking them to join him in the abduction of the President. Both men were former soldiers. Both had fought in the Confederate ranks. Arnold had left the colors because of illness;

MARY E. SURRATT, 48, the owner of the boarding house in Washington, the meeting place of the conspirators. Though the trial had not established her guilt, Mrs. Surratt received the death sentence.

DAVID E. HEROLD, 23, a feeble-minded former drugstore clerk with the mental age of an eleven-year-old, accompanied Booth on his flight to Virginia. He received the death sentence and was executed.

PIRATORS
IR FATE

O'Laughlin had deserted. When Booth sought them out in Baltimore, they were working for their brothers. Over drinks the scheme was discussed; Arnold and O'Laughlin, flattered that Booth had asked them and hopeful of his money, promised their help. They believed the idea to kidnap Lincoln was a capital one.

From that time on Booth worked out

JOHN H. SURRATT, 20, the son of Mary, a Confederate spy, was the only one of the conspirators who was able to flee the country.

MICHAEL O'LAUGHLIN, 27, a schoolmate of Booth and a Confederate Army deserter, received a life sentence. He died in prison.

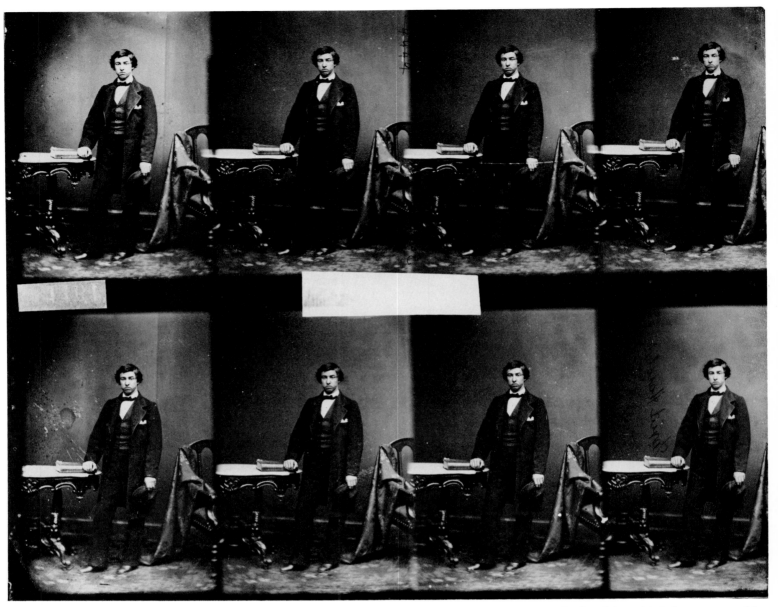

EIGHT PICTURES OF A CONSPIRATOR, on a single plate. The infantile David Herold, who lived with his mother and seven sisters in Washington, photographed by Brady's multiple-lens camera. After the first four pictures, the plateholder was moved for the next four.

DR. SAMUEL A. MUDD, 31, a doctor from Maryland, who bandaged Booth's wounded leg, was sentenced for life imprisonment.

the details of the plot. Like a general before a battle, he evolved a strategy. He wanted to capture Lincoln in a theatre, tie him up, and take him to the Confederate capital where he would be handed over to the authorities, who in turn would exchange him for Southern prisoners, or, with the President in their hands, force a negotiated peace. Booth made a careful inspection of the route which he was to travel. It would be across the Anacostia River, through Surrattsville to Port Tobacco, from there on a ferry across the Potomac and then to Richmond.

In a letter addressed to his brother-in-law, he wrote: "My love (as things stand to-day) is for the South alone.

Nor do I deem it a dishonor in attempting to make for her a prisoner of this man, to whom she owes so much misery."

During a trip to Maryland, he made the acquaintance of a country doctor, Dr. Samuel Mudd, the man who later introduced him to John Surratt in Washington, the third one to join the plot. Surratt brought in two others—George Atzerodt, a coachmaker at Port Tobacco, who regularly ferried contraband across the Potomac to Virginia, and David Herold, a stupid youth, who admired Booth. But the last recruit was the most important of all. It was Lewis Paine, the son of a Baptist minister, a tall, strong, dull-witted

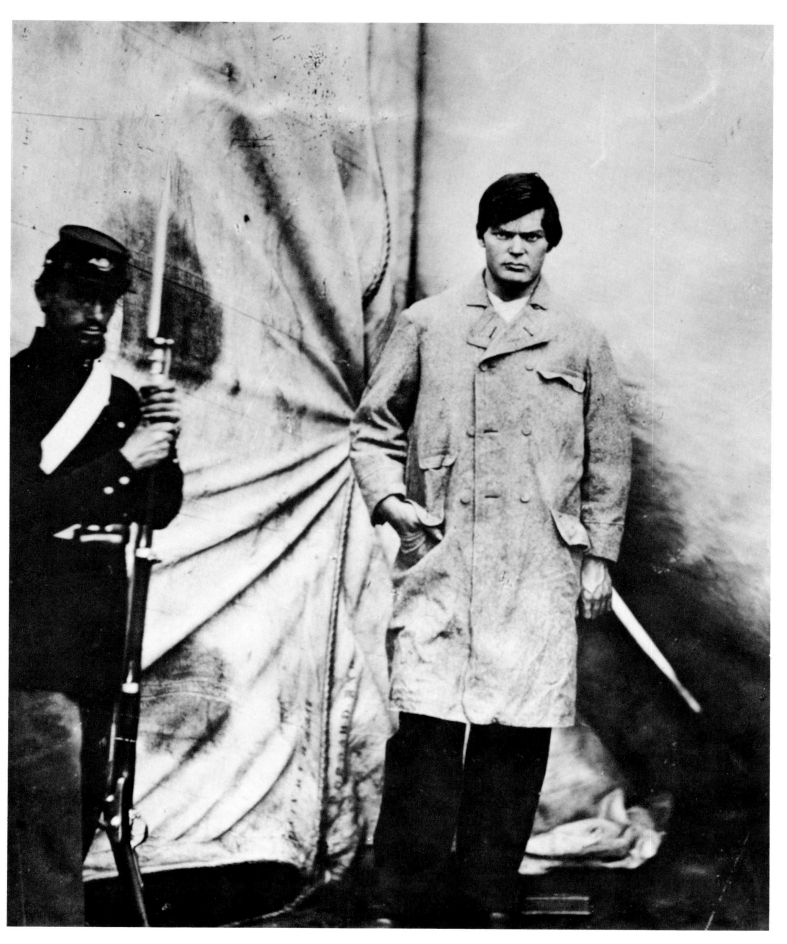

"SUSPICION OF INSANITY" was a doctor's verdict after he examined Lewis Paine, the most brazen of the conspirators. Paine (born as Lewis Thornton Powell), wounded in the Battle of Gettys-burg, was captured, but escaped and flew to Baltimore, where he was arrested for beating up a colored maid. On the evening of Lincoln's assassination, he tried to murder Secretary of State Seward.

THE MILITARY COMMISSION which tried the conspirators. From left to right: Brigadier General T. M. Harris; Major General David Hunter; Brevet Major General August V. Kautz; Brevet Brigadier General James A. Ekin; Major General Lewis Wallace, who later won fame as the author of *Ben Hur*. Standing on the right is John A. Bingham, one of the assistant Judge

From Harper's Weekly, *June 10, 1865*

fellow, with an insane streak in his make-up, who joined the plotters in February, 1865. Paine had had a checkered career. He was wounded as a Confederate soldier in the Battle of Gettysburg, and was taken prisoner. After his release he became involved with the law in Baltimore because of beating up a colored maid, and was ordered out of the city.

On March 17, 1865, the conspirators met in a Washington restaurant —with Booth paying for food and drinks—to discuss the abduction plot. Within a short while they were in each

THE TRIAL was held before a military commission in Washington's Old Penitentiary. The prisoners were sitting on the platform at the far end of the courtroom.

Advocates.—On the picture above are, in the usual order, Brigadier General Joseph Holt, Judge Advocate of the U.S. Army, who was appointed by President Johnson to be Judge Advocate and Recorder of the commission; Brigadier General Robert S. Foster; Brevet Colonel H. L. Burnett; Brevet Colonel C. H. Tomkins, the other assistant Judge Advocate.

other's hair. Surratt insisted that the President could not be abducted, as he was too closely guarded. But Booth would not abandon the plan, which was put to test three days later. The conspirators were to ambush the President and capture him as he was driving to the Soldiers' Home. However, Lincoln changed his plans, and was not in his carriage. Thus the abduction plot came to nothing and the would-be abductors dispersed. O'Laughlin returned to Baltimore, Arnold to Old Point Comfort in Virginia. John Surratt took up his old job and carried

THE PLAN OF THE COURTROOM where the trial was held. The military commission was faced by a table of reporters, while the prisoners were sitting in the dock.

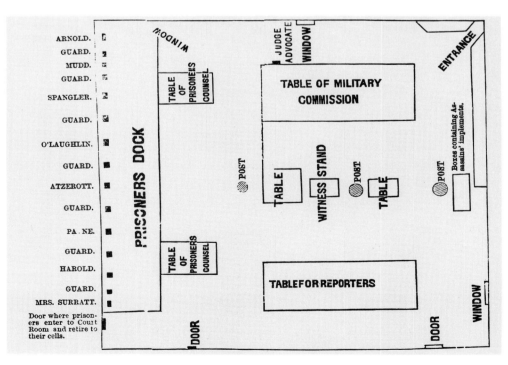

dispatches between Richmond and Montreal.

Paine, Herold, Atzerodt and Booth stayed in Washington. On April 9 General Lee surrendered to Grant. John Wilkes Booth still believed that the war against the North would go on, and he was ready to help the Confederate cause. Involved in his mad dreams he now concocted the idea which, if successfully carried out, was to paralyze the Federal government.

The scheme called for the death of three men: the President, the Vice-President and the Secretary of State. Paine was to murder Seward; Atzerodt was to assassinate Johnson; Booth was to kill Lincoln.

At about the same time that Booth entered the box at Ford's Theatre, Paine rang the bell at Secretary of State Seward's residence. A few days before Seward had been thrown from his carriage, fracturing his jaw and

breaking his arm. Ever since then he had been in bed.

Paine told the colored servant who let him in that he had brought some medicine from the doctor with instructions to hand it personally to the patient, then rushed up the steps. At the head of the staircase he faced the eldest son of Seward, Frederick. Paine repeated his story to him and was told again that he could not see the Secretary. The intruder began to

THE LAST HOURS OF THE FOUR CONDEMNED

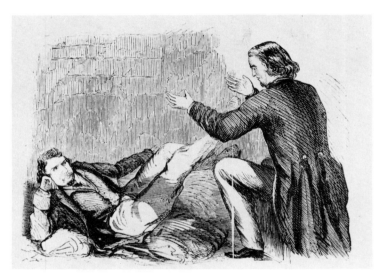

GEORGE ATZERODT WITH HIS SPIRITUAL ADVISER.

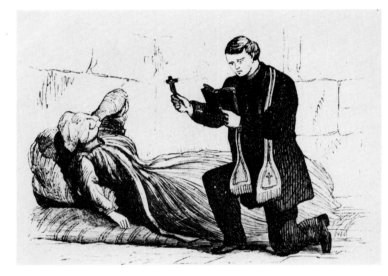

THE PROSTRATE MRS. SURRATT LISTENS TO THE GOSPEL.

LEWIS PAINE WAITING FOR THE LAST CALL.

DAVID HEROLD'S FAREWELL TO HIS SISTERS.

These drawings appeared in Frank Leslie's Illustrated Newspaper, *July 22, 1865*

Photograph by Alexander Gardner

FRIDAY, JULY 7, 1865. In the prison yard of Washington's Old Penitentiary, the scaffold is ready. A presidential order set the time of the execution between the hours of ten and two. Already, Captain Rath, the executioner, had tested the gallows with bags of shot.

walk down the steps, but suddenly turned around and jumped at Frederick Seward. Hit by the butt of Paine's revolver, the Secretary's son fell to the floor. Paine was now in the sickroom where he stabbed the Secretary of State, wounding him at several places. The noise brought another son of Seward into the room. He and the male attendant pushed Paine toward the door. The intruder was now on the run. Racing down the stairs, he shouted: "I'm mad! I'm mad!"

That night Washington was agog with rumors. But by late morning the people of the capital learned the truth. President Lincoln had been murdered,

Secretary of State Seward wounded.

Within a short time the men who were suspected in the conspiracy were arrested. Edman Spangler, the stagehand, George Atzerodt, the would-be killer of the Vice-President, and Lewis Paine, the assailant of Seward, were taken prisoners. So were Samuel Arnold and Michael O'Laughlin.

The two who were still free were Booth and Herold. Where were they?

After Booth left the theatre he rode across the Navy Yard bridge and reached Surratt's Tavern around midnight. Davy Herold took the same route, joined him, and together the two men kept on riding. But the pain in

Booth's leg got worse. Thus, about four o'clock in the morning, "with the bone of my leg tearing the flesh at every jump," they reached Dr. Mudd's house in Bryanton and asked him for help. The doctor put a splint on the injured leg and made a crutch. At four in the afternoon—after learning that the Federal troops were chasing them—the two were off again. They followed an abandoned wagon trail through Zekiah Swamp, where they were lost for hours. At last a colored man directed them to the home of Samuel Cox, a Southern sympathizer. Arriving there at four in the morning—by then it was April 16 —they were taken in by Samuel Cox

287

and his half-brother, Thomas A. Jones. On the 21st they crossed the Potomac in a fishing skiff. On the 23rd they were in Virginia, on the bank of Gambo Creek. Confederate soldiers led them across the Rappahannock to Richard Garrett's farm, between Port Royal and Bowling Green. Here they were given shelter. By then detachments of soldiers were hard on their heels. The soldiers reached the tobacco barn at Garrett's farm—the hiding place of Booth and Herold—on the 26th of April. The commander of the troops, Lieutenant Baker, ordered the men inside the barn to surrender, or the building would be set on fire. From the barn came the pleading voice of Booth:

"Let us have a little time to consider

it." The time was given and after a while Booth called out:

"Captain, I know you to be a brave man, and I believe you to be honorable; I am a cripple. I have got but one leg; if you will withdraw your men in one line one hundred yards from the door, I will come out and fight you." Lieutenant Baker would not entertain such a suggestion. "Well, my brave boys, prepare a stretcher for me," cried out Booth from the barn. Not much later, the soldiers heard arguing voices from inside. "You damned coward, will you leave me now? Go, go; I would not have you stay with me," shouted Booth. Then he called out to the soldiers: "There's a man in here who wants to come out." Slowly the barn door opened, and the

PREPARING FOR THE END. Already General Hartranft has read the death warrant. Now the assistants of the executioner adjust

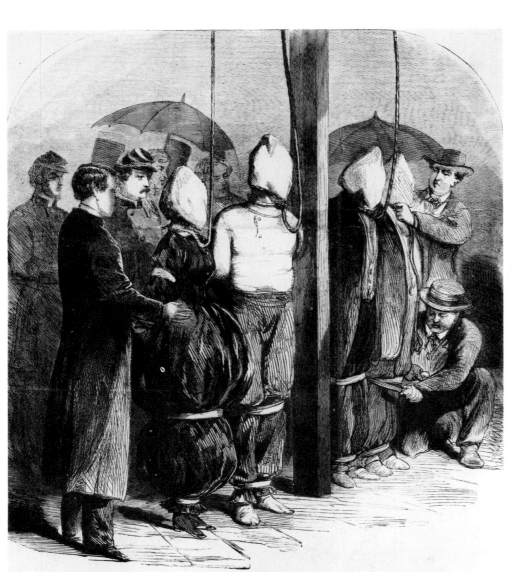

A sketch in Frank Leslie's Illustrated Newspaper, *July 22, 1865*

THE LAST PREPARATIONS BEFORE THE EXECUTION, as sketched in the yard of Washington's Old Penitentiary for the title page of *Frank Leslie's Illustrated Newspaper.*

trembling Herold surrendered himself.

Now the soldiers lit the brush outside the building and the dry pine boughs caught fire. In an instant the barn was aflame. Through the cracks between the planks a dark figure became visible as it moved toward the

288

Photograph by Alexander Gardner

the ropes, while under the scaffold the four soldiers are ready to spring the trap. The three clergymen have finished their prayers. The prisoners are bound and hooded. It is a hot, suffocating day. The sun beats down mercilessly. The four condemned are shaded by umbrellas—what irony. A few more seconds—and they will have no need of it. A few more seconds and they will be dead.

door—the figure of John Wilkes Booth. At this moment a shot was fired and Booth fell to the ground. The soldiers rushed into the barn and carried him out, laying him underneath a locust tree. The wounded man's lips moved. "Tell mother I die for my country," he whispered in a barely audible voice. Soon he breathed his last.

As President Lincoln's assassination was considered a military crime—the Commander-in-Chief fell "in actual service in time of war"—the conspirators were not tried by a jury in a civil court, but by a military commission.

The trial began on May 9 and lasted till June 30, when the sentences were pronounced. It was a strange procedure, conducted in the postwar hysteria. The prisoners' deed was linked with deeds of the Confederate government, their names linked with that of Jefferson Davis. Irrelevant charges, in no way connected with the crime, were brought in. Witnesses testified about the starvation of Union prisoners, about the introduction of pestilence during the war, about the plot to burn New York City, about the starvation in the notorious Andersonville Prison and other unrelated subjects. On the other hand, people who should have been investigated, people who should have been called as witnesses, were not asked to testify. John F. Parker, who had left the President unguarded in the theatre, was neither reprimanded nor dismissed from the police force. He was not asked to appear before the Court; neither was Thomas A. Jones or Samuel Cox, the two who harbored Booth for a week. Mrs. Surratt was convicted on the testimony of two unreliable characters, one a drunkard and the other a liar.

The military tribunal sentenced Mrs. Surratt, Paine, Atzerodt and Herold "to be hanged by the neck." Dr. Mudd, Arnold and O'Laughlin were to be imprisoned for life; Spangler was to receive six years of hard labor. John Surratt, who escaped, could not be tried.

On a sweltering summer day the four condemned were executed. Until the last it was hoped that Mrs. Surratt would be pardoned, but when no word came from the President she was hanged with the other three conspirators. Of the four who received prison sentences, O'Laughlin died in captivity two years later; Dr. Mudd, who saved many lives during a yellow-fever epidemic in the penitentiary, was pardoned by President Johnson in 1868; and a year later, in 1869, Arnold and Spangler were set free.

Photograph by Alexander Gardner

THE END. Dangling on the ropes in the noon sun are Mrs. Surratt, Lewis Paine, David Herold and George Atzerodt. Until the last it was thought that Mrs. Surratt would be pardoned. Paine told the executioner: "If I had two lives to give, I'd give one gladly to save Mrs. Surratt. I know that she is innocent, and would never die in this way if I hadn't been found at her house. She knew nothing about the conspiracy at all. . . ." But when no reprieve came for her, Mrs. Surratt was executed with the three other conspirators, the first woman in the country's history to die on the gallows.

APPENDIX A:
A PICTORIAL BIBLIOGRAPHY

Photography was invented in 1839, when Abraham Lincoln was thirty years old. Not until the summer of 1840 did itinerant "daguerreotype artists" reach the West with their box cameras. Therefore no photograph of him could exist before 1840—the time of Tippecanoe's election to the Presidency. As it happened, Lincoln did not sit for a daguerreotypist until seven years later—when he was a member of the 30th Congress. Thus 1847 is the limiting date on one side, while his death in 1865 is on the other; all Lincoln's photographs were made within the span of these eighteen years.

There are certain clues to determine the dates of the pictures. As Lincoln was without a beard until his election, all his cleanshaven portraits must be dated before November, 1860, all the bearded ones later.

At the time he left Springfield for

Washington his beard was heavy, but the barbers of the capital went at it until they reduced it to almost nothing. The early presidential pictures show him with a full beard, the later ones with a light one.

His collar is another help. In his early pictures he wore a collar with a stocklike effect and a very full bow tie. As a candidate he sported a rolling collar with points and an abbreviated tie. As President-elect his collar was a high overlapping one, while during the presidential years it was low.

Photographic processes by which the pictures were made give further hints. Daguerreotypes (sheets of copper plated with silver) began to go out of fashion about 1853, when photographers switched to wet-plate negatives. These had the advantage that any number of copies could be made from them, while daguerreotypes and ambrotypes

(a negative plate on a black surface, viewed by reflected light) gave only a single likeness. One can say that most of Lincoln's portraits after 1854 were made on wet plates.

The late Frederick Hill Meserve was the first to begin the systematic collection of Lincoln photographs. Starting at the turn of the century, he spent much time and money tracking down plates, negatives, and prints, doing the magnificent work of a pioneer. For this the gratitude of all Lincoln students will be everlasting.

However, a critical look at his classification reveals flaws. In his privately printed book, *The Photographs of Abraham Lincoln,* published in 1911, Mr. Meserve enumerates one hundred different Lincoln photographs. Since then four supplements have been issued: No. 1 in 1917, No. 2 in 1938, No. 3 in 1950, and No. 4 in 1955. Each of these supplements contains eight additional pictures, bringing his total of Lincoln photographs to 132.

After the author of this volume published his *Lincoln: His Life in Photographs* in 1941 Meserve followed with his *The Photographs of Abraham Lincoln* in 1944, containing his numbers but placing the photographs in the chronological order suggested by the Lorant book. An example: 22 is followed by 109, then 4, 32, 112, and 111.

An examination of the Meserve list shows that some of his pictures listed under different numbers are not different at all, but one and the same. Meserve 101 is an enlargement of his 6; 10 is a "harder" enlargement of his 11; 15 is a retouched detail of 14; 18 is a touched-up enlargement of 26; 19 is an enlargement of 20; and 30 is an enlargement of 29. By eliminating the above duplicates, the beardless photographs are reduced by six.

Going through Meserve's classification of the bearded photographs, one finds that his 118 is the same exposure

A MULTIPLE-LENS CAMERA. An instrument which Mathew Brady used in photographing Lincoln. Such *carte-de-visite* cameras made four images on a single plate; by moving the plate holder the number was doubled. The prints from such plates—especially if the image on the extreme left is paired with the image on the extreme right are placed next to each other give a three-dimensional impression if seen with a viewer.

A PHOTOGRAPH . . .
On this Alexander Gardner photograph, taken in November, 1863, the background was added by an artist. The two photographs of

. . . GETS A BACKGROUND
Lincoln with his son Tad also have variants with painted-in backgrounds. They may look different but they are the same.

as 68, taken by a multiple-lens camera. The pairs 49 and 50 and 73 and 74 were also made by such a camera; therefore they should not be counted twice. Similarly 51, 52, and 114 were made by one exposure, as were 75, 107, and 115 and also 81, 82, and 83.

By the simple method of enlarging and superimposing one negative over another, one found that Meserve 62 was an enlargement of 63; 60 was an enlargement of his 57; 94 was a retouched enlargement of 100; and 108 was an enlargement of 87.

There are other duplications. No. 96, showing Lincoln with Tad, was made from the same negative as 95 (with the background painted in). Meserve's 40, 41, and 127 and the greatly repainted and doctored 126 were made from the same negative as 39 (Lincoln with Tad). Of the photographs taken outdoors, No. 48 (Lincoln with McClellan) is a heavily touched-up print of 47.

Three items (125 plus A and B)

in Meserve's fourth supplement—one supposedly showing Lincoln with the Clay battalion (125) and in the others supposedly posing with a group of soldiers (A) and supposedly inspecting the building of the Aqueduct (B)—cannot be regarded as Lincoln photographs, as the top-hatted man in the pictures is not Lincoln. (See further notes on pages 308 and 311.)

To sum up: the Meserve list of 132 (130 plus A and B) Lincoln photographs should be reduced by 28, leaving it with 104 different listings.

When the above findings were presented by the author of this volume in 1957 they were accepted by the Lincoln community. Not a single critical remark has challenged them, and they were not contradicted by Mr. Meserve.

So the matter of classification seemed to rest. But in 1963 a New York bookseller and a commercial artist from the Middle West, Charles Hamilton and Lloyd Ostendorf, pub-

lished their $19.50 volume, *Lincoln in Photographs.* The compilers were neither historians nor experts in photography. With their hodgepodge of undigested data, misleading information, and wild guesses, they brought renewed confusion to the classification of Lincoln photographs. Their work seems to be more a self-advertisement for one of the compilers, whose name in full and in abbreviation appears no fewer than 669 times, than a serious study of Lincoln pictures.

In their book they list 119 Lincoln photographs, or fifteen more than the revised Meserve classification.

Of these, eleven represent three events: the Philadelphia flag-raising ceremony and the first and second inaugurals. In the majority of these photographs Lincoln cannot be seen. (To help this deficiency one of the compilers painted in the President's face and retouched his figure on numbers 110 and 111. The same liberties were taken with their number 102, in which Lincoln's head was drawn in.)

Of the picture showing soldiers with a top-hatted man they assert that it is Lincoln, though Meserve was not so certain. He wrote that the figure "conceivably may be President Lincoln." It is not.

Now to the duplicates. Their number 37 is a somewhat retouched version of 36; 41 and 42 are one and the same photograph (even the strings of the tassels of the photographer's curtain match exactly); 45 is an unretouched print of 44; 113 is an unretouched version of 112 (see identical white triangle under the collar).

The naïveté and ignorance of the compilers led them into ridiculous pitfalls. They relate the finding of an "undiscovered" Lincoln photograph in an old print- and book-shop in New York and its acquisition for $8. Apparently this sent their imaginations soaring. Because the label on the back of the carte-de-visite had Edward Bierstadt's name on it, they concluded that it was he who took the picture (though in his long life Bierstadt never once referred to photographing Lincoln—an event which surely could not have

escaped his mind. There is a letter from 1882 in which Bierstadt asks the Secretary of War for a Brady negative of Lincoln. Surely he would not have asked for the plate twenty-one years later if he had had one of his own.) The compilers claim that the picture is the first known photograph of Lincoln as President. If they had looked a bit closer and if they had had more knowledge about photographers retouching the prints of their competitors (to escape copyright suits), they would have found that their "undiscovered" Lincoln photograph is nothing but a retouched copy of the well-known portrait which Lincoln inscribed to Lucy Speed on October 3, 1861. Placing the outlines of the two pictures over each other, they match perfectly.

Their claim about their other "undiscovered" photograph is even more grotesque. They say that it is a retouched "photographic copy of an ambrotype." One would like to know: what ambrotype? Who owned it? Who has seen it? Who copied it? Who retouched it? But no documentation is given. The picture looks more like a painting than a photograph. And if one compares it with the 1860 E. B. and

E. C. Kellogg lithograph, one recognizes that the "undiscovered" ambrotype is nothing but a heavily retouched copy of that print. The outlines of Lincoln's figure and his head, the distances between his eyes, nose, mouth and ears are the same in both pictures; they cover each other exactly.

One would feel more generosity toward their elementary errors if they were not so positive about their "new discoveries." Here are a few examples:

On page 154 they print a scene at Gettysburg with the legend: "The crowd awaits Lincoln's address," implying that the photograph was taken on November 19, 1863, when Lincoln delivered his address. But in the picture the women wear summer dresses and carry parasols to shade their faces from the sun. It could not have been taken on a cold, wintery November day. It wasn't. It was taken six years later on July 1, 1869, at the unveiling of a stone shaft marking the historic site.

On pages 200 and 201 under the two full-page photographs it is asserted that the pictures show the crowd waiting for the ceremonies of the second inaugural. In reality they are not from Lincoln's inauguration, but from

THE PLATEHOLDER WAS QUICKLY MOVED to yield the triple image on this Brady plate. These pictures were probably taken with a single-lens camera, in which the plateholder was moved between exposures, while Lincoln sat motionless during the three exposures.

1 + 1 = 1. The two portraits, believed to be different ones, turned out to be the same when prints of exactly the same size were superimposed over each other (see third photograph). Brady often made enlargements, thus producing a flow of "new" Lincoln pictures.

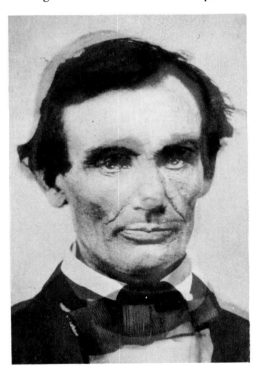

1 + 1 = 2. The first and second portrait (the second one heavily retouched) show some resemblance. However, their superimposed enlargements, as can be seen in the third picture, proved that these originals have been made from two different negatives.

Grant's. One can enumerate the mistakes and misrepresentations ad infinitum, but why go on?

If one omits the compilers' duplicate Lincoln photographs and their fake pictures, their list is reduced by eight. And if one omits seven of the eleven "event" photographs in which the figure of Lincoln can only be imagined (leaving four, the same number as

Meserve), their list is reduced to 104 —the very figure as in the corrected Meserve classification.

In the 1957 edition of the present work 102 different photographs were listed. Since then the author has become convinced that two of the almost identical pictures (Meserve 78 and 84) were not taken at the same exposure, but separately. Thus he added them to

his list. To this comes the newly found Gardner picture, which is published for the first time here. It brings the canon of Lincoln photographs up to 105.

Research during the past decade has unearthed some new data on the photographs and the photographers, in many cases changing the chronological sequence. Thus the former numbers have been revised in line with the findings.

MATHEW B. BRADY (1823–96), THE ENTERPRISING PHOTOGRAPHER, AS TAKEN BY A MULTIPLE-LENS CAMERA.

APPENDIX B:

THE PHOTOGRAPHER OF LINCOLN

He was sixteen when he became the pupil of the celebrated Samuel F. B. Morse, who had just returned from Paris with his new daguerreotype camera. Morse taught the young man the new art of taking pictures. By 1844 Brady had his own gallery in New York, and five years later he opened his "daguerrean rooms" in Washington.

Ambition fired him; he wanted to record the faces of the famous, to hold them for posterity. With the introduction of the wet-plate process, which allowed the making of many copies, he prospered. His costly lifesize pictures as well as his inexpensive carte-de-visite photos were much sought after. To be posed by him was the fashion.

When the war came he dreamed of capturing its drama for posterity, and he organized teams of photographers and followed the troops. But this ambitious enterprise proved too expensive; by 1872 he was forced into bankruptcy. When two years later he could not pay a $2,840 warehouse bill, the Secretary of War paid it to rescue some of his negatives. Then in 1875 Congress finally bought his other plates—5,712 of them—for $25,000 "as an act of great mercy to a suffering and worthy man."

But the money came too late. His Washington gallery closed in 1881. For the next decade and a half he worked for other firms. Pained by rheumatism, sick and lonely, he took to the bottle. He died, disillusioned and forgotten, in a New York charity hospital early in 1896.

A DAGUERREOTYPE OF MATHEW B. BRADY WITH HIS WIFE, JULIA HANDY (ON THE LEFT), AND A FRIEND.

BRADY after his return from Bull Run on July 22, 1861.

APPENDIX C:
THREE-DIMENSIONAL PICTURES

George Eastman House

MATHEW B. BRADY OWNED THIS STEREOSCOPIC CAMERA and used it during the years of 1861 to 1870. It is a somewhat cumbersome instrument. Before each exposure the wet plate had to be prepared. The camera is now in the possession of Graflex, Inc.

The search for three-dimensional Lincoln pictures began in 1941. In that year Louis A. Warren wrote an article on Lincoln stereos (*Lincoln Lore*, No. 632), and in the same year the author of this volume printed two examples of three-dimensional pictures in his *Lincoln: His Life in Photographs*.

Ever since, the speculation about "three-dimensional Lincolns" goes on. How many are there? Some say there are more than thirty; others hold that most of them are not *real* stereos but *incidental* ones.

What is a stereoscope? The principle behind it had been understood as early as the time of Euclid, about 300 B.C., but the first scientists to come up with an instrument allowing the observation of such plastic effects were the Englishmen Charles Wheatstone in 1833 and James Eliot in 1839. Mayo, in his *Outline of Human Physiology* (1833),

A REAL STEREO, probably taken by a photographer of the New York firm of E. & H. T. Anthony, which was the leader in the making of such pictures. Taken and distributed in 1865, the year of the assassination, it had wide circulation among stereoscope owners.

explains the three-dimensional principle this way: "A solid object, being so placed as to be regarded by both eyes, projects a different perspective figure on each retina. Now if these two perspectives be actually copied on paper, and presented, one to each eye, so as to fall on corresponding parts, the original solid figure will be apparently reproduced in such a manner that no effort of the imagination can make it appear as a representation of a plane surface." He of course spoke of stereoscopic drawings.

After photography was invented in 1839 the scope of three-dimensional effects was vastly enlarged. By 1849 Sir David Brewster had come up with a double-lens camera—soon to be introduced in the United States—which took stereoscopic photographs.

The earliest stereoscopes were printed on glass or on a thin, unmounted paper. Oliver Wendell Holmes disliked the glass stereos; he found that "twenty-five glass slides well inspected in a strong light, are good for one headache." For him the paper ones were easier to view—they

were "a leaf torn from the book of God's recording angel." He saw a promising future for these pictures and prophesied: "The next European war will send us stereographs of battles. It is asserted that the bursting shell can be photographed. The time is perhaps at hand when a flash of light as sudden and brief as that of lightning which shows a whirling wheel standing stock

still, shall preserve the instant of the shock of contact of mighty armies."

It would be some time before his prophecy came true and the camera could record "the bursting shell," but in the 1860's stereos offered all kinds of scenes, even from the battlefield. They became fashionable; they caught the people's imagination. One could get views of cities, of streets, of buildings,

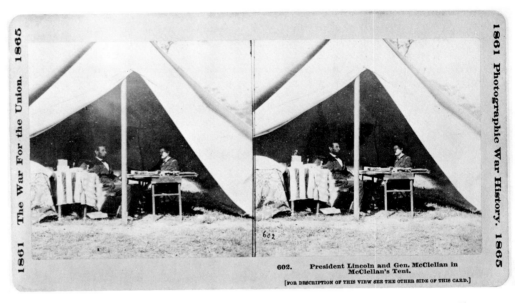

THE FIRST STEREOSCOPE of Lincoln with General McClellan at the General's tent at Antietam, taken a year after Oliver Wendell Holmes constructed his first stereoscopic viewer.

ANOTHER EARLY STEREOSCOPE taken by Alexander Gardner on the same occasion as the one above—October 3, 1862—before the tent on the Antietam battlefield. Viewed through the two lenses of a stereoscope the photograph reveals a third dimension—depth.

A NEW FIELD IN LINCOLN PHOTOGRAPHIC RESEARCH: Pairs of photographs giving a three-dimensional effect. Brady and Gardner often posed Lincoln before a four-lens *carte-de-visite* camera, so that the production of prints could be made faster—one plate yielding four pictures. On occasion, by moving the plate holder this number on a single plate was doubled (see page 296). With the image on the left of the plate placed next to the image on the right side, a three-dimensional stereoscopic effect could be obtained.

LINCOLN IN THE ROUND. Another set of Lincoln pictures, taken by Brady in 1863 with the multiple-lens camera and showing a three-dimensional effect. This pair was made up by the National Archives of Washington and is in the collection of Elias Barkey of Brooklyn.

with two lenses, one for each eye, placed about 2½ inches apart. But in 1861 Oliver Wendell Holmes came up with a small, lightweight apparatus that could be held in one hand. When Joseph Bates improved upon this discovery he marketed it under the felicitous name "The Holmes Stereoscope." By the turn of the century there was hardly an American middle-class home without such a stereoscope viewer.

Of Abraham Lincoln we have two kinds of stereos. One is the *real* stereo photograph, taken by the regular two-lens stereo camera, while the other one is an *incidental* one, achieved by the multiple-lens camera.

The first true stereo photographs of Lincoln were taken by Alexander Gardner on October 3, 1862, at the time the President visited General McClellan in Antietam. The two were photographed in the General's tent as well as with some others at the General's headquarters. The figures on this stereoscope, from left to right, show Buck Juit, Lamon, Ozias Hatch, Gen. R. B. Marcy, Capt. Wright Rives, Gen John McClernand, the President, Lt. Col. Andrew Porter, McClellan, Joseph Kennedy, John Garrett, and Col. Thomas Mather. (Curiously, one man sits while Lincoln stands; it is Ward Hill Lamon, nursing a game leg.)

We know that both Mathew Brady and Alexander Gardner used the

of the countryside, and of natural wonders. And there were cards of ladies with hoop skirts, as well as of floods, of children, of fires. One series of twelve stereos related the story of a whaling voyage, even though no photographer went to sea to take the pictures—the boats and whales were models and the sea was imitated by a crumpled cloth.

The early stereoscopic viewers were bulky boxes and elaborate trays fitted

ONE OF THE FEW DOZEN PAIRS

multiple-lens camera frequently. The reason for it was obvious: Such cameras, with two lenses above and two lenses below, recorded four images on the same plate, thus four pictures could be printed at once.

Now, as the lenses of the multiple-lens camera were approximately as far apart as on the stereoscopic ones, these pictures, if properly matched (pairing the lower left photograph with that on the lower right), gave a three-dimensional effect.

Frederick S. Lightfoot wrote, in the article "The Stereoscopic Portraits of Lincoln" (*Image*, February, 1957): "The separation of the lenses on a carte-de-visite camera was about 2¼ inches, considerably less than the separation of lenses on the standard stereo cameras of the 1860's, but quite close to the separation considered ideal on modern stereo cameras, which is 2½ inches. The main drawback to stereos made from cartes was the 2¼ inch width. When they were mounted on the standard stereo card, which was designed to take stereo print halves 3 inches wide, an abnormal ¾ inch blank margin appeared between them. [With such a wide, empty space it was harder to see the three-dimensional effect in a standard stereoscopic viewer.] This shortcoming did not prevent the leading publishers of cartes and stereos of celebrities—the An-

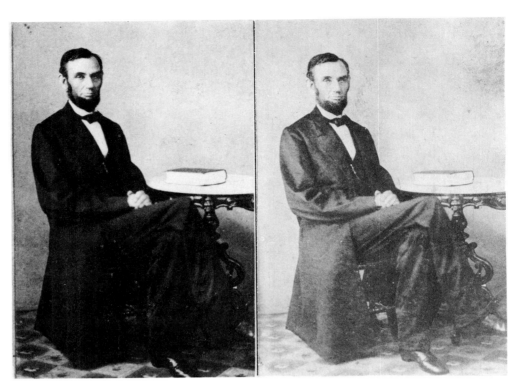

CARTES DE VISITE, which if placed side by side give a three-dimensional effect. Stefan Lorant published these sets of Alexander Gardner's photographs for the first time in 1941.

ANOTHER SET OF CARTES DE VISITE, taken by Alexander Gardner, which shows Lincoln three dimensionally. On the left photograph the glasses were painted out— still the exposure was made at the same time as the picture on the right.

WITH THE MULTIPLE-LENS CAMERA.

thonys, Frederick, Gurney, and others —from producing stereos of this type in the early 1860's."

While Lincoln was alive only a few such cards were on the market. The craze to pair up these incidental stereos is a recent one; only in the last few years have Lincoln enthusiasts "discovered" them. Matching these multiple-lens pictures grew into a hobby; to conjure a three-dimensional Lincoln became a fascinating game.

APPENDIX D:
THE FAMILY

THOUGH MANY PICTURES SHOW THE LINCOLNS, THEY HAD NEVER BEEN PHOTOGRAPHED TOGETHER.

A CURRIER & IVES LITHOGRAPH of the Lincolns, published after the President's death, had been made up from two different photographs, one showing Lincoln with Tad (at the right), the other Mary by herself.

right:
AN ENGRAVING OF THE WHOLE FAMILY after a painting by F. Schell. The artist copied the photograph of Lincoln with Tad.

THE LINCOLNS IN 1861. A lithograph after Francis B. Carpenter's painting in the New-York Historical Society shows the three Lincoln boys—Willie, Robert Todd, and Tad—with their parents.

THE LINCOLNS AFTER WILLIE'S DEATH. Lincoln with Tad before Washington's bust; Willie's picture is behind Robert Todd. This lithograph was published by Haskell & Allen of Boston.

A BRADY PHOTOGRAPH TAKEN IN 1863 . . .   **. . .AND A PROBABLE ANTHONY PHOTOGRAPH TAKEN IN 1863. . .**

He loved her and she loved him.

Much has been said about how difficult she was. But he was no easy man to live with either. Physically, mentally, emotionally, they were at opposite poles. She was small of stature, highly strung, quick-tempered; he was a tower of a man inside and out and in steady control of his emotions. She had a good education, spoke French, played the piano, was brought up amidst the niceties of life, while his background was harsh, his formal education cursory. What he learned was from a few books he read and from the people he met.

Sensitive about the difference in their height, Mary did not relish her husband's teasing "here is the long and short of the Presidency." Perhaps it was because of this that they were never photographed together.

And, curiously, no original photo-

. . . ADD UP TO THIS CARTE-DE-VISITE.
The two photographs on the top prove that this one is a montage, with the photographs of Lincoln and his wife pasted together.

graph exists of the whole family either. They were never posed together, though at one time his picture was taken with Tad (at a Brady sitting on February 9, 1864), and another time (on April 10, 1865) Alexander Gardner made a picture of the two. And we have a charming daguerrotype of Mary with her two smaller sons (see page 116) taken in Springfield before their departure for Washington.

The group pictures of the family which have come down to us are either paintings or photomontages; the best-known among the paintings were done by S. P. Waugh (engraved by William Sartain) and by Francis B. Carpenter (engraved by J. C. Buttre). In most of the engravings of the family the artists copied the Brady photograph of Lincoln with Tad, adding to it the figures of Mary, Robert, and Willie.

303

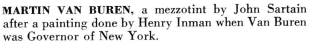

MARTIN VAN BUREN, a mezzotint by John Sartain after a painting done by Henry Inman when Van Buren was Governor of New York.

Lincoln's coat and tie as well as his head, drawn after

an 1864 photograph by Wenderoth & Taylor (see left), were put on Van Buren's body. The artist erased the State Capitol in Albany from the Van Buren engraving and substituted the Capitol in Washington.

APPENDIX E:

LINCOLN'S HEAD ON OTHER BODIES

When he received the nomination, his features were hardly known in the country. He had spoken in New York only one time, when he addressed an audience at Cooper Union early in 1860. And had he taken a stroll in San Francisco not one person in a hundred would have recognized him. Even some of those who nominated him were not certain whether his first name was Abram or Abraham. He had to set them straight; it was Abraham.

Thus, when the party chose him as its nominee, requests for his likeness poured in. People wanted to see what the new Republican candidate looked like. Brady had photographed him while he was in New York, and this photograph was copied by the pictorial weeklies for their woodcuts and by Currier & Ives for their lithographs.

Other firms entered into competition. They obtained his photographs taken in the previous years and made engravings and prints from them. Bufford in Boston brought out a print with Lincoln's likeness taken from the 1858 Christopher German photograph; Blodgett & Bradford in New York reproduced his mussed-up-hair portrait taken

PRESIDENT ANDREW JACKSON, engraved by Alexander A. Ritchie after a painting by Dennis M. Carter. Lincoln's head, taken from an 1864 Brady photograph (see right) is superimposed on Jackson's body.

The background was obliterated by a bust of Washington and the goose quill imperfectly erased, but otherwise, except for Lincoln's watch chain, the drawing remained the same; even Jackson's glasses were retained.

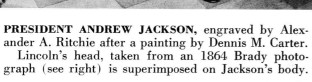

left:
FRANCIS BLAIR, JR., an engraving by Boyle. Lincoln's head was drawn after a Brady photograph (above) and placed on the body of Blair.

JOHN C. FRÉMONT BECOMES . . .
The first Republican candidate for President in an engraving by J. C. Buttre. Lincoln's head was drawn and superimposed on Brady's Cooper Union photograph in 1860.

. . . ABRAHAM LINCOLN.
The picture (at left) was reversed to make it fit Frémont's body. The globe on the table was changed into a lamp and the sundial removed, but everything else was left.

by Hesler in Chicago; Currier & Ives copied the ambrotype made by one of the Cole Brothers in Peoria; E. B. & E. C. Kellogg in Hartford lithographed the Hesler photograph made in 1860.

But most publishers reverted to the Brady photograph taken in New York on February 27, 1860, the day of his Cooper Union address. In the pioneering work of Winfred Porter Truesdell, *Engraved and Lithographed Portraits of Abraham Lincoln* (privately printed in 1933), no fewer than twenty-five pages (45 to 71) were given to the list of prints which were modeled after

Brady's Cooper Union picture.

To meet the spiraling demand, publishers and politicians dispatched artists to Springfield posthaste to paint him so that prints could be made from their works and distributed among the voters. On some mornings while he opened his correspondence in the State House half a dozen artists were sitting around him painting his portrait. Charles Barry, sent by prominent Republicans in Massachusetts, was there, as was John Henry Brown, who was to make a miniature for Judge Read in Philadelphia. Alban Conant arrived

with the money advanced by William McPherson of St. Louis; and also Thomas H. Johnston, who was to make a painting for Brainard, the Boston publisher.

On the campaign posters showing the two candidates—Lincoln and Hamlin —the artists used the old photographs as models and redrew them. As there was no time to make a full engraving of Lincoln, his head was taken from the Brady photograph and put on the figure of Henry Clay, probably because the publisher had a plate and Lincoln's head fitted the figure.

JOHN C. CALHOUN BECOMES . . .
An engraving in E. A. Duyckinck's *National Portrait Gallery of Eminent Americans* after a painting by Alonzo Chappel. Lincoln's head was taken from the famous 1864

. . . ABRAHAM LINCOLN.
Brady photograph which is on the $5 bill and reversed; thus the mole appears on the wrong cheek. The papers in the Calhoun engraving were altered to Northern slogans.

After the heat of the campaign, the demand for his pictures slackened. Brady and Gardner photographed him again and again, and from their photographs the weeklies made their woodcuts. All his portraits in *Harper's Weekly, Frank Leslie's Illustrated Newspaper*, and the publications outside the country like the *Illustrated London News* or the German *Leipziger Illustrierte* were drawn after them.

Curiously enough, during his Presidency only a few engravings of him were issued. But after April 14, 1865, his martyrdom created another huge

demand for his likeness. Publishers of prints, eager to benefit by the sudden upsurge of his fame, needed new plates of him, and needed them in a hurry. Thus almost overnight, engravings with the bodies of Andrew Jackson, John C. Calhoun, and Martin Van Buren received new heads—that of Lincoln. No one seemed to notice the deception, let alone mind. These engravings found their way into countless American homes, where they had a hallowed place next to glass-encased flowers, prayer desks, and globed kerosene lamps.

For a long time scholars speculated about these engravings. They saw that in them the body was not Lincoln's but someone else's. The question was: on whose figure was the President's head grafted? It took persistent research— and some luck—to find the originals showing the original bodies with the original heads. Five pairs of plates have come to light so far: Lincoln's head on Henry Clay's body, and his features on the bodies of President Jackson, President Van Buren, as well as on John C. Calhoun and Francis P. Blair. There must be some more.

APPENDIX F:

IS THIS LINCOLN?

Americans have a fondness for imitating their Presidents; they like to model themselves after him. Thus when Lincoln grew a beard many men in the country followed suit, and because he wore a stovepipe hat they too began to wear them.

During Lincoln's Presidency scores of photographs were taken of tall men with beards and top hats. When people found these pictures later in their attics and in old family albums, they invariably "recognized" the tall man as Lincoln. They asserted that the man in the top hat posing with his folded umbrella at Hanover Junction was no one else but Lincoln on his way to Gettysburg, and that the peaceful-looking gentleman sitting under a tree with a group of soldiers was of course the President—who else?—as was the tall bearded man nonchalantly viewing the building of an aqueduct. And nobody could talk them out of their conviction.

But was it really he? If one enlarged the photographs to study the details, and if one did some research on the circumstances under which the picture was taken, the result was always the same: it was not.

Lincoln National Life Foundation

IS THE TOP-HATTED MAN LINCOLN? A stereoscope taken at the Great Falls aqueduct in 1861. On the back of it was penciled "A. Lincoln"—the only hint that the man may be Lincoln. He is not.

IS THIS LINCOLN?

An enlarged detail of the oval picture below taken by photographer O. Pierre Havens, Ossining, New York, sometime in 1862 or 1863. The man in the top hat under the tree is supposed to be the Great Emancipator.

left:

IS IT REALLY HIM?

One of those self-appointed picture experts asserts that it *is*, and that Lincoln is photographed with soldiers of the Fifth New York Cavalry Regiment. It is doubtful that the young soldiers would have been allowed to pose in such informal attitudes with their Commander-in-Chief and that the colored man with the straw hat should be sitting in the foreground. If the top-hatted man were Lincoln, the photographer would have placed him in the center of the group and facing the camera; it would have made the picture more salable.

Library of Congress

IS LINCOLN IN THE PICTURE?

1   **A RAILROAD PHOTOGRAPH FROM THE 1860's ...**

National Archives

Hanover Junction in Pennsylvania in the 1860's or 1870's with a top-hatted man holding an umbrella before the station. He is supposed to be Lincoln. Sometime ago the photograph received wide circulation; newspapers and magazines claimed that it actually pictured the President on November 18, 1863, while he was changing trains to Gettysburg.

2   **... AND AN ENLARGEMENT OF ITS CENTER SECTION.**

We know that on November 18, 1863, the President's train reached Hanover Junction around five o'clock in the afternoon; on that day the sun set at 4:42. Yet in the picture the sky is light, and the figures are clearly visible.

We also know that Lincoln was accompanied on his journey by his staff and his political family (Secretary of State Seward, Secretary of Interior Usher, and Postmaster General Blair were on the train, as were the President's secretaries, John G. Nicolay and John Hay). But where are they? None of them can be seen in the picture.

And where was Brady, who supposedly took the photograph? He did not make the trip to Gettysburg, but stayed in New York to make pictures of the officers of the visiting Russian fleet. On the very day he supposedly photographed Lincoln at Hanover Junction the *Dollar Newspaper* of Washington reported: "Brady had taken off the heads of the Russians, photographically." Poor Brady! Like many others of his day he believed that Lincoln's visit to Gettysburg to dedicate a battlefield cemetery was less significant than the Russian fleet's visit to New York.

3   **A FURTHER ENLARGEMENT SHOWS CLEARLY ...**

4

... THAT THE MAN WITH THE UMBRELLA IS NOT LINCOLN.

IS THIS LINCOLN? A collector insists that the picture shows Lincoln after his death. Where it was taken, the expert does not reveal. Needless to say, it is not Lincoln.

ANOTHER "LINCOLN" IN HIS COFFIN?

But the President was never laid out on a bed; he was not photographed in his coffin, save by Gurney in New York's City Hall, and even then the plates and prints were confiscated on the orders of Secretary of War Stanton.

Besides, at the time of the assassination Lincoln's beard was short—much shorter than the dead man's— nor was his hair so stylish as the coiffure of the corpse.

IS THIS LINCOLN IN HIS COFFIN? The *Saturday Evening Post* on February 15, 1941, featured an article with the photograph of a dead man supposed to be Lincoln. The ambrotype, so the article suggested, was taken by the photographer Jeremiah Gurney, Jr., in New York's City Hall on April 23, 1865.

It is true that Lincoln's body was lying in state in City Hall on that day and that Gurney took photographs of the occasion (see page 174). But in the *Saturday Evening Post* picture the man is obviously not Lincoln. When Gurney took his photograph Lincoln was in his casket, whereas in the *Post* picture the corpse is stretched out on a bed. Furthermore, Lincoln was buried in his black suit, a white shirt with collar attached, and a black tie—not in a white tie as is the dead man of the *Post*. Observing the man's face one misses Lincoln's characteristics.

A final indication that the man is not Lincoln is that the original plate is an ambrotype. Gurney, a professional photographer, took his images on glass negatives from which prints could be easily obtained. Why should he have made an ambrotype—a single plate?

IS LINCOLN IN THE PICTURE? The citizen-soldiers of the Cassius M. Clay Battalion, photographed at the rear of the White House by a government photographer on April 29, 1861. The top-hatted figure in the center (standing before the third column from the left) is supposedly Abraham Lincoln, and the shadowy figure in the third window from the left on the second story is Mrs. Lincoln, What imagination is necessary to think so!

IS THIS LINCOLN? The magazine photographer Leo Stashin found this exquisite half-plate daguerreotype in a New York antique shop in 1968 and bought it for $28, convinced that it was an early likeness of the Great Emancipator. Stashin and his wife, an anatomist, made a thorough study of Lincoln's facial characteristics and also arranged a scanning test at the Itek Data Analysis Center. And when all the evidence was in they concluded that the man in the daguerreotype was indeed Abraham Lincoln. So far they have not been able to convince the Lincoln experts; not a one agrees with the Stashins.

IS THIS TOP-HATTED MAN LINCOLN? Did he pose here before Beauregard's fortifications at Manassas in the summer of 1862? And is the man at the left the photographer Alexander Gardner? If the two men had been standing closer to the camera the questions might be answered easily . . .

AN ENLARGEMENT OF THE FIGURES reveals clearly that the man on the right is not Lincoln; he is not tall enough. Besides, what was the Commander-in-Chief doing in shirtsleeves on the battlefield? As for the other man, it might possibly be Gardner.

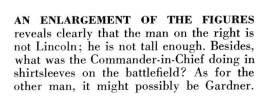

1   1847
Daguerreotype by N. H. Shepherd, Springfield

This is the earliest-known likeness of Lincoln. He is thirty-eight years old and a Representative in the 30th Congress. This daguerreotype (reversed here to show his features accurately) was supposedly taken by Nicholas H. Shepherd, an itinerant daguerreotypist. It is in the Library of Congress.

2   SATURDAY, FEBRUARY 28, 1857
Photograph by Alexander Hesler, Chicago

This picture was taken at the request of Lincoln's lawyer friends. Hesler, the photographer recalled that "His hair was plastered down smooth over his forehead. In conversing and studying his face I found it very interesting. I ran my fingers through his hair and made the negative."

3   PROBABLY SUNDAY, APRIL 25, 1858
Ambrotype by Samuel G. Alschuler, Urbana

Henry C. Whitney in his *Life on the Circuit with Lincoln* (p. 70) relates that Lincoln came to the studio in a linen coat. When the photographer suggested that he change it, he said he had no other with him, so Alschuler lent him his own velvet-collared black coat to wear for the picture.

4   FRIDAY, MAY 7, 1858
Ambrotype by A. M. Byers, Beardstown

This print is made from the original ambrotype, which the photographer's wife willed in 1947 to the University of Nebraska. Taken on the day Lincoln cleared Duff Armstrong of the charge of murder, with the aid of an almanac, it is one of the best portraits of lawyer Lincoln.

5   SUNDAY, JULY 11, 1858
By Schneider or von Schneidau, Chicago

Lincoln spoke on July 10 at the Tremont House, answering Stephen A. Douglas, who had delivered the first speech in the senatorial campaign. In his hand he holds a copy of the Chicago *Press & Tribune*, whose editors—Dr. Charles H. Ray and Joseph Medill—gave him their ardent support.

6   THURSDAY, AUGUST 26, 1858
Ambrotype by T. P. Pearson, Macomb

This portrait was made five days after Lincoln's first joint debate with Douglas at Ottawa, Illinois. Richard Watson Gilder, the well-known editor of the *Century Magazine*, owned the plate, which was lost when the Century Building in New York was destroyed by fire in 1888.

7   **FRIDAY, OCTOBER 1, 1858**
Ambrotype by Calvin Jackson, Pittsfield

During the senatorial campaign, after Lincoln had made a two-hour speech in the public square, he was asked by his friend, attorney D. H. Gilmer, for a picture. He obligingly posed for the itinerant ambrotyper Jackson, who probably made two plates. This one he presented to Gilmer.

8   **MONDAY, OCTOBER 11, 1858**
Ambrotype by W. J. Thompson, Monmouth

Taken two days before the sixth debate with Douglas at Quincy, Ill., where a large crowd met Lincoln at the station. The Republicans gave him a "splendid torchlight procession." Before this portrait was taken, Lincoln made a three-hour speech to an enthusiastic audience.

9   **SOMETIME IN 1858**
Ambrotype by Preston Butler, Springfield

The debates were over—Lincoln's name was known throughout the country. When he gave an address at Atlanta, Ill., his host, Sylvester Strong, asked him for a photograph. Returned to Springfield, Lincoln sent him an ambrotype, from which this somewhat retouched print was made.

10   **PROBABLY APRIL, 1858**
Ambrotype by Amon T. Joslin, Danville

Clint Clay Tilton, the late president of the Illinois State Historical Society, established the fact that this picture was taken in the latter days of April, 1858, and not on November 13, 1859, as previously supposed. Lincoln was then attending the Vermilion Circuit Court.

11   **SOMETIME IN 1858**
Place and photographer unknown

There is hardly any information about this picture. One guesses that in all probability it was made in the second half of the year 1858, or perhaps in the beginning of 1859. Frederick Hill Meserve, the eminent Lincoln student and photograph collector, discovered the print.

12   **PROBABLY IN 1858**
By one of the Cole Brothers, Peoria (?)

Several ambrotypes exist of this portrait, and the owners disagree on the date. Some say it is from 1858, others that it was taken in 1859, and still others hold that it was made in 1860. Some evidence indicates it may have been done by one of the Cole brothers, Peoria photographers.

13   LATE IN 1858?

Probably by C. S. German, Springfield

This portrait, which in all probability was originally done as an ambrotype, was presented by Lincoln to Harriet Chapman, Dennis Hanks's daughter, with the words: "This is not a very good-looking picture, but it is the best that could be produced from the poor subject."

14   PROBABLY OCTOBER 4, 1859

Photograph by S. M. Fassett, Chicago

Lincoln was in his fifty-first year when this portrait was taken. Alexander Hesler, the Chicago photographer, said he made it. But D. B. Cooke wrote to the Chicago *Tribune* that he had accompanied Lincoln to Samuel Fassett's gallery for the sitting. The negative perished in the Chicago fire.

15   MONDAY, FEBRUARY 27, 1860

By Mathew B. Brady, New York

This photograph was taken on the very day Lincoln delivered his Cooper Union address in New York City and when he visited the new gallery on the corner of Broadway and Tenth Street to sit before Brady's camera for the first time. The portrait became Lincoln's favorite one.

16   EARLY IN 1860

Photographer unknown

Before the Cooper Union Speech Lincoln dined in Brooklyn at the house of George B. Lincoln. Among the dinner guests was Colonel William L. Bramhall, who later asked Lincoln for a profile. He received the above picture, which served as a model for George H. Lovett's campaign medal.

17   TUESDAY, MAY 8, 1860

Photograph by E. A. Barnwell, Decatur

Taken a week before the Chicago convention assembled to nominate Lincoln as a presidential candidate, the portrait came to light when Grace Barnwell, the photographer's daughter, presented it to the Decatur Public Library. This new reproduction was specially made for this volume.

18   SUNDAY, MAY 20, 1860

Photograph by W. Church (?), Springfield

A day after Lincoln received formal notice of his nomination for the presidency, Marcus Ward, later Governor of New Jersey, asked him for a photograph. Lincoln replying that he had no good portrait but would gladly sit for one, the two went to the photographer—and this was the result.

19 **SUNDAY, MAY 20, 1860**
Photograph by W. Church (?), Springfield

This is another pose taken at the same time as the previous one. On the evening before, Lincoln had received the Republican notification committee in the north parlor of his Springfield home and responded briefly to the short address of Chairman George Ashmun of Massachusetts.

20 **SUNDAY, MAY 20, 1860**
Photograph by W. Church (?), Springfield

And this is the third pose done by William Church. Whether the photographer made other exposures, we do not know. There is perhaps a fourth negative which has not yet been found. The notion is also advanced that the photographer's name might have been William Marsh and not William Church.

21 **SUNDAY, JUNE 3, 1860**
By Alexander Hesler, Springfield

This is one of the four known negatives Hesler made at Springfield. The glass plates of this and the following photograph were damaged in the mail in 1933. The Goverment, after paying damages to the sender of the package, gave the broken plates to the Smithsonian Institution.

22 **SUNDAY, JUNE 3, 1860**
By Alexander Hesler, Springfield

After his nomination, Lincoln was asked by Hesler to sit for a portrait. Lincoln replied that he intended to stay near home during the campaign and could not come to Chicago, but if Hesler would visit Springfield, he would willingly pose and would even get "dressed up" for him.

23 **SUNDAY, JUNE 3, 1860**
By Alexander Hesler, Springfield

This is one of the poses Hesler made of Lincoln. Of this and the preceding portraits more than 100,000 prints were distributed during the campaign months. And while his pictures went into American homes, the candidate stayed in Springfield, keeping his lips shut on political matters.

24 **SUNDAY, JUNE 3, 1860**
By Alexander Hesler, Springfield

The portrait Hesler made of Lincoln in 1857 (No. 2) was not a winning one, and something more flattering was needed by his friends and campaign managers to show the electorate that Lincoln was not a bad-looking man. Thus Hesler was put on his mettle to get a better likeness.

25 **PROBABLY JUNE, 1860**
Photograph by Joseph Hill, Springfield

This is a print from one of four different negatives, all of which were destroyed by fire. Unfortunately, there are no more facts about this sitting. It is very hard to determine the exact time when this portrait was taken. It resembles some others that were made in 1860.

26 **SUMMER OF 1860**
Photographer unknown, Springfield

There is nothing more known about this portrait. It is very similar to another whichWilliam Seavey took in Springfield in 1860, but it is not sure if the two photographs were taken at the same sitting. H. W. Fay claimed that it was the work of Frederick Gutekunst of Philadelphia.

27 **PROBABLY IN 1860**
Ferrotype by an unknown photographer

Miss Ida Tarbell published this photograph in *The Early Life of Abraham Lincoln* (New York, 1896), believing it to have been made in 1856. But this could not be right; it must have been taken later. Josephine Cobb thinks the date may be either 1858 or early in 1859.

28 **SUMMER OF 1860**
Photographer unknown, Springfield

There are not many facts about this portrait either. Miss Ida Tarbell wrote in *McClure's Magazine*, February, 1896, that the photograph was taken at the request of M. C. Tuttle, of St. Paul, and that it was widely used in the presidential campaign, but this is all we know.

29 **SUMMER OF 1860**
By William Shaw (?), Chicago

It is similar to the previous photograph, so it may be one of the negatives taken at the same time. Frederick Hill Meserve says that a similar portrait was made by Tresize's Enterprise Gallery in Springfield. On the back of a contemporary print the name of the photographer William Shaw is printed.

30 **SUMMER OF 1860**
Photographer unknown, Springfield

There is the same absence of data about this Lincoln photograph as about the two previous ones. It is not unlike Nos. 28 and 29, so it might have been made by the same photographer either in Springfield or in Chicago, but this is no more than guesswork. Research could uncover no real facts.

316

31   **SUMMER OF 1860**

Photographer unknown, Springfield

A print of it was found among the effects of J. Henry Brown, the artist who painted Lincoln in 1860, came into the hands of Ida M. Tarbell, the Lincoln biographer, who in turn left it after her death to Allegheny College, Meadville, Pa., by whose courtesy it is here reproduced.

32   **MONDAY, AUGUST 13, 1860**

Ambrotype by Preston Butler, Springfield

This plate, 4 by 5 inches in size, was given to J. Henry Brown, the artist, who used it as a model to make a miniature on ivory. Five days before it was taken, a Republican rally was held to celebrate the party's candidate. As Lincoln had no desire to make a speech, he escaped on horseback.

33   **SUMMER OF 1860**

By William Seavey, Springfield

The negative was lost when the Seavey Gallery was burned. Only this seems to be also certain: William Seavey, who had a photographic studio in Canton, Ill., visited Springfield and took the photograph; Lincoln's appearance indicates that it must have been made sometime in the summer of 1860.

34   **SUMMER OF 1860**

Photographer unknown, Springfield

This is the first photograph of Lincoln showing him full figure, all 6 feet 4 inches of him. It is thought that the Republican candidate posed for it to oblige Leonard W. Volk, the sculptor, who needed it to model his busts after as a supplement to the sittings Lincoln gave him.

35   **SUNDAY, NOVEMBER 25, 1860**

By Samuel G. Alschuler, Chicago

Shortly after his election, the first photograph was made of Lincoln with a beard, The New York *Herald* reported under the dateline of November 25: "On Sunday Lincoln and Hamlin attended church. Lincoln also sat for a photographer, the result being a unique half-bearded portrait."

36   **JANUARY, 1861**

By Christopher S. German, Springfield

The sculptor Jones relates that he accompanied Lincoln to a photographic gallery "to pose him for some pictures he desired to present to a very dear friend." As this happened on a Sunday late in January, it must have been the 13th or 20th, as Lincoln autographed a print on January 26th.

37 SATURDAY, FEBRUARY 9, 1861
By C. S. German, Springfield

This is the last portrait made of Lincoln in Springfield, two days before he left for Washington. On February 11 he visited his law office and said to Herndon: "Give our clients to understand that the election of a president makes no change in the firm of Lincoln and Herndon."

38 SATURDAY, FEBRUARY 9, 1861
By C. S. German, Springfield

The family had already broken up housekeeping and was staying at the Chenery House, waiting for the day of departure. Everything was packed and Lincoln himself had labeled the baggage: "The White House, Washington." This photograph was taken at the same time as the previous one.

39 SUNDAY, FEBRUARY 24, 1861
By Mathew B. Brady, Washington

Lincoln arrived in Washington at six in the morning on February 23. Probably a day later he went to Mathew Brady's Photographic Parlor on the corner of Pennsylvania Avenue and Seventh Street to have his picture taken. The painter George H. Story, who was present, told a New York *World*

40 SUNDAY, FEBRUARY 24, 1861
By Mathew B. Brady, Washington

reporter later that Brady wanted to "pose" Lincoln, but Story said to make the exposures just as the President-elect was sitting at the table. The painter recalled that Lincoln seemed to him elegant in dress and appearance, his clothes being made of the finest broadcloth, and that he sat quietly and deep

41 SUNDAY, FEBRUARY 24, 1861
By Mathew B. Brady, Washington

in thought while Brady and Alexander Gardner made their preparations. To Story he gave the impression of a man "who was overwhelmed with anxiety, and fatigue, and care." He was deep in thought, oblivious of the surroundings.

The photographers took him in different

42 SUNDAY, FEBRUARY 24, 1861
By Mathew B. Brady, Washington

poses, some of the exposures being quickly repeated after moving the plateholder in the camera, thus fixing Lincoln's image several times on the same negative. According to Story a second camera, holding 11 x 14-inch glass plates, was also used the day this photograph was made.

318

43 **SUNDAY, FEBRUARY 24, 1861**
By Mathew B. Brady, Washington

A couple of months later, on April 27, *Harper's Weekly* printed a woodcut copy of No. 42 saying: "We publish herewith from a photograph, just taken expressly for this paper, a portrait of the President. It is the first accurate portrait that has been published since he began to grow a beard."

44 **SUMMER, 1861**
Photographer unknown

Lincoln inscribed this portrait on October 3, 1861: "For Mrs. Lucy G. Speed from whose pious hand I accepted the present of an Oxford Bible twenty years ago." Mrs. Speed was the mother of Joshua and James Speed, Lincoln's lifelong friends, at whose home he was always welcome.

45 **ABOUT 1862**
By Mathew B. Brady, Washington

For many months Lincoln was not photographed. These are the first pictures of him taken by Brady after he became President. Now that he knew Lincoln better, Brady took greater liberties with his subject than at the first sittings in Washington. He now posed the President "artis-

46 **ABOUT 1862**
By Mathew B. Brady, Washington

tically," and Lincoln, in an obliging mood, did not seem to mind. The above picture probably was made by a huge camera holding a negative of 16¼ x 19 inches, if it is not an enlargement. These photographs show marked changes in Lincoln's features. In the short space of a year the furrows

47 **ABOUT 1862**
By Mathew B. Brady, Washington

had grown deeper, the eyes sadder: the anxieties and trepidations of the first war year had left their marks on his face.

The sitting took place in the year of his moving annual message to Congress: "Fellow citizens, we cannot escape history. We of this Congress

48 **ABOUT 1862**
By Mathew B. Brady, Washington

and this administration, will be remembered in spite of ourselves. No personal significance, or insignificance, can spare one or another of us. The fiery trial through which we pass, will light us down, in honor or dishonor, to the latest generation. We *say* we are for the Union. The world

49　　**ABOUT 1862**
By Mathew B. Brady, Washington

will not forget that we say this. We know how to save the Union. The world knows we do know how to save it. We—even *we here*—hold the power, and bear the responsibility. In giving freedom to the *slave*, we *assure* freedom to the *free*—honorable alike in what we give, and what

50　　**ABOUT 1862**
By Mathew B. Brady, Washington

we preserve. We shall nobly save, or meanly lose, the last best hope of earth. Other means may succeed; this could not fail. The way is plain, peaceful, generous, just—a way which, if followed, the world will forever applaud, and God must forever bless."

51　　**PROBABLY 1863**
By Mathew B. Brady, Washington

The Emancipation Proclamation was issued on January 1, 1863. It was during this year that Lincoln visited Mathew Brady's studio for the third time since he came to Washington. The photographers at the studio—as was the custom—made several exposures, using among others a multiple-

52　　**PROBABLY 1863**
By Mathew B. Brady, Washington

lens camera, yielding four exposures at once.
　In some of the Brady plates in the National Archives Lincoln's image is fixed on the negative three times (see page 294). This was accomplished —according to Professor Robert Taft, author of *Photography and the American Scene*—by moving

53　　**PROBABLY 1863**
By Mathew B. Brady, Washington

the plateholder rapidly between exposures. Beaumont Newhall, the Curator of George Eastman House, states that the negatives were not made with a multiple-lens camera because Lincoln's features "do not show relief when they are looked at with a stereoscope." He believes the triple

54　　**PROBABLY 1863**
By Mathew B. Brady, Washington

prints are copy negatives. This very well may be so.
　From some poses Brady made enlargements by "blowing up" the head and "matting out" the body. At a hurried glance, these *carte de visite* heads seem to appear different from the photo-

320

55   PROBABLY 1863
By Mathew B. Brady, Washington

graphs which show Lincoln sitting in the chair. Actually they are identical (see page 295)—they may have been enlarged from plates which have disappeared. Only one such head shows enough difference to be considered as a separate pose from this sitting.

56   SUNDAY, AUGUST 9, 1863
By Alexander Gardner, Washington

It is said that Lincoln was Alexander Gardner's first client when that photographer opened his studio in Washington. Gardner, a Scotchman, was probably brought to America by Brady in 1856. Robert Taft's *Photography and the American Scene* offers the spare facts on the photographer's

57   SUNDAY, AUGUST 9, 1863
By Alexander Gardner, Washington

life. Taft says that Gardner had training in the collodion process abroad, where it was practiced extensively before it was adopted in the United States. He also knew the secret of how to make enlargements, which at the time was a rather cumbersome and difficult undertaking.

58   SUNDAY, AUGUST 9, 1863
By Alexander Gardner, Washington

Gardner became the head of Brady's Washington gallery, and he was in charge of it from 1858 until 1863, the year when he opened his own studio on the corner of Seventh and D Streets, over Shephard and Riley's Bookstore. The first advertisement of his establishment appeared in the

59   SUNDAY, AUGUST 9, 1863
By Alexander Gardner, Washington

National Intelligencer, Washington, on May 26, 1863, and said: "To avoid the fault so generally and justly complained of, the 'Light' has been constructed so as to obviate all heavy and unnatural shadows under the eyebrows and chin. All the chemical department has been brought to such

60   SUNDAY, AUGUST 9, 1863
By Alexander Gardner, Washington

perfection that the sitting for a *carte de visite* rarely exceeds five seconds! Oftener not more than one or two!" On Lincoln's first visit to the gallery, Gardner used at least two cameras. The smaller one was most probably the then fashionable double-lens camera, which threw two images

61 SUNDAY, AUGUST 9, 1863
By Alexander Gardner, Washington

on the negative. Nos. 57 and 59 were certainly taken that way, as prints were found which show slight differences in the space between Lincoln's leg and the table beside which he sat. The photographs seem to have given satisfaction—they were widely distributed during the second campaign.

62 SUNDAY, AUGUST 9, 1863
By Alexander Gardner, Washington

First publication of a newly found photograph. Lincoln gave it to his secretary, John Hay, who presented it to his son, Clarence. And when Clarence died in 1969 the brown-toned 13 x 16 enlargement came to his son, another John Hay.
It is published here through his courtesy.

63 NOVEMBER 8 OR 15, 1863
By Alexander Gardner, Washington

On Sunday, November 8, 1863, John Hay wrote in his diary: "Went with Mrs. Ames to Gardner's Gallery & were soon joined by Nico and the Prest. We had a great many pictures taken. . . . Nico & I immortalized ourselves by having ourselves done in group with the Prest." But Noah

64 NOVEMBER 8 OR 15, 1863
By Alexander Gardner, Washington

Brooks wrote in his *Washington in Lincoln's Time* (p. 285): "One November day—it chanced to be the Sunday before the dedication of the national cemetery at Gettysburg [making it November 15]—I had an appointment to go with the President to Gardner, the photographer, on

65 NOVEMBER 8 OR 15, 1863
By Alexander Gardner, Washington

Seventh Street, to fulfill a long-standing engagement. Mr. Lincoln carefully explained that he could not go on any other day without interfering with the public business and the photographer's business, to say nothing of his liability to be hindered by curiosity-seekers 'and other seekers'

66 NOVEMBER 8 OR 15, 1863
By Alexander Gardner, Washington

on the way thither. . . . The President suddenly remembered that he needed a paper, and, after hurrying back to his office, soon rejoined me with a long envelop in his hand in which he said was an advance copy of Edward Everett's address to be delivered at the Gettysburg dedica-

67 NOVEMBER 8 OR 15, 1863
By Alexander Gardner, Washington

tion. . . . A disaster overtook the negative of that photograph, and after a very few prints had been made from it, no more were possible. In the picture which the President gave me, the envelop containing Mr. Everett's oration is seen on the table."

68 TUESDAY, FEBRUARY 9, 1864
A Brady photograph, Washington

This was perhaps the most elaborate sitting Lincoln granted to Brady. Some of these poses were taken with a multiple-lens camera. There are other examples of these profiles which will show relief when the pairs are matched in a stereo viewer. But these two profiles—in spite of a

69 TUESDAY, FEBRUARY 9, 1864
A Brady photograph, Washington

great similarity—do not seem to have been fixed by the four-lens camera. The differences are clearly seen by comparing the shirt fronts and Lincoln's left eyebrows.

Lincoln took his son Tad with him and the photograph of the two was soon in many thousands

70 TUESDAY, FEBRUARY 9, 1864
A Brady photograph, Washington

of homes. The picture of Lincoln with his son was used by painters as the basis of their portraits of the Lincoln family. In his book, Carpenter recalls that one day in 1864 "some photographers from Brady's Gallery came up to the White House to make some stereoscopic

71 TUESDAY, FEBRUARY 9, 1864
A Brady photograph, Washington

studies for me of the President's office. They requested a dark closet, in which to develop the pictures; and without a thought that I was infringing upon anybody's rights, I took them to an unoccupied room of which little 'Tad' had taken possession a few days before, and with the aid of

72 TUESDAY, FEBRUARY 9, 1864
A Brady photograph, Washington

a couple of servants, had fitted up as a miniature theatre. . . . Everything went on well, and one or two pictures had been taken, when suddenly there was an uproar. The operator came back to the office, and said that 'Tad' had taken great offence at the occupation of his room without his

73 TUESDAY, FEBRUARY 9, 1864
A Brady photograph, Washington

consent, and had locked the door, refusing all admission. The chemicals had been taken inside, and there was no way of getting at them, he having carried off the key. (In the midst of this conversation, 'Tad' burst in, in a fearful passion. . . . Mr. Lincoln had been sitting for a photo-

74 TUESDAY, FEBRUARY 9, 1864
A Brady photograph, Washington

graph, and was still in the chair. He said very mildly, 'Tad, go and unlock the door.' Tad went off . . . refusing to obey . . . no coaxing would pacify him." Lincoln suddenly rose and strode off. Directly he returned with the key to the theatre, which he unlocked, then resumed his seat.

75 WEDNESDAY, APRIL 20, 1864
A Brady photograph, Washington

The author of this volume found in the painter Francis B. Carpenter's diary this entry, written on April 26, 1864: "Today, Mr. Berger from Brady's came up and took several pictures for me of Mr. Lincoln in the Cabinet room. Succeeded very well." Carpenter needed photographs to serve

76 WEDNESDAY, APRIL 20, 1864
By Berger, Brady's assistant, Washington

as models for his painting. This and the previous one were discovered among the belongings of Francis B. Carpenter and were first published by the author. (They were in the possession of the artist's grandson, Emerson Carpenter Ives.) The cut-out head was pasted in his

77 TUESDAY, APRIL 26, 1864
By Berger, Brady's assistant, Washington

scrapbook. Why it was cropped is not known; it may be that Carpenter placed it over his sketch of Lincoln's body to see the effect.

In the two photographs of Lincoln at the table the President holds the same position in which he is painted in Carpenter's large canvas,

78 TUESDAY, APRIL 26, 1864
By Berger, Brady's assistant, Washington

"Reading the Emancipation Proclamation." Carpenter had asked Anthony Berger, an assistant of Brady, to come to the White House and photograph Lincoln that way so that he could use the pictures as models. The legs on the right of one of the photographs belong to Carpenter, who sat on

324

79 **TUESDAY, APRIL 26, 1864**
By Berger, Brady's assistant, Washington

a chair as he would paint Seward (see pages 162 and 163). The watch chain of Lincoln in the sitting pose and in the broken-plate pose shows a different pattern. Thus it is surmised that the pictures were taken not on the same day but on different occasions.

80 **PROBABLY IN 1864**
By Lewis E. Walker, Washington

This exquisite portrait of Lincoln was probably taken in the White House, around the time of his renomination. Circumstances of the sitting are not known; one surmises now that the photographer was Lewis E. Walker, and not Thomas Walker, as formerly believed.

81 **PROBABLY IN 1864**
By Wenderoth & Taylor, White House

These two portraits were made in the White House sometime during the year of 1864, when Lincoln was running for re-election and when matters looked dark for him and for the Union. The exact date could not be ascertained, nor could the circumstances under which they were taken.

82 **PROBABLY IN 1864**
By Wenderoth & Taylor, White House

However, we do know that the photographs were made by the firm of Wenderoth & Taylor, who had a well-known gallery at Philadelphia. They caught Lincoln in a pensive mood, his eyes clear and hard, his features sharply drawn in the technically excellent portraits.

83 **PROBABLY EARLY 1865**
By Thomas Walker, Washington

This photograph and the next one were put on the market as stereoscopes by E. & H. T. Anthony. Originally it was believed that it was Brady who took the pictures, but later research indicated that the photographs may have been taken by Thomas Walker, a Treasury Department employee.

84 **PROBABLY EARLY 1865**
By Thomas Walker, Washington

The exact date of the sitting is uncertain; one's guess is that they were taken shortly before the second inauguration, probably in February, 1865, when Grant was pressing Lee before Petersburg and the end of the hostilities was in sight, although the strain of the office had not yet abated.

85 MONDAY, MARCH 6, 1865
By Henry F. Warren (?), Washington

On March 4 Lincoln was inaugurated for the second time and two days later photographer Warren of Waltham, Mass., supposedly took this portrait in the White House. But nothing shows that Warren was in Washington at that time—there is no record that he received a pass.

86 MONDAY, APRIL 10, 1865
By Alexander Gardner, Washington

On Sunday, April 9, Lincoln returned from City Point to Washington. On board the *River Queen* he relaxed, reading aloud from *Macbeth*, in particular, the verses following Duncan's assassination. These tell the torments of Macbeth when he became king after the murder of Duncan.

87 MONDAY, APRIL 10, 1865
By Alexander Gardner, Washington

The Marquis de Chambrun, a member of the President's party, recalled: "Mr. Lincoln paused here while reading, and began to explain to us how true a description of the murderer that one was; when, the dark deed achieved, its tortured perpetrator came to envy the sleep of the victim."

88 MONDAY, APRIL 10, 1865
By Alexander Gardner, Washington

Deep in meditation, when his French companion mentioned his home town, Lincoln roused: "Springfield! How happy, four years hence, will I be to return there in peace and tranquillity!"
On that very day the war ended; General Lee surrendered to Grant at Appomattox.

89 MONDAY, APRIL 10, 1865
By Alexander Gardner, Washington

And once more Lincoln repeated the lines:
Duncan is in his grave;
After life's fitful fever he sleeps well;
Treason has done his worst; nor steel, nor poison,
Malice domestic, foreign levy, nothing
Can touch him further.

90 MONDAY, APRIL 10, 1865
By Alexander Gardner, Washington

These were his last photographs, four days before his assassination. They show a face "furrowed and harrowed by infinite perplexities, while over all was a simple dignity more than sacerdotal—a peculiar set-apart look . . . never seen in any other man."

PHOTOGRAPHS OF LINCOLN
NOT TAKEN IN THE STUDIO

91   **AUGUST 8, 1860**
Photographer unknown, Springfield

A detail of the photograph, which is printed on page 110, showing Lincoln standing in front of his Springfield house, surrounded by well-wishers.

92   **1860**
By A. J. Whipple of Boston

The Boston photographer A. J. Whipple came to Springfield some time during the summer of 1860, to take pictures of the Republican candidate. Lincoln, with one of his younger sons obligingly posed for him before his home. The photographer erected his camera across the street, taking in the whole of the house.

93   **1860**
By A. J. Whipple of Boston

This is a detail of another exposure. The blurry little figure outside the fence is Isaac R. Diller, a friend of the Lincoln children.

94   **FRIDAY, FEBRUARY 22, 1861**
By F. De B. Richards, Philadelphia

One of the photographs at the flag-raising ceremonies before Philadelphia's Independence Hall. Lincoln is on the left, holding his hat above the single star. There are two other views of this Washington's Birthday celebration—unfortunately, they do not show Lincoln too well; one of them is reproduced on page 120.

95   FRIDAY, OCTOBER 3, 1862
By Alexander Gardner

Detail from a group picture, which is printed on page 170, showing Lincoln at the battlefield of Antietam with McClellan and other generals.

96   FRIDAY, OCTOBER 3, 1862
By Alexander Gardner

Detail from another photograph. This time General McClellan is at Lincoln's left. This picture was taken with a stereo camera. (See page 299.)

97   FRIDAY, OCTOBER 3, 1862
By Alexander Gardner

The President poses with the detective Allan Pinkerton and Major General John A. McClernand on the battlefield at Antietam, Maryland.

98   FRIDAY, OCTOBER 3, 1862
By Alexander Gardner

Another photograph of Lincoln with Allan Pinkerton and John A. McClernand taken before a tent at the army headquarters in Antietam.

99   FRIDAY, OCTOBER 3, 1862
By Alexander Gardner

Detail of a photograph, which is printed on page 171, showing Lincoln with General McClellan in the army commander's tent at Antietam.

100   FRIDAY, OCTOBER 3, 1862
By Alexander Gardner

A second exposure of Lincoln with McClellan at Antietam. The windblown newspapers before the President's chair indicate the difference.

101   NOVEMBER 19, 1863
By an unknown photographer,

Detail of a photograph from Gettysburg greatly enlarged (see page 202). The negative from which this print was made was discovered by Josephine Cobb, the iconographer of the National Archives.

102   MARCH 4, 1865
Probably by Alexander Gardner

About seven different exposures were made of the ceremony. In this one Lincoln sits, in another he stands (see page 275). In the remaining pictures he can hardly be seen.

103   APRIL 24, 1865
By Gurney & Son, New York

The only photograph of Lincoln in his coffin, taken at New York's City Hall while his body lay in state there. The original print was confiscated by the Secretary of War.

CONTENTS AND BIBLIOGRAPHY

GENERAL WORKS

Jay Monaghan's *Lincoln Bibliography* (1945) lists 3,958 books and pamphlets on Lincoln through the year 1939.

The main source of all these books is Lincoln's writings, which are in *The Collected Works of Abraham Lincoln* (1953, 1955). These eight volumes and index prepared by the Abraham Lincoln Association supersede all previous compilations.

Of the important biographies of Lincoln, here are a few: John Locke Scripps (1860), Josiah Holland (1866), Ward Hill Lamon (1872), Isaac N. Arnold (1885), William H. Herndon and Jesse W. Weik (1889), Ida M. Tarbell (1900), William E. Barton (1925), Carl Sandburg (1926 and 1939), Albert J. Beveridge (1928), James G. Randall (1945).

Among the one-volume biographies, the popular ones are: Lord Charnwood (1912), Benjamin Thomas (1952), Carl Sandburg (1954), Stefan Lorant (1954), Reinhard Luthin (1961).

CHRONOLOGIES

The pioneering listing of the day-by-day activities of Lincoln was issued by the Abraham Lincoln Association of Springfield in four volumes: *Lincoln 1809–1839* (ed. by Harry E. Pratt, 1941), *Lincoln 1840–1846* (ed. by Harry E. Pratt, 1939), *Lincoln 1847–1853* (ed. by Benjamin P. Thomas, 1936) and *Lincoln 1854–1861* (ed. by Paul M. Angle, 1933). They were revised and continued by the Sesquicentennial Commission in 1958: *Lincoln Day by Day: A Chronology, 1809–65*, 3 vols., (ed. by Earl Schenk Miers, 1960).

AS HIS CONTEMPORARIES SAW HIM

Herbert Mitgang compiled newspaper extracts for *Lincoln as They Saw Him* (1956). *Lincoln Among His Friends* (1942) and *Intimate Memories of Lincoln* (1945), edited by Rufus Rockwell Wilson, and *The Lincoln Reader* (1957), edited by Paul M. Angle, provide selections from contemporary accounts.

9–11 THOMAS LINCOLN TAKES A WIFE

On Lincoln's forebears: J. Henry Lea and J. R. Hutchinson's *The Ancestry of Abraham Lincoln* (1909); Marion Dexter Learned's *Abraham Lincoln: An American Migration* (1909); William E. Barton's *The Paternity of Abraham Lincoln* (1920); and Louis A. Warren's *Lincoln's Parentage & Childhood* (1926). A biography of his mother is *Nancy Hanks Lincoln* (1953) by Harold and Ernestine Briggs.

Christopher Graham's recollections are from Ida M. Tarbell's *The Early Life of Abraham Lincoln* (1896).

12–13 THE CABIN WHERE LINCOLN WAS BORN

Dennis Hanks's recollections are from Eleanor Atkinson's interview in *The American Magazine*, February 1908, and

Library of Congress

THE FIRST INAUGURAL. Though Lincoln is on the platform, his figure cannot be detected. There is at least one other photograph of the ceremonies, but it too was taken from afar, as an assassination attempt was feared and the security arrangements were strict.

Courtesy King V. Hostick and Gene Snack

THE SECOND INAUGURAL. Some half a dozen or more exposures were taken from the same position. Unfortunately, the camera was a good distance from the platform; while it recorded the crowd and the background, it was not near enough to capture with clarity the features of the President.

from her book, *The Boyhood of Lincoln* (1908).

Roy Hays's "Is the Lincoln Birthplace Cabin Authentic?" is in *The Abraham Lincoln Quarterly*, September 1948. About the cabin, see *Lincoln Lore*, Nos. 1016 and 1019.

14–15 THE SEVEN YEARS IN KENTUCKY

Lincoln's memories of the Knob Creek place, as told to Dr. Jesse Rodman, are in Tarbell's *The Early Life of Abraham Lincoln*.

16–19 MOVING TO INDIANA

His father's proposal to Sarah Johnston is from Ward Hill Lamon's biography. Louis A. Warren in *Lincoln's Parentage and Childhood* and *Lincoln's Youth: Indiana Years* (1959) deals with his life in that state. Adin Baker and Mary E. Lobb's "The Lincoln Log Cabins" in *Lincoln Herald*, Spring 1969, discuss the Lincoln cabins in Indiana as does Edwin C. Bearass in a monograph for the National Park Service.

Lincoln's stepmother recalls his love of reading in Hertz's *The Hidden Lincoln* (pp. 350–53).

20–21 THE FOURTEEN YEARS IN INDIANA

Sarah Bush Lincoln's recollections are in Hertz's *The Hidden Lincoln* (p. 350), as are Nat Grigsby's (p. 353) and Elizabeth Crawford's (p. 365).

22–23 MOVING TO ILLINOIS

See Dennis Hanks's interview with Eleanor Atkinson and Lincoln's own 1860 life sketch.

24–25 FLOATING DOWN THE MISSISSIPPI

John Hanks described this flatboat trip. See Hertz's *The Hidden Lincoln* (pp. 345–50).

26–35 AT NEW SALEM

Benjamin P. Thomas' *Lincoln's New Salem* (1934 and 1954) and Thomas P. Reep's *Lincoln at New Salem* (1954) are the best books on the life of the village.

Zarel C. Spears and Robert S. Barton's *Berry and Lincoln* (1947) argues for William Berry. Kunigunde Duncan and D. F. Nickols' *Mentor Graham* (1944) makes the best of sparse facts.

The Ann Rutledge myth is discussed

by Louis A. Warren in *The Lincoln Kinsman* of May 1941 and in *Lincoln Lore*, No. 830. James G. Randall, in the second volume of *Lincoln the President*, has a detailed appendix, "Sifting the Ann Rutledge Evidence." Jay Monaghan's "New Light on the Lincoln-Rutledge Romance" is in the September 1944 *The Abraham Lincoln Quarterly*; "The Rutledge Family" in *Lincoln Lore*, No. 149; a "Directory of New Salem and Environs" in *Lincoln Lore*, No. 473; Lincoln's "Six Years at New Salem" in *Lincoln Lore*, No. 522; and "The Restoration of New Salem" in *Lincoln Lore*, No. 238.

36–37 LEGISLATOR IN VANDALIA
William E. Baringer's *Lincoln's Vandalia* (1949) and *Lincoln's Preparation for Greatness: The Illinois Legislative Years* (1965) by Paul Simon are the best studies on the subject.

38–41 IN LOVE WITH A FAT GIRL
R. Gerald McMurtry's "Appendix" in Olive Caruthers' *Lincoln's Other Mary* (1946) deals with the affair thoroughly. The statements of Mary Owens (later Mrs. Jesse Vineyard) and her son B. R. Vineyard are in Hertz's *The Hidden Lincoln*.

42–45 MOVING TO SPRINGFIELD
Paul M. Angle's *Here I Have Lived* (1950) is an excellent book of Lincoln's Springfield. Harry E. Pratt's "Springfield's Public Square in Lincoln's Day" is in the *Illinois Bar Journal* of May 1952.

46–51 TO MARRY OR NOT
Mrs. Abraham Lincoln (1932) by W. A. Evans is a doctor's critical survey of her unhappy life; *Mary, Wife of Lincoln* (1928) by Katherine Helm, Mrs. Lincoln's niece, is based on recollections of Mary's half-sister Emily; *Lincoln and His Wife's Home Town* (1929) by William H. Townsend covers Mary's years at Lexington. Carl Sandburg and Paul M. Angle, in *Mary Lincoln, Wife and Widow* (1932), reproduce many of her letters.
Robert L. Kincaid's *Joshua Fry Speed: Lincoln's Most Intimate Friend* (1943) records the Lincoln-Speed story. Ruth P. Randall's *Biography of a Marriage* (1953), *Lincoln's Sons* (1956), and *The Courtship of Mr. Lincoln* (1957) provide good material about his relation to Mary.

52–53 PRACTICING LAW AND POLITICS
Frederick Trevor Hill's *Lincoln the Lawyer* (1906), Albert A. Woldman's *Lawyer Lincoln* (1936), Henry C. Whitney's *Life on the Circuit with Lincoln* (1892), and John J. Duff's *A. Lincoln: Prairie Lawyer* (1960) cover the circuit days.
Harry E. Pratt's *The Personal Finances of Abraham Lincoln* (1943) is well documented.

54–55 CONGRESSMAN
Donald W. Riddle's *Lincoln Runs for Congress* (1948) and *Congressman Abraham Lincoln* (1957) treat this period.

56 INVENTOR
Thomas I. Starr's "The Detroit River and A—— L——" in the *Bulletin of the Detroit Historical Society*, February 1947.

57 OFFICE SEEKER
Thomas Ewing's "Lincoln and the General Land Office" in the *Journal of the Illinois State Historical Society* (1932).

58–61 FAMILY RELATIONS
Ruth P. Randall's three volumes, cited above, give the facts.

62–65 RIDING THE CIRCUIT
The volumes on Lincoln's law activities have previously been mentioned. John M. Palmer's *The Bench and Bar of Illinois* (2 vols., 1899) paints the background. Two articles by Harry E. Pratt—"The Genesis of Lincoln the Lawyer" in the *Abraham Lincoln Association Bulletin*, No. 57, and "Lincoln's Supreme Court Cases" in the *Illinois Bar Journal*, September 1943—are thorough studies.
A full account of the Lincoln of this period is *Prelude to Greatness: Lincoln in the 1850's* (1962) by Don E. Fehrenbacher.

66–69 BACK IN THE POLITICAL ARENA
See Paul M. Angle's introduction to *Lincoln, 1854–1861*. *Lincoln's Lost Speech* (1962) by Elwell Crissey is an intensive study of the Bloomington address.

70–71 DEFENDING A FRIEND
Stefan Lorant in *Life* magazine (February 9, 1948), "A Day in Lincoln's Life," re-creates the Armstrong trial.

72–73 NOMINATED FOR THE SENATE
See William E. Baringer's *Lincoln's Rise to Power* (1937).

74–79 DEBATING WITH DOUGLAS
The speeches are in *The Lincoln-Douglas Debates of 1858* (Illinois State Historical Library Collections, 1908), edited by Edwin E. Sparks.

80–81 GROWING INTO A CANDIDATE
See Paul M. Angle's introduction to *Lincoln, 1854–1861* and Baringer's *Lincoln's Rise to Power*.
Biographies of two of Lincoln's political friends: Jay Monaghan's *The Man Who Elected Lincoln* (1956), about Charles H. Ray, and Willard L. King's *Lincoln's Manager: David Davis* (1960).

82–83 HE WRITES OUT HIS LIFE STORY
See *Abraham Lincoln's Autobiography* (1948) by Robert Dale Richardson, the great-grandson of Jesse W. Fell.

84–85 SPEAKING IN NEW YORK
Andrew A. Freeman describes it in *Abraham Lincoln Goes to New York* (1960). Richard Cunningham McCormick's recollection of the Cooper Union address is in the New York *Evening Post* of May 3, 1865.

86–87 CAMPAIGNING IN NEW ENGLAND
Elwin L. Page's *Abraham Lincoln in New Hampshire* (1929).

88–93 THE REPUBLICANS CHOOSE THEIR CANDIDATE
Stefan Lorant's *The Glorious Burden* (1969) gives a concise account of the happenings, in text and pictures. Murat Halstead's reports of the conventions are *in Caucuses of 1860* (1860) and *Three Against Lincoln* (issued in 1960).

94–95 A LIFE MASK IS MADE
Leonard Wells Volk recounted the story for the *Century Magazine*, December 1881.

96–97 SCULPTORS MODELED HIM
About the Volk statues, see *Lincoln Lore*, Nos. 1421–25. On the Jones bust, see *Abraham Lincoln and Others in the St. Nicholas* (1968) by Wayne C. Temple.
F. Lauriston Bullard's *Lincoln in Marble and Bronze* (1952) is about sculptors who have created heroic statues of Lincoln.

98–99 AFTER THE NOMINATION
Allan Nevins' *The Emergence of Lincoln* (1950–52) gives the story to 1861.

100–5 ARTISTS CAME TO PAINT HIS PORTRAIT
L. Gerald McMurtry's *Beardless Portraits*

of *Abraham Lincoln* (1962) reprints articles which appeared in *Lincoln Lore*.

Thomas Hicks's recollections are in Allen Thorndike Rice's *Reminiscences of Abraham Lincoln* (1889). Charles A. Barry's were in the Boston *Transcript*, reprinted in Wilson's *Intimate Memories of Lincoln* (pp. 307–10). Alban Jasper Conant's recollections were printed in *McClure's Magazine*, March 1909.

106–13 THE PRESIDENTIAL CAMPAIGN
Reinhard H. Luthin's *The First Lincoln Campaign* (1944) is a comprehensive study. Albert Shaw's *Abraham Lincoln* (2 vols., 1929) reproduces numerous political cartoons, as does Rufus Rockwell Wilson's *Lincoln in Caricature* (1953).

114–15 WHY A BEARD?
See *Lincoln Lore*, No. 98.

116–19 FAREWELL TO SPRINGFIELD
William E. Baringer's *A House Dividing: Lincoln as President Elect* (1945) portrays Lincoln between the election and the inauguration.

120–21 THE BALTIMORE PLOT
See Norma B. Cuthbert's *Lincoln and the Baltimore Plot, 1861* (1949). Victor Searcher's *Lincoln's Journey to Greatness* (1960) covers the trip to Washington.

122–23 AT BRADY'S WASHINGTON STUDIO
The recollections of George Story are from an undated New York *World* clipping. See also Josephine Cobb's superb study, "Mathew B. Brady's Photographic Gallery in Washington," in the *Columbia Historical Society Records*, Vols. 53–56, pp. 3–44.

Many of Brady's negatives passed from his nephew, L. C. Handy, to the Library of Congress.

124–27 THE INAUGURATION
Margaret Leech's *Reveille in Washington: 1860–1865* (1941) catches the mood of inauguration day. The controversial record, *The Diary of a Public Man* (1945), gives a vivid description of the event.

128–29 FORMING THE CABINET
William E. Baringer's *A House Dividing* reveals the difficulties of choosing the Cabinet; the *Diary of Gideon Welles* (3 vols., 1911) has many pertinent data; *The Autobiography of Thurlow Weed* (1893) gives the Republican politician's story.

130–31 THE CARTOONISTS COMMENT ON THE NEW PRESIDENT
An introduction to Lincoln cartoons is Wilson's *Lincoln in Caricature*. Lithographic cartoons were issued by Currier & Ives, and wood-engraved cartoons can be found in *Frank Leslie's Illustrated Newspaper*, *Harper's Weekly*, and *Vanity Fair*.

132–35 THE WAR BEGINS
Battles and Leaders of the Civil War (4 vols., 1884), edited by Robert Underwood Johnson and Clarence Clough Buel, contains the participants' accounts, as does *The Blue and the Gray* (2 vols., 1952), edited by Henry Steele Commager.

For the considerations in the Cabinet, *The Diary of Edward Bates, 1859–1866* (1933), edited by H. K. Beale, and *Inside Lincoln's Cabinet: The Civil War Diaries of Salmon P. Chase* (1954), edited by David Donald, were useful sources.

David M. Potter's *Lincoln and His Party in the Secession Crisis* (1942) deals with the period from November 1860 to April 1861.

On Lincoln as a politician, statesman, diplomat: James G. Randall's *Constitutional Problems Under Lincoln* (1926 and 1951), Jay Monaghan's *Diplomat in Carpet Slippers* (1945), H. J. Carmen and R. H. Luthin's *Lincoln and the Patronage* (1943), Allan Nevins' *The Statesmanship of the Civil War* (1953) give the basic facts.

136–37 WASHINGTON PREPARES FOR THE WORST
John G. Nicolay and John Hay's *Abraham Lincoln: A History* (10 vols., 1890) and Margaret Leech's *Reveille in Washington* treat the "hysteria" in the capital.

138 A YOUNG HERO DIES
Luther Robinson's article "Ephraim Elmer Ellsworth" in the *Transactions of the Illinois State Historical Society*, 1923. John Hay's "Personal Reminiscences of Col. E. E. Ellsworth" is in *McClure's Magazine*, Vol. VI, p. 357.

139 THE FIRST BATTLE OF THE WAR
William H. Russell wrote his reports for the London *Times*, many of which appeared as *My Diary North and South* (1863, reprinted in 1954).

140–43 THE NEW COMMANDER
T. Harry Williams' *Lincoln and His Generals* (1952) and Colin R. Ballard's *The Military Genius of Abraham Lincoln*

(1926) deal with the President's gift for strategy.

McClellan's Own Story (1887) and the memoirs of the men who served with the General (such as the Comte de Paris) make, of course, a case for "Little Mac."

144–45 TROUBLES IN THE WEST
The fullest work on Frémont's life is Allan Nevins' *Frémont, the West's Greatest Adventurer* (1928).

146 ORDERING AN OFFENSIVE
See *The War of the Rebellion: Official Records of the Union and Confederate Armies* (128 vols., 1880–1901) and the *Records of the Union and Confederate Navies* (26 vols.).

147–49 WILLIE DIES
The Vinton visit is described by Francis B. Carpenter in *Six Months at the White House* (1867). Episodes of the Lincoln children are in Julia Taft Bayne's *Tad Lincoln's Father* (1931) and Ruth Randall's *Lincoln's Sons*. Elizabeth Keckley related her memories through the pen of a ghost writer in *Behind the Scenes* (1931).

"The Mortality of the Five Lincoln Boys" by Milton H. Shutes in the *Lincoln Herald*, Summer 1953, is a well-researched piece.

150–51 THE SECOND BRADY SITTING
Lincoln Lore, No. 211, discusses this sitting. Stefan Lorant's article in the *New York Times Magazine*, February 13, 1949—"His Photographs Conceal the Real Lincoln"—discuss his behavior before the camera.

152–57 THE PENINSULAR CAMPAIGN
McClellan's Own Story reveals the General's mind. *Anecdotes of the Civil War in the United States* (1884) by E. D. Townsend, McClellan's aide, is what the title implies.

Life and Letters of General Thomas J. Jackson (1891), edited by Mary A. Jackson, reveals the character of Jackson. The best biography is *Mighty Stonewall* by Frank Vandiver (1957).

158–59 HORACE GREELEY AND HIS "PRAYER OF TWENTY MILLIONS"
Lincoln's and Greeley's relations are recorded in James R. Gilmore's *Personal Recollections of Abraham Lincoln and the Civil War* (1898). William Harlan Hale's *Horace Greeley: Voice of the People* (1950) is a vivid biography.

160–61 THE BATTLE OF ANTIETAM

Bruce Catton's trilogy—*Mr. Lincoln's Army* (1951), *Glory Road* (1952), *A Stillness at Appomattox* (1953)—and his recent volumes are masterly works on the Civil War.

162–67 THE EMANCIPATION PROCLAMATION

Thomas T. Eckert's recollections are in David H. Bates's *Lincoln in the Telegraph Office* (1907). Carpenter's *Six Months at the White House*, Salmon P. Chase's *Diary* (in the *Annual Report of the American Historical Association*, 1903), and Gideon Welles's *Diary* record the diarists' impressions.

Stefan Lorant's "A Rare New Find of Lincoln Material" in the *Saturday Evening Post* of July 19, 1947, recounts the painting of the picture.

168–69 THE ATTACKS OF A BALTIMORE DENTIST

Van Dyk MacBride's article "Eight Etchings by Dr. Adalbert J. Volck" appeared in the *Lincoln Herald*, Fall 1954.

170–71 LINCOLN VISITS ANTIETAM

McClellan's Own Story gives the General's account.

172–73 BURNSIDE SUCCEEDS McCLELLAN

Ben: Perley Poore's *The Life and Public Services of Ambrose E. Burnside* (1882) is a laudatory biography.

174–75 THE CAMPAIGN IN THE WEST

T. Harry Williams' *Lincoln and His Generals* is a lucid account of the Northern strategy.

176–77 AN ENGLISH WEEKLY ATTACKS LINCOLN

The prints are from the original issues of *Punch*.

178–79 THE BATTLE OF FREDERICKSBURG

Fiasco at Fredericksburg (1961) by Vorin E. Wham is a thorough study of the Union command.

182–83 THE BUTT OF RIDICULE

For Lincoln cartoons, the periodicals of the time—*Frank Leslie's Illustrated Newspaper, Harper's Weekly, Punch, Vanity Fair*, and the *London Fun*—have been consulted.

184–85 HOOKER SUCCEEDS BURNSIDE

William E. Barton's *Abraham Lincoln and the Hooker Letter* (1928) is about that famous letter.

186–87 HOOKER'S DEFEAT AT CHANCELLORSVILLE

The visit of the President is reported in Noah Brooks's *Washington in Lincoln's Time* (1895), which also tells how he received the news of the disaster.

James P. Smith, Jackson's aide-de-camp, describes the death of the general in *Battles and Leaders of the Civil War*, Vol. III, pp. 211–14.

188–89 THE BATTLE OF GETTYSBURG

Meade's Headquarters, 1863–1865: Letters of Colonel Theodore Lyman (1922) and the *Life and Letters of George Gordon Meade* (2 vols., 1913) offer the high command's views. Richard A. Brown's *Gettysburg* (1948) gives combatants' recollections.

190–91 A HITHERTO UNKNOWN PHOTOGRAPH AND A BIT OF DOGGEREL IN HIS OWN HAND

Lincoln and the Civil War in the Diaries and Letters of John Hay, edited by Tyler Dennett (1939).

192–93 VICTORIES AT LAST

Grant's and Sherman's *Memoirs* are the prime sources. "With Grant at Vicksburg—From the Civil War Diary of Captain Charles E. Wilcox" is in the *Journal of the Illinois State Historical Society*, January 1938.

194–95 HUSBAND AND WIFE

The Diary of Orville Hickman Browning (2 vols., 1925), edited by Theodore C.

AUTOGRAPHED LINCOLN PHOTOGRAPHS ARE EXTREMELY RARE;

THIS LINCOLN PORTRAIT, taken by Alexander Hesler of Chicago (Lorant #2), was sold at the Barrett auction in 1952 for $550. It is now in the possession of Dr. Paul B. Freeland, Nashville, Tennessee.

LINCOLN AUTOGRAPHED this picture (Lorant #13), now in the Illinois State Historical Library, Springfield, for George F. Smith, a dry-goods salesman from Plantsville, Conn., four days before his election.

$750 WAS PAID for this photograph (Lorant #24) at the Barrett auction in 1952. Originally President Lincoln gave the picture to Arnold Robinson, a crier of the U.S. Court in Springfield, Illinois.

Pease and James G. Randall, and John Hay's *Diaries*—and also the diaries of other contemporaries—throw light on Lincoln's married life. Elizabeth Keckley's memoirs and Ruth P. Randall's three books were cited previously.

Stefan Lorant in his "Where Are the Lincoln Papers?" (*Life* magazine, August 25, 1947) presents the evidence that Robert Todd destroyed his parents' correspondence.

196–205 THE GETTYSBURG ADDRESS
William E. Barton's *Lincoln at Gettysburg* (1930, reprinted 1950) and Louis A. Warren's *Lincoln's Gettysburg Declaration* (1964) are the most comprehensive accounts.

206–7 SOUTHERN ATTACKS ON THE PRESIDENT
Martin Abbott's "President Lincoln in Confederate Caricature" in the *Journal of the Illinois State Historical Society*, Autumn 1958, Richard B. Harwell's "Confederate Anti-Lincoln Literature" in the Fall 1951 *Lincoln Herald*, and Dwight L. Dumond's *Southern Editorials on Secession* (1931) contain material against Lincoln.

208–13 A BRADY SITTING IN 1864
Noah Brooks's *Washington in Lincoln's Time* recalls his remarks about the Bible.

John L. Cunningham's recollections are from his diary—*Three Years with the Adirondack Regiment* (1920).

213 THE POMEROY CIRCULAR
T. Harry Williams' *Lincoln and the Radicals* (1941) treats Lincoln and his antagonists within his party.

214–15 LINCOLN FINDS HIS GENERAL
Kenneth P. Williams' *Lincoln Finds a General* (4 vols., 1949–56) is a scholarly work of the first order.

216–19 THE WILDERNESS CAMPAIGN
See Grant's *Memoirs* and Horace Porter's *Campaigning with Grant* (1897).

220–21 HIS DAILY ROUTINE
Carpenter's *Six Months at the White House* abounds in anecdotes and incidents, as do Hay's *Diaries*; *The Life and Letters of John Hay* (2 vols., 1908), edited by William H. Thayer, and *Lincoln's Third Secretary: The Memoirs of William O. Stoddard* (1955), edited by William O. Stoddard, Jr.

222–23 A FRENCH MERCHANT SKETCHES LINCOLN
The Morand sketches are discussed in "A Portfolio of Original Lincoln Sketches" in the *Bulletin of the Missouri Historical Society*, April 1953.

224–25 SIGNED UNSEEN
John Hay wrote about the signing of the document in his *Diaries* (pp. 237–38).

226–29 CAMPAIGN CARTOONS ASSAIL LINCOLN
Stefan Lorant's *The Glorious Burden* has many cartoons, as does Rufus Rockwell Wilson's *Lincoln in Caricature*.

230–31 AN ANTI-LINCOLN CAMPAIGN BIOGRAPHY
The booklet is in the Library of Congress.

232–33 SHERMAN TAKES ATLANTA
See the *Memoirs of General William T. Sherman* (1875). A good account of the siege is in *Marching with Sherman, Passages from the Letters and Campaign Diaries of Henry Hitchcock* (1927), edited by M. A. DeWolfe Howe. Passages from other diaries are in Earl Schenk Miers' *The General Who Marched to Hell* (1951).

234–35 THE 1864 CAMPAIGN
Stefan Lorant's *The Glorious Burden* includes pictures and cartoons of the campaign. An early account is Arthur C. Cole's "Lincoln and the Presidential Election of 1864" in the *Transactions of the Illinois State Historical Society* (1917). Also see H. M. Dudley in the *Mississippi Valley Historical Review*, 1932, pp. 500–18.

THESE SIX PICTURES ARE SOME OF THE FEW KNOWN ONES.

THE LONGEST AUTOGRAPH is under the photograph which Lincoln gave Mrs. Lucy G. Speed (Lorant #44). The picture is a prized possession of the J. B. Speed Memorial Museum, Louisville, Kentucky.

THE USUAL SIGNATURE under a *carte-de-visite* photograph. There are a number of such autographed pictures in existence. This one belonged to Elmer E. Robinson of San Francisco, who donated it to Stanford University.

THE ONLY AUTOGRAPH OF ITS KIND. Lincoln inscribed this Brady photograph (Lorant #71) to Gustav Matile, White House clerk. It is now in the collection of the Green Bay, Wisconsin, Public Library.

236 THE BIXBY LETTER
F. Lauriston Bullard discusses the circumstance in *Abraham Lincoln and the Widow Bixby* (1946).

237 RE-ELECTED
The cartoons are reproduced from the original publications.

238–39 LINCOLN'S SUPREME COURT
David Silver's *Lincoln's Supreme Court* (1957) is a recent study.

240–41 ANOTHER LIFE MASK IS TAKEN
Articles based on the Clark Mills mask are T. D. Stewart's in the *Smithsonian Report* (1952) and Harry L. Shapiro's in *Natural History*, February 1953.

242 MARCHING THROUGH GEORGIA
The recollections of Captain Daniel Oakey are in *Battles and Leaders of the Civil War*, Vol. IV, pp. 675–78.

243 THE 13TH AMENDMENT
James G. Randall's *Constitutional Problems Under Lincoln* (1926, reprinted 1951) discusses the amendment.

244–47 THE SECOND INAUGURAL
Noah Brooks's *Washington in Lincoln's Time* gives a vivid description.

248–49 THE INAUGURAL BALL
Noah Brooks and Margaret Leech picture the ceremonies.

250–55 PREPARING THE FINAL BLOW
Captain Augustus Brown tells the excitement at Petersburg in his *Diary of a Line Officer* (1906). The siege and Lee's surrender are in Grant's *Memoirs*.

256–57 LEE SURRENDERS
The scene at Appomattox is described in *An Aide-de-Camp of Lee: Being the Papers of Colonel Charles Marshall* (1927), edited by Sir Frederick Maurice.

258–59 THE LAST DAYS
In *Reveille in Washington* Margaret Leech describes those days after the surrender of Lee.

260–71 GOOD FRIDAY, APRIL 14, 1865
Accounts of the tragic night are in David H. Bates's *Lincoln and the Telegraph Office* and the *Diary of Gideon Welles*. William H. Crook, Lincoln's bodyguard, wrote "Lincoln's Last Day" for *Harper's Monthly* (1907). Moorfield Storey gives Stanton's and Sumner's recollections in *Atlantic Monthly* (1930). Dr. Charles Sabin Taft's "Abraham Lincoln's Last Hours" is in the *Century Magazine*, February 1893.

272–73 LINCOLN'S ASSASSIN
On Booth and his deed: George S. Bryan's *The Great American Myth* (1940).

274–79 THE NATION MOURNS
The Lincoln Legend (1935) by Roy B. Basler and *Myths after Lincoln* (1929, reprinted in 1957) by Lloyd Lewis.

280–81 THE CONSPIRATORS AND THEIR FATE
Benn Pitman's transcript of the trial has been reissued as *The Assassination of President Lincoln and the Trial of the Conspirators* (1954). Robert J. Donovan's *The Assassins* (1955) and Jim Bishop's *The Day Lincoln Was Shot* (1955) are popular accounts.

292–95 A PICTORIAL BIBLIOGRAPHY
See Stefan Lorant's *Lincoln, His Life in Photographs* (1941), Frederick Hill Meserve's *The Photographs of Abraham Lincoln* (1944), Lorant's *Lincoln, A Picture Story of His Life* (1952 and 1957), and Charles Hamilton and Lloyd Ostendorf's *Lincoln in Photographs* (1963).

See also Jay Monaghan's "A Critical Examination of Three Lincoln Photographs" in the *Journal of the Illinois State Historical Society*, Spring 1959.

296–97 THE PHOTOGRAPHER OF LINCOLN
Robert Taft's *Photography and the American Scene* (1938 and 1967) has the source material on Brady. G. A. Townsend's "An Interview with Brady" appeared in the New York *World* on April 12, 1891.

Roy Meredith's *Mr. Lincoln's Camera Man* (1946) and James D. Horan's *Mathew Brady: Historian with a Camera* (1953) are two popular books on the famous photographer.

298–301 THREE-DIMENSIONAL PICTURES
"Stereoscopic Pictures of Lincoln" is in *Lincoln Lore*, No. 632. Frederick S. Lightfoot in *Image*, February 1957, wrote a good piece on the Lincoln stereos. Harold F. Jenkins' *Two Points of View, The History of Parlor Stereoscopes* (1957) is an interesting short book.

302–3 THE FAMILY
On Lincoln family portraits, see *Lincoln Lore*, No. 439.

304–7 LINCOLN'S HEAD ON OTHER BODIES
See Winfield P. Truesdell's *Engraved and Lithographed Portraits of Abraham Lincoln* (1933, privately printed).

308-11 IS THIS LINCOLN?
The photograph of the Clay Battalion was first published in *Old Cane Springs, A Story of the War Between the States in Madison County, Kentucky* (1936–37) by Dr. Jonathan T. Dorris.

On the Hanover Junction photograph, see Stefan Lorant's letters to the New York *Herald Tribune*, October 19, 1952; *Time* magazine, November 10, 1952; *Newsweek*, November 17, 1952; and E. John Long's article in *Trains and Travel*, November 1953.

WHEN *PUNCH* RECANTED
After Lincoln's assassination the English weekly which had cruelly caricatured him ran this sympathetic cartoon by Tenniel on May 6, 1865. But a long poem by *Punch's* future editor, Tom Taylor,

BRITANNIA SYMPATHISES WITH COLUMBIA.

made a greater impression on America. Taylor, the author of "Our American Cousin," which Lincoln saw on the night of his death, chided the paper and its "mocking pencil" for so belatedly coming to recognize his greatness.

INDEX

LINCOLN, ABRAHAM, (continued)

of Atlanta, 242; signs the Thirteenth Amendment, 243; the second inaugural, 244–247; the inaugural ball, 248; the last conferences of the war at City Point and aboard the River Queen, 250–255; entry into Richmond, 255; telegraphs Grant about the possibilities of Lee's surrender, 256; sits for Gardner, 258, 259

The days before the assassination, 258; his premonition of death, 260; the assassination, 264–267, 270, 271, 277–279; deathbed scenes, 266–269; funeral ceremonies, 274–279

life masks
by Leonard Volk, 94, 95
by Clark Mills, 240, 241

manuscripts in his hand
A page from his schoolboy exercise book, 19; discharge notice for a soldier in the Black Hawk war, 34; a post office receipt, 35; a survey, 35; a suggested resolution for the Illinois assembly, 37; letters to Mary Owens, his first sweetheart, 38–41; affidavit for his first lawsuit, 44; bill for the use of the office as a jury room, 44; entries in the Stuart-Lincoln account book, 45

Letters to Speed about his decision to marry, 46, 47; contract for the purchase of his house in Springfield, 50; petition for a patent, 56; letters refusing the post of secretary of Oregon, 57; seeking the job as Commissioner of the General Land Office, 57; letter to his stepbrother at the time of his father's death, 59; rebuking his stepbrother, 61; brief defending an alleged slanderer, 62; instructions to the jury in another slander suit, 65; the "Now, vere ish my hundred tollars" note, 65; letters on the slavery question, 68, 69; instructs the jury in the Armstrong trial, 70

Accepting Douglas's terms for the debates, 76; annotated scrapbook of the speeches in the debates, 77; notes for a campaign speech, 78; the question put to Douglas–can slavery be excluded, 79; five letters pondering a campaign for the Presidency, 80, 81; an autobiographical sketch, 82, 83; the note sent along with his autobiography to Jesse W. Fell, 83; notes for a speech at Hartford, 86; a pre-convention letter, 88; accepting the Republican nomination, 92; a letter suggesting campaign policy to Judge Davis, 112; answer to the girl who suggested he grow a beard, 114; bill of sale for some of his furniture, 117; the farewell address given in Springfield, 119; asking Buchanan to the inaugural ball, 126

Rebuke to Seward's initial attempt to frame Presidential policy, 129; instructions to the commander of Fort Sumter, 133; proclamation calling for 70,000 militia against the South, 135; letter of sympathy to the parents of Col. Ellsworth, 138; "memorandum of military policy" after the defeat at Bull Run, 140; two letters in response to Frémont's proclamation freeing slaves in the West, 144, 145; General War Order No. 1, 146; letters in June 1862 to McClellan, 154; letters of June 28, 1862, to McClellan and Seward, 156

Answers to Greeley's "Prayer of Twenty Millions," 158, 159; draft of the Emancipation Proclamation, 166, 167; two dispatches to McClellan, 172, 173; note congratulating Grant, 174; letter in January 1863 to Hooker, 184, 185; doggerel ridiculing Lee, 191; the Fourth of July message after Gettysburg, 192; thanks to Grant after Vicksburg, 193; four letters to his wife, 194, 195; first draft of the Gettysburg Address, 199; letter to

Everett after the address, 204; letter to Meade in 1863, 205; answers Chase's offer to resign, 213; letter to Grant before 1864 campaign, 217

The document which cabinet members endorsed without seeing, 223; calculation of the electoral vote in 1864, 234; comparison of the 1864 popular vote with that of 1860, 235; the controversial Bixby letter, 237; reply to Sherman after the capture of Atlanta, 242; responding to congratulations on the second inaugural address, 244; manuscript of the address, 246, 247; letter to Grant just before Lee's surrender, 256; memo to Seward on the day before his assassination, 258

photographs
falsely described as showing Lincoln, 87, 308–311; a chronological sequence, 312–329

portraits painted or drawn from life
by Thomas Hicks, 100; by Charles A. Barry, 101; by John Henry Brown, 102; by A. J. Conant, 102; by Lewis P. Clover, 103; by Thomas Johnston, 104; by George Frederick Wright, 105; by Pierre Morand, 222, 223; by Albert Hunt, 254

illustrating scenes from his life
at home in Kentucky, 14; at home in Indiana, 17; attending his mother's funeral, 18; earning his first dollar, 20; as a railsplitter, 21; moving to Illinois, 22; his first view of slavery, 24; on a Mississippi flatboat, 24, 25; as a storyteller, 26; the wrestling bout with Jack Armstrong, 29; as a circuit lawyer, 53; as a circuit rider, 63; the debate with Douglas at Galesburg, 74; the debate at Charleston, 74; the farewell speech at Springfield, 118; the passage through Baltimore, 120; views of the first inaugural, 124, 126; reading the Emancipation Proclamation, 162, 163; reviewing the army of the Potomac, 187; taking the Presidential oath a second time, 247; meeting with military leaders, 253; entering Richmond, 255; deathbed scenes, 266–269

Lincoln, Edward Baker (his second son), 51, 116
Lincoln, Mary Todd (his wife), 46–49, 57, 116–118, 147, 149, 192, 194, 195, 248, 249, 251–253, 265, 270, 302, 303
Lincoln, Robert Todd (his first son), 86, 147, 149, 267, 302
Lincoln, Sarah (his sister), 12, 15, 18, 20, 23, 24
Lincoln, Thomas (his father), 9–18, 22, 23, 58–61
Lincoln, Thomas "Tad" (his fourth son), 51, 108, 116, 147–149, 194, 209, 258, 302
Lincoln, William Wallace "Willie" (his third son), 51, 108, 116, 147–149, 302
Littlefield, John H., 268
Logan, Stephen T. (his law partner), 52, 53
"Long Nine," the Sangamon County delegation, 36
"Lost speech" in Bloomington, 67, 68
Lowe, Prof. T. S. C. (balloonist), 152, 153

McClellan, Gen. George B., 140, 141, 143–146, 152–156, 160, 161, 170–173, 207, 226–229, 234
McCormick, Andrew, 36
McDowell, Gen. Irving, 139, 146
McLean, John, 81, 90, 93
Meade, Gen. George G., 188, 189, 214, 216, 252
Medill, Joseph, 90, 92
Meserve, Frederick Hill, 292–295, 316
Mills, Clark (sculptor), 240, 241
Monitor, 152
Moore, Clifton, 64
Mudd, Dr. Samuel A., 282, 290

Nasby, Petroleum V. (David R. Locke, the humorist), 75, 78, 237, 265
Nast, Thomas (artist), 120, 251
New Salem, Illinois, 26–35

Nicolay, John G. (his secretary), 119, 122, 197, 200, 274, 293

Offutt, Denton, 24–27
O'Laughlin, Michael (conspirator), 281, 285
Owens, Mary, 38–41, 45

Paine, Lewis (conspirator), 280, 283–291
Peninsular Campaign, 152–157
Pinkerton, Allan, 120, 121
Pomeroy Circular, 213
Pope, Gen. John, 160
Pope, Nathaniel, 64
Porter, Adm. David D., 248, 253
Punch, the English weekly, 176, 177, 235

Rathbone, Maj. Henry Reed, 262, 269, 270
Ray, Charles H., 90
Raymond, Henry J. (of the New York Times), 181, 205
Ritchie, A. H., 163, 268
Roosevelt, Theodore, 274
Rutledge, Ann, 28, 32–35
Rutledge, Mary Ann (mother of Ann), 28

Schurz, Carl, 77, 78, 108–110, 119
Scott, Gen. Winfield C., 124, 125, 139, 141–143, 162, 163, 167, 199, 200, 203, 205, 207, 225, 258
Seward, William H., 80, 88, 91–93, 128, 129, 131, 142, 283, 286, 287
Sherman, Gen. William T., 232, 233, 242, 248, 262
Short, James, 28
Slavery question, 54, 66, 69, 73–79, 84, 108, 145, 162
Smith, Caleb Blood (his Secretary of the Interior), 90, 128
Southern cartoonists attack the President, 206, 207
Spangler, Edman (conspirator), 278, 280, 290
Speed, Joshua Fry, 43–51, 53
"Spot resolutions" of Congressman Lincoln, 54
Springfield, Illinois, 42, 43, 48
Stanton, Edwin (his Secretary of War), 154, 155, 162, 163, 179, 183, 246, 254, 255, 261, 266, 267, 269, 272, 274
Stevens, Thaddeus, 220, 226
Stone, Dan, 36, 37
Story, George H., 123, 318
Strother, David H. ("Porte Crayon"), 182
Stuart, John T. (his law partner), 34, 42–45, 48, 50, 52
Sumner, Charles (Massachusetts Senator), 158, 248, 267, 269
Supreme Court, 238, 239
Surratt, John T. (conspirator), 281, 285, 290
Surratt, Mrs. Mary (conspirator), 281, 286–291

Taney, Roger B. (Chief Justice), 68, 69, 126, 238
Tenniel, John (cartoonist for Punch), 176, 177, 235
Thirteenth Amendment, 243
Treat, Samuel H., 64
Trumbull, Lyman (Senator from Illinois), 64, 81

Usher, John Palmer (his second Secretary of the Interior), 199, 269

Vandalia, Illinois, 36, 37
Volck, Dr. Adalbert Johann (as a caricaturist), 121, 168, 169
Volk, Leonard Wells (sculptor), 94, 95, 96, 97

Wade-Davis Manifesto, 224
Waud, Alfred R. (artist), 187, 260
Weed, Thurlow (the political boss), 88, 128, 129, 131, 244
Welles, Gideon (Secretary of the Navy), 128, 129, 160, 162, 163, 183, 246, 267, 269
Wilderness Campaign, 216–219
Wills, David (of Gettysburg), 196, 199, 200
Wilson, Robert Lang, 36
Wright, George Frederick (painter), 105